CW01219713

SUGARLAND

SUGARLAND
THE TRANSFORMATION OF THE COUNTRYSIDE
IN COMMUNIST ALBANIA

Artan R. Hoxha

CEU PRESS

Central European University Press
Budapest-Vienna-New York

Copyright © by Artan R. Hoxha 2023

Published in 2023 by
CENTRAL EUROPEAN UNIVERSITY PRESS
Nádor utca 9, H-1051 Budapest, Hungary
Tel: +36-1-327-3138 or 327-3000
E-mail: ceupress@press.ceu.edu
Website: www.ceupress.com

All rights reserved. No part of this publication may be reproduced, stored in a retrieval system, or transmitted, in any form or by any means, without the permission of the Publisher.

ISBN 978-963-386-616-0 (hardback)
ISBN 978-963-386-617-7 (ebook)

A catalogue record for this book is available from the Library of Congress.

Table of Contents

List of Illustrations ... vii
Acknowledgments ... ix

INTRODUCTION ... 1

CHAPTER 1
The Making of the Sugar Scheme: Transitioning from Empire to Nation ... 23
   The Plain of Maliq in Ottoman Times ... *23*
   Conceiving the Reclamation of the Maliq Swamp ... *27*
   The Maliq Scheme and the Quest for Nation-Building and Self-Sufficiency ... *35*
   Albania's American Frontier ... *45*
   The Maliq Scheme and Fascism's Grand Colonial Project in Albania ... *60*

CHAPTER 2
The Making of Maliq's Landscape: Modern and Stalinist ... 67
   Maliq's Landscape Between "Good" and "Bad" Governments ... *67*
   Uncompleted Reclamation ... *70*
   "For the Factory and Your Country": Maliq and the Nation ... *86*
   Inscribing the Tabula Rasa: Gridding the Stalinist Landscape ... *99*

CHAPTER 3
Sugar and the Communist Construction of Spatial Inequalities in Maliq ... 113
   Sugar Production and the Communist Project of Social Transformation ... *113*
   Building and Peopling Where Once Only the Fishermen Could Go ... *117*
   Building Socialism, Spatializing Inequalities ... *128*
   Love for the Plain ... *142*

CHAPTER 4
Maliq and the World ... 151
   A Tapestry of Transnational Exchanges ... *151*
   Maliq and Its East-West Economy of Knowledge ... *158*
   Sugar Consumption and Cross-Border Exchanges ... *183*

CHAPTER 5
Communism and After: From Sugar to Ruins   195
  Ruins and the Angel of History   *195*
  Building a Regional Integrated Economic Web   *199*
  The Fall of Communism and the Unraveling of the Web   *211*
  Maliq Today: Ruins, Marginalization, and Memory   *223*

EPILOGUE   237

Bibliography   247
Index   287

List of Illustrations

FIGURE 1.   28
Photo of the swamp of Maliq taken by USAF recognizance on September 14, 1943
[NARA RG 242: Target Dossier – Balkans, SO Series, OKL—Southeastern Europe, Box SO 10-407]

FIGURE 2.
1943's German military map of the plain of Korça and Maliq   37
[NARA RG 373, ON059531 T153948285, B 8131 (Picture 5095)]

FIGURE 3.   71
The Minister of Construction, Spiro Koleka, inspects the swamp of Maliq (September 14, 1946)
[ATSH (Albanian Telegraphic Agency), Collection "Construction," year 1946, photo 1861]

FIGURE 4.   75
Digging the drainage canal of Maliq
[ATSH (Albanian Telegraphic Agency), Collection "Construction," year 1946, photo 1864]

FIGURE 5.   75
Bare feet workers transporting stones during the construction of the drainage canal of Maliq
[ATSH (Albanian Telegraphic Agency), Collection "Construction," year 1946, photo 1863]

FIGURE 6.   77
Using human muscles for the reclamation of the plain of Maliq
[ATSH (Albanian Telegraphic Agency), Collection "Construction," years 1949–1950, photo 6651]

FIGURE 7.   80
Using heavy machinery for draining the swamp of Maliq
[ATSH (Albanian Telegraphic Agency), Collection "Construction," years 1949–1950, photo 6656]

FIGURE 8.   82
The map of the Soviet-Albanian Project for the full reclamation of the swamp of Maliq
[AQSh, Collection no. 490 (Council of Ministers), year 1959, file 457, sheet 10]

FIGURE 9.   103
Maliq's orthogonal plots
[AQSh, Collection no. 490 (Council of Ministers), year 1982, file 543, fl. 12-13. Section of the Project of 1982 for the improvement of the plain of Maliq's drainage system]

FIGURE 10.   107
Tractors plowing the plain of Maliq
[ATSH (Albanian Telegraphic Agency), Collection "Agriculture," year 1968, photo 37361]

FIGURE 11. 120
The sugar town in the making
[ATSH (Albanian Telegraphic Agency), Collection "Construction," year 1950, photo 10480]

FIGURE 12. 125
A new village in the reclaimed land of Maliq
[ATSH (Albanian Telegraphic Agency), Collection "Construction," years 1953–1954, photo 15840]

FIGURE 13. 139
Young woman working in the laboratory of the sugar factory of Maliq
[ATSH (Albanian Telegraphic Agency), Collection "Industry," year 1952, photo 13243]

FIGURE 14. 162
Moments from the construction of the sugar factory of Maliq
[ATSH (Albanian Telegraphic Agency), Collection "Construction," years 1949–1950, photo 6663]

FIGURE 15. 200
Filling and weighing sacks of sugar
[ATSH (Albanian Telegraphic Agency), Collection "Industry," year 1952, photo 13247]

FIGURE 16. 203
Storage points of sugar beet
[ATSH (Albanian Telegraphic Agency), Collection "Industry," year 1949–1951, photo 6885]

FIGURE 17. 204
The refinery after its reconstruction in the late 1970s
[AQSh, Collection no. 490 (Council of Ministers), year 1979, file 400, sheet 12]

FIGURE 18. 229
The sugar factory of Maliq. September 2017.
Photo by author

*I dedicate this book to my parents,
Roland Hoxha and Raimonda Naçi,
for everything, always with love*

Acknowledgments

In writing this book, I am indebted to many people but first of all to Gregor Thum, who represents an inspirational personal and academic role model. During my years in Pittsburgh he was my mentor, my friend, and my colleague. It was with him that I conceived my study of Sugarland. One late afternoon in the winter of 2016, in his office, Maliq came out of our heads, pretty much like Zeus gave birth to Athena. It was he who accompanied me along the trajectory of writing and publishing the story of Maliq.

Diego Holstein, Lara Putnam, and John Markoff read my manuscript, gave precious advice, and relentlessly stimulated me to keep writing. Many heartfelt thanks and gratitude go to Mary Neuburger, Shannon Woodcock, and Konrad Clewing who helped me to improve this book and raise it to the level at which it now comes into the readers' hands. Many thanks go to Sabrina Ramet, who helped me immensely in the initial stage of publication. Leslie Hammond, Niklas Frykman, Molly Warsh, David Montgomery, Neil Doshi, Raja Adal, Rob Ruck, Vincent Leung, Pernille Røge, and Michel Gobat engaged in many different ways with my project. Their ideas have been precious. Liljana Đurasković and Sadria Kalezi were a second family to me while I was writing this book. Ermal Aliu was and is a close friend. With him I discussed many of the ideas that permeate this study. Jennifer Boum Make, Bethany Wade, José Andrés Fernandés, Bryan Paradis, Jacob Pomeranz, Philipp Kröger have been friends, attentive listeners, and engaged readers. The constant exchanges with them have been a blessing. Many thanks go to archivists Evis Reçi, Fjoralba Vukatana, Roza Stavre, Eda Qazolli, Pranvera Prendi, Isa Xhaferi, Endri Musaj, Armando Boçe, Mirela Mihali, Blerina Mihalçka, and Brandy Oswald. Fatime Hoxha occupies a special place in the writing of this book. Without her, this book would have not been completed.

My sisters, Arlinda and Genta, and my parents, Roland and Raimonda, have always been with me. And, finally, I am indebted to Olta Shehu, who was with me during the years I wrote this book.

Introduction

On an early Monday morning, in mid-September of 2017, I headed from Tirana to Korça, the largest city in southeast Albania, traveling in a cherry-red Ford Transit passenger van. The van passed the ring of mountains that surround the capital from the east and drove eastward through the beautiful and meandering valley of the Shkumbini River. Once it reached the pass of Thana, close to the state borders of the Republic of North Macedonia, the van turned southward and crossed the breathtaking scenery of Lake Ohrid. After more than three hours, the minibus entered the northern part of the plateau of Korça, called the plain of Maliq. At that moment, I recalled the first time I had heard of Maliq. It was in the late 1980s, when as a little child, I heard my grandmother say that the sugar we consumed was refined in Maliq. In fact, the plain was Albania's center of sugar production for forty years, from 1951 to 1991. In the mid-1990s, not long after communism's demise, Maliq's sugar industry collapsed.

That early morning, the plain's captivating landscape was covered by the glimmering smile of the rising sun. I could see the perfect rows of poplars, which like silent ghosts, aligned along the plain's ditches and canals. To the west stood the brownish and bare hills and mountains of the regions of Gora; on the east, the giant dark silhouette of the Dry Mountain (Mali i Thatë) rose up, while the pulsating electrical lights of the villages scattered across the plain signaled the beginning of a new day. At that moment, the beauty of the scenery loaded with contrasts between the flatness of the plain and the crown of mountains that surrounded it fully unfolded between the shredded cloak of the retreating night and the dim veil of the gleaming dawn.

The plain of Korça was formed during the Pliocene, sometime between 5 and 2.5 million years ago, by powerful tectonic activities at the northern end of the Pindus Mountains. Surrounded by a ring of mountains and hills, the basin looks

Introduction

like a giant lopsided cauldron. In the north, the hills of Çërrava separate it from the Ohrid basin. In the east and southeast, the tall wall of the Dry Mountain, at 2028 meters, and Morava Mountain, at 1800 meters, cut the plain off from the basins of the Prespa and the Devoll. The eastern wall breaks into two halves at the Cangonj Pass. Here, the Dry Mountain ends abruptly with a stark rupture, while the Morava elevates gradually and softly toward the sky. In this narrow valley, the Devoll River flows through the plain of Korça. In the south, the hills of Qarr close off the plain and link the Morava to the western wall, which consists of the highlands of Voskopoja, Opar, and Gora. These mountain chains, which rise in a series of peaks up to 2,400 meters, close off the ring around the basin. There are no ruptures in the western wall, except for the narrow gorge close to the small hilly village of Maliq. It is here that the Devoll River, after traversing the plain, pursues its journey westward to the Adriatic.

The plateau of Korça occupies an area of 300 square kilometers. With an average altitude of 820 meters above sea level, it is 35 kilometers long, while its width oscillates from 1 to 16 kilometers in a south–north direction. The plateau reaches its maximum extension between the pass of Cangonj and the gorge of Maliq, which is also called the plain of Maliq, where, as a result of subsiding tectonic activity, the altitude is 812 meters above sea level—the lowest point of the entire plateau. This area is the center of gravity of the entire drainage system of the Korça basin and the mountains around it. In this natural sink, the Devoll River was joined by a multitude of creeks, which filled it up with their water, creating the swamp of Maliq in the late glacial era, between 13,000 and 10,000 years ago. Another important factor that helped in the formation of the large pond was the uneven distribution of rainfall. The region's Mediterranean subcontinental climate is distinguished by dry summers and heavy rains in the autumn and spring. A huge mass of water from melting snow and rainfall pours straight into the plain of Maliq in a very short time. Before World War II, the narrow gorge jammed the draining of this vast body of water, which remained blocked in the plain. Stretching for roughly 14 kilometers in length and around 6 kilometers in width, the swamp area varied throughout history between 40 and 80 square kilometers, although during summers and dry years, its water cover shrank even further.[1]

---

1 On the geological and climatological history of the Korça basin see: Eric Fouache et al., "Palaeogeographical reconstructions of Lake Maliq (Korça Basin, Albania) between 14,000 BP and 2000 BP," *Journal of Archaeological Science* 37, no. 3 (2010): 525–535; Eric Fouache et al., "Man and environment around lake Maliq (southern Albania) during the Late Holocene," *Vegetation History and Archaeobotany* 10, no. 2 (2001): 79–86; Michelle Denèfle et al., "A 12,000-Year Pollen Record from Lake Maliq,

Introduction

Maliq has a long history of human presence. The climatic transformations that occurred during the Mesolithic transformed it into an ideal place for the thriving of human life. From the Early Neolithic, many communities settled around the swamp, which became the epicenter of their life. They practiced hunting, fishing, and agriculture. The lake not only provided abundant sources of food but also building materials and protection. The prehistoric settlers used mud and reeds to build large huts with two rooms and, by the Late Neolithic, many of them lived in stilt villages—the oldest in Europe.[2] In historical times, the area had been under the control of many states: the Illyrian and the Macedonian kingdoms, as well as the Roman, Byzantine, Bulgarian, and Ottoman empires ruled for centuries. During these millennia, the old polytheistic religions faded away, and the universal monotheistic faiths took the stage. Pagan gods retreated under the expansion of the Eastern rite of Christianity. With the arrival of the Ottomans, it was the turn of Orthodoxy to become defensive under the pressure of Islam's expansion. Mosques replaced many churches, and the muezzins' songs began to compete with the ringing of church bells.

In the meantime, the lake was always there, indifferent to all the societal transformations. Many things changed in the lives of the people that lived by its shores, but many others remained the same. The peasants tilled the land with wooden plows and used the swamp to collect reeds for building houses and producing mats. As an archeologist observed in the 1960s, the twentieth-century dwellings built with reeds and straw were similar to those of the Eneolithic era.[3] Until the first half of the twentieth century, the marsh, with its murky mantel of canebrakes and islands of thick groves of alders, beeches, and poplars that coated three-quarters of its area, was still critical to the sixteen villages that lived around

---

Albania," *Quaternary Research* 54, no. 3 (2000): 423–432; Jean-Jacques Dufare et al., "Tectonics and geomorphological evolution: the example of the Korçë basin (Albania)," *Géomorphologie: relief, processus, environment* 5, no. 2 (1999): 111–128; Amandine Bordon et al., "Pollen-inferred Late-Glacial and Holocene climate in southern Balkans (Lake Maliq)," *Quaternary International* 200, nos. 1–2 (2009): 19–30.

2   On Maliq's prehistry, Frano Prendi, "La civilization prehistorique de Maliq," *Studia Albanica* 1 (1966): 255–280; Frano Prendi, "The Prehistory of Albania," in *The Cambridge Ancient History*, vol. 3, Part I, ed. by John Boardman et al. (Cambridge: Cambridge University Press, 1982), 187–237; Neritan Ceka, *Ilirët* [The Illyrians] (Tirana: Ilar, 2001), 27–38; Zhaneta Andrea, *Kultura ilire a tumave në pellgun e Korçës* [The Illyrian culture of Korça's basin tumuli] (Tirana: Akademia e Shkencave e RPSh, 1985); Gjerak Karaiskaj & Petrika Lera, "Fortifikimet e periudhës së parë të hekurit në pellgun e Korçës" [The fortifications of the early Iron Age in the Korca basin], *Kuvendi I i studimeve ilire* [The first convention of the Illyrian studies], 263–273.

3   Frano Prendi, "Përfundoi punimet ekspedita arkeologjike e Maliqit" [The archaeological expedition of Maliq has ended], *Zëri i rinisë* [The youth's voice], October 6, 1962, 4.

3

it. Besides the very rich fauna of fishes, eels, ducks, geese, and many other birds, which inhabited the area, herds of wild horses also roamed across the swamp. The peasants caught these powerful sprinters in late spring, used the sheer force of their muscles for threshing in summer, and let them free into the wild in autumn. Other parts of the picture were the huge water buffalos that reclined in the swamp's mud and the herds of cattle that pastured peacefully by the edge of its waters. A full portrait of Maliq could not miss the shallow boats with fishermen making their way through the dense curtain of reeds or the hunters looking for wild hogs, woodcocks, and wildfowl. To the rich and colorful tableau of everyday life, one should add the oxcarts, moving slowly on the dusty roads along the shores of the swamp, as if carrying, like Atlas, the burden of eternity.

Inseparable components of the panorama were the peasants' plots that surrounded the swamp with a mosaic of irregular shapes. In the spring, the oxen dragged plows reined by men dressed in large dark pants, woolen jerkins, and white Albanian hats—*qeleshe*. In the majority of cases, these peasants owned their land and did not pay rent to any lord, although sharecroppers were not uncommon. Behind these men with strong hands walked the women: when young, they wore clothes with vivid colors, and when old, were garbed in black. They sowed the seeds of grain and corn in the deep and long wounds that the plows opened in the dark sandy-clay soil of Maliq. Landlords, rich peasants, state bureaucrats, and urbanites in European attire appeared regularly in the plain and added new elements to the cultural layers deposited across the centuries in this locality of southeastern Albania. The mountaineers of Gora and Mokra further enriched the human landscape. On Saturdays, they descended from their hamlets to exchange in the market of Korça the few things they produced. Their long mustaches, white skirts (called *fustanella*), black waistcoats, white shirts with wide sleeves, and heavy grey or black cloaks hanging on their shoulders showed the face of Albania's highlands.

The bucolic blend of nature, animals, and humans was neither idyllic nor heroic. The daily existence was filled with hardships and scarcity, burdened with dues, and lived with blood and sweat. With few exceptions, the peasants in the villages of the plain used mud and reeds as construction material, and their houses had no pavement. Here and there, tall buildings popped up with thick walls of stone: they were the landlords' houses, who marked their power with size and strength. The inventory of the peasants' houses consisted of a few wares and stools, no beds, a table only on rare occasions, small windows, and a hearth. Beginning in the late nineteenth century, the massive emigration to the United States marginally improved the economic situation of the peasants and intensified their connections with the cash economy. However, their economic condition hung on a fine thread, and the cause of this was the swamp, which, while being a source of livelihood, also tormented the rural communities around it. Quite often, a mist of gases emitted from its decomposed vegetation caused serious damage to agriculture. Moreover, the floods during the rainy seasons caused immense suffering to the local population. They destroyed crops, drowned animals, and inundated houses. Endemic malaria caused by the armies of marsh mosquitoes that had dominated Maliq were the cherry on the cake.[4] By the 1940s, Maliq had become, in the eyes of many young Albanian modernizers, synonymous with fever and malaria. Among them, the most committed were the communists.

Everything changed after World War II when the Albanian Communist Party (ACP) came to power. Like all revolutionary and authoritarian modernizers, the Albanian communist leadership had a Manichean conceptualization of time, opposing past and future. Considering the past as dark, they were committed to cleaning it off and transforming the country into a tabula rasa, where they could inscribe the script of a bright future. The vision of modernization and its concomitant temporal dichotomies defined the horizon of the Albanian communists' political goals and informed the way they understood the Soviet model and their embracement of it. Indeed, for the ACP's elite, socialism meant, among other things, modernizing the country and overcoming what it perceived as the trap of backwardness that Albania inherited from the past. The communists considered their takeover as the beginning of a new chapter in Albania's history and a rupture with its past.

---

4   I based this depiction on Andromaqi Gjergji, *Mënyra e jetesës në shekujt XIII-XX: përmbledhje studimesh* [The way of life through the thirteenth to the twentieth century: A collection of studies] (Self-published, Tirana, 2002), 70–89, 129–155, 184–196, 197–240; Ligor Mile, *Zejtaria fshatare shqiptare gjaë Rilindjes Kombëtare* [Albanian rural handicraft during the national awakening] (Tirana: Marin Barleti, 2001), 9–29 and 64–99; Ligor Mile, *Çështje të historië agrare shqiptare: fundi i shek. XVIII – vitet 70 të shek. XIX* [Issues of the Albanian agrarian history: The end of the XVIII century through the 1870s] (Tirana: Akademia e Shkencave të RPSSh, 1984), 319–407; Nathalie Clayer, *Në fillimet e nacionalizmit shqiptar: Lindja e një kombi me shumicë myslimane në Europë* [At the beginning of Albanian nationalism: the birth of a nation with a Muslim-majority in Europe], trans. Artan Puto (Tirana: Përpjekja, 2012), 106–116; Fatmira Musaj, *Gruaja në Shqipëri (1912–1939)* [The woman in Albania (1912–1939)] (Tirana: Akademia e Shkencave e RSh, 2002); Gazmend Shpuza, *Kryengritja Fshatare e Shqipërisë së Mesme, 1914–1915* [The peasant uprising of Central Albania, 1914–1915] (Tirana: Akademia e Shkencave të RPS të Shqpërisë, 1986), 46–76; Spiro Shkurti, "Sprovë për klasifikimin e parmendave shqiptare" [Essay for the classification of Albanian plows], *Etnografia Shqiptare*, 13 (1983): 101–139; Thimi Mitko, "Topografi e Korçës" [Topography of Korça] in Thimi Mitko, *Vepra* [Works] (Tirana: Akademia e Shenkcave të RPSSH, 1981), 569–572; Anton Ashta, *Malarja në Shqipni* [Malaria in Albania] (Tirana: Mihal Duri, 1961), 8–9; Melville Charter, "Albania, Europe's Newest Kingdom," *The National Geographic Magazine* 59, no. 2 (1931): 131–182.

Introduction

What would better represent this historical caesura than the swamp's reclamation? According to the Albanian communists' modernist worldview, the swamp represented the most prominent symptom of bad government; social, economic, and cultural backwardness; stagnation; and a lack of positive transformation. The swamp of Maliq, with its malaria and continuous floods, was one of the most emblematic quagmires symbolizing the legacy of the past, which the ACP wanted to change and erase. For the communists, Maliq stood for the country's misery and lag and embodied what history stood for. Was there any better way to inaugurate the program of the wholesale transformation of the country and give substance to the claim of the new than the draining of the Maliq swamp? The communists believed so. Only a year and a half after taking over the reins of power, they started the reclamation of the bog. It was the first large-scale infrastructural project of the communist era.

The Maliq project was, in its essence, an enterprise of internal colonization. The communist power apparatus considered the plain of Maliq as empty and unutilized space. They did not recognize the use that the peasants of the area had made of the swamp. In fact, the quagmire demonstrated the lack of any rational and productive exploitation. The ACP's structure had its own concepts about what land use meant, and for it, reclamation meant not only the expansion of arable land but also the beginning of the implementation of the modernization program. Besides a space for economic use, it also became a site for the transformation of the people of the area whom the communists equated with the metaphor of the swamp: they were backward and lived in darkness. The fertile sandy-clay soil and subcontinental climate of the plain were ideal for the cultivation of sugar beet. Soon after completing the reclamation of the swamp, the communist authorities, with the financial and technological support of the Soviet Union, transformed the plain into the center of sugar production in Albania. Close to the gorge of Maliq, the regime built a sugar refinery, which gradually expanded into an integrated industrial complex, which, besides refining sugar, specialized in the production of alcohol, molasses, starch, refreshing beverages, and other products. Next to the refinery, the regime built a small town for its workers and specialists, while in the plain, it built a series of villages inhabited by people coming from the uplands. The latter supplied the necessary workforce to cultivate the labor-intensive sugar beet.

From a swampland, Maliq became Albania's land of sugar. Such a transition implied a total metamorphosis of the landscape and people's everyday lives, which reflected the new forms of economic organization and the specialization of the plain in sugar production. The state's continuous investment in the building of irrigation and drainage systems drastically transformed the outlook of the plain. Tractors and combines gradually replaced the oxen, although the latter were still used well into the 1970s. New types of houses built in brick and richly furnished supplanted those of adobe. In addition, clinics, and especially houses of culture and communist committee centers, appeared in almost all the villages of the plain, while churches and mosques disappeared under the relentless atheistic policies of the regime. The attire changed, too. Both men and women dressed in modern garb. The peasants of the plain continued to work in agriculture, which was organized in cooperatives. Many of them worked in the sugar refinery as well. Soon, Maliq became a coveted destination for the entire rural population of Korça district and a demonstration of the communists' modernizing project. However, in the 1990s, soon after the collapse of communism, the sugar industry closed down. It did not survive global competition. Additionally, while the temple of socialist modernity, the factory, had been reduced to a heap of ruins thanks to globalization, Christian and Muslim shrines re-emerged again in the villages of the plain.

From the late 1940s, the plain of Maliq had undergone immense transformations, always called transitions, consistently heading toward different destinations, and still failing to reach any of them. What exactly did these broad visions of transformation consist of? How did these visions shape Maliq? How have Maliq and its people shaped these visions? Generally speaking, historians still think of the second half of the twentieth century as a period when Europe was divided into fundamentally opposing systems. In addition, the academic literature tends to reproduce the narrative constructed by the Soviet-type regimes, which still treats the communist period as an abrupt historical rupture. Can we unearth from Maliq's history shared historical processes and patterns of transformation common to the second half of the twentieth century? Do the stories of those in places like Maliq, who dedicated their energies to the pursuit of the dream of modernization, allow us to not only understand communism but also assess and grasp the historical processes that followed its demise? On a September morning in 2017, I was traveling to Korça to answer these questions. My goal was to situate Maliq's story within a global context and see in a specific site how broad historical processes, which otherwise remain abstract concepts, play out on the ground. By zooming into a single place, we can better understand large patterns of transformations by analyzing how they impact upon and are impacted by local circumstances.

Introduction

This work is the result of a full year of fieldwork and archival research. I have collected reports, correspondence, speeches, minutes of meetings, projects, studies produced by the local and central state apparatus, maps, photos (including aerial and satellite images), and information on geological activity. I have also used statistics on the use of TVs and radios, marriage patterns and migration, and data on education, consumption, and revenues. My fieldwork also includes wanderings in Korça and its surroundings, many visits to Maliq and its villages, and countless discussions with locals, always accompanied by coffee and cigarettes. The long conversations with peasants, agricultural specialists, engineers, tractor and bulldozer drivers, actors, doctors, and people of all types of professions, combined with my explorations, allowed me to establish an intimate relationship with Maliq and its history—a region I had not known before. In this informal ethnography, I heard how the people that had lived and worked in Maliq made sense of the communist period and what followed it, and how they situated their lives within broader national and global narratives. My goal was to go beneath the surface of the documents' written words and to contextualize them within Maliq's world. It was a priceless experience, and the opinions of local inhabitants have shaped much of this work. To me, this locality became an access point and a litmus to twentieth-century history, especially of the communist period.

Rather than pursuing the path of multi-sited research as a form of making connections across space and exploring global trends, I preferred zooming in on a locality and subsequently understanding the wider world from there. Focusing on one single place allowed me to gain an intimate connection to Maliq's microworld and history, to access its horizon in a way that only context-based research can give to a scholar. The historical layers of one place record over their surface transformations that are simultaneously local and global. By peeling them back, it is possible to both understand the specific and the general, and how local circumstances have participated in translating worldwide trends and processes into local contexts. The goal of this study is to understand exactly how these links and the exposure to worldwide processes affected Maliq's history and how the specific circumstances, human and ecological, changed large dynamics and patterns in turn.

Placing my lens on this corner of the Balkans has permitted me to explore broad historical processes from the vantage point of a periphery. Studying the infrastructural, economic, social, and cultural transformations in Maliq created an opportunity to build up knowledge of the whole from the parts. This approach avoids hierarchical spatial dichotomies that juxtapose the center to the periphery. Thinking in terms of wholeness and parts provides a flexible and dynamic conceptualization of interactions across space that avoids the creation of maps that divide the space between hubs which create models and marginal areas that import and consume them. Instead of spatial hierarchies, the analysis of the relations between the global, or the whole, and the parts, or the local, avoids binaries and highlights the interdependence of the mosaic's pieces.

Studying circumscribed localities provides a strategy permitting a closer examination of the dynamics of transformations in a specific place and how they are connected to broader historical patterns. I use Maliq's transformation during the second half of the twentieth century as a magnifying glass for exploring broad historical processes. Pursuing this methodological approach does not mean that the locality under study is a replica of some broader abstract model. Nor does it seek, as many microhistories do, to exclusively highlight the particular and different, which is exceptional from the norm, so as to unravel the grand narratives that prioritize generalization.[5] Instead, the local and the global are interdependent. As the British geographer Doreen Massey has stated, the uniqueness of a place is relational: it is constructed by the links with the broader world and by the relations of its history to that of other places.[6] Focusing the lens of analysis on a single place, it is possible to trace both the interconnections with the wider world and how broad historical processes have been adopted and adapted to specific non-replicable local circumstances. The close examination of the intersection between local conditions and worldwide trends, of connections and what is connected, may raise new questions, pose new problems, and propose a rereading of the generalizations that take place among historians.[7]

To explore how Maliq was connected to the world and to look beyond the East–West divide, which dates back to the Cold War era, I use the concept of entangled history that explores networks and border crossings. As a modus ope-

---

5   On the use of microhistory either to seek the monad of the world or as an instrument to question the generalizations of macrohistories, see John-Paul A. Ghobrial, "Introduction: Seeing the World Like a Microhistorian," *Past & Present* 242, Supplement 14 (2019): 13–14; Giovanni Levi, "On Microhistory," in *New Perspectives on Historical Writing*, ed. Peter Burke (University Park, PA: The Pennsylvania State University Press, 1992), 94–95; Carlo Ginzburg and Carlo Poni, "The Name and the Game: Unequal Exchange and the Historiographic Marketplace," in *Microhistory and the Lost Peoples of Europe*, ed. Edward Muir and Guido Ruggiero, trans. Eren Branch (Baltimore: Johns Hopkins University Press, 1991), 1–10.
6   Doreen Massey, "Questions of Locality," *Geography* 78, no. 2 (1993): 145 and 148.
7   Giovanni Levi, "Frail Frontiers?" *Past & Present* 242, Supplement 14 (2019): 45.

randi, it identifies the threads weaved in the tapestry of an interconnected world.[8] Entangled history serves as a polyvalent lens, able to grasp the larger picture without losing attention to detail. Under its scope, Maliq does not come out as a project shaped by forces that originated somewhere else as an imitation. Instead, it was produced and reproduced from the interplay of local factors, contemporary patterns of thinking and understanding, and the political goals of the communist top-elite. Rather than repositories, passive receivers, or the ending point of a continuum, Maliq and Albania emerge as part of global circuits of knowledge, ideas, and technologies that were involved in perpetual movement and adaptation. To use Charles Tilly's view of the world as a composition of not well-bounded vast and small networks, Maliq was a crossroad of various nested networks, enmeshed at different levels at the local, national, and global level.[9]

Thus, investigating the dynamics of Maliq's infrastructural, economic, social, and cultural transformations provides a series of important clues. First, this work questions the assertion of an alleged passive periphery with respect to models generated in the center. Rather, it opts for a model that looks at Maliq as part of a larger conjuncture that is not centered in any specific geographical location, but is disseminated and produced simultaneously in many different locations, regardless of their social–economic systems. Approaching the whole from the parts helps us avoid the trap of ethnocentrism and spatial hierarchies. Moreover, such a take identifies similarities and points of contact between Maliq and many other places across Europe, which raises serious question marks over the alleged irrec-

---

8   Diego Olstein, *Thinking History Globally* (London: Palgrave Macmillan, 2015), 13–14, 35–36, 178–180; Michael David-Fox, "Introduction: Entangled Histories in the Age of Extremes," in *Fascination and Enmity: Russia and Germany as Entangled Histories, 1914–1945*, eds. Michael David-Fox, Peter Holquist, and Alexander M. Martin (Pittsburgh, PA: University of Pittsburgh Press, 2012), 1–12; Hartmut Kaelble, "Between Comparison and Transfers – and What Now? A French-German Debate," in *Comparative and Transnational History*, eds. Heinz-Gerhard Haupt and Jürgen Kocka (New York: Berghahn Books, 2009), 33–38; Philipp Ther, "Comparison, Cultural Transfers, and the Study of Networks: Toward a Transnational History of Europe," *Ibid*, 204–225; Michael Werner & Bénédicte Zimmermann, "Beyond Comparison: *Histoire Croisée* and the Challenge of Reflexivity," *History and Theory* 45, no. 1 (2006): 30–50; Liliane Hilaire-Pérez & Catherine Verna, "Dissemination of Technical Knowledge in the Middle Ages and the Early Modern Era: New Approaches and Methodological Issues," *Technology and Culture* 47, no. 3 (2006): 536–540; Constantin Iordachi, "'Entangled Histories:' Re-thinking the History of Central and Southeastern Europe from a Relational Perspective," *Regio – Minorities, Politics, Society*, English edition, 1 (2004): 113–147; Deborah Cohen & Maura O'Connor, "Introduction: Comparative History, Cross-National History, Transnational History—Definitions," in *Comparison and History: Europe in Cross-National Perspective*, eds. Deborah Cohen and Maura O'Connor (London: Routledge, 2004), ix–xxiv.
9   Charles Tilly, *Big Structures, Large Processes, Huge Comparisons* (New York: Russell Sage Foundation, 1984), 147.

oncilability of the models implemented on both sides of the Iron Curtain. In this way, this study destabilizes longstanding and taken-for-granted paradigms that consider the socialist and capitalist blocs as essentially and diametrically different from each other.

This work, which builds its argument based on economic, social, environmental, demographic, transnational technology transfer, and cultural analyses, approaches Albanian history from a new perspective. Generally speaking, Albania has attracted the attention of scholars as an idiosyncratic case that stands out from the norm, especially when it comes to the communist regime and Enver Hoxha's leadership. The harshness, the professed loyalty to Stalin, and the relative isolation of the country from Europe after the break with the Soviet Union in 1960 have puzzled many observers. A good illustration of what many Cold War-era specialists thought of communist Albania is an article published in May of 1975 in *The New York Times*. It compared it to Cambodia, a communist country isolated even from the communist world, which was depicted as a closed safe box.[10] The image of the strongbox represents better than anything else the collective imagining of Albanian history during communism. Different scholars have considered the country during the Hoxha years as the epitome of isolationism, xenophobia, mysterious self-seclusion, and ruthless authoritarianism: all symptoms of psychological aberration or tribal xenophobia.[11] The country's postsocialist rocky road to liberal democracy has reinforced these stereotypes, which have been brushed over many times with Orientalist colors. Of course, such conclusions stem from simplistic historical analyses that seek the roots of historical phenomena and reduce their subject, in this case, the communist era, to a mere reflection of a deeper collective and cultural essence.

Such essentialization regarding authoritarianism, indeed, has been widely used for all the countries of southeastern Europe. Maria Todorova has already argued that in the last three centuries, travelers, diplomats, and scholars from Western

---

10 Jonathan Steele, "Xenophobic Albania is Not Likely to Change," *The New York Times*, May 18, 1975, E3.
11 Oliver Jens Schmitt, *Shqiptarët: Një histori midis Lindjes dhe Perëndimit* [The Albanians: A history between East and West], trans. Ardian Klosi (Tiranë: T & K, 2012), 182–197; Paolo Rago, *Tradizione, nazionalismo e comunismo nell'Albania contemporanea* (Rome: Nuova Cultura, 2011); James S. O'Donnell, *A Coming of Age: Albania under Enver Hoxha* (New York: University of Columbia Press, 1999); Jon Halliday, ed., *The Artful Albanian: the Memoirs of Enver Hoxha* (London: Chatto & Windus, 1986). Bernd J. Fischer, who has studied the history of interwar Albania, views Zog's authoritarianism as an outcome of the alleged tribal structure of Albanian society. In reality, the situation in Albania was more complex than this explanation. For more, see Bernd J. Fischer, *King Zog and the Struggle for Stability in Albania* (New York: Columbia University Press, 1984).

Europe have constructed an image of the Balkans as the alter ego of an imagined civilized Europe. While still a part of Europe, the Balkans have represented a space that has also stood outside of the old continent, exposed to Asian influences, and hence is polluted—a hybrid, not fully European.[12] Considered the powder keg of Europe for the entire twentieth century, historians' attention has been mainly focused on finding the root of the region's virulent nationalism and the accompanying wars and ethnic cleansing. The works that have emphasized authoritarianism and violence as the essential denominators of Balkan history consider them as part of the region's traditions—proof of the shallowness of its Europeanness.[13]

The dominant paradigm in Western European and North American scholarship has explained southeastern Europe's twentieth-century history as an outcome of the interaction of modernity and local traditions. While the ideas and institutions imported from Western Europe were positive, the indigenous cultures opposed them, which meant they were negative. The seeds of modernity were planted in unsuitable soil, and the fruits differed substantially from those that bloomed in their place of origins. The traditions and history of the region shaped the new imports, and the result was a century filled with wars, bloodshed, genocides, ruthless dictators, weak civil society, and corrupted institutions. It is important to note here that similar arguments, rearticulated within the explanatory framework of multiple modernities, have also been made for the history of the Soviet Union.[14] In both cases, the Balkans and Russia are imagined as transitioning spaces between Europe and Asia, and as a result, spaces of liminality that distort the Western European imports. Needless to say, these narratives have only reinforced the exceptionality of Western Europe vis à vis the rest of the world, including regions that are geographically part of Europe. Much of the scholarship on the modern history of the Balkans has critically engaged with these claims.

---

12   Maria Todorova, *Imagining the Balkans* (Oxford: Oxford University Press, 2009).
13   Among the most representative works of this group are: Bernd J. Fischer, ed., *Balkan Strongmen: Dictators and Authoritarian Rulers of Southeast Europe* (West Lafayette, IN: Purdue University Press, 2007); Joseph S. Rouček, *Balkan Politics: International Relations in No Man's Land* (Stanford, CA: Stanford University Press, 1948); Charles and Barbara Jelavich, eds., *The Balkans in Transition: Essays on the Development of the Balkan Life and Politics Since the Eighteenth Century* (Berkeley and Los Angeles: University of California Press, 1963). In the latter work, there is a more nuanced approach to the problem. However, the paradigm has remained untouched. See also Alina Mungiu-Pippidi & Wim Van Meurs, eds., *Ottomans into Europeans: State and Institution-Building in South Eastern Europe* (New York: Columbia University Press, 2010).
14   Michael David-Fox, "Multiple Modernities vs. Neo-Traditionalism: On Recent Debates in Russian and Soviet History," *Jahrbucher fur Geschichte Osteuropas*, Neue Folge, Bd. 54, H. 4 (2006): 535–555; Terry Martin, "Modernization or Neo-Traditionalism? Ascribed Nationality and Soviet Primordialism," in *Stalinism: New Directions*, ed. Sheila Fitzpatrick (London: Routledge, 2000), 348–367.

Introduction

Since the 1980s, the Greek sociologist Nicos Mouzelis has challenged the idea that authoritarianism and violent politics in the Balkans were not related merely to indigenous factors but also to global economic structures. By using world-system analysis and comparing the Balkans to the southern cone of South America, Mouzelis concluded that the economic dependence and legacy of imperial domination created a fertile soil for anti-democratic regimes in these two regions.[15] However, his work soon fell into oblivion. The wars in the ex-Yugoslavia demonstrated the importance of culture and nationalism and showed the limits of Mouzelis' analysis. By the late 1990s, historians Mark Mazower and John R. Lampe pursued another path to integrate the modern history of the Balkans into the wider European context. Rather than identifying the root of the region's troubled history in any alleged tradition in Balkans societies, these authors found it in the very nature of modernity. They especially point the finger at nationalist programs and their monolithic conceptualization of a nation. According to these historians, nation-state policies of imposing cultural, linguistic, and religious homogenization disrupted the century-old fabric of Ottoman diversity with catastrophic consequences. It is their becoming more European, they claim, that made the history of the Balkan countries more violent.[16] While avoiding the trap of Orientalism and the essentializing of the region, both these authors have reduced modernity and nationalism into an assemblage of ideologies, institutions, and practices that only generate violence. The bulk of the academic works on the region explores the building of national identities, institutional frameworks, and the myths that have fed, sustained, and reproduced nationalism. This has also been the case with the history of Albania.[17] As far as the latter is concerned, the

---

15 Nicos P. Mouzelis, *Politics in the Semi-Periphery: Early Parliamentarism and Late Industrialization in the Balkans and Latin America* (London: Macmillan, 1986).

16 John R. Lampe, *Balkans into Southeastern Europe, 1914–2014: A Century of War and Transitions* (New York: Routledge, 2014); Mark Mazower, *The Balkans: A Short History* (New York: The Modern Library, 2002). See also Mark Mazower's superb book on the city of Salonika and its violent transitioning from an imperial to a national setting: Mark Mazower, *Salonica, City of Ghosts: Christians, Muslims and Jews, 1430–1950* (New York: Alfred A. Knopf, 2005).

17 The list is too long, but I will cite here some of the most important works on national identity in the Balkans. For more, see Theodora Dragostinova, *Between Two Motherlands: Nationality and Emigration among the Greeks of Bulgaria, 1900–1949* (Ithaca, NY: Cornell University Press, 2011); Maria Todorova, ed., *Balkan Identities: Nation and Memory* (New York: New York University Press, 2004); John R. Lampe & Mark Mazower, *Ideologies and National Identities: The Case of Twentieth-Century Southeastern Europe* (Budapest: CEU Press, 2004); Mary Neuburger, *The Orient Within: Muslim Minorities and the Negotiation of Nationhood in Modern Bulgaria* (Ithaca, NY: Cornell University Press, 2004); Vjekoslav Perica, *Balkan Idols: Religion and Nationalism in Yugoslav States* (Oxford: Oxford University Press, 2002); Irina Livezeanu, *Cultural Politics in Greater Romania: Regionalism, Nation Building & Ethnic Struggle, 1918–1930* (Ithaca, NY: Cornell University Press, 1995); Ivo Banac &

Introduction

only exception is the recent study of the American-based historian Elidor Mëhilli, who avoids the trap of nationalism and narrates the history of communist Albania as part of a larger communist ideological *oikumene*.[18]

By investigating the transformation of the Albanian countryside during the communist era and contextualizing it into a broader European and global historical landscape, my work departs from the scholarship on the Balkans. While my study analyzes the issue of authoritarian modernization, it does not focus on the debates on state and ethnic violence, nor on those that explore the construction of national identity. The violence tied to nation-building and the engineering of homogenous societies has been present in the bulk of the world during the twentieth century. Not accidentally, Eric Hobsbawm called the period between 1914 and 1991 the age of extremes.[19] Rather than an exception, the Balkans are part of the rule. Regardless of the prominence of large-scale and organized violence, we cannot reduce this century to only one identifier.

Consequently, this study will not seek to identify the root of what has generally been characterized as negative aspects of the history of the countries of the Balkan Peninsula. Finding the first cause is counterproductive because it pushes scholars into presentism or teleology. According to both sides involved in this debate, the implementation of the Western European model in the Balkans either destroyed the alleged Ottoman harmony, or created explosive cocktails when merging with local traditions. The competing narratives that attempt to define who is the victim and who is the perpetrator have positioned Balkan societies at the end of the trail. Either active or passive, the latter are always receivers. Balkan historians Maria Todorova and Theodora Dragostinova have already criticized this approach that denies the synchronicity of historical processes in the societies of southeastern Europe.[20] In this study, I will demonstrate how the proj-

---

Katherine Verdery, eds. *National Character and National Ideology in Interwar Eastern Europe* (New Haven, CT: Yale Center for International Area Studies, 1995); Katherine Verdery, *National Ideology under Socialism: Identity and Cultural Politics in Ceaușescu's Romania* (Berkeley, CA: University of California Press, 1991). On Albania, see Stephanie Schwander-Sievers and Bernd J. Fischer, eds., *Albanian Identities: Myth and History* (Bloomington, IN: Indiana University Press, 2002); Roberto Morozzo della Rocca, *Nazione e religione in Albania* (Lecce: Besa, 2000).

18 Elidor Mëhilli, *From Stalin to Mao: Albania and the Socialist World* (Ithaca, NY: Cornell University Press, 2017).

19 Eric J. Hobsbawm, *The Age of Extremes: A History of the World, 1914–1991* (New York: Vintage Books, 1996).

20 Maria Todorova, "The Trap of Backwardness: Modernity, Temporality, and the Study of Eastern European Nationalism," *Slavic Review* 64, no. 1 (2005): 140–164; Theodora Dragostinova, "Studying Balkan State-Building: From the 'Advantage of Backwardness' to the European Framework," *European History Quarterly* 48, no. 4 (2018): 708–713.

ects of the local and central elites, either in Korça or Tirana, belonged to broader European and global visions and programs. Investigating the circulation of ideas, technologies, people, and goods in a small locality such as Maliq, we discover a complex historical landscape that defies the simplified models of the narratives focused on authoritarianism and extreme nationalism.

Mary Neuburger and Theodora Dragostinova have already started to walk in this path. In her latest book, Dragostinova explores the cultural diplomacy of the Bulgarian communist regime in the 1970s and 1980s. Rather than a Soviet satrapy in the Balkans, Bulgaria emerges as an ambitious actor, part of a larger worldwide web of cultural exchanges and contacts that reached out to both the West and the Global South. Her study defies the inherited Cold War view of a bipolar world and instead exposes a more complicated picture in which small countries such as Bulgaria played a role in the global scene during the last two decades of the communist era.[21] In her book *Balkan Smoke*, Mary Neuburger shifts away from cultural history and explores Bulgaria's tobacco industry as a lens to study the country's nineteenth- and twentieth-century history from a transnational and global perspective.[22] In her study, Neuburger demonstrates not only the role of tobacco in the Bulgarian economy but also how the Bulgarians were important players in the powerful global networks of this industry, including the Cold War era. My study likewise uses a technology, in this case the sugar industry, as a point of connection between Albania and the world. In contrast to Neuburger, though, my work focuses on a single place and investigates not only the global connections weaved around a single industry but also how its development transformed the locality, its social fabric, and landscape.

Gregor Thum's book on the metamorphosis of the German city of Breslau into the Polish Wrocław offers a great example of how the interaction between global trends and local factors configured the physical and social landscape of a specific place. Centering his attention on one place, Thum simultaneously writes the history of the city, central Europe, and genocide in one of the most violent moments of twentieth-century history.[23] His multilevel analysis and dexterous movement across different geographic and temporal scales provide a very good

---

21 Theodora K. Dragostinova, *The Cold War from the Margins: A Small Socialist State on the Global Cultural Scene* (Ithaca, NY: Cornell University Press, 2021).
22 Mary C. Neuburger, *Balkan Smoke: Tobacco and the Making of Modern Bulgaria* (Ithaca, NY: Cornell University Press, 2013).
23 Gregor Thum, *Uprooted: How Breslau Became Wrocław during the Century of Expulsions*, trans. Tom Lampert and Allison Brown (Wrocław: Via Nova, 2011).

example of how I could use Maliq's transformation as a litmus test to trace broad historical processes. More importantly, lurking below the blanket of disparateness, there are important common elements that undergird the postwar story of Wrocław and Maliq.

The Polish and Albanian authorities approached Wrocław and Maliq, respectively, from the same perspective: the Soviet-type regimes of Warsaw and Tirana considered both of these sites as battlefields where they could wage war against history, erase the past, and materialize their visions of the future by building the latter from scratch. Whether reclaiming the alleged Polishness of Wrocław, on the one hand, or Maliq from the swamp, on the other, both projects sought to make a clean break with the past. In essence, the metamorphoses of Breslau and the plain of Maliq belonged to the post-World War II endeavors to build new societies. The driving vision that informed the communist projects of social engineering in both Poland and Albania constructed a sharp temporal opposition between the past and the present. Building socialism meant breaking every link with the immediate past by obliterating any marker of historical continuity. As I will explain later, although at an incomparably smaller degree than Wrocław, in Maliq, the erasure of the past and the building of the future were pregnant with violence. However, the making of the land of sugar, and the broad historical processes it was part of, should not be identified with and reduced to violence. Maliq's story holds for us many other valuable gems, which rather than reinforcing existing stereotypes, better explain the past and present of Albania and the Balkans.

The large transformative enterprises that sought to revamp societies were part of those developmental projects in the years that followed the end of World War II, when the entirety of Eastern Europe became a construction site of socialism-building and modernization. As Artemy Kalinovsky shows in his book on the Nurek dam on the Vahksh River, while Moscow was seriously engaged in the Sovietization of its European allies, it also continued efforts to radically transform its Asian peripheries and make them showcases of development.[24] The Maliq scheme was no different. The Albanian communist authorities did not conceive the establishment of the sugar industry from only a utilitarian perspective, although its building was not devoid of economic calculations. It was also an instrument for transforming the periphery, engineering the society and modern-

---

24 Artemy M. Kalinovsky, *Laboratory of Socialist Development: Cold War Politics and Decolonization in Soviet Tajikistan* (Ithaca, NY: Cornell University Press, 2018).

izing it, and serving as conveyor belt for transmitting the center's power to the plain of Maliq and the district of Korça.

Stephen Kotkin's book on the steel town of Magnitogorsk, built from scratch during the first stage of Stalin's reign, suggests that this model had already taken shape in the Soviet Union in the 1930s. More importantly, he argues that Stalin's goals to modernize the economy and remake the social fabric were part of a much broader phenomenon that transgressed ideological boundaries. While Kotkin considers Magnitogorsk an expression of Stalinism's distinct cultural, economic, and social organization, he also locates it squarely within the global conjuncture of the interwar era. Large-scale production and mass consumption, known as Americanism, set the tone for those years.[25] The transformation of Maliq was likewise not merely an enterprise tied to the Albanian communist regime but part of a larger global history that transcended the rigid ontology of regional, ideological, and periodization boundaries. Its history belongs to the twentieth century's modernizing programs that sought to build utopias, forge new societies, usher in nation-building, and reshape landscapes, imbuing them with new meanings.

The bulk of the important works writing on the history of places during the communist era belong to the genre of urban history and focus especially on steel towns and heavy industry, the epitome of Soviet power and social engineering.[26] In contrast, my study of Albania's Sugarland contributes to the field of communist and Eastern European studies by exploring the development of light industry and its impact on a predominantly rural locality. On the other hand, the bulk of the historical works that study the countryside during the communist era concentrate on collectivization. These studies explore the ideological and power ra-

---

25 Stephen Kotkin, *Magnetic Mountain: Stalinism as a Civilization* (Berkeley, CA: University of California Press, 1995). See also, Stephen Kotkin, "Modern Times: The Soviet Union and the Interwar Conjuncture," *Kritika: Explorations in Russian and Eurasian History* 2, no. 1 (2001): 111–164.

26 For other works on communist steel towns, see Katherine Lebow, *Unfinished Utopia: Nowa Huta, Stalinism, and Polish Society, 1949–56* (Ithaca, NY: Cornell University Press, 2013); Lennart Samuelson, *Tankograd. The Formation of a Soviet Company Town: Cheliabinsk, 1900s–1950s* (London: Palgrave Macmillan, 2011). Among these works, there is also that of the historian Visar Nonaj, who, focusing on the metallurgical plant "Steel of the Party," has inquired about the inherent inefficiencies of centralized planning and the failure of the communist regime to use heavy industry as an instrument to create the "New Man." Visar Nonaj, *Albaniens Schwerindustrie als zweite Befreiung?: "Der Stahl der Partei" als Mikrokosmos des Kommunismus* (Munich: De Gruyter Oldenburg, 2021). Another study that focuses on everyday life, which exposes the limits of the totalitarian rule, especially its chronic inefficiencies, but also the ability of the Albanian communist regime to impart a sense of resignation in the population, is that of Idrit Idrizi, *Herrschaft und Alltag im albanischen Spätsozialismus (1976–1985)* (Munich: De Gruyter Oldenburg, 2019).

tionales that drove the communist elites' program to collectivize agriculture, and the strategies and stages they pursued to attain this goal. The latter is widely considered a disciplinary instrument and a political tool to extend the reach of the state. The communist authorities used collectivization to fundamentally alter the property relations in the countryside and, through it, to increase their ability to control the rural population. By expropriating the peasants, the communist regimes consolidated their ability to extract all the surplus they wanted from agriculture and transformed the rural population into a rustic proletariat that depended on the state's distribution of resources.[27]

Collectivization has sparked the interest of scholars of Eastern Europe for two main reasons. First, it has been an important device for Sovietizing the socialist bloc. Exploring the entire process of decision-making provided a window for understanding the relationship between Moscow and the Eastern European communist elites and how the latter conceived the socialist transformation of their respective countries. Second, collectivization provides historians with a lens for investigating the operation of communist power in the countryside. This is especially true for Eastern Europe where the communist regimes were less harsh than the Soviet authorities, and besides the stick, they widely used the carrot as well. Although there is no study yet to thoroughly investigate collectivization in Albania, the process followed patterns similar to those of the other Balkan countries, where the communist state negotiated its power rather than merely imposed it.[28] Collectivization, however, was not the only instrument that the Soviet-type regimes used to include the countryside within the socialist system.

---

27 Constantin Iordachi and Arnd Bauerkämper, eds., *The Collectivization of Agriculture in Communist Eastern Europe: Comparison and Entanglements* (Budapest: CEU Press, 2014); Gail Kligman and Katherine Verdery, *Peasants under Siege: The Collectivization of Romanian Agriculture, 1949–1962* (Princeton: Princeton University Press, 2011); Constantin Iordachi and Dorin Dobrincu, eds., *Transforming Peasants, Propriety and Power: The Collectivization of Agriculture in Romania, 1949–1962* (Budapest: CEU Press, 2009); Lynne Viola, *Peasant Rebels under Stalin: Collectivization and the Culture of Peasant Resistance* (Oxford: Oxford University Press, 1996); Lynne Viola, *The Best Sons of the Fatherland: Workers in the Vanguard of Soviet Collectivization* (Oxford: Oxford University Press, 1989); Sheila Fitzpatrick, *Stalin's Peasants: Resistance and Survival in the Russian Village after Collectivization* (Oxford: Oxford University Press, 1994); David A. Kideckel, *The Solitude of Collectivism: Romanian Villagers to the Revolution and Beyond* (Ithaca, NY: Cornell University Press, 1993).

28 Örjan Sjöberg, "'Any Other Road Leads Only to the Restoration of Capitalism in the Countryside:' Land Collectivization in Albania," in *The Collectivization of Agriculture in Communist Eastern Europe*, 369–397; Nigel Swain, "Eastern European Collectivization Campaigns Compared, 1945–1962," *Ibid*, 497–534; Örjan Sjöberg, *Rural Change and Development in Albania* (Boulder, CO: Westview Press, 1991), 86–96.

Introduction

My study traces how the infrastructural investments and industrialization of the countryside included the rural population within the national economy, thus extending the state's ability to control it. The reclamation of the swamp, the building of the refinery in Maliq, and the specialization of the plain's agriculture in the cultivation of sugar beet linked the communities of the locality to the other regions of Albania. In other words, the creation of Sugarland played a powerful role in the process of nation-building. As explained above, studies on twentieth-century Balkan history have primarily focused on the cultural policies and identity-building that national governments and intellectual elites pursued to forge homogenous societies. As is known, this process, which was based on the exclusion of the "Other" and the crushing of any form of regional particularism, has often been extremely violent. In contrast to previous scholarship, my study inquires into the use of the economy as a mechanism of nation-building and complicates the entire dynamic of this process. I show how the Albanian governments, during both the interwar and communist eras, sought the establishment of a cohesive national unit by stimulating the regionalization of production. In the vision of the Albanian political elites, regional specialization would undermine local self-sufficiency and increase the interdependencies between different districts. The effectiveness of cultural policies and the increase in the state's role and the success of its social engineering depended, among other things, on the economic integration of the new nation.

To conclude, this study provides a series of contributions to the historical debate on communist Eastern Europe. First, my research questions the East–West divide of the Cold War era. Instead of separate and hermetic boxes, we see wide, cross-European interactions and circuits that make Europe seem less divided than has been thought up to now. Even Albania, the least open country of the socialist bloc, was connected in many invisible ways to broader trends that were taking place simultaneously on both sides of the ideological divide. Second, I argue against the idea of a historical break between the communist period and the interwar era. Despite the substantial transformations that took place, there were also important continuities, especially the commitment to modernization. Indeed, as the case of Maliq shows, the communist authorities took over projects that had been conceived during the interwar era, and even in the late Ottoman period, and implemented them. Third, my study highlights the spatial synchronicity and decentralization of the production of the models of modernization. Although a peripheral country, Albania was not a mere consumer of models produced in core areas. Instead, the country fully participated in fashioning templates of modernization. Fourth, up to this point, most scholars have used cities as lenses for exploring physical, social, economic, and cultural transformations during the communist era. In contrast, my work investigates these historical dynamics in the countryside. Fifth, unlike the bulk of works on the history of the Balkans, which focus on extreme nationalism, genocide, and authoritarianism, this study focuses on global patterns of modernization in the countryside and the industrialization of agriculture. Thus, this study expands the horizon of the historical investigation of southeastern Europe.

This work is organized into five chapters. In the first chapter, I question the narrative of the establishment of the communist regimes as a historical break. Did the communists really totally break with the past, or did they just continue with projects conceived before their takeover? What can we learn from the Maliq scheme, and what does it inform us about the processes of continuity and change? Should we think of the communist regimes in Eastern Europe as faithful implementers of the Soviet blueprint or as autonomous actors whose goals were informed by that very past, which they claimed to erase? This chapter aims at reconstructing the diachronic extension of the Maliq scheme, and through it, to gauge the influence the modernizing ideologies that had preceded the establishment of Albania exerted over the policies of Albanian communist leadership. Indeed, the Maliq project was part of a larger trend that had started in the late decades of the 1800s. The communists, however, had the commitment and ruthlessness to use all the means at their disposal to implement it.

The second chapter explores the function of the Maliq project within the larger modernizing project of the Albanian communists. I argue that the sugar scheme was not merely an economic enterprise, although it did play important symbolic functions in the communist-led nation-building process. The Albanian Stalinist leadership used local circumstances akin to its broader goal of the regionalization of production as an instrument for building a cohesive society. Did the Albanian Soviet-type regime leave its signature in Maliq and project inequalities and privileges in Maliq?

The third chapter extensively discusses the sugar scheme and the uneven regional development. The communist regimes sought to solve the urban/rural conflict and the unequal regional development that was so typical of the capitalist economies. The industrialization of the countryside and the equal distribution of investments regardless of economic profitability were solutions that the Soviet systems sought in order to fix spatial inequalities. Yet, notwithstanding the consistent improvement of the standard of living in the villages of Maliq which the establishment of the sugar industry triggered, it did not level the inequalities between the city of Korça and the plain's rural communities. On top of this, despite the claims of the communist regime to dilute the spatial inequalities between the lowlands and highlands, the huge infrastructural investments and pouring of resources into the area of Maliq accentuated the inequalities within the countryside.

An additional reason why the regime continuously invested capital in Maliq would be autarky. Driven by a mentality of war, the Albanian communist elites insisted on achieving full economic self-sufficiency, especially in basic goods. Sugar was one of them. Did they really have the luxury to seal themselves off from the continent? In the fourth chapter I argue that the communist regime, facing a constant increase in consumption and a demographic boom, could not afford to isolate itself from Europe. Indeed, Albanian industry depended on importing technologies from countries located on both sides of the Iron Curtain, and technologies are not ideology-free. Despite declarations of autarky and loyalty to Stalinism, Albania was not as isolated as we have been made to believe. In Maliq, I trace the cultural and scientific orientations of Albania before and after the break with Moscow in 1961, and I argue that the sugar industry connected the country to Western and Eastern Europe.

Lastly, what was the role of the sugar industry in the regional economy? Answering this question is important in order to understand the impact that the closing of the refinery had on the communities of Maliq following the demise of the communist regime. The fifth chapter scrutinizes the making of the sugar industry during the communist era and the price local communities paid for its dissolution during the transition from planned to market economies. The collapse of the Maliq sugar scheme reflects broader contemporary historical processes that are tied to the shift toward globalization, the turn toward flexible production, and the end of investments in fixed capital. The post-communist history of Maliq gives important lessons for this new century, especially on how global networks of capital movement, national policies, and local circumstances interplay with each other.

This study starts with the reclamation of the Maliq swamp and ends with images of its dilapidated sugar refinery. The history of Albania's Sugarland, of its creation and ruin, mirrors the historical trajectory of the communist utopia. Maliq's transformation started with great expectations. Reclaiming the swamp, which represented the past, meant transforming the plain into a land of promise, into a land that produced not merely sugar but also hopes for a bright future. The abandoned refinery is what remains of those sweet dreams. This is also the history of communist Albania and of many other countries around the world that have struggled to attain the utopia of a developed countryside. Today, some of the old buildings are being reused by "Rozafa" fishing company, which will transform the ex-sugar factory into a processing plant. Hence, from a town of sugar, Maliq is transitioning into a town of fish. The history of the Maliq scheme, like many similar schemes across the world, shows the many forms which the project of modernization assumes in different socio-economic and political regimes. Meanwhile, the local population keeps dreaming of achieving development.

CHAPTER 1

The Making of the Sugar Scheme: Transitioning from Empire to Nation

The Plain of Maliq in Ottoman Times

When the Ottomans took control of the plain of Korça in the 1430s, it had no urban center. Korça was a small, fortified settlement at the foot of Mount Morava, having little more than a market and thirty houses. The village next to it, Peshkëpi (meaning "the Bishop's residence"), had about seventy houses and a handful of fourteenth-century Byzantine churches. The Ottomans merged the two villages and preferred the name Korça, making it the administrative center of Kaza (district). Korça, though, would not grow into a city until the late eighteenth-century.[1] The majority of the plateau's villages was concentrated in its northern part, around the swamp of Sovjan, as the locals called it, before the Ottomans' arrival. After the inclusion of the area under the jurisdiction of the Sublime Porte, the villages became *timars*, feudal estates granted in exchange for services to the Ottoman state, and distributed to *sipahis*, who were the fief-holders. The overwhelming majority of the servicemen were Islamized Albanians, but there were Orthodox Christians until at least the sixteenth century. By the seventeenth century, with the gradual erosion of the Sultan's power, the feudal lords that controlled the plain asserted themselves against the central authority and transformed their *timars* into private property, which they inherited regardless of their services to the Ottoman state. A group of powerful feudal families owned the villages of the plain. The peasants, who all had the status of *reaya*, the lower

---

1   Pirro Thomo, *Korça: urbanistika dhe arkitektura* [Korça: Urban planning and architecture] (Tirana: Akademia e Shkencave të Shqipërisë, 2002), 28–31.

class of taxable subjects, paid from one third to half of their production to the *beys*—feudal lords—along with dues in labor. Their obligations also included working the personal plots of the *timar* owners, the *timariots*, including doing their harvesting and other tasks. In addition to these dues, the villages around the swamp also supplied their masters with fish and eels.[2]

By the seventeenth century, due to the tax and legal discrimination of the Christian population, poverty, opportunities for upward mobility in the Ottoman bureaucratic system, and migration from the uplands, Islam expanded in the majority of the plain's villages. The conversion, though, did not improve the status of the rural population vis à vis the nobles and did not alleviate their tax burden. With Islamization, a new Muslim toponymy also made its way into the plain. For centuries, the swamp had been called the non-Islamic name of "Lake of Sovjan," after the village with the same name. However, gradually, the locals started calling the bog after the village of Maliq—from the Arabic and Quranic name Malik—which was built into the slopes of the hills, right over the gorge where the Devoll River starts its journey into the highlands of Gora.

During the eighteenth century, local beys exploited the inability of Istanbul to control its western peripheries in the wake of continuous military defeats of the Ottoman armies; the local beys consolidated their power base. Commanding small armies of hundreds of highlanders, they ruled over the plain as sovereigns. By entering into tangles of competing alliances centered around important feudal families, these beys challenged the undisturbed power of the Sublime Porte and its local administration, which was under the total control of these warlords.[3] Centralizing reforms that started in the early nineteenth century under Sultan Selim III were finalized in the later decades under Mahmood II and brought to an end the immense power of these local nobles. Istanbul waged a rabid war against the bulk of the southern Albanian beys, who had been defying the Sultans' power for more than a century. In the plain of Korça, the Ottoman authorities, through military force, disbanded the personal armies of the local feudal lords and destroyed the power base of these warlords. The nineteenth-

---

2   AIH, A.III.323, *Defteri i Përmetit dhe i Korçës* [The Ottoman register of Përmet and Korça for the years 1431–1432], trans. Vexhi Buharaja, fl. 48. In his memoires, written in the early 1510, the Albanian nobleman Gjon Muzaka explains that the peasants of the area fished very good eels in the lake. See, Gjon Muzaka, *Memorje* [Memoires], transl. Dhori Qiriazi (Tirana: Toena, 1996), 28.

3   On the Albanian nobility and the broader Balkan pattern of center-periphery relations, see Fikret Adanir, "Semi-Autonomous Provincial Forces in the Balkans and Anatolia," in *The Cambridge History of Turkey*, vol. 3, *The Later Ottoman Empire, 1603–1839*, ed. Suraiya N. Faroqhi (Cambridge: Cambridge University Press, 2006), 157–185.

century Ottoman reforms, known as the *Tanzimat*, abolished the peasants' dependency on land, and recognized private property and the legal equality of all subjects regardless of their religious affiliation.[4]

The region's geographic location and the accompanying administrative gravity of the district of Korça significantly influenced the impact of the broad legislative and political transformations of the nineteenth century, especially in the area of the plain. Since the beginning of their rule, the Ottomans integrated the region of Korça administratively and religiously within the vilayet of Monastir—today's Bitola in the south of the Republic of North Macedonia. Both the Orthodox episcopate and the Muslim institutions depended on their respective centers located in Monastir. For the length of the Ottoman rule, the area was economically linked with the multiethnic territories within the vilayet of Monastir, inhabited by Slavic-speakers, Greeks, Vlachs, and Jews. The main maritime gate that connected the region of Korça to the world was the city of Salonika, today's Thessaloniki, one of the most important ports of the eastern Mediterranean. The bulk of the regional trade mainly took place in an eastern and southern direction, along the most important communication routes of the European regions of the Ottoman Empire, which connected the northern Balkans and central Europe to Istanbul. On the other hand, contacts with the administrative units in the west and north, areas densely inhabited by Albanian speakers, were not as intensive, and sometimes, very sparse.[5]

With the implementation of the *Tanzimat* and the greater protection it gave to the Christian Orthodox groups, the peasants of the region of Korça started to emigrate from the empire in the late 1800s, especially to the United States. Being in geographic proximity and having close contact with both the Slavic-speakers and the Greeks of their vilayet, the Orthodox Christian peasants of the region of Korça integrated themselves into the extensive migratory networks of these groups. They successfully used the newly gained right to leave their villages,

---

4   For a concise description and analysis of Tanzimat, see Carter Findley, "The Tanzimat," in *The Cambridge History of Turkey*, vol. 4, *Turkey in the Modern World*, ed. Reşat Kasaba (Cambridge: Cambridge University Press, 2008), 11–37.

5   The territories inhabited by Albanians from the early nineteenth century to the Balkan Wars were divided into four vilayets, the name for the Ottoman administrative units. More specifically, these were: the vilayet of Scutari (or Shkodra) in northwest Albania; the vilayet of Skopje, which included the territories of present-day eastern Albania and Kosovo, as well as a good part of the present-day Republic of North Macedonia; the vilayet of Bitola, which included the region of Korça, the southern part of the present-day Republic of North Macedonia, and parts of present-day northern Greece; and the vilayet of Ioannina, which was composed of the territories of present-day northwestern Greece and southwestern Albania.

and especially the monetarization of the economy, which took off in the nineteenth century, to migrate and work for wage labor. The Muslims of the region, especially those in the villages of the plain of Korça, followed suit. Exploiting the continuous erosion of the power of the beys and their intense involvement in the market economy, the peasants used the cash accumulated from emigration to buy their land. By the early 1900s, the majority of them owned their land, though there were still many sharecroppers until the end of World War II.

Though the Tanzimat crippled the power of the local beys, those in the coastal plains of the Adriatic fiercely resisted Istanbul's centralizing policies and preserved their grasp over the land. Unlike in the plain of Korça, these regions were geographically far from the principal communication routes that crossed the hinterland of the Balkans through contemporary Kosovo and North Macedonia. In addition, the coastal areas of the Albanian vilayets had no major port city, and urban life was marginal. As a result, the market economy and the concomitant transregional communications were poorly developed. Additionally, in the western lowlands, there were much fewer free peasants that owned their land, with a majority of Christian Orthodox and Muslim peasants working the beys' farms as sharecroppers until the interwar era. The geographic location of the western plains, with the tall mountains in the east and the deep blue sea on the west, kept the peasants relatively isolated from the broader transethnic networks of emigration and trade. The market economy advanced slower, and most peasants remained loosely connected with the market economy.[6]

The geographic position that facilitated integration into broader imperial circuits boosted Korça's growth. In the nineteenth century, the city became one of the most important trading centers of the vilayet of Monastir. The breaking of the local nobles' power and the intensification of trade during the Tanzimat era boosted the rapid growth of Korça's population. The majority of newcomers were Christian Orthodox. Following an Ottoman pattern of the religious division of labor, the local trade fell into the hands of the Christian Orthodox, while the Muslims controlled the state bureaucracy and army. Korça's merchants not only controlled a large share of their vilayet market, but they also successfully integrated into the formidable circuits of Ottoman Christian Orthodox merchants,

---

6   On the regional variations in the patterns of agricultural economy in the Albanian-speaking vilayets during the eighteenth and nineteenth centuries, Clayer, *Në fillimet e nacionalizmit shqiptar*, 106–116; Mile, *Zejtaria fshatare shqiptare gjatë Rilindjes Kombëtare*, 9–29 and 64–99; Mile, *Çështje të historië agrare shqiptare*, 319–407; Gazmend Shpuza, *Kryengritja Fshatare e Shqipërisë së Mesme, 1914–1915*, 46–76.

who, since the late eighteenth century, controlled the bulk of Ottoman trade. Demographic growth was not limited only to the city of Korça. Indeed, the number and size of the villages of the plain grew as well.[7] After the establishment of the Albanian state in 1912, the plain of Korça was one of the most densely populated areas of the country.

Conceiving the Reclamation of the Maliq Swamp

Demographic growth, especially in Korça, increased pressure on the environment and disrupted the ecological balance. Housing and heating augmented the need for timber, while a swelling population ballooned the herds of goats in the area as the need for protein increased. This combination of excessive logging and goat pasturing deforested the mountains around the plain and increased soil erosion through the nineteenth century.[8] During the rainy seasons, the creeks and the Devoll River deposited vast amounts of inert matter, blocking the gorge of Maliq. The level of the waters increased, and the swamp expanded and transformed large tracts of surrounding groves and land into a permanent fen. In the winters, it covered the whole plain and flooded the villages around it every year, causing massive damage. The local Ottoman authorities cleared the gorge of the detritus when necessary, but did not make comprehensive interventions for solving the problem permanently. The marsh's destruction of harvests caused a local bread crisis in the late 1870s. The intense rainfalls and the swamp's water level destroyed the crops, forcing the merchants to import grain from Egypt. The problem persisted in the later years. As a consequence, in the last two decades of the nineteenth century, the peasants of the villages around the swamp and the local elites started discussing its reclamation.[9]

---

7   On the role of Orthodox Christian merchants in Ottoman trade, see Bruce Masters, "Christians in a Changing World," in *The Cambridge History of Turkey*, vol. 3, 186–206. On the growth of the rural population in the plain of Korça during the nineteenth century, see Andromaqi Gjergji, "Fshati si territor banimi dhe si bashkësi shoqërore (Në fushën e Korçës)" [The village as a residential territory and a social community – in the plain of Korça], in *Mënyra e jetesës në shekujt XIII–XX*, 129–155; Andromaqi Gjergji, "Jetesa në një fshat të fushës së Korçës (shek. XIX–XX)" [Life in a village in the plain of Korça during the nineteenth and twentieth centuries], in *Mënyra e jetesës në shekujt XIII–XX*, 197–240.
8   Gjon Fierza, "Pyjet, kullotat dhe Shërbimi Pyjor i Shqipërisë në vështrimin historik" [Forests, pastures, and the Albanian Forest Service: A historical overview], in *Pyjet dhe Shërbimi Pyjor Shqiptar në vite* [Forests and the Albanian Forest Service through the years], eds. Gjon Fierza, Kolë Malaj, and Janaq Mele (Tirana: Graphic Line-01, 2013), 25–26.
9   AIH, A.IV.275, *Korça: kqyrje historike* [Korça: An historical review], fl. 2; AIH, A.IV.305, Charallamb Karmitses, *Gjeografia e Korçës dhe e rrethit* [The geography of Korça and its district] (Thessaloniki,

CHAPTER 1

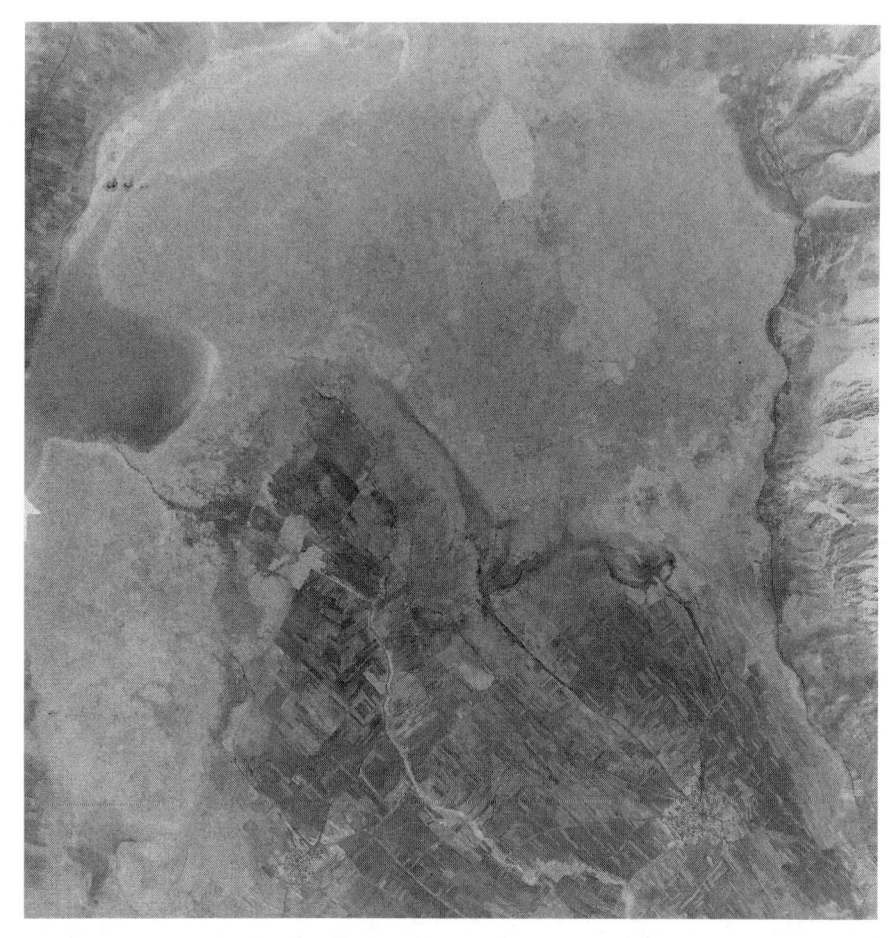

FIGURE 1. Photo of the swamp of Maliq taken by USAF recognizance on September 14, 1943

However, it was the Ottoman state that started the project of reclamation. During these same decades, the Sublime Porte embarked on an ambitious modernizing program for revitalizing the empire that included a series of reclamations, which had the expansion of agricultural land and the eradication of malaria as goals. These efforts were not simple responses to political agitations or the floods that the swamp caused but also reflected a broader trend that had appeared in the Mediterranean in the second half of the 1800s and continued through the 1960s. The new nation-states of Southern Europe, and an Ottoman state that was strug-

---

1888), trans. Niko Çane, fl. 20–21; Nuçi Naçi, *Korça edhe katundet e qarkut* [Korça and the villages of its county] (Korça: Dhori Koti, 1923), 55–56; Gjergji, "Jetesa në një fshat të fushës së Korçës," 207–208.

gling to regenerate its crumbling imperial structure, were all committed to mimicking the industrial and agricultural revolution in Germany and Northwestern Europe.[10] They started a series of infrastructure projects, where waterworks and the reclamation of swamps occupied a prominent place. These initiatives were not limited to the southern fringe of Europe. Around the same time, England and France started reclamations and other hydrological projects in their empires, as was the case with Egypt and Vietnam.[11] State authorities and private actors were all taken away by the fever of the expansion of the internal frontier and started reclaiming many swamps that infested the coasts or inland plains.[12]

By the second half of the nineteenth century, the modernist approach toward nature that had emerged since the eighteenth century in northern Europe made inroads in southern Europe. By the late 1800s, the emerging groups and social segments that held power embraced the vision of nature as feminine, wild, uncivilized, untamed, and chaotic. It had to be conquered, disciplined, civilized, tamed, and ordered.[13] In an age that juxtaposed civilization to barbarity, the promoters of the modern centralized state considered the alleged wilderness of nature as unacceptable and its taming as a duty to civilization.[14] This attitude to-

---

10 On Germany see David Blackbourn, *The Conquest of Nature: Water, Landscape, and the Making of Modern Germany* (New York: W. W. Norton, 2006).

11 On Egypt and Italy, John R. McNeill, *Something New Under the Sun: An Environmental History of the Twentieth-Century World* (New York: W. W. Norton, 2000), 166–177. On Greece, Maria Kaika, "Dams as Symbols of Modernization: The Urbanization of Nature between Geographical Imagination and Materiality," *Annals of the Association of American Geographers* 96, no. 2 (2006): 283; Maria Kaika, *City of Flows: Modernity, Nature, and the City* (London: Routledge, 2005), 112. On Spain, Erik Swyngedouw, "Modernity and Hybridity: Nature, *Regeneracionismo*, and the Production of the Spanish Waterscape," *Annals of the Association of American Geographers* 89, no. 3 (1999): 443–465. On Vietnam, David A. Biggs, *Quagmire: Nation-Building and Nature in the Mekong Delta* (Seattle: University of Washington Press, 2010), 23–52.

12 Many of these marshlands of the Mediterranean were created from the sixteenth to the eighteenth century. In the same way, the nineteenth-century trend to reclaim them was also pan-Mediterranean in scale, when all the states of the area started similar hydraulic projects. For more, see Faruk Tabak, "Economic and Ecological Change in the Eastern Mediterranean, c. 1550–1850," in *Cities of the Mediterranean: From the Ottomans to the Present Day*, eds. Biray Kolluoglu and Meltem Toksöz (London: I. B. Taurus, 2010), 23–37.

13 For more on this subject, see Neil Smith, *Uneven Development: Nature, Capital, and the Production of Space* (Athens, GA: University of Georgia Press, 1990), 10–48.

14 Stefania Barca argues that in Italy, until the 1860s, the approach to nature was not defined by these dichotomies. She argues that the Italian elites considered nature as a source that supported improvement and well-being. The situation changed in the last three decades of the nineteenth century when the dichotomies between nature and progress were equated to the binary between civilization and barbarity. Stefania Barca, "A 'Natural' Capitalism: Water and the Making of the Italian Industrial Landscape," in *Nature and History in Modern Italy*, eds. Marco Armiero and Marcus Hall (Athens, OH: University of Ohio Press, 2010), 215–230.

ward nature was anthropocentrism *in extremis* that regarded everything as an object of transformation and manipulation. Disciplining nature meant organizing it according to a superior human-made order. What is most important is that the utilitarian outlook, which considered nature a function to human ambition, did not limit itself within liberal democracies. The Promethean vision of humanity liberated from the fetters of nature's tyranny and mastering the universe was central to the communist and fascist regimes as well.[15]

The reclamation of Maliq was part of these broader trends that penetrated the Ottoman Empire in the last phases of its existence. For the entire nineteenth century, the technocratic elites of the Sublime Porte tried to reform the empire following the model of the modern Western European territorial states. Although the Ottoman modernizers failed to transform the "sick man of Europe" into a healthy first-rate power, they did attain considerable success. However, the reclamation of the swamp of Maliq was part of those many unsuccessful enterprises. A lack of funds and corruption of the local authorities inhibited any significant steps in preventing the floods, indicating the limits of the Ottoman modernizers' ability to successfully meet their lofty goals.[16]

The local imperial apparatus's procrastination to reclaim the swamp prompted some entrepreneurs from Korça to independently continue the project. Some wealthy merchants of the city saw an excellent opportunity to invest their capital in the reclamation and lobbied in Istanbul to secure the Sultan's authorization.[17] In March 1912, the Ottoman Imperial Ministry of Public Works granted the concession to a group of local entrepreneurs who were well connected to influential political circles in Istanbul.[18] It was too late, though, and the works never

---

15 On Fascism, see Federico Caprotti and Maria Kaika, "Producing the Ideal Fascist Landscape: Nature, Materiality, and the Cinematic Representation of Land Reclamation in the Pontine Marshes," *Social & Cultural Geography* 9, no. 6 (2008): 617–618. On Stalin's Soviet Union, see John McCannon, "Tabula Rasa in the North: The Soviet Arctic and Mythic Landscapes in Stalinist Popular Culture," in *The Landscape of Stalinism: The Art and Ideology of Soviet Space*, eds. Evgeny Dobrenko and Eric Naiman (Seattle: University of Washington Press, 2003), 241–260.

16 On nineteenth-century Ottoman history, see M. Şükrü Hanioğlu, *A Brief History of the Late Ottoman Empire* (Princeton, NJ: Princeton University Press, 2008); Donald Quataert, *The Ottoman Empire, 1700–1922* (Oxford: Oxford University Press, 2005). On the failure of the Ottoman authorities to reclaim the swamp, see AQSh, F. 149, Kryeministria, 1920, d. III–66, fl. 1. Letter of appeal of the peasants of the villages of the plain of Maliq sent to the Prime Minister's Office for reclaiming the swamp of Maliq; Naçi, *Korça edhe katundet*, 55–56; Gjergji, "Jetesa në një fshat," 207–208.

17 AQSh, F. 51, Sami Frashëri, n.d., d. 14, fl. 1-4. Draft by Sami Frashëri on the reclamation of the lake of Maliq.

18 AQSh, F. 143, Koleksion dokumentesh, 1912, d. 1274, fl. 1-5. Act of concession and Sultan Mehmed Reshad's decree on the approval for the reclamation of the swamp of Maliq.

started. In October 1912, the First Balkan War began. The military alliance between Bulgaria, Greece, Montenegro, and Serbia, forged with the blessing of Russia, brought an end to the Sublime Porte's control over the Balkans.

With the support of Austria-Hungary, the archenemy of Russia and its Balkan allies, Serbia and Montenegro, a group of Albanian nationalists proclaimed the independence of Albania on November 28, 1912. At the 1912 Conference of Ambassadors in London, the highest international forum of the era decided the peace in the Balkans and drew new state borders between the belligerent parties. After continuous threats from a German-backed Austria to invade Serbia, the conference decided to recognize the establishment of an independent Albania. Italy supported the Habsburg policy on Albania not out of loyalty but to prevent any country from controlling the Albanian coast. Lying across the Strait of Otranto, the Italians considered control over the Albanian coast of vital interest. On July 29, 1913, the Conference of Ambassadors in London recognized the existence of an independent Albania with the same state borders it has today. The European Concert proclaimed Albania a neutral state and guaranteed its sovereignty collectively. These guarantees aimed to prevent the country from slipping under the influence of one of the powers and disrupting the geostrategic balance of the region.[19]

After the two Balkan wars and the Conference of the Ambassadors, the *vilayet* of Monastir was split between three different countries: Albania, Greece, and Serbia. The latter annexed the city of Monastir, which changed its name to Bitola (which in Slavic means monastery), and the northern regions of the ex-Ottoman vilayet. Greece conquered all the southern coastal districts, including the port city of Salonika, and changed its medieval name to the more ancient and Greek name of Thessaloniki. Korça, meanwhile, much coveted by Greece, became part of Albania. Although both Greece and Bulgaria claimed to take all the vilayet for themselves and had been contending for it since the late nineteenth century, its territories, which had constituted an economically integrated

---

19 On the complicated issue of Albanian independence and the encroaching interests of the Great Powers, see Arben Puto, *Pavarësia e Shqipërisë dhe Diplomacia e Fuqive të Mëdha (1912–1914)* [Albanian independence and Great Powers diplomacy (1912–1914)] (Tirana: 8 Nëntori, 1976); Miranda Vickers, *The Albanians: A Modern History* (London: I. B. Tauris, 2001), 53–76; Bernd J. Fischer, "Albanian Nationalism in the Twentieth Century," in *Eastern European Nationalism in the Twentieth Century*, ed. Peter F. Sugar (Washington, DC: American University Press, 1995), 25–34; Barbara and Charles Jelavich, *The Establishment of the Balkan National States, 1804–1920* (Seattle: University of Washington Press, 1977), 222–234. On the Balkan Wars, see Egidio Ivetic, *Le guerre balcaniche* (Milan: Mulino, 2007).

melting pot, dissolved. The new state borders broke the old unity of regional markets and social networks built over the centuries of Ottoman control. While the region of Korça, because of its affluence and participation in the larger flows of people, goods, capital, and ideas, was one of the most important centers of Albanian nationalism, its integration in the Albanian state was extremely difficult economically.

As with other Balkan states, the European Great Powers chose a German prince for the newly born state and assigned Wilhelm von Wied as its sovereign. The beginning of hostilities in World War I marked the end of the European Concert, the main guarantor of the existence of Albania as a newly established state. Wied's career as the prince of Albania, who arrived in Albania in March 1914, did not last more than six months. Facing immense domestic difficulties, including a rebellion induced by Serbian and Greek gold and its neighbors' commitment to undermining the newly established state, Wied lacked the much-promised international support. After the beginning of hostilities, regardless of Vienna's pressure to fight against Serbia and Montenegro, Wied reiterated Albania's neutrality. Left without support and with empty coffers, he headed to Germany and joined the Prussian army as a private citizen, without, however, abdicating the Albanian throne.[20]

Albania became a battlefield of opposing armies. Italy, whose interests conflicted with Austria over the Italian-speaking minorities within the Habsburg's realm and the latter's dominance over the Adriatic, clashed with Vienna over control of the Albanian coast. After World War I began, Rome did not renew its alliance with the Central Powers and sided with the Entente Cordiale. The latter saw the establishment of Albania as a launching pad for Austrian and German interests. To lure Italy into their alliance, France, the United Kingdom, and Russia agreed to concede full control over central Albania and its Adriatic coast to it. In London, where two years prior the European Concert had decided the establishment of an Albanian state, the Entente was signed with Italy on April 26, 1915. The Secret Treaty of London sealed the fate of Albania. Besides fulfilling Italy's requests, this accord divided north Albania between Serbia and Montenegro while giving the south, including the region of Korça, to Greece.[21]

---

20 On Wied's reign, see Ferdinando Salleo, *Albania. Un regno per sei mesi* (Palermo: Sellerio Editore, 2000); Joseph Swire, *Albania: The Rise of a Kingdom* (New York: AbeBooks, 1971).

21 On the secret treaty of London and Albania, as well as broader issues concerning the diplomacy of the great powers toward Albania during World War I, see Arben Puto, *Historia diplomatike e çështjes shqiptare, 1878–1926* [The diplomatic history of the Albanian question, 1878–1926] (Tirana: Albin,

However, events did not proceed smoothly for the Entente's new southern allies. While Italy took control of southwestern Albania, strategically closing off the Habsburg fleet in the Adriatic, Greece nearly slipped into civil war between pro-German and pro-Entente supporters. The internal turmoil did not allow the Greeks to consolidate rule over the regions they had received in the Treaty of London. The pro-Entente party, led by the Hellenic Prime Minister Eleftherios Venizelos, established its headquarters in Thessaloniki and asked for the support of its great allies. Soon, the French Armée d'Orient disembarked in the port city. By 1916, the Habsburg forces, after crushing the tenacious Serbian and Montenegrin resistance, crashed through northern and central Albania, the Austro-Hungarian military halted its advance only in the southern districts already where they encountered the Entente's troops. The Italian army had been controlling the southeastern regions of Albania since 1914 and the detachments of the Armée d'Orient had captured the district of Korça.

The French army, based in Thessaloniki, occupied the southeastern regions of Albania to prevent the Austro-Hungarian divisions from both threatening their positions in the Aegean port city and joining their forces with the pro-German Greek King, Constantine, based in Athens. After units of the Armée d'Orient entered Korça in October 1916, they immediately started, in colonial style, their *mission civilatrice* in this corner of the Balkans. Besides guns, cannons, and soldiers, the French army also brought administrators and scientists. They played concerts and movies for the servicemen, built roads with mobilized labor—mainly war prisoners—collected taxes, and explored the region's resources. Entertaining their soldiers was important for the French commanders, but the roads and taxes were even more critical for their military operations. During the three and a half years of its administration, the French command tried to limit the swamp's floods, which not only devastated the population but also hampered the movement of the troops. In addition, one of the principal goals was to limit malaria's effects on military units—similar to other French efforts in Thessaloniki. For that reason, the French used war prisoners to clear the gorge of Maliq of the detritus and partially drain the high water of the swamp.[22]

2003); Arben Puto, *Çështja shqiptare në aktet ndërkombëtare të periudhës së imperializmit: përmbledhje dokumentesh me një vështrim historik* [The Albanian question in the international proceedings of the age of imperialism: document collection with a historical overview], vol. II (Tirana: 8 Nëntori, 1984); Muin Çami, *Shqipëria në marrëdhëniet ndërkombëtare (1914–1918)* [Albania in international affairs (1914–1918)] (Tirana: Akademia e Shkencave e RPS të Shqipërisë, 1987).

22 On the issue of the French military intervention in Greece and the diplomatic chess game between the Quai d'Orsey, their Greek supporters, and the Albanians, see Nicola Guy, *The Birth of Albania:*

CHAPTER 1

Following the blueprint that the Armée d'Orient's headquarters applied in Thessaloniki, its branch in Korça did not limit itself exclusively to military matters. Thinking of themselves as an outpost of France in the Balkans' heartland (which to them meant outside of Europe), the French command in Korça exploited the opportunity to project their country's power. Opening a Lycée in the city, where Enver Hoxha would teach French in the 1930s, was not enough to convey the benefits of the French civilization, however. Looking at the area of Korça through the same Orientalist lenses they had used in Macedonia, the French officers and scientists located in the region considered it a space abundant with unused potential due to passivity and mismanagement. During their time in Korça, a group of French scientists studied the ecology, geography, fauna, and geology of the region. Although they did not study the swamp, the French discovered that the sandy-clay clay soil of the plain was optimal for the cultivation of sugar beet and the development of a sugar industry.[23]

At the end of the Great War, the winners gathered in Paris to decide the post-World War I European order. With the Entente's triumph, the implementation of the Treaty of London became a real possibility, and the independence of Albania hung on a very thin thread. After witnessing the annexation of half of the Albanian-speaking population by the neighboring countries, Albanian nationalists were not willing to concede any further territory. In 1920, they organized their own government in Tirana, a city located safely within the 1913 borders. What the nationalists considered as temporary became the country's permanent capital. The new government did not recognize the Treaty of London and pro-

---

Ethnic Nationalism, the Great Powers of World War I and the Emergence of Albanian Independence (London: I. B. Tauris, 2012), 125–151; Muin Çami, "Veçori të Lëvizjes Kombëtare në krahinën e Korçës (gjatë Lufës së Parë Botërore)" [Characteristics of the national movement in the region of Korça during World War I], in *Shqipëria në rrjedhat e historisë, 1912–1924* [Albania through the currents of history, 1912–1924] (Tirana: Onufri, 2007), 76–88; Muin Çami, "Ushtarakët francezë në Korçë mbështetës të aspiratave të popullit shqiptar" [The French military in Korça, supporters of the aspirations of the Albanian people], *Ibid*, 127–150; Muin Çami, *Shqiptarët dhe francezët në Korçë: 1916–1920* [The Albanians and the French in Korça: 1916–1920] (Tirana: Dituria, 1999). On the activity of the French army in the region of Korça, AIH, A-IV-149, Mediha Jasa, *Republika e Korçës 1916–1918* [The Republic of Korça 1916–1918], unpublished study in the Archive of the Institute of History, Tirana. On the French engineering works, AQSh, F. 177, Ministria e Punëve të Botore, 1920, d. 10, fl. 5. Report of the engineer of public works of the prefecture of Korça concerning the problem of the reclamation of the swamp of Maliq. July 29, 1920.

23 AIH, A-IV-149, Jasa, *Republika e Korçës 1916–1918*; Jacques Bourcart, *Shqipëria dhe shqiptarët* [Albania and the Albanians], trans. Asti Papa (Tirana: Dituria, 2004), 117–127. On the French *Mission Civiliatrice* in Thessaloniki during World War I, see Mazower, *Salonica, City of Ghosts*, 295–298.

claimed that it adhered to the decision of the now-defunct European Concert and started preparing to defend its borders.

Soon after the war was over, the allies became enemies as they fought for the spoils of World War I. Yugoslavia replaced Austria-Hungary as Italy's principal competitor in the Adriatic, and neither of them were willing to split Albania and have a border with each other in the south. For both of them, a weak Albania seemed to be the better option. Greece, meanwhile, had embarked upon its Turkish adventure, and after its crushing defeat in Anatolia, was too drained of resources and energy to start another war with the very determined Albanian nationalists. What saved Albania, though, was the energetic intervention of Woodrow Wilson. The American president went to Paris with the slogan of new diplomacy and crusading against secret treaties, including those signed in London in April of 1915. During this time, it was the active lobbying of the Albanian nationalists—and especially Wilson's strong support of Yugoslavian policy—that played an essential role in his decision. He also received positive reports from the American envoys in Albania, who favored the country's existence. Adhering to the principle of self-determination, one of the most important points of his program, Wilson flatly rejected the implementation of the Treaty of London and the ensuing disintegration of Albania in February 1920, making him a hero of Albanian nationalists. In May of the same year, the Conference of Versailles recognized the existence of an independent Albanian state with the borders established by the European Concert back in 1913.[24] Soon after recognizing Albania's independence and Korça as part of it, the French troops left the region. Their idea of sugar industry, though, remained.

The Maliq Scheme and the Quest for Nation-Building and Self-Sufficiency

The collapse of the Ottoman Empire and the refashioning of the political borders of the Balkans dissolved the old imperial administrative structure and their fragments were absorbed into new political frameworks. Territories that had few contacts and exchanges until that point, now coexisted under the umbrella of

---

24 On the Paris Conference of 1919, the discussion of the Albanian question, and Wilson's intervention in favor of Albania's independence, see Haris Silajdzic, *Shqipëria dhe ShBA në arkivat e Uashingtonit* [Albania and the USA in the Washington Archives], trans. Xhelal Fejza (Tirana: Dituria, 1999); Puto, *Historia diplomatike e çështjes shqiptare, 1878–1926*; Margaret Macmillan, *Paris 1919: Six Months that Changed the World* (New York: Random House, 2002), 357–164.

the nation-state. Centuries-old links unraveled, and new ones, oriented toward national centers, emerged. The new demarcation lines between the states of southeastern Europe erected walls of customs barriers and protectionist policies that crippled the flow of people, goods, and capital along the old trade routes. Amid the reframing of the political map of the Balkans, Korça's traders and merchants lost a good part of their old markets and trade connections, along with access to Thessaloniki. The most pressing problem that the region faced was the dependence on imported foodstuffs, especially cereals; a pattern that had persisted since the second half of the nineteenth century. With the closing of the old trade routes, the price of grain spiked. Supplies now arrived from the coastal areas of the Adriatic, but the poor road network affected the price of grain, which in Korça was three times higher compared to the western lowlands. The lack of food also meant social trouble, as in 1921 and 1923, when bread demonstrations erupted among Korça's poor.[25]

Heavy rains in the early 1920s caused increased flooding and damaged the local peasants' holdings, forcing them to ask the government's immediate intervention to clear the gorge of Maliq.[26] The government had the will to take immediate action but lacked the financial resources.[27] The wealthy merchants and urban landlords of Korça saw the bread crisis and the devastations of the swamp as business opportunities and took over the challenge of reclamation. By the early 1920s, local elites were adjusting themselves to the new national context and were looking for opportunities to revitalize their capital. They planned a series of ambitious projects, which also included the building of a hydropower station on the Devoll River that aimed at both exploiting the region's resources and connect-

---

25 "Mbi shtrentësirën e kësushme" [On actual high prices], *Posta e Korçës* [Korça's mail], August 30, 1921, 1; "Çështja e ditës" [The issue of the day], *Zëri i Popullit* [The people's voice], March 17, 1923, 2; Kristaq Misha, *Lëvizja punëtore në Shqipëri* [The workers' movement in Albania] (Tirana: Naim Frashëri, 1970), 88–91.
26 AQSh, F. 149, Kryeministria, 1920, d. III-66, fl. 1. Letter of appeal of the peasants of the villages of the plain of Maliq sent to the Prime Minister's Office for reclaiming the swamp of Maliq; AQSh, F. 177, Ministria e Punëve të Botore, 1920, d. 10, fl. 5. Report of the engineer of public works of the prefecture of Korça concerning the problem of the reclamation of the swamp of Maliq. July 29, 1920; "Liqeni i Sovjanit" [The lake of Sovjan], *Posta e Korçës*, October 25, 1921, 1.
27 AQSh, F. 152, Ministria e Punëve të Brendshme, 1922, d. 390, fl. 1-16. The order of the Ministry of the Interior to issue credit for the reclamation of the swamp of Maliq and respective correspondence. January 1, 1921–October 29, 1922; AQSh, F. 152, Ministria e Punëve të Brendshme, 1922, d. 713, fl. 1-4. Correspondence of the Ministry of the Interior and the prefecture of Korça regarding the reclamation of the swamp of Maliq. December 7-12, 1922; AQSh, F. 177, Ministria e Punëve Botore, 1922, d. 71, fl. 1-83. Correspondence between the Ministry of Public Works and the Ministry of Finance concerning the reclamation of the swamp of Maliq and the destruction caused by the Devoll floods. January–September 1922.

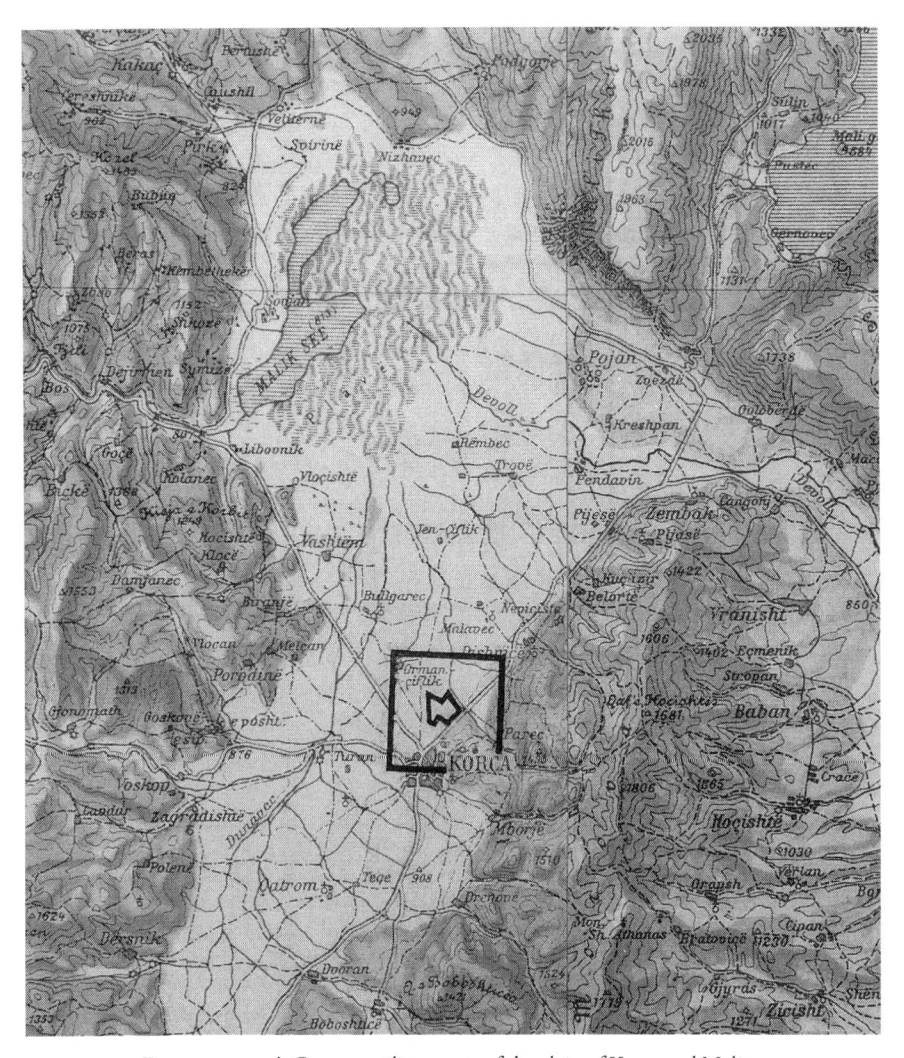

FIGURE 2. 1943's German military map of the plain of Korça and Maliq

ing it to the western lowlands. It was a vision of the future that tried to integrate regional ambitions and aspirations within broader modernizing plans of the national state. The entrepreneurs of Korça used hydrological projects as platforms for social and economic transformation, similar to the development schemes of the 1930s and the post-World War II era.

The reclamation of the Maliq swamp was to be the first of these projects because their implementation depended on the draining of the marshland and controlling the Devoll's flow. According to the plans of the entrepreneurs, they would cultivate the reclaimed land with wheat to meet local demand. The returns from this investment would support the other subsequent projects.[28] So great was the enthusiasm in Korça for the reclamation of Maliq that the future French Minister of Health, Justin Godart, while visiting Korça in 1921, recorded in his diary that everybody in the city was talking about it.[29] Such an undertaking needed time, and it was only finalized in 1924 with the establishment of the Maliqi joint-stock company. The government, which expressed support for the project since its conception, granted the company a five-year concession for the swamp of Maliq in 1925.[30] However, by the mid-1920s, improvements to road and transportation systems lowered grain prices from the western lowlands. Reclaiming the swamp in order to cultivate it with wheat was no longer profitable, but the owners of the Maliqi company did not give up on the project and looked for other profitable undertakings. Indeed, they already had one left behind by the French military expedition during World War I. The company brought specialists from France, who confirmed that the soil of the area around the swamp was still suitable for the cultivation of sugar beet.[31]

In the meantime, the increase in sugar consumption during the interwar era made such an enterprise very profitable. From 4 kg per person per year in 1921, the annual per capita consumption of sugar reached the figure of 6 kg by the mid-

---

28 AQSh, F. 177, Ministria e Punëve Botore, 1924, d. 165, fl. 4-5. Report of Friedrich Rudolph, specialist in the Ministry of Public Works, on the Maliqi company. February 25, 1924; *Ibid*, fl. 6-8. Report of Friedrich Rudolph on the participation of the state in the project for the reclamation of the swamp of Maliq. March 26, 1924; *Ibid*, letter of the Commission of Initiators of the Maliqi company sent to the prefecture of Korça regarding the reclamation of the swamp of Maliq. April 4, 1924; "Kapitali i vendit dhe liqeni i Maliqit" [The national capital and the lake of Maliq], *Zëri i Popullit*, August 18, 1923, 2.
29 Justin Godart, *Ditarët shqiptarë: shënimet e udhëtimeve nga marsi 1921 deri në dhjetor 1951* [The Albanian diaries: traveling notes of March 1921 to December 1951], transl. Asti Papa (Tirana: Dituria, 2008), 77 and 91.
30 On the need to establish a company with joint capital for the reclamation of the swamp, see "Kapitali i vendit dhe liqeni i Maliqit," 2. On the establishment of the Maliqi company, "Shoqëria Anonime "Maliq" [Maliqi joint-stock company], *Gazeta e Korçës* [The Korça gazette], April 19, 1924, 3. On the government's support and granting of the concession, AQSh, F. 177, Ministria e Punëve Botore, 1924, d. 165, fl. 1-19. Correspondence between the Ministry of Public Works and the prefecture of Korça concerning the requests of the Maliqi company and its project to reclaim the swamp of Maliq. February 25–April 19, 1924; AQSh, F. 177, Ministria e Punëve Botore, 1925, d. 106, fl. 56-59. Decree of the Ministry of Public Works for the right of the Maliqi company to reclaim the swamp of Maliq. February 4, 1925; AQSh, F. 317, Prefektura e Korçës, 1925, d. 99, fl. 1-11. Correspondence between the Prime Minister's Office, the Ministry of the Interior, and the prefecture of Korça regarding the concession to the Maliqi company for reclaiming the swamp of Maliq. April 30, 1925–January 2, 1926; AQSh, F. 146, Parlamenti, 1925, d. 58, fl. 1-24. Approval from the Parliament of the government's concession to the Maliqi company for the reclamation of the swamp of Maliq. November 11–December 15, 1925.
31 "Shoqëria 'Maliq'" [Maliqi company], *Koha* [Time], no. 249, December 5, 1925, 2.

1920s. In 1926, Albania imported 5000 tons of sugars—loaves, half processed, molasses, and granulated—and reached its peak in 1930 with 5500 tons. The Albanian government realized the growing importance of sugar and, in the late 1920s, considered it, together with rice, flour, coffee, and kerosene, one of the most important commodities that the country imported. As an Albanian newspaper noted in 1930, sugar, salt, and kerosene were the basic stuff of any shop in Albania. Two Italian sugar specialists working for the Albanian government shared the same opinion. In a report they wrote in 1933, they observed that "Albania is a strong consumer of sugar for the extensive use of coffee, tea, and Turkish delights." Under the weight of the Great Depression in the 1930s, Albania decreased its imports of sugar. However, according to Italian estimates, by the end of the decade, sugar consumption was 5.2 kg per capita. The economic crisis did not impact peoples' desires.[32]

The shareholders of the Maliqi company were eager to put their hands on the 2 million gold francs—approximately USD 500,000—of sugar imports. After confirmation by French researchers that the soil of the plain of Maliq was suitable for the cultivation of sugar beet, the company's shareholders realized the potential for a sugar industry. It would not take them long to give the project a new direction by cultivating the reclaimed land with sugar beet and building a sugar refinery in Korça.[33] Thus, in the mid-1920s, the swamp's reclamation and the development of the sugar industry merged into one single project. By the 1930s, the Maliqi company started negotiations with a Hungarian firm to build a refinery with shared Albanian and Hungarian capital. Besides producing sugar for the domestic market, the entrepreneurs of the Maliqi company planned to expand their business and produce chocolates and bonbons, for which demand was continually increasing in Albania.[34]

---

32 On the Albanian authorities considering sugar as one of the most important commodities the country imported, see AMPJ, 1928, d. 167, fl. 14. Explanatory list of the Ministry of Foreign Affairs regarding the imports of Albania. On the press considering sugar as one of the most important imports of the country, "Monopolet dhe konçesionet – monopoli i sheqerit" [Monopolies and concessions – the monopoly of sugar], *Shqipëria e Re* [New Albania], no. 446, November 21, 1930, 1. On the Italians' observations on the consumption of sugar in Albania, AQSh, F. 171, Ministria e Ekonimisë (Drejtoria e Bujqësisë), 1933, d. 833, fl. 4. Report of Giovanni Lorenzoni and Pier-Francesco Nistri on the establishment of the sugar industry in the region of Korça. On the Italian estimations of sugar consumption in the 1930s, AQSh, F. 161, Mëkëmbësia e Përgjithshme, 1939, d. 1060, fl. 1. Report on the project for the construction of two sugar factories, one in Korça and one in the plain of Myzeqe.
33 M. Frashëri, "Një shpjegim për çështjen e liqenit të Maliqit" [An explanation on the issue of Maliq's lake] *Gazeta e Korçës*, no. 181, May 2, 1925, 4; "Shoqëria 'Maliq'," 2.
34 On the focus on sugar production in the 1920s, see "Tharja e liqenit të Maliqit" [The reclamation of Maliq's lake], *Koha*, nr. 220, May 9, 1925, 2; "Inagurimi i tharjes së liqenit Maliq" [The inauguration

CHAPTER 1

The shareholders of the Maliqi company, eager to fill the lacunae of domestic production and exploit the national market to the maximum of their advantage, started plans to transform the plain of Maliq into Albania's land of sugar. These entrepreneurs saw an opportunity in national projects and readily exploited them as a platform to redefine regional economic life by supplying the domestic market with specialized products. The regional specialization of Korça in the production of sugar and sweets was taking place within the context of the nation-state.

There were other critical factors that made the plain of Maliq a designated place for the development of the sugar industry. Besides the suitable climate and soil composition, the swamp solved the problem of land, which was the major challenge for the cultivation of sugar beet. Its reclamation guaranteed the necessary contiguous arable land, large enough to allow large-scale farming and the application of at least a three-year crop rotation to preserve its fertility. Sugar beet is a labor-intensive crop, and its cultivation needs the use of modern mechanized means for deep plowing, so to produce yields high enough to respond to the sugar refinery's needs. According to the Albanian government, for the production of 6000 tons of sugar for the domestic market, 10,000 hectares of land were necessary.[35]

---

of the reclamation of Maliq's lake], *Zëri i Korçës* [The voice of Korça], no. 206, July 12, 1927, 4; "Industrija e tanishme në barabitje me industrinë q'i duhet Shqipërisë" [Today's industry compared to the industry that Albania needs] *Shqipëri' e re* [New Albania], no. 325, June 3, 1928, 2. On the project for the building of a refinery with shared Albanian and Hungarian capital, AQSh, F. 171, Ministria e Ekonomisë (Drejtoria e Tregtisë dhe Industrisë), 1934, d. 676, fl. 3. Report on the proposal of the Hungarian engineer Tibor Kevesh, representative of Hungarian companies, for the selling of machinery for the processing of beet sugar. December 31, 1934; "Projekte për ndërtimin e disa fabrikave" [Projects for the constructions of some factories], *Gazeta e Korçës*, no. 2132, January 2, 1935, 1. The statistics of the Ministry of Finance demonstrate a huge increase of imported cocoa and chocolates during the interwar era, an indicator of the increase in consumption in Albania of the goods of this category. For more, see the statistics released by the Albanian government on foreign trade during the 1920s and 1930s: *Statistika Importatjon – Exportatjone vjetës 1921 e Shtetit Shqyptár* [Statistics of the Albanian state on imports and exports for the year 1921] (Shkodra: Ministrija e Financavet, 1922), 4; *Statistika Tregtare e Importacjon – Eksportacjon-it prej 1 Kallnuerit deri më 31 Dhetuer 1926* [Commercial statistics on imports and exports for the year 1926] (Tirana: Ministria e Financavet, 1927), 11; *Statistikë e Tregtis së Jashtëme: Viti 1927* [Statistics on foreign commerce for the year 1927] (Tirana: Ministria e Financavet, 1928), 51; *Statistikë e Tregtis së Jashtëme: Viti 1928* [Statistics on foreign commerce for the year 1928] (Tirana: Ministria e Financavet, 1929), 49–50; *Statistikë e Tregtis së Jashtëme: Viti 1935* [Statistics on foreign commerce for the year 1935] (Tirana: Ministria e Financavet, 1936), 23–24.

35 AQSh, F. 171, Ministria e Ekonomisë, 1934, d. 676, fl. 3-4. Report on the proposal of the Hungarian engineer Tibor Kevesh, representative of Hungarian companies, for the selling of machinery for the processing of beet sugar. December 31, 1934; AMPJ, 1935, d. 205, fl. 1. Letter of the Royal Legation of Albania in Trieste in relation to the project for building sugar factories in Shkodra and Korça. January 22, 1935; AQSh, F. 179, Banka Kombëtare, 1937, d. 47, fl. 8. Correspondence between the Directory of the National Bank and its branch in Korça concerning the possibility of the building of a sugar refinery. September 16, 1937.

In the early 1920s, Albania did not have enough arable land—a problem that persists today. It is a mountainous country, and the few plains it had were covered by swamps and bogs. The property structure in the areas under cultivation did not help large-scale agriculture. The land was divided among many small farmers. The tillers were not fully integrated into the market economy and worked their small scattered plots with primitive tools. The swamp of Maliq, with its 4500 hectares covered by water and another 4500 by groves, seemed to offer a solution to these obstacles. Indeed, the marshland provided the sugar industry with a vast area of predominantly unowned arable and fertile land for the implementation of large-scale, mechanized agriculture.[36] Thus, the plain became specialized in the production of a commodity.

Hence, sugar production became a means that fostered the integration of the region of Korça within the national body. The spatial division of labor enabled the construction of a coherent and cohesive national economic system, where different districts, or provinces, complemented each other's needs. The nation is not merely an imagined community built through a symbolic order. The latter, conveyed through schools, books, propaganda, civic celebrations, maps, and censuses, is but only a part of the nation-building process.[37] The symbolic representation of the nation, or its imagined forms, should correspond to an empirical reality which underpins the former. The creation of a cohesive national economic system fills the national map with new and powerful meaning and transforms it into a tapestry of thickly interwoven threads that knit a distinct entity of links, conceptually separable from other countries. In the nationalists' thinking, the connections within the national borders have to surpass, by far, those outside of them. Thus, the nation's map not only becomes a symbolic projection of the territory inhabited by a given group but also emerges as a space of intense interactions and interdependencies. To build the nation and make it more tangible, the national elites added a bedrock of economic interests to the constructed shared identities.

Analyzing the role of the economy in nation-building, the economic historian Andreas Etges has stated that the political economy is just like the nation,

---

36 AQSh, F. 171, Ministria e Ekonomisë (Drejtoria e Tregtisë dhe Industrisë), 1940, d. 251, fl. 2-3. Letter of SASA to the Ministry of the Economy in relation to the construction of a sugar factory in the area of Korça. February 27, 1940.
37 I am referring here to the concept of "nations as imagined communities" coined by Benedict Anderson in his *Imagined Communities: Reflections on the Origin and Spread of Nationalism* (London: Verso, 2006).

an imagined economic community created by the artificial drawing of borders. The thin lines of international borders create national markets out of different pieces, which, before being put together, were not necessarily close to each other. On the contrary, argues Etges, borders can cut regions off from other closer regions with which they have constituted a more "organic" or "natural" economic, social, or cultural unit. "The economic borders," he concludes, "do not follow a market logic but a national logic which nationalizes economic interests and economic policy."[38] This is also the case with the efforts to integrate the region of Korça through economic linkages to the other districts of the country, and the use of the spatial division of labor to create a solid unified national mosaic.

Regional specialization was not imposed from above and did not come exclusively from the state apparatus. As the case of Maliq's sugar industry shows, it was not solely a state-driven process. The initiatives came from the local level as well. The regional specialization of production was not part of a grand strategy defined by an interventionist state. It instead came into light as a local response to a new context created after the collapse of the Ottoman Empire and the establishment of the Albanian national state. The integration process through differentiation was a two-way process, where groups of interests participated in the project of nation-building through market integration. In this way, the Maliqi company was drawing the map of Albania by imbuing the plain of Korça with a new economic meaning and function, which simultaneously acted as a symbol of local identity in the spatial imagination of the country.

Since the early 1920s, non-state actors, entrepreneurs, and workers elaborated on the issue of state protectionism and autarky, including the self-sufficiency of sugar production.[39] Many Albanian public figures, who were not all necessarily politicians, considered the increase in sugar imports as a grave financial problem. For Albania, the annual outflow of two million gold francs was not a negligible matter. In the early 1920s, the primary beneficiary was Italy. By the end of the

---

38 Andreas Etges, "Theoretical and Historical Reflections on Economic Nationalism in Germany and the United States in the Nineteenth and Early Twentieth Centuries," in *Nationalism and the Economy: Explorations into a Neglected Relationship*, eds. Stefan Berger and Thomas Fetzer (Budapest: Central European University Press, 2019), 89.

39 On the requests for economic protectionism and self-sufficiency, see Agim Muçaj, *Lufta e fshatarësisë shqiptare kundër shfrytëzimit çifligaro-borgjez (1925–1939) dhe qëndrimi i klasave ndaj saj* [The struggle of the Albanian peasantry against feudal-bourgeois exploitation (1925–1939) and the attitude of the classes towards it] (Tirana: Shtëpia e Librit Universitar, 1990), 90–91; Iljaz Fishta and Veniamin Toçi, *Gjendja ekonomike e Shqipërisë në vitet 1912–1944, prapambetja e saj, shkaqet dhe pasojat* [Albania's economic condition in the years 1912–1944: Its backwardness, causes, and repercussions] (Tirana: 8 Nëntori, 1983), 99–100; Misha, *Lëvizja punëtore në Shqipëri*, 65–66, 85, 145–146.

decade, Czechoslovakia, which had become the major sugar supplier in the Balkans, displaced the Italians as the principal importer of sugar. However, for the influential circles in Albania, it did not make much difference who was the recipient of the hard cash. Even the considerable decrease in the sugar price in the 1930s did not dilute Albanian nationalists' anxieties.[40]

The Albanian modernizers, for whom the nation was the fundamental category of analysis, understood that the country's development meant, among other things, a growing dependence on other international actors, which could have a high economic and political price. Social–economic modernization was expensive not only for building roads, bridges, and schools but also because of the population's consumption. As Albanians consumed more goods than the country produced, it became harder for the national economy to afford to buy them. The more the country modernized, the more it became entangled in the web of international trade, and the more it depended on foreign economies for goods and services that Albania did not produce. Likewise, the more Albania depended on other economically more advanced states, the more its independence was threatened in the hostile and competitive international environment of the interwar era. There was a conflict between the political imperatives of sovereignty, on the one hand, and consumption and the new needs of the population on the other. The solution was to produce the most important commodities Albanians consumed domestically.

Part of this broader goal was the establishment of a domestic sugar industry. In the spirit of interwar neo-mercantilism, the stated goal from within the state apparatus and the press was to produce all the sugar the country consumed domestically. A noted journalist of the period stated:

---

40 On the Czechoslovak sugar trade in the Balkans, see Frantisek Dudek, "The Crisis of the Beet Sugar Industry in Czechoslovakia," in *The World Sugar Economy in War and Depression 1914–1940*, eds. Bill Albert and Adrian Graves (London: Routledge, 1988), 37 and 41. For the data on sugar imports, see *Statistika Importatjon – Exportatjone vjetës 1921 e Shtetit Shqyptár*, 7; *Statistika Tregtare e Importacjon – Eksportacjon-it prej 1 Kallnuerit deri më 31 Dhetuer 1926*, 12–13; *Statistikë e Tregtis së Jashtëme: Viti 1927*, 42–43; *Statistikë e Tregtis së Jashtëme: Viti 1928*, 50–51; *Statistikë e Tregtis së Jashtëme: Viti 1935*, XX–XXI and 24; *Relacion i Bilançit më 31 Dhetuer 1936 paraqitun Mbledhjes së Përgjithëshme të Aksionistavet më 7 Maj 1937* [Report on the balance sheet for the year 1936 presented at the meeting of the shareholders held on May 7, 1937] (Tirana: Banka Kombëtare e Shqipnis, 1937), 27; *Relacion i Bilançit më 31 Dhetuer 1938 paraqitun Mbledhjes së Përgjithëshme të Aksionistavet më 10 Qershor 1939* [Report on the balance sheet for the year 1938 presented at the meeting of the shareholders held on June 10, 1939] (Tirana: Banka Kombëtare e Shqipnis, 1939), 33; *Albania* [Geographical Hand Book Series] (London: Naval Intelligence Office, 1945), 256.

When talking about the question of sugar, we mean: it is one of the most important factors for the improvement of the economy of any state and the preservation of its independence from foreign markets... Thus, sugar must be produced domestically.

Embracing the age's tendency of state interventionism, the journalist continued:

...we must say that the production of sugar in the country is an excellent trade, needs extensive capital of at least 3-4 million gold Francs, and without the encouragement and support of the government no one can undertake such an enterprise. Therefore, it is a fundamental maxim of the civilized and advanced world that the state should always encourage any capitalistic private institution that has as a goal the production or manufacture of a thing being made within the state for the first time, which it should support with the issuance of concessions, protections, insurances, subventions, etc.[41]

According to the author of this article, it was the national government's duty, with its paternalistic policies, to lead and guarantee autarky. Politicians and other influential personalities in interwar Albania were not seeking to cut the country off from the world but to preserve its independence. In the widely shared opinion of the time, Albania would be able to maintain its political sovereignty by achieving self-sufficiency in its most important commodity. According to public opinion, domestic production was necessary for keeping precious capital in the country, fostering the domestic economy, and diminishing alleged harmful dependency. This opinion did not consider openness to the European market, the reference model of the Albanian interwar elites, and autarky as mutually exclusive. On the contrary, economic self-sufficiency was a means for Albania to join the group of privileged and civilized nations of Europe.

The beliefs of the Albanian modernizers were grounded in and shaped by contemporary European ideas. Not by accident, the new states of Eastern Europe championed autarky. Their weakness vis à vis the aggressive and revanchist powers that squeezed them from West and East created the perceived need to prepare their nations for war and, consequently, for autarky.[42] As the Czechoslovak

---

41 Nebil Çika, "Çështja e sheqerit: Pjesa I" [The question of sugar: Part 1], *Rilindja e Arbënisë* [The reawakening of Arbëria], no. 50, November 16, 1930, 1.
42 Kenneth Jowitt, "The Sociocultural Basis of National Dependency in Peasant Countries," in *Social Change in Romania, 1860–1940: A Debate on Development in a European Nation*, ed. Kenneth Jowitt

consul in Tirana argued to some members of the Albanian government, there was a need to produce their own sugar, because World War I demonstrated how critical it was for a country to domestically produce all primary commodities, among which he listed sugar. The Bohemian diplomat did not have to convince his Albanian counterpart, who shared the same apprehensions.[43]

The Albanians' approach to partial self-sufficiency falls squarely within the models that all its Balkan neighbors had embraced by that time. The post-Ottoman states of southeastern Europe, which were points of reference for Tirana, had pursued autarkic policies since the early twentieth century.[44] The historical conjuncture of the interwar era that saw the emergence of alternative models that challenged the market economy and promoted an increasing role of the state as a regulator of social–economic life made its inroads in Albania too.[45] Ultimately, the enormous political, economic, and cultural influence of fascist Italy over the small Balkan country during the interwar years had a long-lasting impact on the strategies of development the Albanians pursued. The fascists' endless diatribes about autarky, which was the economic doctrine of Rome, reinforced the worldview of many Albanians, including that of sugar production.

Albania's American Frontier

In October 1922, Pompeo Amadei, an Italian engineer who worked in the Albanian Ministry of Public Works, wrote an article on the reclamation of the swamp of Maliq for a newspaper in Korça. To the local audiences, he said: "Fun-

---

(Berkeley, CA: University of California Press, 1978), 3; István Deák, "How to Construct a Productive, Disciplined, Monoethnic Society: The Dilemma of East Central European Governments, 1914–1956," in *Landscaping the Human Garden: Twentieth-Century Population Management in a Comparative Framework*, ed. Amir Weiner (Stanford, CA: Stanford University Press, 2003), 213.

43 AQSh, F. 177, Ministria e Punëve Botore, 1925, d. 161, fl. 48. Letter of the consul of Czechoslovakia sent to the Albanian government regarding the proposal of a Czechoslovak firm to develop the sugar industry in Albania. October 25, 1925; *Ibid*, fl. 12. Response from the Ministry of Public Works to an inquiry of the Prime Minister's Office regarding a Czechoslovak offer to build a sugar refinery in Albania. December 10, 1925; AQSh, F. 149, Kryeministria, 1926, d. III-896, fl. 5. Correspondence between the Ministry of Public Works, the Prime Minister's Office, and the Ministry of Justice regarding the offer of a Czechoslovak firm to establish a sugar industry in Albania. December 16, 1925.

44 John R. Lampe and Marvin R. Jackson, *Balkan Economic History, 1550–1950: From Imperial Borderlands to Developing Nations* (Bloomington, IN: Indiana University Press, 1982), 13.

45 Stephen Kotkin, "Modern Times: The Soviet Union and the Interwar Conjuncture," *Kritika: Exploration in Russian and Eurasian History* 2, no. 1 (2001): 111–164; Daniel Chirot, "Ideology, Reality, and Competing Models of Development in Eastern Europe Between the Two World Wars," *Eastern European Politics and Societies* 3, no. 3 (1989): 378–411; Michael R. Dohan, "The Economic Origins of Soviet Autarky 1927/1928–1934," *Slavic Review* 35, no. 4 (1976): 603–635.

damentally, it should be known that you have an America in your house, but it is necessary that it be exploited with wisdom."[46] Amadei's words echoed his contemporary Italian discourse of "integral reclamation" and "internal colonization" that sought to fix the problem of demographic excess and prevent the emigration of the surplus labor force to the United States by reshaping space. Rome's political elites were devising projects of expanding the arable land through large reclamation enterprises and to use their human resources to strengthen the country's international posture.[47] This effort, which culminated with Mussolini's reclamation of the Agropontine marshes located south of Rome, aimed at replacing overseas America with another America within Italy. Since the nineteenth and the first half of the twentieth centuries, in Europe, America symbolized not only a land of fresh beginnings and a new page in history but also a space of expansion.[48] It was an example of the power of civilization that tamed barbarity and nature, and that created order out of the chaos of the wild. While the swamp represented untamed and uncivilized nature, the wisdom Amadei summoned represented the rationality of civilization. By exploiting the reclaimed land with wisdom, the Albanians would show that they had embraced the values of modern civilization. Like the American West, Maliq became a borderland, a space of expansion. By civilizing it, the Albanians would show that they deserved their independence and membership in the family of European nations.

The only difference was that this frontier did not lie outside of the country's borders but within it. Maliq was an internal frontier, and civilizing it was as much a marker of triumph as was the conquest of the Americas by the Europeans. Taking the land away from the waters and using it, thrusting the plow in it, and shaping and ordering it was an act as virile and civilizational as was the conquest of the Americas. As a new nation, the Albanians had to show efficiency and the ability to conquer new lands. To become part of the civilized world, they had to tame the wilderness. In the spirit of the nineteenth century, still strong after

---

46 Pompeo Amadei, "Për tharjen e gjolit të Maliqit" [On the reclamation of Maliq's lake], *Posta e Korçës*, October 24, 1922, 2.
47 Lorenzo Veracini, "Italian Colonialism through a Settler Colonial Studies Lens," *Journal of Colonialism and Colonial History* 19, no. 3 (2018): no page numbers.
48 On the impact of American western expansion in the German imaginary, especially in the projects of the revitalized *Drang nach Osten*, see Gregor Thum, "Seapower and Frontier Settlement: Friedrich List's American Vision for Germany," in *German and United States Colonialism in a Connected World: Entangled Empires*, ed. Janne Lahti (London: Palgrave Macmillan, 2021), 17–39; Robert L. Nelson, "The Fantasy of Open Space on the Frontier: Max Sering from the Great Plains to Eastern Europe," *Ibid*, 41–62; Robert L. Nelson, "From Manitoba to the Memel: Max Sering, Inner Colonization, and the German East," *Social History* 35, no. 4 (2010): 439–457.

World War I, the Albanians had to find their own America to expand in and to demonstrate to the European powers that they were a nation of civilizers.

The reclamation of the Maliq swamp served as an advertisement for Albanian politicians and nationalists to debunk the many stereotypes that many political circles in Western Europe had for the country and its people. Meaningful is an anecdote that Mehdi Frashëri, the future Prime Minister of Albania and its representative at the League of Nations during the 1920s, told the crowds gathered to celebrate the beginning of the reclamation on July 11, 1927. Frashëri, who had represented Albania at the Conference of Versailles in 1920, recounted that during the meetings in Paris in 1919, many Albanians personally went to France's capital to ask the Entente Powers to recognize the existence of Albania. Among them, he continued, there was also an old man, to whom a Western diplomat told that if the Albanians were allowed to have an independent country, they would make it a slaughterhouse. "I wish I had an airplane to bring the diplomat here to Maliq," concluded Frashëri, "so he—the Western diplomat—could see the slaughterhouse for himself and how the land is calling for its reclamation and the progress of Albania."[49]

Mehdi Frashëri's story may be apocryphal, but what is important is that Albanian politicians integrated the reclamation of Maliq within the broader discourse of progress. The significance of this undertaking was not restricted to state-building but was also about representing Albania to the world. It was the first enterprise undertaken by an Albanian company with Albanian capital. The project bore the name of the nation; it carried the name of Albania on it and constructed the image of the newly established state according to the norms of progress established in Western Europe—norms that circulated even in the early years of the twenty-first century, when specialists of international affairs linked the so-called "failed nation-states" of the Global South with the inability of their societies to master the environment.[50] The speech of Albanian politicians, rather than expressing frustration with the criteria Western diplomats used to stereotype the Albanians, revealed an eagerness to prove Western European political circles wrong on the grounds that the Albanians could progress. Rather than making their country a slaughterhouse, they were able to keep their house in

---

49 "Inaugurimi i tharjes së Liqenit Maliqi," 4.
50 For more on this issue, see Mark T. Berger, "From Nation-Building to State-Building: The Geopolitics of Development, the Nation-State System and the Changing Global Order," *Third World Quarterly* 27, no. 1 (2006): 11–12.

order and make Albania prosper. In other words, the reclamation of Maliq demonstrated that the Albanians deserved their independent political life.

Unlike the nationalist politicians in Tirana, for whom Maliq was an instrument of nation-building and an advertisement for international consumption, for many people in Korça, the reclamation of the swamp had a more practical and economic importance. The establishment of the state borders and the fixing of the external frontier shrunk the hinterland of Korça. The founders of the Maliqi company considered the swamp's reclamation as an internal frontier, whose expansion would compensate for the losses from the collapse of the Ottoman Empire. The opening of new virgin land would provide resources, increase the revenues of local capital, and solve the demographic pressure that had exacerbated after the United States restricted its immigration quotas in 1917 and 1924.[51] The Maliq swamp was the alternative to America and was the America in the house that Pompeo Amadei was talking about. The reclaimed land of Maliq could become the space within Korça's plain to be tamed and colonized. Korça's elites stepped up to give an example to the entire country on how to expand the internal frontier and increase Albania's size without pushing the state borders further and clashing with their more powerful neighbors. In the context of the nation-state, the reclamation of the swamp was "America in the house," the source of future wealth that would help them press forward with other projects of regional modernization.

However, there were serious challenges to make Maliq "an America in the house." Until the end of World War II, the swamp remained an uncharted site. The French were mainly interested in minerals and military activities and did not produce much knowledge of the swamp. There was no detailed map of it and hardly any geological studies of the composition of the soil. Neither was there any in-depth geobotanic, ecological, topographic, or hydrological knowledge on the swamp.[52] Meanwhile, Albania had no specialists to produce the necessary

---

51   On the external and internal frontier, see Archibald R. Lewis, "The Closing of the Mediaeval Frontier, 1250–1350," *Speculum: A Journal of Medieval Studies* 33, no. 4 (1958): 475–483. On the use of the reclamation as a means of compensating for the shrinking of the hinterland of Korça and as a solution to emigration to the United States, see AQSh, F. 991, Kompania Anonime Maliq, 1943, d. 13, fl. 1. Discussion of the deputy chair of the Maliqi joint-stock company regarding the activity of the company and its conflicts with other subjects. March 14, 1943.

52   AQSh, F. 490, Këshilli i Ministrave, 1950, d. 1637, fl. 3. Memo from the Ministry of Agriculture sent to the Prime Minister's Office and the State Planning Commission regarding the conditions and problems of the new state farms. June 14, 1950; AQSh, F. 490, Këshilli i Ministrave, 1950, d. 1637, fl. 16. Memo from the Ministry of Agriculture sent to the State Planning Commission concerning some problems that emerged for the reclamation of the plain of Maliq. July 24, 1950.

scientific knowledge about the reclamation and exploitation of the plain of Maliq. Neither the Albanian state nor the local entrepreneurs had the instruments to generate control, power, and order.

Most importantly, in real colonial style, the company considered the plain a half "empty" space, devoid of inhabitants—as if it was the old American frontier.[53] While the company called its enterprise an example of enlightened self-interest, the 7500 inhabitants of the 16 villages around it were visible to its gaze only for their dues, but not when it came to their rights. The land around the swamp was not free of ownership. It either belonged to the villages, as communal property, or to individual peasants and larger landowners. The borders of the holdings were very intricate, and as a rule, the families owned a series of scattered plots. Moreover, the cycle of the seasons and rainfalls determined the boundaries and use of the communal land. The peasants used part of the pastures and arable land only during the summers when the swamp was at its lowest level.[54]

The Maliqi company hired a Greek engineer, Konstantinos Vlamos, in 1924, who worked in the Office of Irrigation Projects in Egypt.[55] His project, instead of following the twisted and complicated lines of existing properties, which were the result of centuries of social interactions and human intercourse with nature, pursued rectilinear lines. As a result, the concession that the government approved included—besides the area that was permanently underwater—swaths of land owned by the villages. Moreover, the concession determined that the peasants had to pay the company for improving their arable land.[56] The population of the sixteen rural communities also had to pay for fishing, hunting, and foraging rights. Besides violating the property borders, the project disturbed the

---

53   On the invisibility of Native Americans and Poles to the North American and German imperial gaze, respectively, see Robert L. Nelson, "Emptiness in the Colonial Gaze: Labor, Property, and Nature." *International Labor and Working-Class History* 79, no. 1 (2011): 161–174.
54   On the claim of enlightened self-interest on the part of the company and the state, see "Inaugurimi i tharjes së liqenit Maliq," 1–2. On the number of the inhabitants in the plain of Maliq, see Teki Selenica, *Shqipria më 1923* [Albania in 1923] (Tirana: Ministria e P. Mbrendshme, 1923), 98–99.
55   "Lajmë enetersante e Liqenit" [Interesting news concerning the lake], *Gazeta e Korçës*, August 26, 1924, 2.
56   According to the concession, the peasant had to pay the company 6 napoleons (the Albanian currency at that time) per dynym (a unit of measurement equal to 1000 square meters). AQSh, F. 155, Ministria e Drejtësisë, 1926, d. II-854, fl. 6. The exchange rate of the napoleon to the dollar for that period was approximately 1 napoleon to 4 dollars ["Kursi i Monedhave në Korçë" (The monetary exchange rate in Korça), *Zëri i Korçës*, 6 February 1926 (59): 4]. This means that the price for 1000 square meters was equal to $24, which—when converted into today's currency—would be equal to $325. Meanwhile, the average area of land owned by families in the plain exceeded 20 dynyms. This meant at least $6500. For populations loosely connected to the market and with a very low standard of living, such an amount was stratospheric.

whole basis of the local rural economy because it excluded the peasants from the natural resources they had always used.

After the project became known to the local population, petitions against the "injustices of the Maliqi Company to the detriment of the pauper people" flooded the government. They asked for protection from the "predatory and ruthless tendencies of the capitalists organized around the joint-stock company." According to the petitions' authors, the company was robbing the "pastures we have owned without any contestation for hundreds of years," thus endangering their "ownership and miserable bread." The Turkish regime, they recalled, did not strip them off their land when it started to partially drain the swamp. The petitions appropriated the language of nationalism of the era and its anti-urban language to their advantage. They defined their interests and rights as Albanians vis à vis the "Other," whom they identified as urban capitalists: exploiters not rooted in the land, who only chased their gain. Thus, one of the telegrams labeled the company as an agglomerate of ruthless capitalists whose only goal was to earn millions.[57] By pointing out that the company was behaving worse than the Turks against the Albanians, they were appealing to the Albanian state to defend them against a group that the petitioners considered alien capitalists.

The telegrams used the idiom of the moral economy. They insinuated a relationship built upon mutual liabilities and benefits that defined a horizon of expectations from both sides involved. By emphasizing the peasants' rights to subsistence and the state's obligation to guarantee it, the petitions' authors tried to determine what was just, and thus legitimize their requests. In speaking on behalf of the rural communities and their customary rights, and the state's responsibility to defend them, these petitions aimed at making the peasants visible to the state's gaze and pointed out the latter's obligation to protect them. In this way, the appeals constructed a discourse that undermined the company's claim, legitimizing its project with the ideology of progress and national modernization. To maximize their gain, the petitioners made full use of moral

---

57   On the petitions to the government to defend the peasants against the company, see AQSh, F. 149, Kryeministria, 1926, d. III-4054, fl. 1-5. Telegram of complaint of Adem Vila and his associates on behalf of the sixteen villages located around the swamp of Maliq, May 25, 1926. On the telegram that considered the government the only salvation for the peasants, see AQSh, F. 149, Kryeministria, 1926, d. III-898, fl. 35-37. Telegram of complaint of Adem Vila and his associates on behalf of the sixteen villages located around the swamp of Maliq. October 14, 1926; AQSh, F. 155, Ministria e Drejtësisë, 1926, d. IV-182, fl. 4. Request of the peasants of the villages around the swamp of Maliq regarding the redefinition of the boundaries of their properties. May 22, 1926.

dichotomies centered upon the subsistence ethos, which distinguished the just from the predatory.[58]

While considering the company as the "evil" force, they cajoled the government as the only salvation of the people, which they hoped would not sell out thousands of Albanians to the capitalists.[59] The petitions defined the state as a distant and benign force, a pastoral power, conceived as a shepherd, whose goal was not only to milk the cattle but also defend them from the wolves—in this case, the capitalists. By victimizing themselves and portraying their position as powerless subjects without agency, totally dependent on the grace of the center, the petitioners tried to manipulate the government and dictate the latter's stance toward the conflicting parties.[60] Additionally, more importantly, the telegrams attempted to define the state's action. The company had very powerful shareholders, including Pandeli Evangjeli and Kostandin Kotta, two wealthy merchants from Korça, who served as Albania's prime ministers during the 1930s. The telegrams tried to prevent the state structures from being used as an instrument in the company's vested interests. By outlining how the state had to handle the conflict, the petitions strove to prompt the authorities to act in their favor.

The petitions hit their target, and the Ministry of the Interior started an investigation, which confirmed that the peasants were telling the truth. Vlamos's project, wrote the prefect of Korça to his superiors in Tirana, had illegally included hundreds of already-owned hectares within those under the company's control. However, it was evident that the government and parliament had approved this concession as a result of lobbying on the part of influential Korça's politicians. The peasants, on the other hand, had started a series of small-scale irrigations in 1924, in order to change the situation in their favor. The prefect urged the Ministry of the Interior to negotiate the conflict in the interests of all the parties involved. In 1926, the president of the country, Ahmet Zog, the strongman that dominated Albania's political life during the interwar era and who, on

---

58 On the moral economy of the peasants, see James G. Carrier, "Moral Economy: What's in a Name?" *Anthropological Theory* 18, no. 1 (2018): 18–35; James C. Scott, *The Moral Economy of the Peasant: Rebellion and Subsistence in Southeast Asia* (New Haven, CT: Yale University Press, 1976). See also, Edward P. Thompson, "The Moral Economy of the British Crowd in the Eighteenth Century," *Past & Present* 50 (1971): 76–136; Jaime Palomera and Theodora Vetta, "Moral Economy: Rethinking a Radical Concept," *Anthropological Theory* 16, no. 4 (2016): 413–432.

59 AQSh, F. 149, Kryeministria, 1926, d. III-898, fl. 35–37. Telegram of complaint of Adem Vila and his associates on behalf of the sixteen villages located around the swamp of Maliq. October 14, 1926.

60 On the use of petitions to manipulate the state authorities, see Golfo Alexopoulous, "The Ritual Lament: A Narrative of Appeal in the 1920s and 1930s," *Russian History/Histoire Russe* 24, nos. 1–2 (1997): 117–129; Verdery and Kligman, *Peasants under Siege*, 264–266.

September 1, 1928, proclaimed himself King, approved the proposal of Korça's prefect. He and the Council of Ministers created a committee and ordered it to revise the concession and bring the conflict to an end.[61]

The peasants were overwhelmingly illiterate. They signed the petitions with their fingerprints and sometimes in Arabic letters. So, who wrote the telegrams? Among the names of the peasants, the names of Adem Vila, Emin Pojani, Sadik Qyteza, and others stand out as rich landowners of the region, and they had actually penned the telegrams. They all owned lands around the swamp and were losing properties in its reclamation. Rather than being used as a means of communication between peasants and state elites, the petitions, which utilized the conceptual arsenal of moral economy, were deployed by local elites to gain the state's support. Traditionally involved in politics, they had intimate knowledge of political conjuncture, knew very well how the state machinery worked, and how to use the language of popular sovereignty to pressure their demands on the government.

However, the vocabulary the authors used in their petitions to couch their requests also had new nuances. The landlords did not construct a dichotomy that juxtaposed modernity to tradition, as they located their discourse squarely within the new national context and attempted to use it to their advantage. Thus, they conflated their interests with those of the rural communities that lived around the swamp. They did not only appeal to the traditional moral order or economy in order to highlight their rights vis à vis the state or other "alien actors," which they wanted to keep at arm's distance from their communities, but in writing on behalf of the people, they employed a trope that did not reject nation and nationalism but rather redefined it. The Maliqi company tried to legitimize its claims by speaking on behalf of the nation and its progress. The big landowners contested this discourse and brought the peasants onto the stage to negotiate their place within the national context and make their voices heard. By juxtaposing the general wellbeing of the community to the egoistic greed of the capitalists, they were formulating the nation's ideology by opposing the people connected

---

61   On peasant irrigation, AQSh, F. 171, Ministria e Ekonomisë, 1931, d. IV-144, fl. 6. Letter of the Maliqi company sent to the Ministry of the National Economy regarding the issue of the conflicts over property boundaries with the peasants of Maliq. April 2, 1931. On the proposal of the prefect, AQSh, F. 149, Kryeministria, 1926, d. III-898, fl. 20–21. On the decision of the President and the Council of Ministers to create a committee, *Ibid*, fl. 26–27. Correspondence between the President of the Republic and the Ministry of the Interior regarding the petitions of the peasants of the plain of Maliq. August 26, 1926.

The Making of the Sugar Scheme

to the land to the rootless capitalist urbanites—not unlike the radical nationalist discourse that was taking place in contemporary Europe.

The government was slow to act, and the committee did not meet. However, in 1930, the five-year concession expired, and the company asked for its renewal. A storm brewed in Maliq, and an avalanche of telegrams from Maliq, similar to those of 1926, flooded Tirana. The petitions asked Zog and the government to revise the concession and cancel it until the enforcement of property lines. They portrayed the company as an entity driven by greed that was illegally looting the pauper peasants. Simultaneously, the telegrams called the King the father of his people who had always cared about the peasants.[62] Besides the petitions, groups of peasants, urged by the landowners, started destroying the border signs that marked the company's property. Especially prominent was Maliq Frashëri, one of the largest landowners in the region, who encouraged the peasants to attack and occupy the company's land by force, and his henchmen attacked settlers that the company had brought into the reclaimed areas.[63]

Unlike the beginning of the reclamation, when the company disregarded the rural population around the swamp, its shareholders now took into full consideration the peasants' interests. After realizing that the requests sent on behalf of the peasants held weight and could not be considered invisible, the company changed course. It leased land in its possession to groups of peasants from the

---

62 On the petitions, AQSh, F. 317, Prefektura e Korçë, 1931, d. 72, fl. 5–6. Letter of the landowners and the councils of the villages around the swamp of Maliq sent to the prefect of Korça regarding the conflict with the Maliqi company; AQSh, F. 171, Ministria e Ekonomisë, 1931, d. IV-144, fl. 16-20, fl. 41-48, fl. 95–96, and 132–133. Complaints against the Maliqi company from the representatives of the sixteen villages located around the swamp of Maliq sent to the Ministry of the Economy. On the destruction of the pyramids, AQSh, F. 319/12, Komuna e Maliqit, 1930, d. 13, fl. 1–2; Letter of the board of directors of the Maliqi company sent to the prefecture of Korça concerning the need it had for the intervention of the state to defend its interests against the attacks against its property. April 11, 1930; AQSh, F. 319/12, Komuna e Maliqit, 1931, d. 23, fl. 1; AQSh, F. 171, Ministria e Ekonomisë, 1932, d. IV-159, fl. 35. Report by the prefecture of Korça sent to the Ministry of the Interior, concerning the conflict between the sixteen villages around the swamp and the Maliqi company. May 30, 1932.

63 On the reports from Korça pointing to Maliq Frashëri's role in the violent acts of the peasants, AQSh, F. 171, Ministria e Ekonomisë, 1931, d. IV-144, fl. 8. Letter of the prefecture of Korça sent to the Ministry of the Economy in relation to the conflict between the Maliqi company and the landowners and peasants of the villages located around the swamp of Maliq. April 4, 1931; *Ibid*, fl. 13. Telegram of complaint of the chair of the Maliqi company, Kristaq Pilika, against the abuses on the part of Maliq Frashëri. April 24, 1931; AQSh, F. 171, Ministria e Ekonomisë, 1932, d. IV-159, fl. 15. Complaint from the Maliqi company against Maliq Frashëri sent to King Zog. May 14, 1932; AQSh, F. 152, Ministria e Brendshme, 1932, d. 404, fl. 37. On Maliq Frashëri's men attacking the company's settlers, AQSh, F. 171, Ministria e Ekonomisë, 1931, d. IV-144, fl. 9. Letter of complaint from the Maliqi company sent to the prefecture of Korça, in relation to the interventions hampering the working and exploitation of the swamp of Maliq. April 2, 1931.

villages around the swamp in exchange for services. Maliqi's shareholders used the peasants' petitions to legitimize their interests and delegitimize those of their opponents. Peasants from the village of Pirg sent a telegram to the government, where they admitted that they were pushed by other people to petition the government against the company. Additionally, others from the villages of Zvirinë, Pertush, and Leshnicë sent telegrams to the Prime Minister's Office, in which they thanked the company for the humanitarian work it had performed to improve their lives, while a petition from the village of Libonik urged the government to renew the company's concession.[64]

The peasants were neither a homogenous group nor puppets of the local elites but actors in their own right. The peasants became visible to the company, which started to entice them to break their ranks and undermine the support they were giving the big landowners. The big local players needed the help of the peasants to legitimate their claims, and the latter made full use of the conflict to see who offered more. The dispute gave many peasants leverage, which they used to their advantage. In the village of Sovjan, some peasants participated in the actions against the company, while others supported the company because it gave them land.[65] The rural population was not a monolithic group, and even single rural communities were divided, with each family having its own interests.

After some hesitation, Zog, who was aware of the role of the big landowners, decided to act and ordered the government to put an end to the conflicts and the violent confrontations.[66] In the end, when the commission succeeded in reaching an agreement, it was the company that lost most. The state sided with the peasants and granted the villagers and landowners the right to own 1000 hectares from those, which according to the concession based on Vlamos' project, were under the company's management. The central authorities, as they admit-

---

64 Telegram from Pirg, AQSh, Collection: Ministry of the Economy, number 171, year 1932, file IV-159, fl. 33–34; Telegram from Zvirinë, Petrush, and Zvirinë, *Ibid*, fl. 39–40; Telegram from Libonik, *Ibid*, fl. 37. Maliq Frashëri tried to debunk these petitions and wrote to the Prefect of Korça that the telegrams sent by the peasants of these villages were all fabricated by the company. *Ibid*, fl. 67.
65 On Sovjan, AQSh, F. 149, Kryeministria, 1936, d. III-3047, fl. 11–12. Petition of the peasants from the village of Sovjan against the Maliqi company. On the peasants supporting the company against the big landowners, AQSh, F. 152, Ministria e Brendshme, 1936, d. 828, fl. 20-21. Appeal of the peasants of the village of Sovjan sent to the Ministry of the Interior in support of the Maliqi company. June 6, 1936.
66 On Zog first dismissing the petitions, AQSh, F. 171, Ministria e Ekonomisë, 1931, d. IV-144, fl. 23. Letter of the Prime Minister's Office sent to the Office of Agriculture of the district of Korça, concerning the complaints of the landowners against the Maliqi company. May 7, 1931. On Zog ordering the Prime Minister to intervene in order to resolve the conflict, AQSh, F. 171, Ministria e Ekonomisë, 1931, d. IV-144, fl. 73. Zog's order regarding the injustices that the Maliqi company was doing against those who owned lands around the swamp of Maliq. June 23, 1931.

ted, sided with the peasants and did not protect the company's interests.[67] The deal of 1932 was not the end, however, as once the agreement was reached, landowners and peasants turned against each other. In the village of Rëmbec, for example, the big landowners confiscated the land of some of the peasants. Moreover, the agreement only appeased a part of the landowning class.

In 1936, the conflict exploded again, and the disgruntled landowners refused to recognize the 1932 agreement because, according to them, the company had failed to drain the lake. The root of the conflict lay in the decision of the company to bring in agricultural settlers. Facing the threat of their land being colonized, the old landlords and peasants found common language again. They petitioned the state authorities and sought to force the company to give the land to them and not allow newcomers to settle. The landowners and peasants started to occupy the company's property once again and attacked the settlers that worked for the company.[68] The government did not concede this time, however, and stuck to the 1932 agreement. The peasants challenged the company's property rights, used the swamp's resources, and grazed their cattle in the areas under its control. Additionally, they resorted to violence and drove the company's agricultural workers off their settlements.[69]

---

67 On the gain of the peasants and big landowners from the arrangement of 1932, AQSh, F. 991, Kompania Anonime Maliqi, 1943, d. 13, fl. 2. Discussion of the deputy chair of the Maliqi joint-stock company regarding the activity of the company and its conflicts with other subjects. March 14, 1943. On the state authorities siding with the peasants, AQSh, F. 152, Ministria e Brendshme, 1936, d. 828, fl. 13. Report of the prefecture of Korça concerning the unjust complaints of Maliq bey Frashëri and some peasants of the village Rëmbec. April 25, 1936.

68 On the peasants' request that the company give them the land AQSh, F. 149, Kryeministria, 1936, d. III-3047, fl. 6–7. Telegram of the village of Sovjan asking the state to intervene with the Maliqi company in order to allow them to work its land. April 5, 1936. On the peasants asking the government to forbid the company from bringing in new settlers, AQSh, F. 177, Ministria e Ndërtimit, 1936, d. 189, fl. 2–5. Appeal of the villages around the swamp of Maliq against the injustices of the Maliqi company. March 19, 1936. On petitioning the government, AQSh, F. 152, Ministria e Brendshme, 1936, d. 828, fl. 14. Report of the prefecture of Korça in relation to the unjust complaints of Maliq bey Frashëri and some of the peasants of the village of Rëmbec. April 25, 1936.

69 On the occupation of the company's land, AQSh, F. 152, Ministria e Brendshme, 1936, d. 828, fl. 46–48. Petition of the Maliqi company sent to the Prime Minister's Office and the Ministry of the Interior for help against the occupation of its land by the peasants. May 14, 1936. On the attack against the settlers, AQSh, F. 152, Ministria e Brendshme, 1936, d. 828, fl. 52. Petition of the Maliqi company against the attack of the peasants of the village of Pojan. April 11, 1936. On the grazing of cattle on the company's land, the collection of reeds, and fishing without paying dues, AQSh, F. 150, Oborri Mbretëror, 1937, d. III-1084, fl. 21. Report of the Chief Superintendent of the Royal Court sent to King Zog on the results of the investigation of the conflict between some large landowners and the Maliqi company. November 12, 1937. On the attack against the settlers by the armed henchmen of a landlord, AQSh, F. 317, Prefektura e Korçës, 1937, d. 53, fl. 54. Petition of the Maliqi com-

CHAPTER 1

During his reign, Ahmet Zog consistently promoted himself as the protector of the people in order to legitimize his power. This was especially true with the peasantry, which comprised 85% of the country's population. In Maliq, both the wealthy landowners and the company, aware of Zog's rationale, used the peasants to increase their leverage in Tirana. The King's support for the peasants, though, did not reflect any ideological identification of the political structure with the peasant classes. It only disclosed that he and his collaborators attempted to negotiate the transformation process. Rather than a partisan of folk nationalism, indeed, Zog was a committed modernizer who preferred a gradualist transformation of the country and its society. It was this approach to change that guided his attitude toward the Maliq conflict. The strongman, rather than being manipulated by the disputing parties, tried to negotiate the process.[70]

It was within this context that the central authorities ordered a revision of the Vlamos project, which the government identified as the source of the conflicts that were taking place in Maliq. To support the company's reclamation while not alienating the peasants, in 1937, the Albanian state hired the Italian engineer, Angelo Omodeo, one of the most prominent hydraulic engineers of his era, to outline a new plan for the reclamation of the swamp.[71] He arrived in Albania early that year and drafted a new project. Omodeo abandoned the full reclamation and anticipated preserving a lake of 800 hectares at the lowest point of Maliq, where the Devoll River and its other tributaries would drain. He argued that the land's depression and the narrowness of the Maliq gorge made full reclamation too expensive for the finances of the company and the Albanian state.[72]

---

pany regarding the violence that the landowners had exerted against the settlers the company had installed in the reclaimed lands. November 10, 1937.

70 Artan R. Hoxha, *Tharja e kënetës së Maliqit dhe ndërtimi i regjimit komunist në periferi të Shqipërisë* [The reclamation of the swamp of Maliq and the building of the communist regime in the Albanian periphery] (Tirana: Onufri, 2021), 42–52.

71 On the flaws of the Vlamos project, AQSh, F. 149, Kryeministria, 1931, d. III-2062, fl. 3. Request of the Maliqi company sent to the Ministry of the National Economy on the extension of the deadline for the completion of the reclamation of Maliq. June 1, 1931; AQSh, F. 150, Oborri Mbretëror, 1935, d. III-776, fl. 9-21. Report of the Italian engineer Luigi Zanuccoli regarding the problem of the reclamation of the swamp of Maliq. September 13, 1935; AQSh, F. 177, Ministria e Punëve Botore, 1935, d. 187, fl. 1-10. Memo of the Ministry of Public Construction regarding the progress made in the reclamation of the swamp of Maliq. September 13, 1935. On the hiring of Angelo Omodeo, AQSh, F. 177, Ministria e Punëve Botore, 1937, d. 138, fl. 1-18. Decision of the Council of Ministers for the release of a special fund for the payment of Angelo Omodeo for the preparation of the project for the reclamation of Maliq. July 22–December 9, 1937. On Omodeo's life see Andrea Filippo Saba, ed., *Angelo Omodeo. Vitta, progetti, opere per la modernizzazione. Una raccolta di scritti* (Roma-Bari: Laterza, 2005), 3–64.

72 AQSh, F. 177, Ministria e Punëve Botore. 1938, d. 172, fl. 1-54. Reports and estimates of the hydraulic systemization of the lake of Maliq. June-August, 1939.

The project was ready in 1938, but the invasion of Albania by Italy in April 1939 and the turmoil of war did not allow the company to restart the reclamation. Omodeo's project remained on paper only.

The Maliq scheme demonstrated how the inefficiency, corruption, property structure, manipulation, and lack of resources and specialists undermined the success of modernization. The failure to foster a fast-track development did not remain without effects, especially when promising alternative paths to modernity had emerged in Europe. Among them was Italian fascism. Its famous project of the Pontine Marshes showcased its alleged success in fostering development. The infamous bogs located to the south of Rome became a site where the fascists could prepare for their future African empire. The reclamation of the Pontine Marshes and the building of new settlements was one of the most important achievements of fascist Italy, and Mussolini used this project to showcase his regime's superiority to its liberal predecessors. The Italian dictator's goal was to prove that the democratic systems were deadlocked in interminable debates and feuds that produced too many words and no action.[73] The success of the fascist authorities was indisputable. Many countries of southern Europe used the Pontine Marshes as a model for fighting malaria. Even the Western democracies recognized it as a significant accomplishment.[74]

Although the Albania of Zog's era was not a democracy, the case of Maliq, with its delays and procrastinations, contrasted with the achievements of Mussolini's Italy. The latter's huge influence over the country during the interwar era provided many young technocrats and intellectuals with an inspirational model of a mobilizing state that ensured fast modernization. The Pontine Marshes and the new settlements in them materialized these aspirations and gave them shape. Thus, when a specialist from the Ministry of Public Construction visited Italy during World War II, he was impressed by what he saw in the district of Littoria, established in the reclaimed area of the Pontine Marshes. For him, the well-regulated plains and new towns built in a place once dominated by swamps dem-

---

73 Federico Caprotti, "Scipio Africanus: Film, Internal Colonization and Empire," *Cultural Geographies* 16, no. 3 (2009): 381–401; Stefan Bo Frandsen, "'The War We Prefer': The Reclamation of the Pontine Marshes and Fascist Expansion," *Totalitarian Movements and Political Religions* 2, no. 3 (2001): 69–82; Caprotti and Kaika, "Producing the Ideal Fascist Landscape," 613–27.

74 Randall M. Packard, *The Making of a Tropical Disease: A Short History of Malaria* (Baltimore, MD: John Hopkins University Press, 2007), 131–132. On the use of the reclamation of the Pontine Marshes for fighting malaria and the ideological underpinnings of this enterprise, see the chapter "Fascism, Racism, and Littoria" in Frank M. Snowden, *The Conquest of Malaria: Italy, 1900–1962* (New Haven, CT: Yale University Press, 2006), 142–180.

onstrated the vitality and dynamism of fascism, which stood in sharp contrast with Albania's relatively slow transformations. The man-made landscape and order were what struck him most.

Fascist Italy's showpiece demonstrated to the Albanian specialist the key for its success: this is what happened when Il Duce commanded his people with an iron fist. The technocrat did not mention the lack of capital, technology, knowledge, and other resources that had inhibited the success of the reclamation in Albania. He focused on the political will as the key to achieving fast modernization. Mussolini did not spend much time with futile debates and led his people with conviction toward progress.[75] The iron fist of a visionary dictator was largely thought of as a solution to compensate for the scarcity of technology, knowledge, and capital. This statement shows the success that the authoritarian regimes and the quest for efficiency and organization had in peripheries such as Albania, which were poor countries with very few resources. In the 1930s, fascism, Nazism, and communism appealed to many restless young modernizers in the peripheries of Europe. In an age dominated by the fever of efficiency, many young Eastern and Southern European modernizers considered the authoritarian regimes as solutions to the barriers that their countries encountered on their way to development. As Erik Swyngedouw has argued, even in the Spain of the 1930s the class of technocrats supported Francisco Franco and his vision of autocratic rule.[76]

It was precisely the success of the authoritarian regimes in promoting projects such as that of the Pontine Marshes that captured the minds of many technocrats in the peripheries. They saw the future in centralized and regimented political orders. The landscape of Littoria reflected the type of political order that created it. It was a tangible example of what Bauman and Weiner have defined as the *garden state*.[77] While these authors have focused on the efforts of the so-called totalitarian regimes to create cohesive conflict-free societies, they have disregarded their efforts to reconfigure space. Littoria was actually a showcase where Mussolini tried to simultaneously create the perfect society and landscape, where ideal fascist communities resided. In the new landscape created from the recla-

---

75 AQSh, F. 172, Ministria e Bujqësisë, Pa vit, d. 102, fl. 1. Report on agricultural reclamation in Italy.
76 Erik Swyngedouw, "Technonatural Revolutions: The Scalar Politics of Franco's Hydro-Social Dream for Spain, 1939–1975," *Transactions of the Institute of British Geographers* 32, no. 1 (2007): 9–28.
77 Zygmunt Bauman, *Modernity and the Holocaust* (Ithaca, NY: Cornell University Press, 1989). Amir Weiner, "Nature, Nurture, and Memory in a Socialist Utopia: Delineating the Soviet Socio-Ethnic Body in the Age of Socialism," *The American Historical Review* 104, no. 4 (1999): 1114–1155; Eric D. Weitz, "Racial Politics without the Concept of Race: Reevaluating Soviet Ethnic and National Purges," *Slavic Review* 61, no. 1 (2002): 1–29.

mation, the fascist regime carved the ideal social organization it was struggling to build. The entire Pontine Marshes project provided a showcase not only of acceleration, but of triumph over both nature and the masses that lived in darkness. More than anything else, it represented a showpiece of ordered and guided development.

Almost twenty years after Amadei had compared Maliq to America, the promised land of bounty was still waiting under water. The interwar era regime and elites had failed to pull out the America that was hiding in Maliq. By the late 1930s, the Pontine Marshes and Littoria had materialized the vision of the land of the future, of how Maliq was supposed to be. The images of order and sanitized land fused aesthetic elements with those of political and economic nature into a materialized example of what progress was. Littoria gave a face to the idea of progress because it operated through stark spatial/temporal contrasts: what the pre-fascist Pontine Marshes used to be and how fascism had transformed them. Together with the new spatial order and the remade landscape, Mussolini's regime also delivered the model that produced it: the monistic antiliberal dictatorship.

What many educated specialists from poor countries located in the margins of Europe, such as Albania, were looking for was an ordered development. Beginning in the 1930s, many Albanian intellectuals were flirting with and promoting the alternative of authoritarian modernization, which was so in vogue in the interwar era in Europe and worldwide.[78] Stigmatizing what they called the Turkish (*turkoshak*) and medieval (*mesjetare*) mentality and identifying tradition as the main source of Albania's backwardness, many young intellectuals, mainly educated in Western and Central Europe, concluded that an "enlightened dictatorship" (*diktaturë e ndritur*) or a fascist-type regime was the only way to dismantle "the remnants of the past" and open the path to the full Europeanization of the country.[79] This discourse also resonated in the words of the Albanian specialist who visited Littoria because it materialized, gave shape, and made

---

78 On the growing appeal of the alternative of authoritarian development across the globe, see Sara Lorenzini, *Global Development: A Cold War History* (Princeton: Princeton University Press, 2019), 13–16.
79 Bashkim Gjergji, *Revistat kulturore në rrjedhën e viteve '30* [Cultural journals in the course of the 1930s] (Tirana: Afërdita & Panteon, 1999), 53–109; Viron Koka, *Rrymat e mendimit politiko-shoqëror në Shqipëri në vitet 30 të shekullit XX* [The social-political currents in Albania during the 1930s] (Tirana: Akademia e Shkencave të RPS të Shqipërisë, 1985), 51–117; Muçaj, *Lufta e fshatarësisë shqiptare kundër shfrytëzimit çifligaro-borgjez*, 84–127.

tangible this drive for order, which was commanded over the population through authoritarian means by a paternalist, benign, and hard-fisted state.

As the Maliq scheme demonstrated, pessimism over the slow progress of the interwar era, the lack of capital and organization, peasant resistance, and the authorities' torpidity gave room to alternatives that exalted the command system and top-down order. Rather than caring about the rural population's moral economy and notions of justice, the young modernizers were concerned about achieving the utopia of development as soon as possible. Indeed, their leaning toward the autocratic model was shaped against the backdrop of and as a response to what they perceived as Albania's social, economic, and cultural backwardness. This attitude was very similar to that of the British and French colonial officials who, during the 1930s, used authoritarian methods to implement their modernizing projects in Africa and Asia.[80] The deliberate use of the iron fist for the sake of development was not limited to the European dictatorships of the interwar era. However, the latter exerted a stronger appeal, especially among many young, educated modernizers, who saw in these hyper-centralized non-liberal regimes an efficient form of governance, able to crack down all the barriers of backwardness through the power of will.[81]

The Maliq Scheme and Fascism's Grand Colonial Project in Albania

After Germany's successful annexations of Austria and the Sudetenland, Mussolini was afraid of Berlin's plans in the Balkans to recreate the defunct Habsburg Empire, and decided to invade Albania. For the Italians, it was both a matter of pride and consolidating their power in the Balkans, which they considered their sphere of influence. The failure of Great Britain and France in protecting the European order they had created in Versailles in 1919 made the Italians bolder. On the other side of the Adriatic, Ahmet Zog resisted becoming a puppet of the Italians and making Albania an Italian protectorate. What worried Mussolini and his Foreign Minister, Count Ciano, most was Zog and his flirtations with the

---

80 Joseph Morgan Hodge, "Writing the History of Development (Part 2: Longer, Deeper, Wider)," *Humanity: An International Journal of Human Rights, Humanitarianism, and Development* 7, no. 1 (2016): 132; Frederick Cooper, *Decolonization and African Society: The Labor Question in French and British Africa* (Cambridge: Cambridge University Press, 1996), 57–109.
81 Besnik Pula has rightly argued that the Albanians intellectuals were not so much attracted by Fascist ideology, but by its authoritarian model to fast modernization. Besnik Pula, "Becoming Citizens of Empire: Albanian Nationalism and Fascist Empire, 1939–1943," *Theory and Society* 37, no. 6 (2008): 567–596.

Germans. In December 1938, the Italians attempted to poison the King of Albania, but the latter discovered the plot. In early April 1939, Mussolini sent Ahmet Zog an ultimatum that asked the full loss of Albania's independence to Italian control. After Zog's refusal, Italy invaded the country on April 7, 1939. That same day, Albania's king left the country with his Hungarian-American wife and their newly-born son.[82] He never returned. He fled first to Egypt and afterward to England, where he remained for the duration of World War II. When the war was over, the communists came to power, and they banned Zog from returning home to Albania. In the early 1950s, he moved to France, where he died in 1961.

In the meantime, the Italian fascist authorities had grand plans for Albania. For them, the invasion of the small Balkan country did not merely represent an action of geostrategic importance for the control of the Adriatic and future expansion in southeastern Europe. Rome's leadership also considered Albania as a space for colonization. The Italian fascists had already started similar enterprises in their African colonies, which had attracted the admiration of the Nazi authorities. The latter monitored their southern allies for their own projects for the colonization of the eastern frontiers.[83] Although not discussed much in academic literature, Albania represented a frontier for the Italians in the southeastern Adriatic, which Rome's authorities planned to colonize with Italian settlers. Unlike Libya, though, the fascists neither applied nor anticipated implementing racist laws to keep the two groups separated from each other. The Italian authorities planned to merge the two ethnic groups rather than keep them apart because their goal was not only to colonize Albania but also to assimilate the Albanians and transform them into Italian subjects.

In the racial categories the Italian fascists had constructed for the world, the Albanians were neither a Semitic race, as was the case with the Libyans, nor black Africans, as was the case with the Ethiopians. In both these Italian colonies, fascist authorities consistently discouraged interbreeding between the Italians and the indigenous populations. Nor were the Albanians Slavic—technically white but, according to the fascist racial categories, still an inferior race. In Albania,

---

82 Bernd J. Fischer, *Albania at War, 1939–1945* (West Lafayette, IN: Purdue University Press, 1999), 8–25.
83 On the influence that the Italian colonization of Africa exerted on Nazi Germany's project of colonization of its eastern frontier, see Patrick Bernhard, "Hitler's Africa in the East: Italian Colonialism as a Model for German Planning in Eastern Europe," *Journ of the al of Contemporary History* 51, no. 1 (2016): 61–90; Patrick Bernhard, "Borrowing from Mussolini: Nazi Germany's Colonial Aspirations in the Shadow of Italian Expansionism," *The Journal of Imperial and Commonwealth History* 41, no. 4 (2013): 617–63.

the fascists encouraged mixed marriages because they considered the Albanians to have similar racial attributes to those of the Italians. Mussolini's regime also invented a legend about the fraternity between Aeneas, the founders of Rome, and the Albanians' ancestors. The construction of this mythic narrative is not significant merely for demonstrating how the fascists used history for legitimating their rule in the eyes of the Albanians. Its real importance lies in the fact that they used the past as a link, as a precedent for merging the two populations, rather than keeping them at a safe distance, as was the norm with the fascist regimes.[84]

The grand project of cultural and ethnic transformation of the country also implied huge infrastructural and economic investments. The Italians borrowed the Maliq scheme from their predecessors and used it in their fascist imperialist project for the Italianization of Albania. In May 1939, roughly a month after the Italian invasion, the Ministry of the Economy of the Albanian puppet government received new petitions against the Maliqi company and its concessions. One of them wrote: "Today... inspired by the valuable principles of fascism, we will enjoy justice from Your Excellency through the fair application of the law for everybody." To the frustration of its authors, the flattering words moved neither the Italian authorities nor their Albanian collaborators. The Ministry of Agriculture rejected their pleas and recognized the concession of 1925.[85] The new fascist authorities had other plans for Maliq.

Six and a half months after the fascist troops marched victoriously in the streets of Tirana, a group of Italian sugar companies pooled their capital and established "La Società Anonima Saccarifera Albanese" (The Albanian Joint-Stock Sugar Company—from now on SASA) on September 21, 1939.[86] In compliance with their project of establishing an autarkic economy in Albania, the Italians

---

84 On Italian attempts to win the hearts and minds of the Albanians and Italianize the country, see Fischer, *Albania at War*, 33–88; Roberto Morozzo Della Rocca, *Nazione e religione in Albania* (Lecce: Besa, 2012), 141–208. On the fascist policies of racial segregation in the Italian African colonies, see Emanuele Ertola, "The Italian Fascist Settler Empire in Ethiopia, 1936–1941," in *The Routledge Handbook of the History of Settler Colonialism*, eds. Edward Cavanagh and Lorenzo Veracini (London: Routledge, 2017), 263–276.

85 Telegram sent to the fascist authorities, AQSh, F. 171, Ministry of the Economy, year 1939, d. VIII-18, fl. 16-17. Petition of the representatives of the sixteen villages located around the swamp of Maliq sent to the Ministry of the Economy against the Maliqi company. May 17, 1939. The rejection of the petitions, AQSh, F. 172, Ministria e Bujqësisë dhe Pyjeve, 1943, d. V-152, fl. 7. Response of the Ministry of Agriculture and Forests to the petitioners from the villages located around the swamp of Maliq. July 13, 1937.

86 AQSh, F. 161, Mëkëmbësia e Përgjithshme, 1939, d. 404, fl. 1. Letter of notification of SASA, sent to the Vicegerent of the Italian Emperor in Albania for the establishment of the company. September 21, 1939.

considered the construction of the sugar refinery as a critical issue.[87] Rome planned to create a self-sufficient Albania, an organ that could stand on its own feet within the Italian Empire. The fascist authorities sincerely believed that they would improve the standard of living of the Albanians, which implied the growth of sugar consumption. Besides, as part of Rome's goal to bring Italian colonists to Albania, the fascist authorities estimated that their arrival would also increase the overall sugar consumption because they used more sugar than the Albanians.[88] Rome would not have been able to convince its subjects to colonize Albania if their quality of life were to decrease.

With capital and the support of the Italian vicegerent in Albania, SASA immediately started to prepare for the construction of the refinery in Korça. The fascist authorities had designated the region for sugar production in Albania.[89] An expedition of two Italian specialists, Giovanni Lorenzoni and Pierfrancesco Nistri, confirmed the suitability of the plain of Korça, especially the area of Maliq, for the cultivation of sugar beet—something that the French and the Albanians had already discovered. In addition, after a general survey of the country, they concluded that this was the only region in Albania suitable for the cultivation of sugar beet. According to them, the plain of Korça combined soil quality, climate, and potential sources for irrigation that would enable the cultivation of sugar beet in both quality and yields comparable to those of northern Italy. The swamp of Maliq, they stated, would provide an area large enough to produce the right amount of sugar beet for Albania's demands.[90]

The administration of SASA complied with these conclusions. In the plots it possessed along the Dunavec River, the company yielded 600 quintals per hectare, twice that of Italy. With the reclamation of the lake of Maliq, SASA would utilize mechanized technology and overcome the problem of the small lands and

---

87 AQSh, F. 171, Ministria e Ekonomisë (Drejtoria e Tregtisë dhe Industrisë), 1940, d. 251, fl. 1. On the request of the Albanian Sugar Company for the obtaining of 35 hectares of land 2 km from the city of Korça, for the building of a sugar refinery. February 20, 1940. On the economic activity of the Italian fascist authorities in Albania during the years of the fascist occupation, see Gian Paolo Caselli and Grid Thoma, "The Albanian Economy during World War II and the First Attempt at Planning," *Journal of European Economic History* 34, no. 1 (2005): 93–119.
88 AQSh, F. 161, Mëkëmbësia e Përgjithshme, 1939, d. 1060, fl. 1. Report on the project for the construction of two sugar factories, one in Korça and one in the plain of Myzeqe.
89 *Ibid.*
90 AQSh, F. 171, Ministria e Ekonimisë (Drejtoria e Bujqësisë), 1933, d. 833, fl. 1-23. Report of Giovanni Lorenzoni and Francesco Nistri on the establishment of the sugar industry in the region of Korça; AQSh, F. 161, Mëkëmbësia e Përgjithshme, 1939, d. 404, fl, 1. Study of Giovanni Lorenzoni and Pierfrancesco Nistri "On the Establishment of a Sugar Refinery in Korça."

CHAPTER 1

primitive tools of the local rural population. The company tried to buy land from the peasants, who agreed to only sell it for stratospheric prices. According to the SASA director, the amount the peasants of the plain of Korça demanded exceeded even that of prime lands with excellent infrastructure in northern Italy. The reclamation of the swamp was a blessing for SASA because it would relieve the company from dealing with the Albanian peasants, and they would pay a much lower price for the land.[91]

However, in order to start production, the company would have to wait for the marsh to be drained. On the other hand, the company needed the peasants. The plain of Korça was one of the most densely populated regions in the country and had the necessary workforce for a labor-intensive crop such as sugar beet. The factory was close to human resources and raw materials. The combination of ecological and demographic factors made the plain of Korça the sugar capital of Italian-controlled Albania.[92] SASA planned to start the production of sugar by the summer of 1941. In 1940, the construction of its factory began a few kilometers north of the city of Korça. Its proximity to the city facilitated the commuting of workers and specialists, which were planned to be brought in from Italy. The company contracted many peasants in the villages of the plain to start cultivating sugar beet. According to Italian specialists who followed the cultivation of sugar beet among the Albanian peasants, the prospects were excellent.[93]

---

91 On the high yields of sugar beet of SASA, AQSh, F. 161, Mëkëmbësia e Përgjithshme, 1942, d. 536, fl. 6. Letter of SASA on the question of the sugar refinery in Korça. October 26, 1942; *Ibid*, fl. 11. Letter of SASA sent to the Provincial Office on the question of the sugar refinery in Korça. September 22, 1942. On the high prices of the Albanian peasants for selling the land, AQSh, F. 479, Shoqëria Shqiptare e Sheqerit, Pa vit, d. 2, fl. 3-5. Criteria for the definition of the price for the lands expropriated in Korça from SASA. On the need to reclaim the swamp to start massive cultivation, AQSh, F. 479, Shoqëria Shqiptare e Sheqerit, 1940, d. 2, fl. 16. Memo of SASA sent to the Ministry of the Economy in Tirana. February 27, 1940.

92 On the designation of the plain of Korça as the area for the cultivation of sugar, AQSh, F. 171, Ministria e Ekonomisë (Drejtoria e Tregtisë dhe Industrisë), 1940, d. 251, fl. 2-3. Memo of SASA concerning the construction of a sugar factory in the area of Korça. February 27, 1940; AQSh, F. 161, Mëkëmbësia e Përgjithshme, 1942, d. 536, fl. 11. Letter of SASA on the question of the sugar refinery in Korça. September 22, 1942.

93 On building the factory next to the city of Korça and the bringing of specialists from Italy, AQSh, F. 479, Shoqëria Shqiptare e Sheqerit, 1940, d. 10, fl. 1-2. Report of the Directory of SASA on the location of the sugar factory of Korça. February 19, 1940; AQSh, F. 479, Shoqëria Shqiptare e Sheqerit, Pa vit, d. 5. fl. 1. Report of the Directory of SASA on the location of the sugar factory of Korça. On the excellent results of the cultivation of sugar beet, AQSh, F. 479, Shoqëria Shqiptare e Sheqerit, 1940, d. 12, fl. 2-5. Report of the Albanian directory of SASA regarding the progress of the sowings of the sugar beet by the Albanian peasants. June 23, 1940.

World War II, though, did not allow for completion of the project. The Greco–Italian war started on October 28, 1940, and the front was not far from Korça, interrupting the building of the refinery.[94] Moreover, the machinery SASA bought from the Czech-based company Škoda—at that time under German sovereignty and ownership—remained in the port of Trieste, because the assemblers in Italy and Bohemia were mobilized for military production. Even the specialist that would operate the refinery could not come to Albania.[95] When the war ended, the swamp still covered the plain of Maliq and flooded the villages around it, while in the outskirts of Korça, the newly built structure of the refinery remained empty. A new stage would start after the war, this time with the communists in charge.

During the interwar era, Albanian private and state capital failed to complete the project. The property structure and lack of capital and specialists undermined the project's success. The Italians borrowed the idea of a sugar industry from their predecessors and furthered the project of territorial integration of Albania through regional economic interdependencies. When the war ended, the country fell under the control of the Albanian Communist Party, renamed the Albanian Labor Party (ALP) in 1948.[96] The communist leadership inaugurated its project of building socialist Albania with the reclamation of the swamp of Maliq. The ALP did not borrow all its ideas from the Soviet Union. Indeed, it continued the state-building process and the spatial integration of the country that had started in the interwar era through projects conceived years before they took over power. The constitution of a cohesive interregional space also meant the reshaping of the local landscape. The communists implemented this double process in Maliq. Although the ALP narrated the story of post-World War II Albania as a historical caesura, in reality, there were substantial continuities with the past, and in Maliq, these links stretched back as far as the late Ottoman era.

---

94 AQSh, F. 479, Shoqëria Shqiptare e Sheqerit, 1941, d. 4, fl. 1. Letter of the construction company of Anastas Pilika sent to the directory of SASA regarding the delay in completion of the refinery of Korça. August 25, 1941; AQSh, F. 161, Mëkëmbësia e Përgjithshme, 1942, d. 536, fl. 9. Letter of SASA sent to the Provincial Office on the question of the sugar refinery in Korça. September 22, 1942.

95 AQSh, F. 161, Mëkëmbësia e Përgjithshme, 1942, d. 536, fl. 6-8. Letter of SASA sent to the Vicegerent of the King of Italy in Albania on the question of the sugar refinery in Korça. October 26, 1942; *Ibid*, fl. 10-11. Letter of SASA sent to the Provincial Office on the question of the sugar refinery in Korça. September 22, 1942.

96 I will use the acronym ALP throughout this work in order to avoid any potential confusion.

CHAPTER 2

The Making of Maliq's Landscape: Modern and Stalinist

Maliq's Landscape Between "Good" and "Bad" Governments

The walls of the "Room of Peace" in Siena's Palazzo Pubblico are covered by frescoes of the *Allegory of Good and Bad Government* painted by Ambrogio Lorenzetti in the late 1330s. Half of this outstanding work depicts good government. People look happy: they sing, dance, and work. The joyous yellowish color of the wheat covers the fields outside of the city's walls, and the regular plots are well kept. Lorenzetti dedicated the other half of the painting to bad government. Dark colors dominate the scene, which is filled with phantasmagoric creatures, starving people, an omnipresent plague, and, above all, barren fields. This fresco is the first representation of the political landscape in European art. Since then, the binary that it elaborates has remained a cornerstone in defining the relationship between the landscape and the type and quality of government. Albanian communists also operated within this dichotomy and used the landscape as an ideological tool to legitimate and consolidate their power.

The transformation of Maliq's landscape occupied an important place in the Albanian Labor Party's iconography and narrative, which located bad and good governments, respectively, in the past and present. Water and the thick blankets of reeds and groves, floods, and malaria symbolized the barren land and the weak and sick society of the past era. Erasing it became a marker of achievement and progress, and this is what the communists accomplished as soon as they took power. In 1951, during the tenth anniversary of the establishment of the ALP, the regime published an album of photos collected from the new socialist Albania. By juxtaposing images from before and after the land reclamation project, it

CHAPTER 2

used Maliq's landscape to deliver the same message as Lorenzetti: the swamp represented the bad government of the past and the country's backwardness. Next to it stood the sugar factory that the regime built in Maliq in 1951.

The refinery supplanted the bog as the center of economic activity in the Maliq plain. The new industrial landscape represented socialism, the modern, and the fulfillment of utopian development. Other albums that were later published by the regime's organs would use images from the plain of Maliq. The clean, geometric, and well-regulated parcels and their lively colors served as proof of the ALP's good government. The reclamation of Maliq showcased the triumph of the Apollonian over the Dionysian, of order over chaos. Considering it a political act, the transformation of the landscape became, in the eyes of the Albanian communist leadership, a critical part of the revolutionary transformation of the political order and society. As a result, the landscape's representation is a lens for exploring the political power that conceives and shapes it, its economy, and its ideology, and Maliq was the embodiment of this.

During the forty-five years of the ALP, the plain of Maliq underwent a thorough metamorphosis. The draining of the swamp, the plowing of the reclaimed land with tractors, the sowing of that land with precision machines, and the harvesting transfigured the face of the plateau. The transformed scenery of Maliq's plain, with its large rectangular parcels, was similar not only to those of the socialist countries, but also to those in Western Germany, the Netherlands, or the American Midwest. Regardless of whether their shape was based on the Eastern or Western side of the Iron Curtain, on socialism or capitalism, these agricultural landscapes shared the same architectural patterns and principles of spatial organization. The plain of Maliq was one of several sites that had been reclaimed from swamps and transformed into arable land ex nihilo in twentieth-century Europe. Some of the most famous cases of this are Agro Pontino and Torviscosa in fascist Italy, and the Zuiderzee scheme and Jura Water Correction in the liberal Netherlands and Switzerland, respectively.[1]

The similarities of these hydrological and agricultural reclamation projects clearly transgressed the ideological boundaries that divided Europe during the twentieth century. Regardless of their differences, the states that implemented

---

1   On Zuiderzee, see Robert J. Hoeksema, "Three Stages in the History of Land Reclamation in the Netherlands," *Irrigation and Drainage* 56, S1 (2007): 113–126. On the Pontine Marshes, see Antonio Linoli, "Twenty-Six Centuries of Reclamation & Agricultural Improvement on the Pontine Marshes," in *Integrated Land and Water Resources Management in History*, ed. Christoph Ohlig (Siegburg: DWHG, 2005), 27–55.

these projects also shared common goals. They conceived these undertakings as answers to demographic pressures on land and as solutions for regional and national development. Their landscapes, crisscrossed by straight roads separating rectangular parcels surrounded by dense irrigation and drainage ditches, look very similar. Liberal democracies have prided themselves on these large and complex schemes, without overloading the engineered landscape with ideological significance, trying to preserve, at least on the surface, the neutrality of nature. This was not the case with the communists, who identified the transformation of nature with socialism. What was, then, socialist about Maliq?

In the 1970s, Henri Lefebvre explored the similarities between the construction of space under capitalism and socialism.[2] However, it was only in the 1990s, when the triumphalism that followed the collapse of Soviet-type socialism ebbed, that scholars started to focus on the similarities rather than the differences between the two competing systems. To overcome the antagonistic divide between liberal democracy and communism which existed between 1945 and 1990, a number of researchers have focused their analysis less on institutions, and more on the microphysics of power, everyday life, and the model of development and social organization. In this way, they continuously navigated between small case studies and broader global perspectives. However, as already mentioned in the Introduction of this book, the authors who have investigated the similarities between shared historical patterns between capitalist and Stalinist experiences have focused mainly on imperial centers, like the US and the USSR,[3] or, when it comes to the small nation states of Eastern Europe, researchers on socialism have explored mainly urban settings, especially the steel towns.[4] Other works have analyzed the symbolic representation of the landscape, while its physical organization has remained out of scholarly attention.[5]

---

[2] Henri Lefebvre, *State, Space, World: Selected Essays*, ed. Neil Brenner & Stuart Elden (Minneapolis, MN: University of Minnesota Press, 2009).

[3] Kotkin, *Magnetic Mountain*; Samuelson, *Tankograd: The Formation of a Soviet Company Town*; Kate Brown, "Gridded Lives: Why Kazakhstan and Montana are Nearly the Same Place," *The American Historical Review* 106, 1 (2001): 17–48; Kate Brown, *Plutopia: Nuclear Families, Atomic Cities, and the Great Soviet and American Plutonium Disasters* (Oxford: Oxford University Press, 2013); Kate Brown, *Dispatches from Dystopia: Histories of Places Not Yet Forgotten* (Chicago: Chicago University Press, 2015).

[4] See footnote 26 in Introduction.

[5] See for example Evgeny Dobrenko and Eric Naiman, eds., *The Landscape of Stalinism: The Art and Ideology of Soviet Space* (Seattle, WA: Washington University Press, 2003); Mark Bassin, "'I Object to Rain That Is Cheerless': Landscape Art and the Stalinist Aesthetic Imagination," *Ecumene* 7, no. 3 (2000): 313–336.

CHAPTER 2

In this chapter, I will argue that the drive to emulate the industrial organization of production in agriculture, which implies efficiency, mechanization, large-scale economies, and mass production, shaped the physical landscape of the plain of Maliq.[6] This drive was limited neither to Albania nor to the communist bloc in general but, indeed, was part of a wider trend that predominated throughout the twentieth century and reached its apex in the three decades that followed World War II. How did Maliq end up sharing a similar outlook to that implanted for other plains that had been reclaimed by fascist or liberal regimes? In what ways did local and national circumstances shape Maliq? Finally, was there any marker in particular that made it a Stalinist landscape?

Uncompleted Reclamation

In April 1945, after a winter of intense rainfall, the Maliq marsh flooded the villages around it. The communist-led government sent a team of specialists to Korça to evaluate the situation. Upon returning to Tirana, they submitted a report asking for an immediate and integral reclamation of "the wounded land" of Maliq.[7] The new authorities ordered work to begin in the area. The reclamation took on a political characteristic. The new authorities used this project to showcase the achievements of the new political order, very similar to how Mussolini tried to prove the superiority of fascism over liberal democracy by reclaiming the Pontine Marshes. Was there a better way to demonstrate the vitality of the new revolutionary regime than to succeed where the previous political elites had failed? Was there a better christening for the Albanian communist modernizers than by taming nature, expanding the internal frontier, and thrusting the plow into a wasteland, thus making it fertile?

---

6   There are two articles that investigate the physical transformations of the landscape in Albania, but none of them engages with Maliq. One of them [Dean S. Rugg, "Communist Legacies in the Albanian Landscape," *Geographical Review* 84, no. 1 (1994), 59–73] is too general and provides the English-speaking reader an overview for an otherwise mysterious country. Besides being overly simplistic, its author conflates rural and urban landscapes into one single concept. The other article [Daniel Müller & Darla K. Munroe, "Changing Rural Landscapes in Albania: Cropland Abandonment and Forest Clearing in the Postsocialist Transition," *Annals of the Association of American Geographers* 98, no. 4 (2008): 855–876] analyzes how the interactions between domestic political actors and global economic forces have shaped the rural landscape after the collapse of socialism.

7   AQSh, F. 494, Ministria e Ekonomisë, 1945, d. 910, fl. 2-3. Report on the damages caused in the plain of Korça by the rivers Devoll and Dunavec, and their systemization. April 26, 1945; AQSh, F. 494, Ministria e Ekonomisë, 1945, d. 439, fl. 43-45. Report on the damages caused in the plain of Korça by the rivers Devoll and Dunavec, and their systemization. April 26, 1945.

FIGURE 3. The Minister of Construction, Spiro Koleka, inspects the swamp of Maliq (September 14, 1946)

Regardless of Tirana's new leadership agenda, the reclamation of the Maliq swamp was part of a broader dynamic of intensified modernization that took place in Europe after World War II. The post-World War II European governments continued to intensify the large-scale campaigns to reclaim marshes that had started in the interwar period, and to do so with increased determination and vigor. Besides the Zuiderzee and Jura schemes, in Italy, the liberal post-fascist governments completed the reclamation of the Mezzogiorno marshlands, which Mussolini's regime had left untouched. The same process occurred in Greece, with the reclamation goals that started in Greek Macedonia in 1920 only being completed in 1970. In Spain, Franco re-initiated "national regeneration" projects after consolidating his power and dedicated special attention to controlling the waterways, especially after the outpouring of American dollars in the early 1950s.[8]

---

[8] On Italy, see Frank M. Snowden, *The Conquest of Malaria*; Graeme Baker & Peter Taylor, "Feudalism and the 'Southern Question' (AD 1500 to the Present)," in *A Mediterranean Valley: Landscape, Archaeology, and Annales History in the Biferno Valley*, ed. Graeme Baker (London: Leicester University Press, 1995), 298–301. On Greece, see Richard C. Smardon, *Sustaining the World's Wetlands: Setting Policy and Resolving Conflicts* (New York: Springer, 2009), 67–69; Neil Roberts & Jane Reed, "Lakes, Wetlands, and Holocene Environmental Change," in *The Physical Geography of the Mediterranean*, 276. On Spain, see Erik Swyngedouw, "Technonatural Revolutions: The Scalar Politics of Fran-

CHAPTER 2

Similar to the post-Ottoman states in the Balkans and the post-colonial states elsewhere, communist regimes borrowed many projects from the pre-communist era and interwove socialist meaning throughout them. Even in the Soviet Union, the Bolsheviks initiated projects that had been planned since the Tsarist period, such as the mammoth White Sea–Baltic canal, the Moscow Canal, and the forestation of southern Russia.[9] In Central Eastern Europe, some of the most prominent examples were those of the steel cities of Nowa Huta in Poland, Ostrava-Poruba in Czechoslovakia, Eisenhüttenstadt in the GDR, and Sztálinváros in Hungary. The communist leadership in Warsaw, Prague, East Berlin, and Budapest borrowed the idea of mega steel cities from the plans of their anti-communist predecessors.[10] Even in Africa, the socialist post-colonial regimes continued the projects of their colonial predecessors, as in the case of the Cahora Bassa dam in Mozambique. In the early stages of their rule, both the Italian fascists and German Nazis also implemented projects that had been conceived and planned by their predecessors.[11]

Despite the narratives of historical caesura held by communist regimes, they all preserved many links with the past. Indeed, as argued by Alexis de Tocqueville in the mid-nineteenth century, in opposition to his contemporaries who concep-

---

co's Hydro-Social Dream for Spain, 1939–1975," *Transactions of the Institute of British Geographers* 32, no. 1 (2007): 9–28; Erik Swyngedouw, "Modernity and Hybridity: Nature, *Regeneracionismo*, and the Production of the Spanish Waterscape," *Annals of the Association of American Geographers* 89, no. 3 (1999): 443–465.

9 Cynthia A. Ruder, *Building Stalinism: The Moscow Canal and the Creation of Soviet Space* (London: I. B. Tauris, 2018), 4; Cynthia A. Ruder, *Making History for Stalin: The Story of the Belomor Canal* (Gainsville, FL: The University Press of Florida, 1998), 14–19; Julie Draskoczy, *Belomor: Criminality and Creativity in Stalin's Gulag* (Boston: Academic Studies Press, 2014), 34–40; Mikhail Morukov, "The White Sea-Baltic Canal," in *The Economics of Forced Labor: The Soviet Gulag*, eds. Paul R. Gregory & Valery V. Lazarev (Stanford, CA: Hoover Institution Press, 2003), 152–153. On Stalin's project for the forestation of southern Russia, see the chapter "Transformation: The Great Stalin Plan for the Transformation of Nature" in Stephen Brain, *Song of the Forest: Russian Forestry and Stalinist Environmentalism, 1905–1953* (Pittsburgh, PA: University of Pittsburgh Press, 2011), 140–167.

10 Dagmara Jajeśniak-Quast, "Nowa Huta, Eisenhüttenstadt and Ostrava-Poruba in Early State Socialism: The Proletarianization and Ruralization of New Cities," in *Mastery and Lost Illusions: Space and Time in the Modernization of Eastern and Central Europe*, eds. Włodzimierz Borodziej, Stanislav Holubec, & Joachim von Puttkamer (Munich: De Gruyter Oldenbourg, 2014), 123–125; Lebow, *Unfinished Utopia*, 20–21; Sándor Horváth, *Stalinism Reloaded: Everyday Life in Stalin-City, Hungary* (Bloomington, IN: Indiana University Press, 2017).

11 On Mozambique, see Allen F. Isaacman & Barbara S. Isaacman, *Dams, Displacement, and the Delusion of Development: Cahora Bassa and Its Legacies in Mozambique, 1965–2007* (Athens, OH: Ohio University Press, 2013), 4. On the fascists and Nazis borrowing projects from their predecessors, see Harald Bodenschatz, "Urbanism and Dictatorship: Expanding Spaces for Thought!," in *Urbanism and Dictatorship: A European Perspective*, eds. Harald Bodenschatz, Piero Sassi, & Max Welch Guerra (Gütersloh, Berlin-Basel: Bauverlag & Birkhäuser, 2013), 17–18.

tualized the great French Revolution as a historical chasm, the reality was that the continuities with the preceding period were substantial.[12] Along the same lines, Peter Holquist, a historian specializing in the history of Russia and the Soviet Union, argues that the Bolsheviks' policies should be understood as a radical extension of rather than a full break with the past.[13] In the previous chapter, I explained how the tendencies of authoritarian modernization had already made inroads in Albania in the interwar era. In his monumental work *Social Origins of Dictatorship and Democracy*, Barrington Moore Jr. said plainly that the road to industrialization and the transition to the modern world was violent. When the ruling elite was not willing to deliver the bill to one social segment, and especially to the peasantry, it opened the gates to a revolutionary transformation, either fascist or communist, with both groups ready to use violence in order to jump to full industrial modernity.[14] The ALP's leadership was not an exception to the rule. The reclamation of Maliq was but another example that proves that the socialist countries of Eastern Europe did not borrow their ideas and projects from the Soviet Union alone. Indeed, they were fertile sites for the cross breeding of old and new ideas, including the determination to radically transform their respective societies by any means possible.

Maliq's reclamation started in May 1946, and it took the regime more than six years to complete the project of the Italian engineer, Angelo Omodeo. The newly established Albanian communist regime faced the same challenges as its predecessors: a lack of financial resources, machinery, skilled workers, technical staff, and knowledge about the swamp and how to reclaim it. However, they had the will to overcome all of these obstacles through mass mobilization and shock work, regardless of the human costs that these strategies incurred. As was the case during the building of Nowa Huta in communist Poland or with the building of Chelyabinsk and Ozersk in the Soviet Union, the Albanian Communist Party compensated for the lack of machinery with human muscles, shovels, pickaxes, and wheelbarrows.[15] Food became a luxury at the Maliq worksite, and the living conditions were terrible. The workers lived in deplorable sanitary condi-

---

12 Alexis de Tocqueville, *The Old Regime and the Revolution*, trans. John Bonner (New York: Harper & Brothers, 1856).
13 Peter Holquist, "Violent Russia, Deadly Marxism? Russia in the Epoch of Violence, 1905–21," *Kritika: Explorations in Russian and Eurasian History* 4, no. 3 (2003): 641–642.
14 Barrington Moore Jr., *Social Origins of Dictatorship and Democracy: Lord and Peasant in the Making of the Modern World* (Boston: Beacon Press, 1966).
15 Lebow, *Unfinished Utopia*, 37–38; Brown, *Plutopia*, 87–114; Samuelson, *Tankograd: The Formation of a Company Town in the Soviet Union*, 90–94.

tions and were packed in small shelters and wooden sheds, or in malaria-infested living quarters. After the administration ran out of tents, many workers slept outside, offering an easy meal to the hungry armies of mosquitos.[16]

One of the major problems was that of supplying the workforce. There were not enough engineers, technicians, and geometers able to lead a project of such magnitude. In addition, there was a serious shortage of skilled workers such as excavator operators, stonecutters, masons, and miners.[17] The scarcity of technicians forced the communist authorities to hire Italian specialists, who had been living in Albania since World War II and whose expertise was critical for the post-war reconstruction.[18] The Albanian communists employed thousands of Italians and at least 1,200 prisoners of war, who were promised a safe return to their home country after the completion of the projects in which they were involved.[19] Many of these Italians worked in Maliq too. Unskilled workers became a rare commodity as well. According to initial estimates, the successful completion of the project required the mobilization of a large workforce of at least 4,000 people per day to compensate for the lack of machinery.[20] In reality, the workforce almost dou-

---

16 AQSh, F. 14/AP, PPSh (STR), 1946, d. 7/1, fl. 9. Telegram of the ALP's Committee of Maliq on some urgent needs for the Maliq construction site. May 11, 1946; *Ibid*, fl. 19 & 23. Telegrams of the ALP's Committee of Maliq on the situation at the Maliq construction site. May 11 and June 2, 1946; AQSh, F. 14/AP, PPSh (STR), 1946, d. 159, fl. 10-11. Report of the ALP's Committee of Korça on the situation at the Maliq construction site. No date; *Ibid*, fl. 47. Report of the Party Committee of Maliq on the progress at the Maliq work site from May to September 1946. September 24, 1946; AQSh, F. 499, Ministria e Ndërtimit, 1946, d. 552, fl. 51. Report of the hospital in Korça on the inspection its doctors had performed at the Maliq construction site. November 23, 1946; AQSh, F. 14/AP (STR), 1947, d. 3, fl. 95. Bulletin of the ALP's Central Committee for the month of June. June 1947; AQSh, F. 14/AP (STR), 1947, d. 323, fl. 13. Telegram of Mihallaq Gjinikasi, Chair of the ALP's Committee of Korça to the ALP's Central Committee concerning the reclamation of the swamp of Maliq. July 20, 1947; *Ibid*, fl. 20. Report on the progress of the works in Maliq. August 4, 1947; AQSh, F. 499, Ministria e Punëve Botore, 1947, d. 43, fl. 5. Report of the Executive Committee of Korça sent to the Ministry of Public Works on the situation at the Maliq construction site. May 23, 1947.
17 AQSh, F. 14/AP, PPSh (STR), 1946, d. 7/1, fl. 44-47 & fl. 49-51. Requests of the administration of the Maliq construction site for skilled laborers. June 8-9, 1946; *Ibid*, fl. 44-47 & fl. 49-51. Requests of the Ministry of Interior for skilled laborers. June 8-9, 1946; AQSh, F. 499, Ministria e Punëve Botore, 1947, d. 431, fl. 58. Report of the technical office of the Maliq construction site sent to the Ministry of Construction. September 26, 1946; AQSh, F. 499, Ministria e Ndërtimit, 1946, d. 547, fl. 1. Information of the State Enterprise of Construction of the district of Korça on the state of the work force at the Maliq construction site. July 19, 1946; AQSh, F. 14/AP (STR), 1947, d. 2, fl. 27. Report of the ALP's Central Committee on the situation at the Maliq construction site. August 22, 1947.
18 NARA 875.00/5-1845. Memorandum of Italian interests in Albania. May 17, 1945.
19 NARA 875.01/6-845. Report of the British Military Mission in Albania. May 22, 1945; Hoxha, *Tharja e kënetës së Maliqit*, 97–99.
20 AQSh, F. 498, Ministria e Bujqësisë dhe Pyjeve, 1945, d. 26, fl. 2-5. Minutes of the meeting of the engineers of the Ministry of Public Works and the Ministry of Economy regarding the necessary preparations for the reclamation of the swamp of Maliq. May 14, 1945.

FIGURE 4. Digging the drainage canal of Maliq

FIGURE 5. Bare feet workers transporting stones during the construction of the drainage canal of Maliq

bled to 7,500.[21] Because the region of Korça could not provide this manpower, the regime was forced to turn to other parts of the country and, as a result, the Maliq worksite became a conglomerate of many languages, accents, and costumes that were unified by the shared experiences of sweat and suffering.

The initial stage of the land reclamation at Maliq stumbled against enormous difficulties due to inexperience coupled with a lack of the necessary financial and technological resources. It was 1946, a crucial historical moment when the division of Europe into antagonistic blocs was looming large. The binaries of the beginning of the Cold War era and the splitting of the continent left their mark on Maliq as well. Possessed by near paranoia of an omnipresent enemy, the Albanian communists accused the top technical staff that led the reclamation project of being saboteurs paid by the American secret services. According to Albania's Ministry of the Interior, engineers and other Albanian, Italian, and Austrian specialists hindered the success of the project in order to discredit the new communist government. Seven of them, including the Croatian wife of an Albanian engineer, were sentenced to death, while eight others ended up in jail.

The draining of the swamp of Maliq started with human sacrifices and continued to claim lives throughout the process.[22] Being short of the necessary manpower, in true Stalinist fashion the Albanian government utilized the forced labor of roughly 900 prisoners.[23] Among them were dissidents sentenced for anticommunist activities. Working and living in inhuman conditions, dozens of political prisoners died in the mud of the swamp while opening irrigation canals. The memories and poetry that some left behind tell of the frightful conditions of the Albanian gulag and the shed blood that stained the process of the reclamation of Maliq.[24]

---

21 AQSh, F. 14/AP, PPSh (STR), 1946, d. 159, fl. 35. Report of the ALP's Committee of Maliq on the situation at the Maliq construction site. September 13, 1946.

22 AMB [Archive of the Ministry of Interior], F. Dosje hetimore gjyqësore, d. 1080; AMB, F. Dosje hetimore gjyqësore, d. 944-A. Files on the investigation and trial of the technical staff at the Maliq hydraulic project.

23 On the entire process of the communist-led reclamation of Maliq, see Hoxha, *Tharja e këneshtës së Maliqit*, 67–123 & 133–186. On the use of forced labor of prisoners in Stalin's Soviet Union, see Ruder, *Building Stalinism*; Ruder, *Making History for Stalin*; Draskoczy, *Belomor*; Paul R. Gregory and Valery Lazarev, eds., *The Economics of Forced Labor: The Soviet Gulag* (Stanford, CA: Hoover Institution Press, 2003).

24 Arshi Pipa, "Canal," in *The Walls Behind the Curtain: East European Prison Literature, 1945–1989*, ed. Harold B. Segel (Pittsburgh, PA.: University of Pittsburgh Press, 2012), 26–27. Sami Repishti, *Nën hijen e Rozafës: Narrativë e jetueme* [Under the shadow of Rozafa: A lived story] (Tirana: Onufri, 2004), 230. Zef Pllumi, *Rrno për me tregue* [Live to tell] (Tirana: Hylli i Dritës, 2001); Makensen Bungo, *Këneta e Vdekjes* [The swamp of death] (Tiranë: Pheonix, 1996); Spartak Ngjela, *Përkulja dhe rënia e ti-*

FIGURE 6. Using human muscles for the reclamation of the plain of Maliq

Inexperience and a lack of organization substantially increased the expense of the project and undermined its rapid progress. Initially, the government estimated that the entire enterprise would cost 100 million ALL (Albanian lekë); ultimately, the state treasury ended up paying over three times as much, i.e., 331 million ALL.[25] Notwithstanding all of the difficulties, setbacks, delays, costs, and human sacrifices, the communist regime managed to complete the Maliq reclamation by 1953. The marshland had disappeared, and what remained of it was a small lake of about 800 hectares, into which the Devoll and Dunavec rivers and a multitude of creeks drained. However, nature was not as malleable as both politicians and engineers thought. Not long after the communists had pulled

---

ranisë shqiptare, 1957–2010, vëll. 2 [The decline and fall of the Albanian tyranny] (Tirana: UET Press, 2012), 153–154; Bujar Leskaj, "Midis dy kënetave: Shënime mbi romanin 'Këneta e Vdekjes' e shkrimtarit Makensen Bungo" [Between two swamps: Notes on the novel "The Swamp of Death" by the writer Makensen Bungo], in Bujar Leskaj, *Muzat e qëndresës* [The muses of resistance] (Tirana: Geer, 2001), 199–218.

25 AQSh, F. 498, Ministria e Bujqësisë dhe Pyjeve, 1951, d. 95, fl. 6. The list of objects built by the Ministry of Construction and their cost. November 12, 1951.

up the iron gates that divided the swamp from the drainage canal, they discovered that the reclamation was not over.

Spanning an area of 5900 hectares, underneath the one-meter thick sandy-clay coat that covered the plain hid a vast deposit of peat, the thickness of which reached a depth of up to ten meters.[26] Peat is an organic matter of plant origin that is mainly deposited in wetlands as a result of the continuous accumulation of decomposed vegetation. When peat comes into contact with oxygen, it is subjected to oxidation, which causes it to shrink. This is exactly what happened in Maliq and in many other areas that had been reclaimed in temperate and tropical climatic zones. The cultivation of peatlands and the draining of the groundwater for agricultural purposes accelerated peat oxidation and caused land subsidence. This phenomenon has caused significant ecological, economic, and social problems in many areas of the world, from the US to Northern Europe, the Mediterranean, and Asia.[27]

Everybody knew about the peat, but nobody, including the author of the reclamation project, Angelo Omodeo, anticipated how it would react once the swamp water no longer covered the plain of Maliq. After the reclamation, it started to decompose, and between 1953 and 1957, the plain subsided by one meter, severely damaging the seepage canals. The drainage lake expanded from the 800 hectares, which Omodeo had anticipated, to 2000 hectares, and a series of other small swamps appeared across the plain. The floods returned, and they left behind a layer of thick mud that inhibited the use of machines for agriculture.[28] Maliq was meant to showcase mechanized agriculture, but the harvest-

---

26 AQSh, F. 14/AP, Komiteti i PPSh (STR), 1958, d. 314, fl. 21. Memo of the Ministry of Agriculture on the full reclamation of the lake of Maliq and the irrigation of the plain of Korça. August 2, 1958; AQSh, F. 490, Këshilli i Ministrave, 1982, d. 39, fl. 8. Memo of the Ministry of Agriculture on the draft-project for the complementary works for the reclamation of the plain of Maliq.

27 Henk van Hardeveld et al., "Supporting collaborative policy process with a multi-criteria discussion of costs and benefits: The case of soil subsidence in Dutch peatlands," *Land Use Policy*, 77 (2018): 425–436; Antoni Grzywna, "The degree of peatland subsidence resulting from drainage of land," *Environmental Earth Sciences* 76 (2017): 559; Jens Leifeld et al., "Peatland subsidence and carbon loss from drained temperate fens," *Soil Use and Management* 27, no. 2 (2011): 170–176; Aljosja Hooijer et al., "Subsidence and carbon loss in drained tropical peatlands," *Biogeosciences* 9, no. 3 (2012): 1053–1071; Francesca Zanello et al., "Long term peatland subsidence: Experimental study and modeling scenarios in the Venice coastland," *Journal of Geophysical Research* 116, F4 (2011): 1–14; Stephan Gebhardt et al., "Shrinkage processes of a drained riparian peatland with subsidence morphology," *Journal of Soils and Sediments* 10, no. 3 (2010): 484–493.

28 AShV Korçë [Local State Archive of Korça], F. 3/1, Komiteti i PPSh Qarku Korçë, 1957, Lista 8, d. 19, fl. 29-32. Reports on the drainage of the marshlands in the cooperative of Plasa and Melçan-Lumalas; AQSh, F. 14/AP, Komiteti i PPSh (STR), 1958, d. 314, fl. 21-22. Memo of the Ministry of Agriculture on the full reclamation of the lake of Maliq and the irrigation of the plain of Korça. August 2, 1958.

ers, which the Albanian regime had imported from the Soviet Union, became stuck in the peat's mud. This time, the inundations did not cause much harm to the private economies of the peasants or their houses, but instead harmed the agricultural cooperatives and, especially, the state farm "Maliqi." The floods and the expansion of the drainage lake occurred within the territory of the farm, which could then use only 1300 out of its 5000 hectares.[29]

In 1958, the Ministry of Agriculture assigned a mixed group of Albanian and Soviet engineers to study how to fully reclaim the Maliq plain. In February 1959, the team, led by the Soviet engineer G. A. Zhukov, submitted the project.[30] Work started in 1960 and finished in 1965. The cost of this new stage of the reclamation reached 400 million ALL, thus exceeding the initial cost of 1946–1953.[31] This time, though, the regime did not resort to the mass mobilization of a workforce. There were delays and setbacks, but the state authorities kept them within limits that did not affect the outcome of the project. By the 1960s, the regime had more dredgers, more tractors, and a plethora of other necessary machinery and equipment. Meanwhile, an entire cohort of engineers, geologists, agronomists, and other technicians that had studied in the Soviet Union and in other Eastern European countries had been assembled. This generation established the University of Tirana and filled all the state institutions with the necessary specialists. During this period, thousands of Soviet and other Eastern European specialists arrived in Albania and trained local technicians. Other COMECON countries provided Albania with financial aid and machinery.[32] Once the communists came into power, the Albanian engineers and technicians not only had more equipment and knowledge, they had also accumulated significant experience in terms of leading large infrastructural projects. The regime was more efficient.

---

29 On the harvesters that stuck in the peat, AShV Korçë, F. 3/1, Komiteti i PPSh Qarku Korçë, 1954, Lista 5, d. 56, fl. 12. Report on the campaign for harvesting, cleaning, and transportation of sugar beet. September 9, 1954. On the expansion of the drainage lake and the limited use of the reclaimed land, AQSh, F. 490, Këshilli i Ministrave, 1959, d. 457, fl. 4. Memo on the full reclamation of the swamp of Maliq. October 21, 1959.
30 AQSh, F. 490, Këshilli i Ministrave, 1959, d. 819, fl. 3. Correspondence of the Prime Minister's Office with the Ministry of Agriculture concerning the full reclamation of the swamp of Maliq. May 2, 1959.
31 AQSh, F. 14/AP, Komiteti i PPSh (STR), 1972, d. 246, fl. 2. Report of the Ministry of Agriculture on some problems of the state farm of Maliq.
32 For a good overview of the aid the countries of the socialist bloc gave to Albania, see Elidor Mëhilli, "Socialist Encounters: Albania and the Transnational Eastern Bloc in the 1950s," in *Cold War Crossings: International Travel and Exchange across the Soviet Bloc, 1940s–1960s*, ed. Patryk Babiracki & Kenyon Zimmer (College Station, TX: Texas A&M University Press, 2014), 107–133; Elidor Mëhilli, "Defying De-Stalinization: Albania's 1956," *Journal of Cold War Studies* 13, no. 4 (2011): 4–56.

CHAPTER 2

FIGURE 7. Using heavy machinery for draining the swamp of Maliq

The peat mineralization did not stop, though, and as it challenged Omodeo in the 1950s, it also challenged Zhukov's project in the late 1960s and into the 1970s. During this period, the level of the plain of Maliq continued to decline to lower depths. Around 3000 hectares had subsided to the level of the riverbed of the Devoll River or below, and it continued to flood.[33] The hydrotechnical specialists concluded that the plain would continue to decrease by at least 1-2 meters over the next decade.[34] A new phase was necessary for land improvements to continue. In 1982, the heads of the ALP's Committee and the Executive Committee of Korça personally expressed their concerns to Enver Hoxha regarding the floods and the need for another round of reclamations.[35] In the meantime, the Ministry of Agriculture had started a new reclamation project. It anticipated deepening the Devoli riverbed by 2.5 meters and widening it by 10 meters. According to the estimates, it was anticipated that in the event of uninterrupted rainfall, 1000 hectares would be flooded in a matter of hours.[36] The Ministry of

---

33 AQSh, F. 490, Këshilli i Ministrave, 1982, d. 39, fl. 8. Memo of the Ministry of Agriculture on the draft-project for the complementary works for the reclamation of the plain of Maliq.
34 Marko Kamenica, *Ulja vertikale e tokave torfike të bonifikuara të Maliqit* [Vertical depression of the reclaimed peatland of Maliq] (Tirana: Ministria e Arsimit dhe Shkencës), 3–9.
35 AQSh, F. 14/AP, Komiteti i PPSh (OU), 1982, d. 55. fl. 10. Minutes of the meeting of the Secretaries of the ALP's Central Committee. March 17, 1982.
36 AQSh, F. 490, Këshilli i Ministrave, 1982, d. 39, fl. 2-3. Memo of the Ministry of Agriculture regarding the draft idea of the reclamation of the plain of Maliq. March 15, 1982; *Ibid*, fl. 10-15. Memo of the

Agriculture estimated that the reclamations would be completed in 1987.[37] However, by that year, the Ministry of Construction had completed less than half of the required work.[38] Budget constrictions hampered the completion of the reclamation, and the regime chose not to compensate for the lack of capital with mass mobilization and forced labor as it had in 1946. Within a few years, the regime had collapsed, and with it the reclamation came to a halt.

Besides reclaiming the swamp, the regime also built a vascular system in the plain: a dense network of irrigation and drainage canals and ditches crisscrossing each other like grid lines on a map. Building this grid was a long and very expensive process. Water remained one of the main problems for the cultivation of the Maliq plain. The reclamation project anticipated the construction of a system comprising drainage canals that were two meters deep and located 200-250 meters from each other. Soon, the engineers and agronomists figured out that the plain contained vast amounts of groundwater, and the humidity that was caused by this groundwater was destroying the crops. They altered the project and constructed denser canal networks: one every 100 meters and up to 2.5 meters deep at points with higher water levels.[39] The work to construct this system continued throughout the 1960s. The magnitude of the entire project and the continuous lowering of the ground level complicated the project but did not keep the regime from utilizing the plain.

Ironically, the plain of Maliq were rich in groundwater but received little annual rainfall. The uneven annual distribution, with 60% falling between October and February, made the problem of irrigation a thorn in the side of agri-

---

Ministry of Agriculture on the draft-project for the complementary works for the reclamation of the plain of Maliq.

37 AQSh, F. 490, Këshilli i Ministrave, 1982, d. 543, fl. 5. Minutes of the meeting of the Council of Ministers concerning the draft-project of the complementary works for the reclamation of the plain of Maliq in Korça. April 12, 1982.

38 AQSh, F. 498, Ministria e Bujqësisë, 1987, d. 59, fl. 1-3. Information of the Ministry of Agriculture on the need to import equipment for the reclamation of Maliq. May 29, 1987.

39 On the construction of the drainage system, AQSh, F. 498, Ministria e Bujqësisë, 1963, d. 57, fl. 23. Tasks regarding the project for the irrigation of the plain of Korça; AShV Korçë, F. 3/2, Komiteti i PPSh Rrethi Korçë, 1967, Lista 23, d. 64, fl. 13. Report of the ALP's Committee of Korça on the systematization of the arable land in the district. On the groundwaters, AQSh, F. 490, Këshilli i Ministrave, 1953, d. 880, fl. 1. Memo of the Ministry of Construction concerning the establishment of a commission for the study of the area of the plain of Maliq. June 10, 1953; AQSh, F. 498, Ministria e Bujqësisë, 1961, d. 110, fl. 36. Memo of the control team of the ALP's Central Committee concerning the intensification of agriculture in the district of Korça. September 10, 1961. On the denser draining grid in the areas with high levels of groundwaters, AQSh, F. 499, Ministria e Ndërtimit, 1964, d. 209, fl. 1-2. Memo concerning the necessary deviations from the project of the reclamation of Maliq. September 12, 1965.

CHAPTER 2

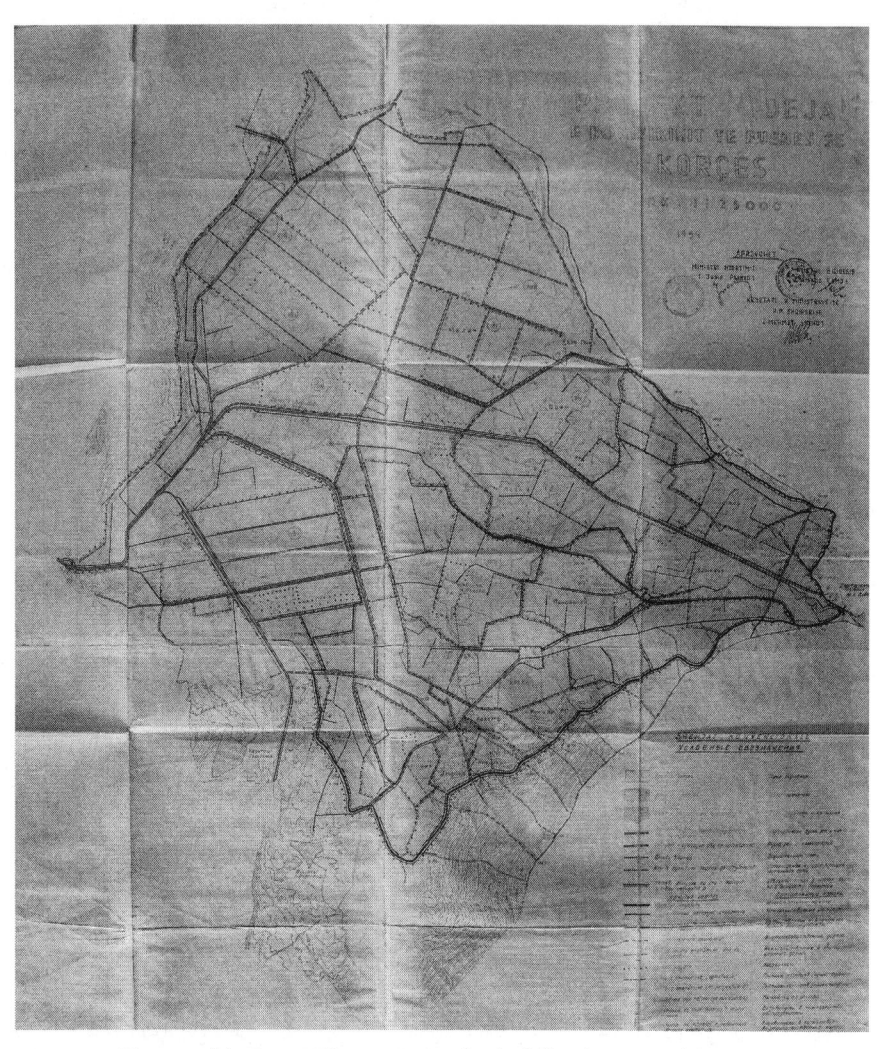

FIGURE 8. The map of the Soviet-Albanian Project for the full reclamation of the swamp of Maliq

culture in the area.⁴⁰ Considering that sugar beet is one of the most irrigation-intensive crops—requiring 1000 cubic meters of water per hectare—the irrigation of the plain became an essential element of the entire Maliq project.⁴¹ In 1954, the regime started a series of irrigation-related projects, and in 1959,

---

40 AQSh, F. 498, Ministria e Bujqësisë, 1959, d. 45, fl. 1. Minutes of the meeting of the Technical Committee of Giprovod'khoz of the Ministry of Agriculture of the USSR. June 11, 1959.
41 AQSh, F. 498, Ministria e Bujqësisë, 1963, d. 57, fl. 23. Tasks regarding the project for the irrigation of the plain of Korça.

the Soviet team led by G. A. Zhukov prepared a comprehensive project that included aspects other than the full reclamation of the swamp and the full irrigation of the plain.[42] Following this and other projects led by Albanian specialists, the local authorities and the central government built a series of reservoirs and a canal that used water from Lake Prespa Minor in the hills around the plain.[43]

Besides the large drainage and irrigation plots and ditches, the regime slowly built a road network 60 kilometers long that traversed the plain.[44] During the harvesting seasons, these roads buzzed with the roar of Czechoslovak Škoda trucks, combines, and tractors as well as buses and vans filled with people. These roads connected the villages of the plain to the region and the country. They were not exclusively used for agricultural purposes, but were also used for the circulation of people, goods, and ideas. The lines of the roads intersected with those of the plots and canals, furthering the molding and fashioning of the physical landscape. They represented other markers in the modern quest for the mastery of the territory.

While the communists did not fully control the plain, they never stopped struggling to tame it, and not without success. The central authorities made sure to have as many specialists as possible working in Maliq. The know-how that they generated allowed the political power and its entire decision-making structure to have a far better understanding of the plain compared to their predecessors. The communists could see beyond the visible surface of the reclaimed land. The underground water, irrigation and drainage canals, peat thickness, land composition, geology, and meteorology were constantly studied by the specialists and

---

42 AQSh, F. 498, Ministria e Bujqësisë, 1959, d. 45, fl. 1. Minutes of the meeting of the Technical Committee of Giprovod'khoz of the Ministry of Agriculture of the USSR. June 11, 1959; AQSh, F. 498, Ministria e Bujqësisë, 1959, d. 153, fl. 4. Memo on the measures for the realization of the production and industrialization of the sugar beet for the year 1959. March 9, 1959.

43 AQSh, F. 14/AP, Komiteti i PPSh, (STR), 1958, d. 314, fl. 21. Memo of the Ministry of Agriculture on the full reclamation of Maliq and the irrigation of the plain of Korça. August 2, 1958; AQSh, F. 498, Ministria e Bujqësisë, 1966, d. 75, fl. 43-45. Decision of the Council of Ministers on the draft project for the irrigation and drainage of the plain of Korça. May 3, 1966; AQSh, F. 495, Komisioni i Planit të Shtetit, 1987, d. 89, fl. 5. Study of the Executive Committee of Korça on the irrigation of the state farm of Maliq. August 6, 1987; AQSh, F. 490, Këshilli i Ministrave, 1989, d. 316, fl. 2. Memo of the Ministry of Agriculture concerning the use of water sprinklers in Maliq. January 13, 1989.

44 AShV Korçë, F. 3/1, Komiteti i PPSh Qarku Korçë, 1957, Lista 8, d. 23, fl. 5. Report on the completion of the overhaul of the sugar combine of Maliq; *Ibid*, fl. 14. Program of the Politburo of the ALP's Committee of the district of Korça for the harvesting, collection, and industrialization of sugar beet; AQSh, F. 497, Ministria e Industrisë së Lehtë Ushqimore, 1977, d. 149, fl. 96. Information on the harvesting, collection, and processing of the sugar beet. October 20, 1977.

scientists who worked for the state research institutions. The decision of the state to intervene and the implementation of their projects were based on this knowledge, which made the plain more transparent in the eyes of the regime.

The mapping of the Maliq plain expresses this new and more in-depth form of knowledge and its crescendo over time very well. However, by the 1950s, the plain stopped being an uncharted space, similar to what was observed in Dino Buzzati's *The Tartar Steppe*. The plain did not appear on maps as a mere part of a larger symbolic projection of space that included the region of Korça or as a component of a more extended spatial formation filled with general visual descriptions. The communist regime produced maps of the plain on their own, which were armed with a rich set of tools that depicted its canals, ditches, roads, coordinates, topography, peatland distribution, soil composition, plots, and reservoirs, conveying to the beholder detailed knowledge about it. These maps demonstrate how the plain changed over time and how its transformation was a result of the growing knowledge that the communist regime had accumulated about it. They reflect order, discipline, and economic utility. Besides their pragmatic utility, these maps were also power-laden texts that demonstrated socialism's triumph over nature and how the ALP's regime succeeded in translating the transformation of the material landscape into a document that conveyed intimate knowledge for practical use.[45]

The reclamation of the swamp and its agricultural systematization transformed the plain of Maliq into a modernist landscape. For Tirana's leadership, it became one of the most emblematic agricultural landscapes of socialist Albania and demonstrated the regime's vitality. The regime's iconography represented the plain to domestic audiences and foreign travelers, showcasing the socialist modernization of the countryside as well as socialism's efficiency and progress.[46] Men and women worked in the plain and drove combines and precision sowing machines while surrounded by a yellowish sea of grain or the greenish leaves of sugar beets.[47]

---

45 On maps as power-laden texts, see John B. Harley, "Maps, Knowledge, and Power," in *The Iconography of Landscape: Essays on the Symbolic Representation, Design and Use of Past Environments*, eds. Denis Cosgrove & Stephen Daniels (Cambridge: Cambridge University Press, 1988), 277–312; Draskoczy, *Belomor*, 137.

46 On showcasing the plain of Maliq to foreign visitors, AMEPJ, viti 1982, d. 1213, fl. 27. Information of the Committee for Cultural Relations with Foreign Countries at the Ministry of Foreign Affairs. March 31, 1982.

47 See for example the images in the album: *Bujqësia* (Agriculture) (Tirana: 8 Nëntori, 1982).

To quote Suzanne Stewart-Steinberg, Maliq was a "techno-natural landscape," a space inhabited by humans and machines.[48] It was a nexus where nature, technology, and social forces became enmeshed. Here, cadres, peasants, agronomists, engineers, doctors, economists, veterinarians, geologists, victims, perpetrators, machinery, tractors, combines, iron and wooden plows, horses, oxen, water buffalo, sugar, sugar beet, peat, water, rainfalls, floods, detritus, and so on, blended into one complex whole. All of these actors interacted in a space that was simultaneously both specifically local but also global. The continuous efforts to reclaim the swamp, the different projects, and specific struggles with peat, subsidence, groundwater, and floods represented the local dynamics of a much larger global historical pattern that Maliq was part of. It is a story of knowledge accumulation and the transition from the poorly charted territory of the pre-World War II era to the communist regime, which provided detailed maps and accurate information.

The reclamation of the swamp represented an effort to erase what was specific about the plain of Maliq and to make them similar to other plains either in Albania or in the other industrialized countries of Europe. However, the disciplining conditions that were implemented within the plain were local. As demonstrated in this section, apart from larger shared patterns that do not differentiate Maliq from other contemporary agricultural landscapes, we can see the resilience of the specific conditions and their role in the transformation of the plain. Although the communist regime tried to obliterate the swamp, its specter constantly haunted it. In his study on the post-World War II transformation of the German city of Breslau into the Polish town of Wrocław, Gregor Thum provides an example of the complexity of historical dynamics, which defy the politics that aim to obliterate the old. Thum argues that despite the efforts of the Polish authorities to treat the city as a palimpsest and to erase the old German presence and supplant it ex novo with a newly-gained Polishness, they could not obliterate the old town. Breslau has always remained covertly present inside Wrocław.[49]

What was true for a social space such as Wrocław was also true for an agricultural space such as Maliq. Besides being a location of social activity and inter-

---

48 Suzanne Stewart-Steinberg, "Grounds for Reclamation: Fascism and Postfascism in the Pontine Marshes," *Differences: A Journal of Feminist Cultural Studies* 27, no. 1 (2016): 103 & 109; Bruno Latour, *We Have Never Been Modern*, trans. Catherine Porter (Cambridge, MA: Harvard University Press, 1993).
49 Gregor Thum, *Uprooted: How Breslau Became Wrocław during the Century of Expulsion*, trans. Tom Lampert & Allison Brown (Wrocław: Via Nova, 2011), 7 and passim.

CHAPTER 2

actions, the latter was also a site where nature was a critical agent. While the Polish communist authorities fought against the ever-present German past, Albanian communist authorities fought the natural factors and tectonic forces that created the swamp, and the ditches and canals were the answer to the swamp's looming threat of return. The struggle to tame nature was part of a piece of global history that took place in the peculiar circumstances of the plain. We can also see the intersection between global trends and local particularities in the specific role that Maliq played in the nation-building process—its sugar scheme.

"For the Factory and Your Country": Maliq and the Nation

Besides its hydrological projects, the communist regime also borrowed the sugar scheme from its predecessors. In 1949, when the swamp reclamation project was close to completion, Tirana's authorities started building a refinery in Maliq and immediately pushed forward its project to transform this plain into Albania's land of sugar.[50] Concomitantly, the government elaborated its plan for the regional specialization of the economy and local agriculture, designating specific regions, in accordance with ecological and geological conditions, to the cultivation and processing of one or two industrial crops. In the summer of 1950, after being authorized by the government, a team from the Ministry of Agriculture devised a general plan. The latter reconfirmed the regionalization of projects from the interwar era and designated the plain of Maliq for sugar beet cultivation. It estimated that the entire plain, which spanned a total of 14,300 hectares, could produce the necessary quantity of sugar beet for a refinery to work.[51]

---

50   The plan of the State Planning Committee to build a sugar factory, AQSh, F. 14/AP, Komiteti i PPSh (STR), 1947, d. 330/10, fl. 11-12. Report of the State Planning Commission regarding the First Five-Year Economic Plan. April 16, 1946. On the establishment of the light industries for which Albania could produce the required raw materials, AQSh, F. 14/AP, Komiteti i PPSh (OU), 1947, d. 12, fl. 10. Discussions in the ALP's Politburo of the plan for economic investments. March 24, 1947; AQSh, F. 14/AP, Komiteti i PPSh (OU), 1947, d. 21, fl. 4. Minutes of the meeting of the ALP's Politburo regarding the principal orientations of the First Five-Year Plan. July 5, 1947; AQSh, F. 14/AP, Komiteti i PPSh (STR), 1947, d. 330/14, fl. 2. Study on the economic situation of Albania during the period of Ahmet Zog's rule.

51   On regional specialization, *Ekonomia politike (socializmi)* [Political economy (Socialism)] (Tirana: Akademia e Shkencave të Shqipërisë, 1981), 54. On the authorization of the Ministry of Agriculture to draft a plan for agricultural regionalization, AQSh, F. 498, Ministria e Bujqësisë dhe Pyjeve, 1950, d. 15, fl. 7. Comments of the Ministy of Agriculture regarding the study on the regionalization of agriculture. February 2, 1950. On the drafting of the plan for regionalization, AQSh, F. 490, Këshilli i Ministrave, 1950, d. 474, fl. 2. Draft-decision on the regionalization of agriculture. August 24, 1950. On the localization of areas subject to regional specialization, AQSh, F. 498, Ministria e Bujqësisë dhe Pyjeve, 1950, d. 15, fl. 9. Draft-decision of the Ministy of Agriculture on the regionalization of agri-

The regionalization of agriculture is similar to what Peter Vandergeest and Nancy Peluso have called internal territorialization. Expanding upon Foucault's argument that the focus of the modern state has been the governing of the masses and their distribution over a territory, Vandergeest and Peluso call internal territorialization the establishment of state control over natural resources and the people who use them. They argue that "all modern states divide their territory into complex and overlapping political and economic zones, rearrange people and resources within these units, and create regulations delineating how and by whom these areas can be used."[52] These principles concerning the territorialization of power over people and natural resources guide the regionalization of agriculture.

After the building of the sugar factory, the first problem that emerged for the planners was that of the sugar beet supply. In the late 1940s and early 1950s, collectivization was still at its beginning stage, and the most significant challenges that the agricultural planners faced were the thousands of private farmers whom the state had contracted to cultivate industrial crops, including sugar beets. In 1948, Spiro Koleka, the then Minister of Industry, expressed his frustration with the poor performance of the peasants in the cultivation of industrial crops. In 1948, they only fulfilled 50-60% of the state's quota. The situation was not much different in terms of sugar beet cultivation. Even in the first year of its cultivation, in 1948, the results were poor.[53]

---

culture. February 11, 1950. On the designation of the plain of Maliq for the cultivation of sugar beet, AQSh, F. 490, Këshilli i Ministrave, 1950, d. 474, fl. 2. Draft-decision on the regionalization of agriculture. August 24, 1950. On the capacities of the plain of Korça to produce sugar beet to supply the refinery, AQSh, F. 498, Ministria e Bujqësisë dhe Pyjeve, 1950, d. 15, fl. 25–26. An outline for the regionalization of cotton, rice, sugar beet, and other industrial crops. July 5, 1950.

52 According to Foucault, governmentality is a form of knowledge (political economy), institutional architecture (the modern state), and technologies of power (police). For more, see Michel Foucault, "Governmentality," in *The Foucault Effect: Studies in Governmentality*, eds. Graham Burchell, Colin Gordon, & Peter Miller (Chicago: Chicago University Press, 1991), 87–104; Peter Vandergeest & Nancy Lee Peluso, "Territorialization and State Power in Thailand," *Theory and Society*, 24, no. 3 (1995): 387. On governmentality see, Tania Murray Li, "Governmentality," *Anthropologica* 49, no. 2 (2007): 275–281; Lorna Weir, Pat O'Malley & Clifford Shearing, "Governmentality, Criticism, Politics," *Economy and Society* 26, no. 4 (2006): 501–517; Nikolas Rose, Pat O'Malley & Mariana Valverde, "Governmentality," *Annual Review of Law and Social Science* 2 (2006): 83–104; Pat O'Malley, "Indigenous Governance," *Economy and Society* 25, no. 3 (1996): 310–326.

53 On the distribution of cultivation among small-holding peasants, AQSh, F. 14/AP, Komiteti i PPSh (OU), 1949, d. 2, fl. 1. Report of Spiro Koleka held at the III Plenum of the ALP's Central Committee regarding the fulfillment of the state economic plan for the period between January–September 1949. October 11–13, 1949. On the contracting of private peasants to cultivate sugar beet, AQSh, F. 14/AP, Komiteti i PPSh (STR), 1948, d. 46, fl. 31. The monthly report of February 1948, of the ALP's Committee of Maliq sent to the ALP's Central Committee. February 29, 1948. On the failure to achieve

CHAPTER 2

The regime responded to the peasants' actions with a legal apparatus that forced these small private farmers to obey the state's central planning directives. It passed a law for the implementation of regionalization, which sanctioned those peasants who resisted the state's plan with severe punishments, ranging from expropriation to jail. Although the local authorities did use the iron fist at times, the regime, notwithstanding its threats, used more carrot than stick. Enver Hoxha and the Secretary for Cadres in the Central Committee, Tuk Jakova, publicly appealed to the peasants of the plains of Maliq, Korça, and Bilisht to work harder and to supply the refinery with the required amount of sugar beet. The two leaders highlighted that the fulfillment of this goal was a great responsibility for all of the rural economies in the plain. They instructed the local authorities to assign the best land to the cultivation of sugar beet and reminded them to use Soviet experience for the best results.[54]

Petitioning the peasants and proposing the magic bullet of Soviet experience were not enough to dilute the effect of the state's policies toward the rural population. In 1945, the ALP authorities imposed compulsory procurements on the countryside, which forced the peasants to sell their surplus production with fixed prices to the state in order to supply the cities.[55] This system openly favored urban and industrial centers over the countryside and immediately backfired. The Minister of Agriculture, Hysni Kapo, pointed out that the peasants were not going to follow state plans without first providing the necessary amount of food for themselves. They regularly hid their surpluses instead of delivering them to the authorities and sold them to the urban market at exorbitant prices.[56]

---

the quota, "Në rrethin e Korçës të bëhen më shumë përpjekje për mbjelljen e shpejtë të panxharit," [In the district of Korça, greater efforts should be made greater efforts for quicker sowing of sugar beet], *Përpara* [Forward], May 15, 1948, 4.

54 On the measures against those who would resist regionalization, AQSh, F. 490, Këshilli i Ministrave, 1950, d. 474, fl. 10. Memo on the regionalization of cotton, sugar beet, rice, and other industrial crops; AQSh, F. 14/AP, Komiteti i PPSh (OU), 1950, d. 53, fl. 31. Draft-decree of the law on the mandatory cultivation of sugar beet and other industrial crops in the regionalized lands. On the plea of Enver Hoxha and Tuk Jakova, "Thirrje e Këshillit të Ministrave dhe e Komitetit Qendror të P.P.Sh. për realizimin e planit të mbjelljeve dhe të arritjes së rendimenteve të larta të panxhar sheqerit" [Call of the Council of Ministers and the Central Committee of the ALP for the realization of the sowing plan and the achieving of a high yield of sugar beet], *Zëri i Popullit* [The people's voice], February 21, 1951, 1.

55 Deko Rusi, *Transformimi socialist i Bujqësisë së RPSh* [The socialist transformation of agriculture in the People's Republic of Albania] (Tirana: Universiteti Shtetëror i Tiranës, 1962), 93.

56 On Kapo's statement regarding peasant deliveries, AQSh, F. 14/AP, Komiteti i PPSh (OU), 1953, d. 2, fl. 8–10. Report on the measures for the improvement and development of agriculture. March 2–3, 1953. On the peasants selling foodstuff in the cities at high prices, AQSh, F. 14/AP, Komiteti i PPSh (OU), 1949, d. 1, fl. 23. Report of Enver Hoxha held at the II Plenum of the ALP's Central Committee. April 28–30, 1949.

In the plain of Maliq, the peasants neglected the cultivation of sugar beet because, according to them, they would otherwise starve. Many of them did not cultivate sugar beet on their land but instead stuck to cereals and legumes, which the peasants used to feed themselves and sell at the market. To the irritation of the Secretary of the ALP's Committee of Maliq, a number of peasants used the reclaimed land designated for sugar beet production to grow corn instead, which they then sold. In 1949, private farmers only met 40% of the sugar beet quotas. According to the ALP's Committee of Maliq, the farmers were more committed to the production of grain, which was far more vital to them, than they were to the cultivation of sugar beet. If this was not enough, the peasants did not even pay attention to the harvesting and conservation of sugar, which are very delicate processes.[57]

Peti Shambli, the head of the ALP Committee of Korça, insisted that the state had to increase the material incentives for the peasants who cultivated sugar beet. Following a study, the State Planning Commission reconfirmed the same conclusion and pointed out that the peasants cultivated their best land with potato crops and cereals because these crops were more rewarding. Even the newly created collective farms did not consider the cultivation of sugar beet worthwhile. The refinery bought the crop at a low price that did not justify the intensive work and high expenses that the plant required. As a response, the state increased the premiums for the peasants.[58]

However, Tirana was not consistent in its use of incentivization, and at times, the local branches of government preferred the use of force. Part of the deal be-

---

57 On the complaints of the peasants, AQSh, F. 14/AP, Komiteti i PPSh (STR), 1948, d. 46, fl. 45. Informative report of the ALP's Committee of Maliq on the first trimester of 1948. April 2, 1948. On the peasants cultivating corn instead of sugar beet, AQSh, F. 14/AP, Komiteti i PPSh (STR), 1948, d. 46, fl. 62. Monthly report of April 1948, of the ALP's Committee of Maliq. May 2, 1948. On the importance of grain for the peasants of Maliq compared to sugar beet, AShV Korçë, F. 3/4, Komiteti i PPSh Rrethi Maliq, 1949, Lista 5, d. 11, fl. 11. Monthly report of February 1949, of the ALP's Committee of Maliq. March 6, 1949. On the lack of attention for the harvesting and conservation of sugar beet, "Në rrethin e Korçës vjelja e panxharit shkon mirë ndërsa grumbullimi i tij është prapa" [In the district of Korça the harvesting of sugar beet is progressing well, but not its storage], *Përpara*, November 17, 1949, 2.

58 On Peti Shambli's proposal, AQSh, F. 14/AP, Komiteti i PPSh (OU), 1953, d. 5, fl. 168. Minutes of the meeting of the IX Plenum of the Central Committee of the ALP. December 24–25, 1953. On the State Planning Commission's study, AQSh, F. 495, Komisioni i Planit të Shtetit, 1955, d. 37, fl. 1. Memo "On the study of sugar beet and some other cultures." On the complaints of the collective farms concerning the cultivation of sugar beet, AQSh, F. 14/AP, Komiteti i PPSh (OU), 1959, d. 32, fl. 93. Memo on the measures for the production and industrialization of the sugar beet. March 23, 1959. On the application of material incentives, Avni Kolaneci, "Punojmë për 380 kv. panxhar sheqeri për hektarë" [We aim to harvest 380 quintals of sugar beet per hectare], *Për bujqësinë socialiste* [On socialist agriculture], no. 7 (1956): 34–35.

tween the state and the peasants was that the former would, in exchange for the cultivation of sugar beet, supply consumption goods that were necessary for the farmers, such as salt, kerosene, maize, thread, etc. By 1952, the state had removed some of these items from the list. Sometimes, the local state organs did not even pay the peasants for their sugar beet crops. When the state did not compensate them with the necessary goods that they needed, the peasants continued to cultivate cereals and to neglect sugar beet. The outcomes were devastating for the operation of the refinery. Thus, of the 4876 economic units that the state contracted, 309 of them did not deliver their quota at all, 1399 had a yield of 50 quintals per hectare, and 55% of the private sector delivered only up to 80 quintals per hectare, whereas the State Planning Commission's quota was 220 quintals per hectare.[59]

In the village of Rëmbec, the peasants became particularly vocal and protested against sugar beet cultivation. According to the local ALP Committee, they wanted to cultivate for the urban market, which was more convenient than selling sugar beet, barley, tobacco, or cotton to industrial enterprises under fixed prices. Even the cadres sometimes did not respond to the ALP's orders. In Sovjan and Novoselë, two villages in the plain of Maliq, the communists did not allow their families to mobilize during the sugar beet harvesting season, while others refused to cultivate it. Clearly, the peasants, whether they were ALP members or not, found potato and cereals to be more profitable than sugar beet.[60] As such, the regime was forced to step back once again. In 1953, Hysni Kapo proposed the reintroduction of the removed items and to increase compensation with both consumption goods and cash for industrial crops. However, the peas-

---

59 On the peasants neglecting the cultivation of sugar beet, AQSh, F. 518, Ministria e Bujqësisë, 1953, d. 107, fl. 1–14. Memo of the Ministry of Agriculture on the increase of the material interests of the peasants for the cultivation of industrial crops. On the discrepancy between the State Plan and the yield, AQSh, F. 14/AP, Komiteti i PPSh (OU), 1953, d. 5, fl. 226–227. Minutes of the meeting of the IX Plenum of the Central Committee of the ALP. December 24–25, 1953.

60 On the convenience of the peasants to cultivate for the local urban market rather than for the industrial enterprises, AShV Korçë, F. 3/2, Komiteti i PPSh Rrethi Korçë, 1956, Lista 12, d. 25, fl. 23. Report on the condition of the ALP's Grassroot Organization in the collective farm of the village of Rëmbec. On the communists that did not join their forces and did not allow their families to mobilize for the harvesting of sugar beet, AShV Korçë, F. 3/1, Komiteti i PPSh Qarku Korçë, 1954, Lista 5, d. 237, document with no page number. Minutes of the meeting of the Politburo of ALP's Committee of Maliq on the analysis of the activity of the party cells in villages of Sovjan and Novoselë. August 19–20, 1954. On the communists who refused to cultivate sugar beet, AQSh, F. 14/AP, Komiteti i PPSh (STR), 1955, d. 70, fl. 28. Report of the Conference of the ALP's Committee of Maliq. May 15–16, 1955. On the profitability of cultivating potato and cereals, AShV Korçë, F. 3/1, Komiteti i PPSh Qarku Korçë, 1955, Lista 6, d. 8, fl. 18. Memo on the study of sugar beet and other crops.

ants still preferred to cultivate potato and cereals. Even the collective farms found that the cultivation of sugar beet was not profitable because the price of 305 ALL per quintal that the combine paid did not justify the intensive work and high expenses the crop required.[61]

The lack of competent specialists regarding sugar production further exacerbated the situation. As Enver Hoxha confessed, the State Planning Commission came up with an unrealistic quota without knowing how to achieve it. Additionally, the government realized how difficult it was to meet the plan only after facing constant failures. Peti Shambli explained to the Central Committee that the average sugar beet quota that the state organs imposed on the peasants totally neglected the complexity of the plain and the variety of soil fertilities. This practice, he continued, undermined the interests of the peasants, who were forced to plant sugar beet, regardless of the quality of their land. This compromised the factory's operation and the peasants' well-being because many of them were impoverished from cultivating sugar beet. Yet, the state sector still fared better than the private farmers did.[62]

The specialists at the Ministry of Agriculture were quick to react to these remarks and admitted that the implementation of regionalization had flaws because it included plots that were not suitable for sugar beet production. In 1954, the Ministry of Agriculture revised the regionalization plan, and instead of assigning the entire plain to sugar beet, it made a more careful selection of those plots to be designated. In a second round, which took place in 1959, teams of geometers and agronomists redefined the areas that were suitable for the regionalization of sugar beet. The new regionalization mandates became more flexible and recognized the lack of pedological uniformity. As such, the teams introduced

---

61 On the peasants preferring to cultivate potato and sugar beet, AQSh, F. 495, Komisioni i Planit të Shtetit, 1955, d. 37, fl. 1. Memo on the study of sugar beet. On the introduction of material incentives, AQSh, F. 518, Ministria e Bujqësisë, 1953, d. 107, fl. 1–14. Memo of the Ministry of Agriculture on the increase of the material interests of the peasants for the cultivation of industrial crops. On the peasants' reluctance to cultivate sugar beet even after the increase of incentives, AShV Korçë, F. 3/1, Komiteti i PPSh Qarku Korçë, 1955, Lista 6, d. 8, fl. 18. Memo on the study of sugar beet and other crops. On the collective farms that did not find the cultivation of sugar beet profitable, AQSh, F. 14/AP, Komiteti i PPSh, (OU), 1959, d. 32, fl. 93. Memo on the measures for the production and industrialization of sugar beet. March 23, 1959.

62 On Hoxha's confession, AQSh, F. 14/AP, Komiteti i PPSh (OU), 1953, d. 2, fl. 126. Closing remarks of comrade Commandant (Enver Hoxha—A.H.) at the VI Plenum of the Central Committee. March 2–3, 1953. On Peti Shambli's complaint about the application of the sugar beet quota, AQSh, F. 14/AP, Komiteti i PPSh (OU), 1953, d. 5, fl. 165. Minutes of the meeting of the IX Plenum of the Central Committee of the ALP. December 24–25, 1953.

a new form of classification that divided the land into different categories based on its suitability for sugar beet cultivation.[63]

The results improved gradually. With advanced collectivization, land consolidation, and the amelioration of services and mechanization, the yields increased. The collective farm system integrated the peasants into the socialist market, and their livelihood no longer depended on their private plots, but on the monetary rewards they received from the performance of their farms instead. Still, the problems between the central planners and the producers in Maliq persisted. Tirana's authorities stuck to autarky, and in the 1970s and 1980s, they dealt with demographic ballooning and increased sugar consumption. For this reason, the State Planning Commission continued to increase the sugar beet quota. In the end, their stubbornness became counter-productive. The need to meet the state quota forced the agricultural enterprises of Korça to cultivate sugar beet in sandy soils, resulting in low yields. While the farms struggled to meet the state plan, the sugar content in the beets showed alarming decreases. In 1975, when this became apparent to the combine specialists, who were already against ever increasing yields as markers of efficiency, they sounded the alarm. They wrote to the government and made it clear that rather than seeking continuous increases in the total sugar beet output, the central authorities would do better to focus on increasing the crop's sugar content.[64]

These continuous tensions between Tirana and Maliq not only show the flaws of central planning and the idea of autarky, but also demonstrate how the sugar industry was a technology of power that connected the plain with the capital and

---

63 On the specialists of the State Planning Committee's admission of the flaws of regionalization, AQSh, F. 498, Ministria e Bujqësisë, 1958, d. 127, fl. 25. Memo concerning the areas cultivated with sugar beet. On the new regionalization, AQSh, F. 498, Ministria e Bujqësisë, 1960, d. 90/1, fl. 48. Report on the development of agriculture in the People's Republic of Albania. On the redefinition of the areas of sugar beet, AQSh, F. 490, Këshilli i Ministrave, 1960, d. 146, fl. 1. Information on the production and industrialization of sugar beet. February 2, 1960. On the new classification of the regionalized land, AShV Korçë, F. 3/2, Komiteti i PPSh Rrethi Korçë, 1959, Lista 15, d. 31, fl. 5–6. Memo on the regionalization of sugar beet.

64 On the cultivation of sugar beet in sandy soils and the low yield, AQSh, F. 495, Komisioni i Planit të Shtetit, 1981, d.146, fl. 2. Information regarding the implementation of the instructions of the ALP's VIII congress for agriculture in the district of Korça. July 16, 1981. On the failure of the cooperatives to meet the state plan, AQSh, F. 495, Komisioni i Planit të Shtetit, 1981, d. 140, fl. 16–21. Memo of the State Planning Commission on the increase of cultivation of industrial crops. October 8, 1980. On the decrease of the sugar content of the beet, *Ibid*, fl. 18. Memo of the State Planning Comission on the increase of cultivation of industrial crops. October 8, 1980. On the letter of the specialists of the sugar combine, AShV Korçë, F. 67, Kombinati i Sheqerit, 1980, d. 19, fl. 4–9. Some opinions of the specialists of the sugar combine of Maliq regarding the construction of a new establishment for the processing of sugar beet. August 15, 1980.

the wider country. The factory was representative of this whole web of production, which, besides refining sugar, also generated the communist power in this part of the country. Very telling is the opinion of a member of a delegation of Soviet kolkhozes that visited the collective farms in the plain of Maliq to teach the Albanian farmers how to cultivate sugar beet and to increase its yield. When, during its missionary tour, the delegation visited the "Shkëndija" (the Spark) cooperative in the village of Rëmbec, one of the Soviet farmers looked toward the factory's smokestacks and said to his Albanian freshmen colleagues: "If you work with advanced farming techniques, I am convinced that you will never be ashamed in front of the new factory and your country."[65]

As this statement points out, the sugar refinery was a shrine of the socialist cult of labor and productivity, which pervaded the entire discourse of all Soviet-type regimes. In Albania, as well as in other communist countries, working was the fetish of the secular religion of progress, which the socialist states transformed into the central tenet of their identity—*labor omnia vincit!* Working was, first and foremost, a political act, and the socialist regimes invested it with ideological meaning. The chimneys, with their long necks that scratched the sky, replaced the belfry and minaret of the churches and mosques and displayed the coming of a new age and new gods. These tall structures with their red bricks established new hierarchies of power and values and reinforced the secular order. The icons, saints, and teachings of prophets lost their appeal. New images of the heroes of progress and labor and of the brave world of industry and development replaced the old idols. The smokestack, along with CO_2 they exhaled into the atmosphere, were part of the Pantheon that represented the new socio-economic system and political power created by the ALP.

The advice of the Soviet farmer makes it clear that besides fabricating the state and its power in the peripheries, as Catherine Alexander has put it, the sugar refinery also fabricated the nation.[66] The factory became the driving force that structured the daily lives of those who worked and lived in Maliq. The combine conveyed the expansion of the state's power, and increased the state's presence in intangible ways. Moreover, in doing so, the sugar industry increased both peoples' participation within the power structure and their dependence on the state. Together with roads, schools, and a common language, and even more effectively

---

65 "Në fushën e panxharit" [In the field of sugar beet], *Shqipëri-BRSS* [Albania-USSR], 10–11(1951): 26.
66 Catherine Alexander, "The Factory: Fabricating the State," *Journal of Material Culture* 5, no. 2 (2000): 177–195.

than them, the production of sugar mediated the relationships of the local communities with the wider social body. In coordination with central planning, the geographical division of labor became part of the invisible but still tangible and powerful forms of indirect relationships that spurred social integration.[67]

Thus, the factory and the collective farms that supplied it were, among other things, a means of communication. While the roads and infrastructure were veins and arteries, Maliq and other similar places pumped blood into them and provided this communication with meaning. It was in the performing of such a role that the refinery tied the people of the community to the national market by supplying the latter with sugar, thus making them dependent on the state. It is by this means that the power of the communist apparatus expanded, disseminated, and reproduced itself at the grassroots level, not by finding ways to permeate and manipulate peoples' consciousness, but by making them part of the system. The latter was not an abstract thing to those who worked in the "sugarland," but was part of their daily existence, something that structured their experience and space of action and allowed them to make a living.

The specialization of the plain of Maliq in sugar production not only connected the area to the center, it also connected it to the other parts of Albania. Indeed, the regional specialization of agriculture was a critical instrument for nation building because it simultaneously avoided competition between regions and sought to establish a spatial organic cohesion of the national territory. Sugar beet cultivation was a means of integrating the peasants of the locality into national life. The refinery, like the magic touch of thaumaturgy, narrowed down the gulf between the state project and those who cultivated and processed sugar beet. It is here that one of the most important political functions of the factory and regional specialization lies. Sugar refining established a symbiosis between industry and nature, which, apart from sweetness, also produced the nation in that corner of Albania.

As seen in the previous chapter, this is a process that had been in motion since the interwar era. The communist leadership borrowed the spatial division of labor project from their predecessors as a means to achieve nation building. The ALP

---

67 On indirect relationships and the role of infrastructure in promoting it, see Craig Calhoun, "The Infrastructure of Modernity: Indirect Social Relationships, Information Technology, and Social Integration," in *Social Change and Modernity*, eds. Hans Haferkamp & Neil Smelser (Berkley, CA: University of California Press, 1992), 205–236; Craig Calhoun, "Indirect Relationships and Imagined Communities: Large-Scale Social Integration and the Transformation of Everyday Life," in *Social Theory for a Changing Society*, eds. Pierre Bourdieu & James S. Coleman (Boulder, CO: Westview Press, 1991): 95–212.

became the political force to complete this process and not derail it. Rather than representing a break with the political regimes of the interwar era, the communists faithfully continued the former's nation-building project. Not only did they borrow the Maliq swamp reclamation, sugar factory construction, and sugar production specialization projects, the communist leadership also appropriated the larger interwar strategy of which these projects were part, namely, their use as nation-building elements. For them, socialism provided a new and alternative framework for achieving the same goals rather than an internationalist ideological platform that neglected the nation. Indeed, the Albanian communists, as was the case with their other Cold War-era eastern European analogues, always denied being merely rootless internationalists. While never denying their internationalist commitment, they relentlessly portrayed themselves as true defenders of the national interests rooted in their respective native lands.

Jennifer Sowerwine rightly points out that no form of spatial organization can obliterate nature from its calculations.[68] The Albanian communist regime, too, used nature for its political goals. The communist revolution meant pushing national spatial amalgamation forward. The ecological conditions of the different regions and the composition of their soil would serve to develop industry and the inclusion of the different regions within a unified national economic system. The regional specialization of agriculture helped to construct the image of a unified nation based on new markers of difference. The regime used climatic and pedological variations to map the nation in a new way, which would foster the fusion and strengthening of social and economic links across space.

The economic organization of space placed the ALP at the center and allowed it to control, direct, and try to merge the peripheries into a larger coherent, but not uniform, unit. In the ALP's worldview, this was a progressive leap from archaic to modern forms of social organization and division of labor. Regionalization organized the country by following the machine model, which Katerina Clark has called the master metaphor for the organization of Soviet society.[69] Each region was a cog: their differences made them simultaneously necessary to each other and enabled the machine of the nation-state to work. Regions would specialize and complement each other, building a centralized economic system

---

68 Jennifer C. Sowerwine, "Territorialisation and the Politics of Highland Landscapes in Vietnam: Negotiating Property Relations in Policy, Meaning and Practice," *Conservation and Society* 2, no. 1 (2004): 99.

69 Katerina Clark, *Petersburg, Crucible of Cultural Revolution* (Cambridge, MA: Harvard University Press, 1995), 245.

that integrated geographical and ecological differences into a coherent whole. As Henri Lefebvre contended, planning the modern economy also includes spatial planning. Fragmentation, he argues, helps centralization. Thus, regional specialization would construct the spatial organization of the nation based on the example of machines, with the system being meant to subordinate each part to the central command.[70]

The communists continued the functionalist spatialization policy in the country, which was explained in the first chapter. By mapping the territory into sections, they envisioned Albania as a body, where each region played the role of an organ within it. The spatial division of labor was meant to overcome localisms by exploding the closed circuit of regional economic connections and placing them in a new national setting. Specialization in one region, in this case, the area of Maliq, meant unraveling older socio-economic links and reshuffling them again, this time knitted into the fabric of the nation. It also meant the establishment of a wider network of regional interdependencies. The specialized regions, which complemented each other, created a framework through which the fragments could be integrated into a whole, conforming to the postulate of the French revolution: "divide to unify". It implied a new gaze of the state over the territory, a new form of understanding, imagining, and ordering. Territorialization, besides the building of an appropriate institutional framework enabling the state to execute its new visions, also implies the delimitation and the classification of resources and the people who make use of them.[71] Maliq was identified not only because it was important for sugar beet and sugar production but also because of its position and utility within the whole.

By establishing one region for sugar, another for cotton, another for steel, another for oil, and so on, the regime constructed fragments that complemented each other and replaced the mostly economically self-contained regions, linking them with the center and with each other via the administrative structure alone. The regionalization of agriculture, which was tied to light industry, created a geographical division of labor that engendered new identities based on technology, economic function, and production, while destabilizing the old regional identities. The peasants now no longer used the land to fulfill their own needs, but

---

70 Henri Lefebvre, "Space: Social Product and Use Value," trans. J. W. Freiberg, in *State, Space, World: Selected Essays*, eds. Neil Brenner & Stuart Elden (Minneapolis, MN: University of Minnesota Press, 2009), 185–195.
71 Phuc Xuan To, "State Territorialization and Illegal Logging: The Dynamic Relationships between Practices and Images of the State in Vietnam," *Critical Asian Studies* 47, no. 2 (2015): 230.

those of the nation. The need to feed the factory's machinery with sugar beet was one of the principal causes of the breaking down of the self-sufficiency of rural households. Regionalization linked the rural economies of the Albanian lowlands with the broader national system not only through a domestic market, but also through the production required to supply it.

Regional specialization displayed the way the central authorities imagined the geography of Albania and its economic development. This geographical epistemology of the spatial distribution of the economy and power helped the ALP's leadership to expand its clout over the peripheries and to pursue the building of a national economic system. The economic, pedological, hydrological, geological, and biota maps that provided detailed scientific categories for the distribution of the resources and regional division of labor within the country expressed more than anything else how the relationship between people and natural resources were an element of central concern for the communist leadership and the construction of its power. Besides the spatial dimension, the regional specialization that was centered on the sugar combine also had a temporal integrative dimension. In addition to displaying the ALP's power over the countryside in full-force, the refinery also marked the extension of industrial time-discipline and organization over the field of agriculture. Henceforth, it was not only the tyranny of the seasons that dictated the rhythm of agriculture, but also the ticking clock of the combine. The peasants of the plain of Maliq could only keep pace with the time of the factory through the use of modern farming techniques.

While the regionalization of agriculture aimed at establishing unity through division from the spatial perspective, its goal from the temporal point of view was to unite Tirana with the peripheries through the synchronization of time. In his "Thesis on the Philosophy of History," Walter Benjamin elaborated upon his concept of "homogeneous empty time," which, according to him, was marked by temporal coincidence and measured by clock and calendar.[72] The simultaneity of time has been a critical device for building modern nations because it connects centers and peripheries into one single temporal dimension. Benedict Anderson dedicated special attention to the platforms that helped to create the simultaneity of time. Among them, he especially highlighted the role that newspapers and novels have played in this process.[73] Besides the whole repertoire of

---

72 Walter Benjamin, "Theses on the Philosophy of History," in *Illuminations: Essays and Reflections*, trans. Harry Zohn (New York: Schocken Books, 2007), 261–262.
73 Anderson, *Imagined Communities*, 22–36.

written texts, which were also instruments of ideological propaganda, in communist Albania, state economic plans served as powerful frameworks for establishing the simultaneity of time between the center and the peripheries.

In terms of industrial crops and factories, in Maliq's case with sugar beet, the regime provided a means of connection. Albanians were now experiencing time in a way that newspapers, gossip, and state institutions had never done before. The state plan treated time differently, and Albanians had to work and live in accordance with the goals of that plan. Through the sugar factory, regionalization connected the rural population of the plain of Maliq and the small sugar-producing town with the entire country. Speaking about the Maliq of the communist era, one of its inhabitants defined it as a buzzing town. During the work season, dozens of trucks unloaded sugar beet and coal or transported sugar across the country.[74] The production of sugar linked Maliq to the nation in real time, and its inhabitants experienced nation not only in the form of symbols but in the form of action too.

Temporal simultaneity was tangible in quintals per hectare and in tons of sugar. Through the sugar factory, regionalization, centralized planning, and mechanization, the communist regime defined the rhythm of everyday life in a part of its southeastern periphery and synchronized it with the time of the nation's center and other parts of the country. Gradually, the regime began building one single temporal grid, which stood together despite local differences and specializations. These territorialization techniques acted as extraordinary instruments for the expansion of the power of the Albanian communist regime into the peripheries, specifically by allowing the ALP's leadership to integrate the provinces into Tirana's time and pace. Anthony Giddens has argued that time is an essential resource in structures of domination. Similar to Marx, he has focused mainly on the correlation between time and labor in order to study class exploitation.[75] The case of Maliq shows that time is not only significant for vertical forms of domination but also for those relationships that stretch horizontally across space. Time is critical for the integration of the peripheries, not merely within the orbit of the center, but also within a broader political and economic structure, which is constructed through the interdependence of different fragments. This is a crucial component of nation-building, the exertion of national territorial control, and governmentality.

---

74 Çelnik Jaupi, informal interview by Artan Hoxha, Maliq, Albania, July 30, 2017.
75 Anthony Giddens, "Time, Space, and Social Change," in *Central Problems in Social Theory: Action, Structure, and Contradiction in Social Analysis* (London: Palgrave Macmillan, 1979), 198–233.

Inscribing the Tabula Rasa: Gridding the Stalinist Landscape

The continuous hydrological works, which were necessary to prevent the swamp from returning, and the transformation of the plain into the center of Albania's sugar industry integrated the area into the larger body of the nation. In fact, what Henri Lefebvre considered to be a characteristic of the capitalist mode of production, which, according to him, integrates while destroying, applies to the Soviet-type regimes as well.[76] By obliterating the marshland, Tirana's state structure absorbed it within its control. After reclaiming the swamp, the regime engraved the plain of Maliq with its inscription through a series of interventions. The chiseling of the landscape, though, was not the outcome of a single blueprint created at the center, but the result of a complex process that was strongly related to sugar production. As Lefebvre rightly argued, the production of space is related to the production of things.[77] Maliq's dense grid of canals and its large rectangular plots were inextricably intertwined with the role the plain played in supplying the sugar refinery.

In 1948, the state contracted the local peasants to supply the refinery with sugar beet. However, the small, scattered, and irregular plots that belonged to the private farmers could hardly meet the state plan, and the direction of production being carried out by thousands of peasant households created constant headaches for the authorities in Tirana. The ALP leadership concluded that the peasants' low productivity undermined the growth of light industry.[78] Mehmet Shehu, the number two man of the regime, stated that there was tension between the small and fragmented private properties of the peasants, who tilled the land with primitive tools, and the state-owned modern industries.[79]

The Albanian communist regime faced the same challenges that the Italian entrepreneurs who wanted to develop the sugar industry in the plain of Korça had experienced. The light industry establishments forced the new authorities in

---

76 Henri Lefebvre, "Space and the State," trans. Alexandra Kowalski et al., in *State, Space, World*, 241.
77 Henri Lefebvre, "Reflections on the Politics of Space," in *State, Space, World*, 171.
78 AQSh, F. 14/AP, Komiteti i PPSh (OU), 1949, d. 2, fl. 1 & 11. Report of the Politburo concerning the realization of the state plan for the period January–September 1949. September 11–13, 1949; AQSh, F. 14/AP, Komiteti i PPSh (OU), 1950, d. 16, fl. 11. Report of the Deputy Prime Minister Mehmet Shehu on the realization of the state plan for the first semester of the year 1950. August 11, 1950.
79 AQSh, F. 14/AP, Komiteti i PPSh (OU), 1950, d. 16, fl. 11. Report of Mehmet Shehu held at the Plenum of ALP's Central Committee. August 11, 1950; AQSh, F. 14/AP, Komiteti i PPSh (OU), 1951, d. 3, fl. 5–6. Report of Mehmet Shehu at the X Plenum of the ALP's Central Committee, regarding the further development of agriculture in Albania. April 9, 1951.

Tirana to confront a series of issues that they were not prepared to deal with. Hoxha himself admitted that he and his collaborators decided to build new industrial establishments without pondering how to supply them.[80] The introduction of new technologies changed how the agricultural policies of the regime worked and created circumstances that it did not anticipate. By 1950, the ALP leadership had come up with a similar solution to that of their Romanian analogues, who started land consolidation projects that same year. This was a solution to the fragmented plots that belonged to the peasants, which was a problem for all of the eastern European communist governments and aimed to establish large contiguous parcels that would allow the use of mechanized farming.[81]

In Albania, land consolidation targeted the areas designated for the cultivation of industrial crops. On September 1, 1950, the government and the ALP's Central Committee issued a joint decree where they stated that, "[t]he peasants are recommended to aggregate the individual plots designed for industrial plants in such a way as to form blocks as large as possible. In this way, it will be easier and more advantageous to make use of mechanical means, water for irrigation, and support and technical control." It also stated that, "[t]he individual (peasant) economies, in order to fulfill their work faster, better, and cheaper than with their oxen, need to contract mechanized means. In order to take advantage of the discounts [applied by the state enterprises that owned the tractors—A.H.], they must design their plots into blocks and take down the fences between them."[82]

Taking down the fences and creating large parcels of land was the answer because it allowed the state to concentrate [its] fixed capital, use mechanized technology, and apply industrial organization to agricultural work. The increase in the productivity of agriculture through the introduction of new technologies and forms of organization was the response to the needs of light industry. Light industry required machines to be used in agriculture. The tractors and harvesting combines, the symbols of productivity and progress in the countryside, dic-

---

80 AQSh, F. 14/AP, Komiteti i PPSh, (OU), 1953, d. 2, fl. 126. Closing remarks of comrade Commandant (Enver Hoxha—A.H.) at the VI Plenum of the Central Committee. March 2–3, 1953.
81 On land consolidation in Romania, see Katherine Verdery, *The Vanishing Hectare: Property and Values in Postsocialist Transylvania* (Ithaca, NY: Cornell University Press, 2003), 63–64; Kligman & Verdery, *Peasants Under Siege*, 128–129. On the problem that small property represented for the governments of Eastern Europe, see the case on the GDR in, Gregory R. Witowski, "On the Campaign Trail: State Planning and *Eigen-Sinn* in a Communist Campaign to Transform the East German Countryside," *Central European History* 37, no. 3 (2004): 406.
82 AQSh, F. 14/AP, Komiteti i PPSh (OU), 1950, d. 53, fl. 24–25. Decision of the Government of the People's Republic of Albania and the ALP's Central Committee on "The Sowing Plan for the Autumn of 1950 and the Spring of 1951." September 2, 1950.

tated the massive proportions of the parcels, allowing the extensive use of mechanization. What mattered for the Albanian authorities was the amassing of parcels and the creation of vast plots where the tractors could thrust in their steel plows and combines could harvest with speed. As a result, the communist leadership did not limit land consolidation to private non-collectivized land only. In November 1950, the ALP's Central Committee ordered all of the collective farms to combine their small plots into larger lots, and harshly criticized those who had not created them yet.[83]

However, the creation of large plots underwent a complicated readjustment process that saw the constant interaction between the peasants, the top echelons of the ALP, and technocrats. Maliq was simultaneously a site and a medium of negotiation between scientific and local knowledge and political agendas. Thus, in the beginning, the area of the plots varied between 20-30 and 60-80 hectares. However, the technicians realized that their size hampered both the drainage and irrigation of the lots.[84] They were too large to preserve the so-called fish-back shape, where the parcel was slightly elevated at the center, which allowed for water drainage toward the edges. Its name came from the peasants of Maliq, who had traditionally created their small plots in this shape, a practice that was later borrowed by agronomists. However, after the merging of the patches, the extensive use of tractors destroyed their contours, which had grave consequences for sugar beet cultivation, and which left many of the beets rotting from lack of drainage. The peasants were able to preserve the shape because they used oxen, but the inexperienced tractor drivers did not pay attention, and with their iron horses and plows of steel, they destroyed the vaulted configuration of the parcels.[85] It was only in the 1960s that the agronomists concluded that in order to preserve the hunchback contours, the plots had to be fifteen hectares in size.[86] From then on, this became the standard size of the parcels in Maliq.

---

[83] AShV Korçë, F. 3/2, Komiteti i Partisë i Nënprefekturës Korçë, 1950, Lista 6, d. 145, fl. 4. Decision of the ALP's Central Committee "On the Situation and Development of the Collective Farms." November 15, 1950.

[84] AShV Korçë, F. 3/2, Komiteti i PPSh Rrethi Korçë, 1965, Lista 21, d. 175, fl. 3–4. Tasks and concrete measures for a better systematization of the plain of Korça.

[85] AShV Korçë, F. 3/2, Komiteti i PPSh Rrethi Korçë, 1967, Lista 23, d. 64, fl. 15–16. Report of the ALP's Committee of Korça sent to the ALP's Central Committee on the systematization of the arable land in the district; AShV Korçë, F. 3/2, Komiteti i PPSh Rrethi Korçë, 1965, Lista 21, d. 175, fl. 7. Tasks and concrete measures for a better systematization of the plain of Korça; AQSh, F. 14/AP, Komiteti i PPSh, (OU), 1972, d. 15, fl. 127. Minutes of the meeting of the ALP's Central Committee. April 24, 1972.

[86] AShV Korçë, F. 3/2, Komiteti i PPSh Rrethi Korçë, 1967, Lista 23, d. 64, fl. 15–16. Report of the ALP's Committee of Korça on the systematization of the arable land in the district.

CHAPTER 2

On other occasions in Maliq, the specialists also used the peasants' knowledge, such as their knowledge regarding soil variations, when designing sugar beet cultivation areas to increase output, and saw very good results. Even high members of Politburo, such as Tuk Jakova, remarked on the usefulness of the centuries-old traditions of the peasants and pressed state planners to take them into account. Enver Hoxha, too, reiterated the same point. In those cases when the technicians and cadres considered this long-term experience, the ALP's leader concluded that the results had been better. Hoxha raised the problem of the lack of grassroots planning, touching upon the fundamental problem of centralized economies, namely, the gulf between the reality in the periphery and the planners in the capital. How was the state plan to be successful in the villages, asked the ALP boss, when those who made the plans did not leave their offices and did not know the reality? None of them had ever gone out there, he continued, and obviously, there was no connection between the plan and the grassroots level.[87]

Communist "high modernism" implied neither the erasure of local knowledge, nor its neglect on the part of technocrats and politicians, but rather its redeployment in interaction with the new scientific disciplines. Contrary to what James Scott has argued in his book *Seeing Like a State*, modern states, including Soviet-type ones, should neither be considered as rigid structures in an antithetical relationship with tradition nor as fanatically sticking to their conceptualization of the world.[88] As the case of Maliq shows for the ALP's regime, the relationships between new and old were complex and nuanced, and the technocrats were not a group that was incapable of reflection and adjustment to local circumstances, as Scott stated.[89] The attitude of the planners and modernizers toward alternative popular forms of knowledge was not uniform, and there were people across the hierarchy of the power structure who both used or neglected it. Rather than monolithic structures, states are corporations that are riddled with tensions

---

87 On the good results of the cooperation between specialists and peasants, AQSh, F. 14/AP, Komiteti i PPSh (OU), 1953, d. 5, fl. 58. Enver Hoxha's report "On the measures for the further raising of the standard of living of the working masses." December 24-25, 1953. On Tuk Jakova's suggestions on the use of the peasants' knowledge, *Ibid*, fl. 173-175. Minutes of the meeting of the IX Plenum of the ALP's Central Committee of the ALP's II Congress. December 24-25, 1953. On Hoxha's critique of armchair planning, AQSh, F. 14/AP, Komiteti i PPSh, (OU), 1953, d. 2, fl. 127. Closing remarks of Enver Hoxha at the VI Plenum of the Central Committee. March 2-3, 1953.
88 James C. Scott, *Seeing Like a State: How Certain Schemes to Improve the Human Condition Have Failed* (New Haven, CT: Yale University Press, 1998).
89 In his critique to James C. Scott, Michael Herzfeld argues that the state cannot function without the use of practical knowledge. See, Michael Herzfeld, "The Political Optics and the Occlusion of Intimate Knowledge," *American Anthropologist* 107, no. 3 (2005): 369-376.

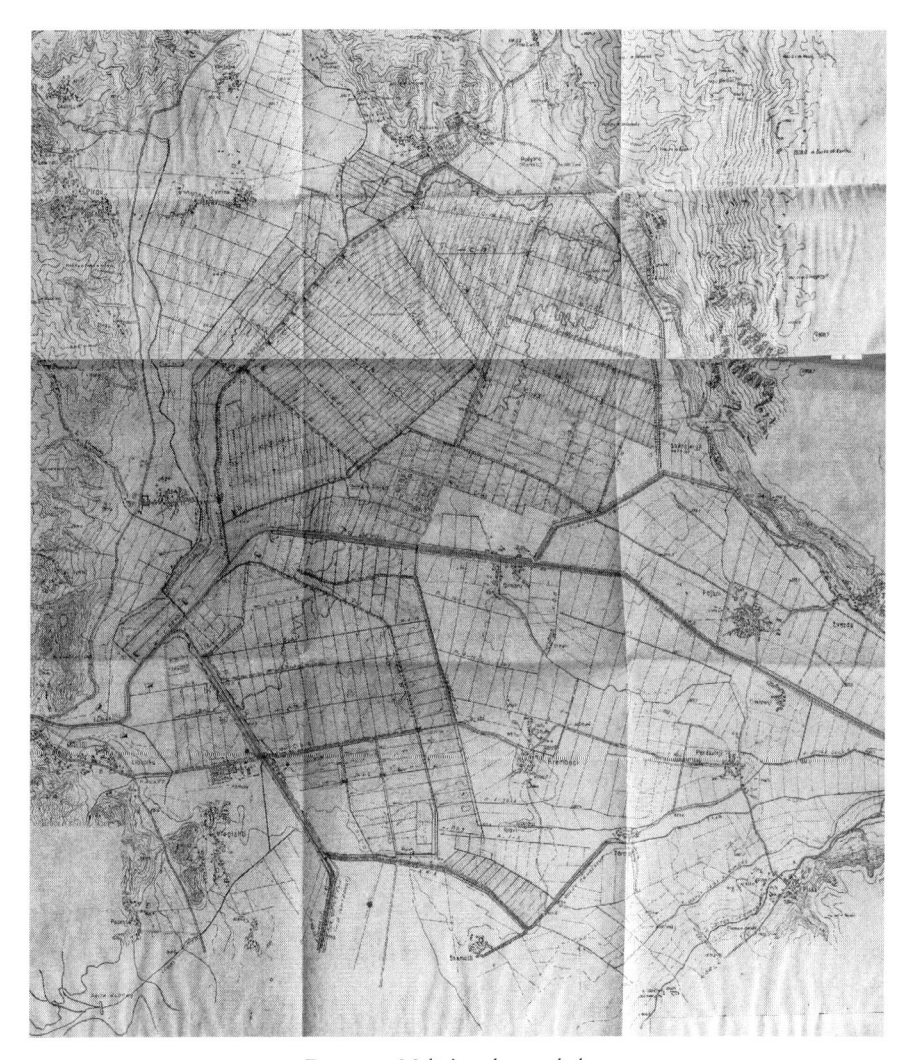

FIGURE 9. Maliq's orthogonal plots

and conflicting views. Hence, it is not accurate to say "seeing like a state" in the singular, as James Scott has, because there is no single way that states see.

The gridded landscape of Maliq is part of a broader twentieth-century European phenomenon that defied the Iron Curtain; it was part of the era of discipline, legibility, mass production, and efficiency. The fields filled with rectangular patches expressed the drive for economic efficiency, which was one of the main denominators of the twentieth century. In Europe, the Cold War never became hot because economic performance was the major battlefield between the two opposing systems. The fact that socialism lost to capitalism does not mean that efficiency was not its priority. It merely means that it was less efficient than capitalism. Moreover, in the post-World War II era, in the liberal democracies, the state, under the banner of Keynesianism, increasingly intervened in agriculture to increase the efficiency of the rural sector.

For example, in the Netherlands, the state reshaped the landscape of the countryside starting in 1924, when Parliament issued the "Law on Re-allotment," which tried to put an end to the fragmentation of land and the subsequent plot shapes that resulted from it. The state ordered the pooling of small patches into larger allotments to help in the mechanization of agricultural processes and to increase the efficiency of the rural sector of the economy. Because of the inseparable assumption that connected efficiency with size, the size of the farms in the Netherlands had doubled by the mid-twentieth century as a result of the re-allotment process. The justification for this law was based on the need for the rationalization of the allotments to facilitate agricultural development.[90]

The vocabulary and concepts of the Dutch lawmakers in the 1920s were not too dissimilar to those of their communist rivals some decades later, whose keywords were rationality, science, and growth. In the Netherlands, the re-allotment process continued well into the 1970s under the banner of "agricultural functionalism." The Netherlands was not alone. France, Germany, and Spain, to mention some other notable cases, also pushed land consolidation forward through the 1950s–1960s under the same drive for modernization and an increase in efficiency. The goal of land consolidation was to restructure and update "outdated and unsatisfactory" land ownership patterns in "new physical and legally-recognizable shapes." A similar process was taking place, under the auspices of the state, in the Socialist bloc, including in Albania, and in Maliq, in particular. In any case, the keyword was the establishment of farms that were adequate in size for mechanized agriculture.[91]

---

90 On the Netherlands, see Kees Doevendans et al., "From Modernist Landscapes to New Nature: Planning of Rural Utopias in the Netherlands," *Landscape Research* 32, no. 3 (2007): 338–342.

91 On the definition of land consolidation and its function, see Robert Dixon-Gough & Erik Stubkjoer, "The Role of Land Consolidation and Land Readjustment in Modern Society," in *The Role of State and Individual in Sustainable Land Management*, eds. Robert W. Dixon-Gough & Peter C. Bloch (Aldershot, VT: Ashgate, 2006), 159; Jørn Rognes & Per Kåre Sky, "Mediation in the Norwegian Land Consolidation Courts," Working Paper 14, North America Series, Land Tenure Centre (Madison, WI: University of Wisconsin-Madison, 1998). On land consolidation in France and Germany, see Terry van Dijk, "Complications for Traditional Land Consolidation in Central Europe," *Geoforum* 38, no. 3 (2007): 505. On land consolidation in Spain, see Daniel Lanero & Lourenzo Fernández-Prieto, "Technology Policies in Dictatorial Contexts: Spain and Portugal," in *Agriculture in Capitalist Eu-*

A similar process occurred in Estonia, which began land consolidation projects in 1919, long before Soviet annexation and the concomitant collectivization of agriculture. Additionally, even in the neighboring country of Greece, which had a rural property structure similar to that seen in other Balkan states, including Albania, the state started to consolidate small, fragmented parcels immediately after the end of World War II. As a result, the number of parcels diminished over the years, and their size increased, although the pace was too slow. The peasants, too, supported land consolidation in order to increase production, but continuous conflicts within rural communities on how to proceed with this process hampered its quick progression. Similar to the Albanian engineer who considered fascism's iron-fisted management of society as the path towards the modernization of the country, the Greek peasants considered authoritarian measures as the only way to complete land consolidation.[92]

During the era of productivism, efficiency in agriculture was strongly related to mechanization, which needed large farms and a concentration of land. Industry and its mass production became a model for agriculture as well. The orthogonal grid was not merely the visual materialization of a vision that preferred geometrical and ordered forms of the man-made landscape to the irregular and chaotic lines of nature. Nor was it merely the spatialization of modern power in the guise of capitalist corporations or the Bolshevik Party either. The rectangular patches that filled the plains of Europe on both sides of the Iron Curtain, with their routinized linearity, were also an outcome of the industrialization of agriculture. All European governments were intervening in and organizing the economies of their countries. They were also gearing their agricultural sectors toward mass production, the concentration of the arable land, and mechanization.

With the end of World War II, the utilitarian ideology of efficiency and productivity triumphed across Europe. It also informed the activity of the governmental bodies in charge of the management of the rural landscape. As Gertruda Andela argues about the Dutch agricultural engineers of the post-World War II era, they were not pursuing any aesthetic principle at the beginning, and their approach to designing the landscape was only guided by economic

---

rope, *1945–1960: From Food Shortages to Food Surpluses*, ed. Carin Martiin et al. (London: Routledge, 2016), 165–184.
92 On Estonia, see Evelin Jürgenson, "Land Reform, Land Fragmentation and Perspectives for Future Land Consolidation in Estonia," *Land Use Policy* 57 (2016): 34–43. On Greece, see Murray E. Keeler & Dimitrios G. Skuras, "Land Fragmentation and Consolidation Policies in Greek Agriculture," *Geography* 75, no. 1 (1990): 73–76; Samuel Popkin, "The Rational Peasant: The Political Economy of Peasant Society," *Theory and Society* 9, no. 3 (1980): 444.

and utilitarian principles. It was only later that they pushed their project to the creation of utopian villages and landscapes.[93] In the beginning, it was the ideology of the tractor, the symbol of the triumph of modernity in the countryside, which, not accidentally, was one of the iconic emblems of Soviet modernization. Across Europe, land consolidation went full steam ahead in the 1950s, precisely at the moment that Paul Bairoch has defined as the beginning of the Third Agricultural Revolution. It was at this historical moment that the Europeans started their extensive use of tractors, and a number of countries on the Old Continent had, for the first time in history, more iron horses than real horses.[94]

Albania had a similar break with the past, although not to the same degree. Even in the 1980s, oxen and horses were a normal part of the rural landscape. Still, the discontinuity with the past was incredible. In 1938, there were only 38 tractors in the whole country, which were owned by some rich landowners and a few Italian firms. In 1958, communist Albania had 2,683 tractors, and ten years later, in 1968, it had 10,000 tractors.[95] In 1968, the district of Korça had only 670 tractors, 81 combines, and 64 threshing machines. The augmentation of agricultural vehicles also increased the area under mechanization. In Maliq, after the adjustment of the large rectangular plots that shaped the architecture of Maliq's landscape, the mechanization of agriculture gradually increased. Thus, in the mid-1950s, 65% of the land comprising the plain of Maliq was tilled with oxen, while in 1960, that area had shrunk to 26%. Both Albania and Maliq had entered the age of the tractor.[96]

---

[93] Gertruda M. Andela, *Kneedbaar landschap, kneedbaar volk. De heroïsche jaren van de ruilverkavelingen in Nederland* [Malleable landscape, malleable people. The heroic years of land consolidation in the Netherlands] (Bossum: THOTH, 2000), 240–242.

[94] For more on the huge agricultural transformation in the first 15 years of the Cold War era, see Juri Auderset & Peter Moser, "Mechanisation and Motorisation: Natural Resources, Knowledge, Politics and Technology in 19th- and 20th-Century Agriculture," *Agriculture in Capitalist Europe, 1945–1960*, 145–164; Laurent Herment, "Tractorisation: France, 1946–1955," *Ibid*, 185–205; Paul Bairoch, "Le trois révolutions agricoles du monde développé: rendements et productivité de 1800 à 1985," *Annales. Économies, sociétés, civilizations* 44, no. 2 (1989): 317–353.

[95] On the number of tractors in 1938, AQSh, F. 498, Ministria e Bujqësisë, 1960, d. 90/1, fl. 67. The development of the agricultural technique in the People's Republic of Albania. On the number of tractors in 1958 and 1968, AShV Korçë, F. 3/2, Komiteti i PPSh Rrethi Korçë, 1959, Lista 15, d. 153, fl. 5. Report on the situation and perspectives of the countryside; AQSh, F. 498, Ministria e Bujqësisë, 1969, d. 5, fl. 22. Report of the Ministry of Agriculture "Intensification – the main path for the development of our socialist agriculture."

[96] On the number of tractors and threshing machines in the region of Korça, AShV Korçë, F. 3/2, Komiteti i PPSh Rrethi Korçë, 1961, Lista 17, d. 88, fl. 19. Memo of the ALP's Committee of Korça concerning the condition and readiness of the tractors in the district. March 9, 1961; AQSh, F. 498,

FIGURE 10. Tractors plowing the plain of Maliq

Specifically, it was the large orthogonal plots that comprised the shop floor of industrialized agriculture. Full reclamation aimed to subordinate the land to the tractor. Regular plots were the alter ego of the swamp in the same way tractors were the antithesis of oxen. Beyond the symbolism they carried, it was the productivity and the rectangular plots marking Maliq's landscape that underpinned the mechanization of agriculture. The full impact became obvious by the mid-1960s, when the production and returns of the state farm noticeably increased. In 1974, Enver Hoxha asked the chair of the State Planning Commission, Abdyl Këllëzi, whether the revenues of the "Maliqi" state farm had covered the investments for the reclamation of the plain. The leader of the ALP found out that the profits of the farm alone had covered state spending multiple times during the two stages of the reclamation.[97]

The collective farms of the plain increased their productivity significantly as well. By the mid-1970s, 70% of the agricultural enterprises of the plain yielded

---

Ministria e Bujqësisë, 1968, d. 90/4, fl. 44. Study on the prospective development of the agricultural sector in the district of Korça for the years 1970–1980. July 1968. On the increase in the rate of mechanization, AQSh, F. 498, Ministria e Bujqësisë, 1960, d. 56, fl. 7. Report on the progression of the agrarian system and propriety in the years 1955–1960.

97 Regarding the costs of reclamation, the total investment of the state was 79 million lekë, while the profit up to 1973, was 230 million lekë. AQSh, F. 14/AP, Komiteti i PPSh (STR), 1974, d. 846, fl. 1. Note of Abdyl Këllëzi sent to Enver Hoxha. March 25, 1973.

more than 40 tons of sugar beet per hectare, and in some sectors, they reached 50 to 70 t/ha. To compare these figures with those of some other countries on both sides of the Iron Curtain, in France, the average sugar beet yield was 44 t/ha; in Poland, it was 32 t/ha; and in Yugoslavia, it was 35 t/ha in the early 1970s. Although the average yield in the plain of Korça dwindled to around 30 t/ha, the figures from the plain of Maliq fostered enthusiasm among the ALP elite because they seemed to materialize their quest of catching up with the rest of Europe.[98] The agricultural economies of the plain increased their cereal output as well. The cooperatives of Pojan and Plasa, located on the eastern fringe of the plain of Maliq, yielded in excess of 5 tons of grain per hectare. This was a record for Albania, where, prior to the communist takeover, the harvests did not exceed 1.8 tons per hectare.[99]

By the 1970s, the systematization of the plain, the mechanization of agricultural processes, the selection of crop varieties, and the extensive use of fertilizers produced impressive results. Thirty years after the first engagement and following continuous adjustments, the Albanian communist regime succeeded in transforming the land of the plain of Maliq, which had once been covered by a swamp, into a granary. The Albanian communist regime did not have a simplified approach to local contexts. Rather than a one-size-fits-all approach, the communist authorities demonstrated a high degree of flexibility and adaptability to specific circumstances. Last but not least, the high modernist landscape of orthogonal plots was not as inefficient as Scott argues. Indeed, the small private farms that made up the small, scattered plots of the pre-socialist era were far less

---

[98] On the increase of productivity of sugar beet by the mid-1970s, AQSh, F. 490, Këshilli i Ministrave, 1976, d. 73, fl. 2. Memo of the Ministry of Agriculture and the Ministry of Food and Light Industry on the price of sugar beet. January 3, 1976. On the yield above 50 t/ha of sugar beet, AQSh, F. 14/AP, Komiteti i PPSh (STR), 1974, d. 934, fl. 9-10. Index of sugar beet harvesting during September 1974. AQSh, F. 497, Ministria e Industrisë së Lehtë Ushqimore, 1976, d. 537, fl. 8. Info concerning the collection of sugar beet up to December 31, 1975. February 6, 1976; AQSh, F. 495, Komisioni i Planit të Shtetit, 1979, d. 133, fl. 2-4. Analysis of the State Planning Commission on the results of the production of sugar beet for the year 1979. January 31, 1980. On the yield of sugar beet in Maliq and the average yield of sugar beet in France, Poland, and Yugoslavia, AQSh, F. 498, Ministria e Bujqësisë, 1973, d. 33, fl. 4-5. Report on some problems related to the planting and cultivation of sugar beet in Yugoslavia, Poland, and France. April 1973. On the importance of the high yield of sugar beet in the plain of Maliq as indicators of the modernization of Albania and catching up to Europe, AQSh, F. 495, Komisioni i Planit të Shtetit, 1978, d. 145, fl. 4-5. Memo on the results of the cultivation of sugar beet in the district of Korça for the year 1978. On the average yield of sugar beet in the plain of Korça, AQSh, F. 14/AP, Komiteti i PPSh (OU), 1974, d. 17, fl. 217. Minutes of the meeting of the Secretariat of the ALP's Central Committee. February 23, 1974.

[99] AQSh, F. 14/AP, Komiteti i PPSh (OU), 1976, d. 96, fl. 20. Minutes of the meeting of the Secretariat of the ALP's Central Committee. September 21, 1976.

efficient than those established by the communist regime. After all, the large parcels were a response to the necessities that the machinery of the sugar refinery imposed on agriculture.

However, a question arises: was there anything Stalinist about the plain of Maliq? Did the communist regime leave its original mark on the plain? The transformation of nature is always a political statement. After exploring the similarities between the socialist and non-socialist agricultural landscapes and the forces that produced these elective affinities, what, then, was the signature of Albanian Stalinism in Maliq? When discussing the Moscow Canal, Cynthia Ruder argues that what made it different compared to the Hoover Dam, the Panama Canal, and other giant hydrological projects completed in the West was the use of brute force and forced labor.[100] Ruder's conclusion might very well apply to Maliq too. The use of an iron fist, forced labor, and violence were commonplace phenomena during the first reclamation. However, Ruder only focuses on the moment of construction. What makes a landscape political, though, is not only the moment of its christening and its transformation, but also the presence of elements that sustain and reproduce power relationships.

What made Maliq's landscape a Soviet-type landscape was not merely the violence and coercive power that were required for its infrastructural transformation. It was not the act of construction, as much as what remained in the plain for the entire length of the regime that distinguished and made it different. What made it state socialist was the "Grove of the Pheasants." While the regime erased all of the hedges that separated the properties of the peasants, it erected fences around this artificial grove, which remained guarded by soldiers. It was a reserve that the communist leadership used for its virile sport of hunting. Nobody could go there except for the leadership. The Grove was a heterotopia, a non-legible space, connected to but also different from the surrounding environment, "a system of opening and closing that isolates and make penetrable at the same time."[101]

The establishment of such places of exclusion was not an Albanian exclusivity, but a widespread phenomenon of the socialist bloc. The communist elites of Eastern Europe had a penchant for hunting in special reserves overstocked with animals, where they, as lords of the Middle Ages, could sharpen their martial skills and shape their sense of manhood. Additionally, in a similar fashion to the

---

100 Ruder, *Building Stalinism*, 56–57 & 261.
101 Michel Foucault, "Different Spaces," in *Essential Works of Foucault. Vol. 2: Aesthetics, Method, and Epistemology*, ed. James D. Faubion, trans. Robert Hurley (New York: The New York Press, 1998), 183.

knights' groves of the feudal era, these hunting grounds were a monopoly of the political elite, and, as a result, markers of privilege and distinction vis à vis society. This small, artificial woodland in the plain of Maliq demonstrated the success of the new regime in excluding the peasants of the area from accessing all of the resources that their environment provided. It explained, in a simple and comprehensible language that was understandable to everybody living in the plain of Maliq, the mechanism of inclusion and exclusion in a system where the state controlled access to resources and benefits. Using space, it projected, with realism, the political order, the power hierarchies, and the differentiation that the ALP's regime had engendered. While dark, foggy, and impenetrable, the grove was also for public consumption.

Places such as the Grove of Pheasants were sites where the top echelons of the Politburo could retreat and stand outside of society's gaze, and hence, out of its reach. To borrow Erving Goffman's definition, these places were back regions, places "where suppressed facts made an appearance."[102] Contrary to the assumption based on the modern state's panopticon, those on the top are always more exposed to the gaze of their subjects than the other way around.[103] This was also true for the communist regimes. The communist leadership used sites such as the Grove of Pheasants as a backstage, a niche where it could conceal patterns of behavior that were not approved of for the public stage. It was in such extra-institutional emplacements that, as Milovan Djilas exposed in his analysis of Soviet-type systems, the communist leadership gathered and made important decisions, making them important locations in which leadership could exercise its power.[104] Indeed, in the latter case, political rule was wielded not only through opening but also through closing of space, and not only through transparency but also, and especially, through opaqueness.

The Grove of Pheasants was a text carved in the space of the political order, a full-force display of the new social hierarchies inscribed in space and embodying the inequalities that the Albanian communist regime engendered. The small hunting ground was a local projection of "Blloku," the enclosed bloc of villas of the ALP's leadership located at the center of Tirana. Betraying the official slogans of

---

102 Erving Goffman, *The Presentation of Self in Everyday Life* (Edinburgh: University of Edinburgh Press, 1956), 69.
103 On this matter, see Anthony Giddens, "Time and Social Organization," in *Social Theory and Modern Sociology* (Stanford, CA: Stanford University Press, 1987), 162–163.
104 Milovan Djilas, *The New Class: An Analysis of the Communist System* (New York: Frederick A. Praeger, 1957), 82–83.

egalitarianism, this segregated residence, where Enver Hoxha and his closest associates lived in luxury and incomparable affluence compared to the rest of Albanian society, was guarded by the army and secret police around the clock.[105] Although it did not have walls, Blloku was, similar to the castles of the Middle Ages, a fortress of the communist lords that separated them from the society they led. The leadership lived isolated in this small neighborhood of large villas. This tiny place represented the cerebral center of power. It was here, away from the eyes of society, where Hoxha and his associates made their decisions about the country and commanded Albania for decades. While within the city, Blloku lay outside the city and the norm. It represented a statement on the exclusion of the people from decision-making and the uneven spatial distribution of power in the communist state. The Grove of Pheasants was a clone of Blloku in the plain of Maliq.

As Michiel Dehaene and Lieven De Cauter explain, heterotopias are spaces that enact the contradictions that societies produce and cannot solve.[106] The Grove of Pheasants reflected the contradictions between ideology and praxis. While socialism promised an egalitarian society and pointed toward the utopia of communism at the discursive level, in practice it undermined these extravagant claims, and, hence, undermined the legitimacy of the regime itself. The Grove demonstrated that Albania was far from the ideal of a People's Democracy. For this reason, the power apparatus erased and suppressed any form of text on or public discussion about the hunting ground. The only exception was the satirical novel *The Rise and Fall of Comrade Zylo* by the renowned Albanian writer Dritëro Agolli, a literary work published in 1973 that caricatures the Albanian high bureaucracy and its privileges. Here, Agolli mentions only in passing how Zylo, a high functionary of the state administration goes with his bosses to the hunting ground of Maliq.[107] But other than that, nobody has ever left a sign marking the grove, and no other document has ever carried any inscription referring to the grove's existence. Similar to the island of Vilm in the Baltic Sea, which served as a residence for the top echelons of the GDR, no map has ever displayed the small artificial woodland.[108] As John B. Harley has argued, maps

---

105 On Blloku, see Fatos Lubonja, "Blloku (pa nostalgji)" [Blloku (without nostalgia)], *Përpjekja* [Endeavor], no. 24 (2007), 11–31; Elez Biberaj, *Albania in Transition: The Rocky Road to Democracy* (Boulder, CO: Westview Press, 1998), 73–74.
106 Michel Foucault, "Of Other Spaces," in *Heterotopia and the City: Public Space in a Postcivil Society*, ed. and trans. Michiel Dehaene & Lieven de Cauter (London: Routledge, 2008), 25n15.
107 Dritëro Agolli, *Shkëlqimi dhe rënia e shokut Zylo* [The rise and fall of comrade Zylo] (Tirana: Naim Frashëri, 1973), 52.
108 I want to thank Philipp Kröger for bringing the case of the island of Vilm to my attention.

are politically constructed and convey power not only through what they make visible but also through what they omit.[109] Silence and silencing are important features of dictatorships.

The muteness that surrounded its existence made this grove a sinister symbol of the Albanian communist regime, a symbol consumed in silence. In fact, the silence that surrounded the grove made it a locus of power. For this reason, it shows how the regime, through spatial language and visible signs, emanated distinctions and hierarchies of power and how it reproduced and maintained them through the silent participation of all. It was a silent acceptance of the center's rule over the periphery. It is precisely this grove and what it represented that singled out the plain of Maliq as a Soviet-type socialist space. Additionally, and more importantly, this tiny place covered by bushes and stocked with pheasants disguised the inequalities that hid behind the orthogonal plots, canals, tractors, and high yields. To return to Lorenzetti's frescoes, the small forest debunked any claim that linked the radical transformation of the plain to good government. However, the well-regulated fields covered with lively greenish and yellowish colors not only veiled inequalities between the center and the periphery, or between the ones at the top and those at the bottom of the social pyramid. The modernist landscape of Maliq also concealed other forms of intraregional socio-economic disparities that betrayed the egalitarian pretensions of socialism and did not necessarily make communism a virtuous political system. The next chapter will explore the subject of geographical disparities further, focusing on the nested inequalities within the area of Maliq.

---

109 Harley, "Maps, Knowledge, and Power," 290.

CHAPTER 3

Sugar and the Communist Construction of Spatial Inequalities in Maliq

Sugar Production and the Communist Project of Social Transformations

On February 8, 1948, the Albanian Communist Party's Central Committee sent a communique to its local branches regarding the cultivation of industrial crops. In this document, the highest forum of the communist regime emphasized: "The expansion of the cultivation of industrial crops is a revolutionary step. [Through it] we are detaching the peasant from the old Oriental mentality of working the land... only for his private interests and sowing only maize... [W]e are introducing him to new advanced agriculture methods and crops. [The] industrial crops will connect agriculture to industry and strengthen the links between the countryside and the city."[1]

Profoundly influenced by the Orientalism of the Balkans' modernizers, the above prognosis expressed the ALP leadership's project of a "civilizing mission" in the countryside.[2] Such a political and cultural undertaking of the communist upper echelons had both economic and technological dimensions and both linked

---

1   AQSh, F. 14/AP, Komiteti i PPSh (STR), 1948, d. 245, fl. 1. Communique of the ACP's Central Committee regarding the new orientation of agriculture. February 8, 1949.
2   On Orientalism in Albania, Enis Sulstarova, *Arratisje nga lindja: orientalizmi shqiptar nga Naimi te Kadareja* [Escaping from the Orient: Albanian Orientalism from Naim Frashëri to Ismail Kadare] (Tirana: Dudaj, 2006). On Orientalism in the Balkans, see John R. Lampe, *Balkans into Southeastern Europe, 1994–2004: A Century of War and Transition* (London: Palgrave Macmillan, 2014); *Ottomans into Europeans: State and Institution-Building in South Eastern Europe*, ed. Alina Mungiu-Pippidi and Wim Van Meurs (New York: Columbia University Press, 2010); Maria Todorova, "The Trap of Backwardness: Modernity, Temporality, and the Study of Eastern European Nationalism," *Slavic Review* 64, no. 1 (2005): 140–164; Mary C. Neuburger, *The Orient Within: Muslim Minorities and the Negotiation of Nationhood in Modern Bulgaria* (Ithaca, NY: Cornell University Press, 2004); *The Balkans*

and subordinated agriculture to industry. The Albanian communist elite considered the connection between the primary and secondary sectors as a means of pulling the peasants out of their alleged isolationism and Asian backwardness. Simultaneously, as explained in the previous chapter, it would also integrate the rural population with the modern national economic system. Maliq would showcase the success of this strategy. In addition to its function as part of the regime's autarkic policies, the refinery meant broader social and cultural transformations. In the hands of the ALP, sugar production would become a political technology for social engineering and a medium for bridging the rural/urban divide. Thus, the Maliq scheme was also a civilizational enterprise.

The success of this strategy was dubious, though. The socialist regime declared that it wanted to erase all of the vertical and horizontal social inequalities. However, in practice, its policies deepened and multiplied these disparities. In Maliq, the sugar industry, rather than obliterating, indeed exacerbated spatial inequalities. As we will see in this chapter, the sugar scheme determined the direction and uneven success of the communist leadership in transforming everyday life in the countryside. The degree and range of social and cultural transformation depended on whether people worked in industry, agriculture, or on the state or collective farms, and whether they lived in the city, the countryside, or in the lowlands or the uplands.

On October 6, 1986, during a visit to the Maliq sugar combine, the Deputy Prime Minister of Albania, Manush Myftiu, reflected on the results of the use of the industrial establishment as an instrument of social engineering. Among other things, he said "In every place, the construction of an industrial establishment brings progress; for example, new streets are opened, the electrical power and pipe water grids extend, etc. But the opposite also happens. With the opening of a well, my village has been left without water."[3] Myftiu was pointing out the Janus-faced impact of the Maliq scheme, which exacerbated, or may have even created, spatial inequalities. The investments that the sugar industry soaked up created capital distribution imbalances, discriminating certain areas and favoring others. Although the regime invested resources for transforming the lifestyles of the peasants and workers, as the case of Maliq shows, they did not produce the same results

---

    in Transition" Essays on the Development of Balkan Life and Politics since the Eighteenth Century, ed. Charles and Barbara Jelavich (Hamden, Conn: Archon Books, 1963).
3   AQSh, F. 490, Këshilli i Ministrave, 1986, d. 246, fl. 2. Minutes of the meeting of the Council of Ministers on the installation of a turbine in the thermal power station of Maliq. October 6, 1986.

everywhere. The ALP not only failed to erase the inequalities between urban centers and the countryside or in the highland lowlands, its policies made them more pronounced instead.

In the previous chapter, I showed how Maliq and socialist Albania undertook a process of spatial integration through regional specialization and functional differentiation, similar to capitalism. In Maliq, a parallel process took place: the creation of spatial hierarchies between different locales that were integrated in a manner that favored the unequal distribution and allocation of resources. While the socialist regimes claimed to have implemented balanced geographic development, they actually generated spatial disparities that were similar to those of capitalism.

Until now, scholars have focused their attention on the spatial inequalities that capitalism has engendered. Authors such as Edward Soya, Neil Smith, and Henri Lefebvre, among many others, have written on the hierarchies in which the capitalist system divide up space, thus projecting its social stratification at a spatial level.[4] According to them, capital is one of the most powerful forces in constructing and shaping the synchronic relationships that produce an uneven distribution of power and wealth across space, dividing the latter into a core and peripheries, into rich and poor places. This approach has been central to the macro-analysis of world historians such as Immanuel Wallerstein, Andre Gunder Frank, and others.[5] While most of the scholarly attention has been on capitalism, the uneven development and spatial inequalities that existed under socialism have received scant consideration.

Historians have mainly scrutinized the emergence of class differentiation under socialism to prove that it betrayed its egalitarian promise. Since the 1970s and 1980s, Vera Dunham and Sheila Fitzpatrick have argued the Stalinist turn toward bourgeoise values and social distinctions in the 1930s. According to them, the turn toward high Stalinism reiterated older social hierarchies and established a tripartite division of society, with the intelligentsia at the top, which projected

---

4 Neil Smith, *Uneven Development: Nature, Capital, and the Production of Space*, third edition (Athens, GA: University of Georgia Press, 2008); Henri Lefebvre, *State, Space, World: Selected Essays*, eds. Neil Brenner and Stuart Elden (Minneapolis: University of Minnesota Press, 2009); Henri Lefebvre, *The Production of Space*, trans. Donald Nicholson-Smith (Oxford: Blackwell, 1991); Edward W. Soja, "The Spatiality of Social Life: Towards a Transformative Retheorisation," in *Social Relations and Spatial Structures*, eds. Derek Gregory and John Urry (London: Macmillan, 1985), 90–127.
5 Immanuel Wallerstein, *World-Systems Analysis: An Introduction* (Durham and London: Duke University Press, 2004); Andre Gunder Frank, *ReOrient: Global Economy in the Asian Age* (Berkeley, CA: University of California Press, 1998).

its values over the other segments of Soviet society.[6] The campaigns for *kul'turnost'*, or "cultured life," expressed the intelligentsia's hegemony in Soviet society of the era.[7] On the other hand, few have explored the spatial inequalities generated by socialism. Sándor Horváth and Kate Brown are among the few historians who have been exploring how class differences constructed space in a socialist context.[8] However, Horváth's work focuses on the urban milieu of the new industrial city of Sztálinváros, while Brown explores urban–rural inequalities, taking the Soviet-closed atomic city of Ozersk in the Urals as a case study.

I intend to explore the construction of spatial inequalities in the countryside and urban–rural inequalities by focusing my lens on the Sugartown of Maliq. Such a choice allows for the exploration of the norm of geographical disparities in the countries that implemented the Soviet model. As a result, "class" is not going to be a central category of my analysis. Although class was one of the most important markers of social difference in socialist systems, other measuring rods also defined privilege and distinction. We need to include the variables of spatial inequalities in the equation in order to understand the inclusion and exclusion mechanisms preventing access to resources and opportunities. I will focus on how technology and investments based on economic profit, which determined the allocation of resources, defined the different scales of social and cultural transformations in Maliq and its surrounding areas. Shedding light on the uneven metamorphosis of the countryside during socialism will help us to better grasp the nature of the challenges that post-socialist societies have faced since the collapse of the communist regimes—especially the rocky road of Albania.

---

6   Vera S. Dunham, *In Stalin's Time: Middleclass Values in Soviet Fiction* (London: Cambridge University Press, 1976), 19–38; Sheila Fitzpatrick, "'Middle Class Values' and Soviet Life in the 1930s," in *Soviet Society and Culture: Essays in Honor of Vera S. Dunham*, eds. Terry L. Thompson and Richard Sheldon (Boulder, CO: Westview Press, 1988), 20–38; Sheila Fitzpatrick, "Becoming Cultured: Socialist Realism and the Representation of Privilege and Taste," in *The Cultural Front: Power and Culture in Revolutionary Russia* (Ithaca, NY: Cornell University Press, 1992), 216–238.

7   On the ideologeme of *kul'turnost'* in the Soviet Union, see Vadim Volkov, "The Concept of *Kul'turnost'*: Notes on the Stalinist Civilizing Process," in *Stalinism: New Directions*, ed. Sheila Fitzpatrick (London: Routledge, 2000), 210–230; Catriona Kelly and Vadim Volkov, "Directed Desires: *Kul'turnost'* and Consumption," in *Constructing Russian Culture in the Age of Revolution, 1881–1940*, eds. Catriona Kelly and David Shepherd (Oxford: Oxford University Press, 1998), 291–313; David L. Hoffman, *Stalinist Values: The Cultural Norms of Soviet Modernity, 1917–1941* (Ithaca, NY: Cornell University Press, 2003), 15–56; Julie Hessler, "Cultured Trade: The Stalinist Turn towards Consumerism," in *Stalinism: New Directions*, 182–209; Sheila Fitzpatrick, *Everyday Stalinism: Ordinary Life in Extraordinary Times: Soviet Russia in the 1930s* (Oxford: Oxford University Press, 1999), 79–89.

8   Sándor Horváth, *Stalinism Reloaded*; Brown, *Plutopia*.

Building and Peopling Where Once Only the Fishermen Could Go

On June 7, 1946, when the regime had just started the reclamation of the swamp, *Bashkimi* [Unity], the press organ of the Democratic Front, published an article where it articulated the communist narrative of progress. Among others, it boasted "In these very fertile lands, some 2000 farming families can be established who, with their work and the healthy climate, will become the happiest farmers of the new Albania."[9] This propagandistic article, part of the regime's narrative of transforming the country into an earthly heaven, carries essential information, not so much regarding what it invents, but for what it omits. The focus of this article is on the future farmers that the regime would install in the reclaimed land, whom the author privileges over the old inhabitants of the sixteen villages around the swamp who remained invisible to him.

By omitting the older communities and concentrating attention only on the prospective farmers, the article expressed the future-oriented characteristics and preferences of the communist elites. It carries the modernizing ideology of the interwar era and its symbolism of internal colonization within the notion of "rebirth," which, as we have already seen in the first chapter, was reinforced even further under fascist influence.[10] Reclaiming the swamp of Maliq would provide space for the emergence of a new type of men and women, this time forged under socialism, in a healthy climate, starting afresh with a blank slate that was uncontaminated by the past. It implied that the oppressive regimes of the past, the unhealthy swamp, and malaria had incapacitated the population of the old villages of the plains, which did not have these new men. The ALP openly preferred the new over the old.

After draining the marshland, the state built the sugar factory next to it, in the small town of Maliq. Additionally, the regime established the "Maliqi" state farm on the 4,500 hectares of newly gained land. The new agricultural enterprise specialized in the cultivation of sugar beet and became the leading supplier of raw material for the refinery.[11] The cooperatives instituted in the older villages

---

9 "Rëndësia e madhe e Maliqit për ekonominë e vendit t'onë" [The great importance of Maliq for our country], *Bashkimi*, June 11, 1946, 3. See also, "Në Maliq, si kudo në Shqipëri po farkëtohet puntoria e re" [In Maliq a new working class is being forged], *Bashkimi*, June 7, 1946, 1.
10 On Fascism and its colonial enterprise as a rebirth, see Patrick Bernhard, "Borrowing from Mussolini: Nazi Germany's Colonial Aspirations in the Shadow of Italian Expansionism," *The Journal of Imperial and Contemporary History* 41, no. 4 (2013): 622.
11 On the specialization of the state farm in the cultivation of sugar beet, AQSh, F. 490, Këshilli i Ministrave, 1951, d. 41, fl. 13. On the decision of the Council of Ministers for the establishment of the state farm of Maliq, AQSh, F. 490, Këshilli i Ministrave, 1950, d. 49, fl. 3.

would play a minor role compared to the agricultural state sector represented by the new farm. In the latter, the communist authorities built three villages in the early 1950s, the inhabitants of which worked on the state farm. The population of these new industrial and agricultural settlements migrated from many different parts of the country, especially from the surrounding highlands.

These newcomers benefited the most from the sugar industry and socialism and were all employed in the state sector and paid with workers' salaries that were considerably higher compared to those paid to the members of the collective farms. The refinery and state farm represented a core economic unit, and together, they formed a center of gravity for the surrounding area. As a consequence, the new settlements, which occupied strategic and privileged positions within the regional economic structure, enjoyed some of the highest standards of living in the district of Korça. However, technical contingencies rather than plans for conceiving utopian communities, as was the case with many projects of the interwar era and the post-World War II years, prompted the Albanian communist authorities to build new towns and villages.[12]

After building the refinery, the regime had to find workers. The main problem, though, was the lack of a labor force. The ALP's leadership decided to swell the ranks of the working class through the mobilization of the allegedly unused rural labor force in the countryside.[13] This strategy was based on the Soviet model of industrialization elaborated by the Soviet economist Yevgeni Preobrazhensky, who assumed that the countryside had a large number of unemployed human bodies. According to this blueprint, the state had to utilize the untapped "disguised labor" hiding in rural regions and use it for the construction of industrial complexes and their operation.[14]

---

12 On the utopian projects of the interwar and post-World War II era, Robert H. Kagon and Arthur P. Molella, *Invented Edens: Techno-Cities of the Twentieth Century* (Cambridge, MA: MIT Press, 2008); Diane Ghirardo, *Building New Communities: New Deal America and Fascist Italy* (Princeton, NJ: Princeton University Press, 1989); Wolfgang Schivelbusch, *Three New Deals: Reflections on Roosevelt's America, Mussolini's Italy, and Hitler's Germany, 1933–1939*, trans. Jefferson Chase (New York: Metropolitan Books, 2006), 104–183; Mia Fuller, "Tradition as a Means to the End of Tradition: Farmers' Houses in Italy's Fascist-Era New Towns," in *The End of Tradition?*, ed. Nezar Alaayyad (London: Routledge, 2004), 171–186; Henry A. Millon, "Some New Towns in Italy in the 1930s," in *Art and Architecture in the Service of Politics*, eds. Henry A. Millon and Linda Nochlin (Cambridge, MA: MIT Press, 1978), 326–341.
13 Demir Durmishi, *Punëtorët në Shqipëri (1944–1960)* [Workers in Albania (1944–1960)] (Tetovo: Album, 2001), 83.
14 Robert C. Allen, *From Farm to Factory: A Reinterpretation of the Soviet Industrial Revolution* (Princeton, NJ: Princeton University Press, 2003), 109–110.

While the USSR had a much larger population and even though the Soviet leadership succeeded in displacing a vast mass of peasants to urban industrial centers during the First Five-year Plan, this was not the case with Albania. As the Maliq case shows, the Albanian rural population did not have a sizeable excessive workforce for the communist regime to use in its numerous projects. There were 21,500 landless families in the entire country prior to 1945. Of these, 13,900 were sharecroppers, and 7,600 had no access to property. It was from these latter families that the pool of 20,000 peasants who sold their labor for money, either for the entire year or during specific seasons, came from.[15] The Agrarian Reform of 1946 further exacerbated the labor shortage because it supplied the landless peasants with arable plots.

The authorities targeted the most impoverished families in the uplands as the pool for expanding the ranks of the working class. The ALP's leadership thought that the lack of available and fertile land made the mountaineers more susceptible to leaving their hamlets for the new industrial centers. The regime started intensive propaganda work to convince the uplanders to undertake such a leap.[16] Hoxha himself invited them to leave the rocks of the mountains and to exploit the opportunities that the state had opened for them in the lowlands.[17] Convincing the peasants to leave their villages and relatives in the uplands was not an easy task. The deplorable living conditions in Maliq, which were similar to those of comparable cities such as Magnitogorsk, Chelyabinsk, Nowa Huta, and Sztálinváros in the early years of their existence, did not facilitate the work of the regime in recruiting workers. The situation of these socialist towns conforms to what Antonio Pennacchi called "post-eventum" cities in his discussion of industrial urban centers built in fascist Italy.[18] First came the factory, while the city along with its roads, apartment buildings, and services were developed later on.

For those who migrated to these industrial centers when urban conditions were still embryonic, life was very hard. The administration of the Maliq refin-

---

15 Naun Guxho, *Zhvillime në strukturën socialklasore në fshat* [Developments in the social class structure in the countryside] (Tirana: 8 Nëntori, 1985), 10–13.
16 On targeting the peasants of the uplands, see Demir Dyrmishi, "Fshatarësia si burim për shtimin e radhëve të klasës punëtore" [Peasantry as a source of the numerical growth of the working class], *Studime historike* [Historical studies] 25, no. 2 (1988): 47–48. On the propaganda among the mountaineers, *Ibid*, 54–55.
17 Enver Hoxha, "Fjala e mbajtur në Kongresin e Parë të Kooperativave Bujqësore" [Speech at the First Congress of the Collective Farms] in *Vepra* [Works], vol. 6 (Tirana: Naim Frashëri, 1971), 24–25.
18 Stephen Kotkin, *Magnetic Mountain*, 136–141; Samuelson, *Tankograd: The Formation of a Soviet Company Town*, 84–94; Katherine Lebow, *Unfinished Utopia*, 55; Horváth, *Stalinism Reloaded*, 63–74; Antonio Pennacchi, *Fascio e martello: Viaggio per le città del Duce* (Roma-Bari: Laterza, 2008), 189.

CHAPTER 3

FIGURE 11. The sugar town in the making

ery did not pay the workers regularly, and the shelter and food were horrible.[19] Although the factory's directory had its share of the blame, the miserable working and living conditions were not exclusively created by it. The low performance of agriculture in the late 1940s and early 1950s shared part of the blame for the food scarcity. During those years, the peasants did not deliver their quota to the state and sold their products in urban markets at high prices. As a result, the government could not supply provisions to the urban and working centers. The refinery administration wrote to the government asking for immediate intervention to fix the problems related to food. A lack of such action, it argued, would leave the workers without sustenance. The combine directory did not

---

19   AShV Korçë, F. 3/1, Komiteti i PPSh Qarku Korçë, 1954, Lista 5, d. 107, fl. 6. Report of the ALP's Committee of Maliq on the work of the organs of justice. February 11, 1954; AShV Korçë, F. 3/1, Komiteti i PPSh Qarku Korçë, 1954, Lista 5, d. 113, fl. 5-8. Report of the Office of Prosecution of the district of Korça on the violation of the workers' rights. March 1, 1954. On the irregular payment of workers, AShV Korçë, F. 3/2, Rrethi Korçë, 1953, Lista 9, d. 148, fl. 4. Report on the work in the Party organization in the sugar combine in Maliq.

wait for the center to fix the problem. The refinery management established its own supporting agricultural economies and, similar to the Soviet practice in the 1930s, provided its workers with 80 square meters of arable land per family member to allow them to provide for themselves and not depend on the market or state supplies.[20]

The minimal budget that the directory of the refinery had for housing further aggravated the situation. The pace of building remained slow, and dwelling problems persisted for years. Even those cadres with important positions had to struggle for shelter—in 1956, the staff of the Executive Committee slept in their offices because they had no apartments. The administration of the factory patched up a series of sheds into houses for bachelors and families, who lived in extremely unhygienic conditions. Approximately ten families, and in many cases, entire families, sometimes with many children, lived in a single room. Further aggravating these conditions was the fact that these improvised shelters had no kitchens or sewage.[21]

The first years, which were marked by a shortage of shelters, bad pay and little food, long working hours, and the administration's authoritarian behavior, did not make Maliq a very alluring place to settle in. The lack of water supply

---

[20] On supplying the urban and industrial centers with food, AQSh, F. 14/AP, Komiteti i PPSh (OU), 1953, d. 5, fl. 63-64. Report "On the measures for the further raising of the standard of living of the working masses," given by Enver Hoxha at the meeting of the IX Plenum of the Central Committee of the ALP. December 24–25, 1953. On the request of the refinery to the government regarding the issue of food, AShV Korçë, F. 67, Kombinati i Maliqit, 1952, d. 2, fl. 11. Letter from the director of the sugar combine to the Minister of Industry, Adil Çarçani. On establishing support for agricultural economies, AShV Korçë, F. 3/2, Komiteti i PPSH Rrethi Korçë, 1952, Lista 8, d. 64, fl. 3. Report on the inspection the ALP's Committee of Korça conducted in the sugar combine in Maliq. October 7, 1952. On distributing 80 square meters of land per person to the workers' families, AShV Korçë, F. 3/4, Komiteti i PPSh Maliq, 1954, Lista 7, d. 17, fl. 16. A report on the enforcement of legality in the economic enterprises of the district of Maliq. On the Soviet practice of the 1930s of giving workers plots for private use, see Elena A. Osokina, "Economic Disobedience under Stalin," in *Contending with Stalinism: Soviet Power and Popular Resistance in the 1930s*, ed. Lynne Viola (Ithaca NY: Cornell University Press, 2002), 173–174.

[21] On the refinery's limited budget for housing, AShV Korçë, F. 67, Kombinati i Sheqerit Maliq, 1962, d. 2, fl. 13. Report of the directory of the sugar combine on the fulfillment of the collective contracts during the year 1961. January 6, 1962. On the staff of the Executive Committee sleeping in their offices, AShV Korçë, F. 3/4, Komiteti i PPSh Rrethi Maliq, 1956, Lista 9, d. 10, fl. 20. Memo on the composition of the staff of the ALP's Committee of Maliq for the year 1956. January 1, 1956. On the conversion of sheds and the hygienic conditions, AQSh, F. 14/AP, Komiteti i PPSh (OU), 1957, d. 349, fl. 2-3. Memo on housing conditions in the city of Maliq. March 3, 1957. On the poor hygienic conditions, AShV Korçë, F. 3/2, Komiteti i PPSh Rrethi Korçë, 1952, Lista 8, d. 190, fl. 3. Report on the activity of the Industry and Communication section during the first trimester of 1952. April 8, 1952. On large families living in one room, AShV Korçë, F. 3/4, Komiteti i PPSh Rrethi Maliq, 1956, Lista 9, d. 24, fl. 15. Memo on the issue of housing in the city of Maliq. September 15, 1956.

worsened the already dangerous situation created by overcrowding and the lack of hygiene, and in 1957, cases of typhus appeared. The extended working hours deteriorated the workers' health. In shared spaces where many people were packed together, conflicts over the use of water, electricity, and sanitation facilities became common and often devolved into violent confrontations. The poor quality of the buildings, something that Enver Hoxha himself admitted, worsened the situation further. Roofs leaked, walls had mold, and there were even cases where restroom windows were connected to bedroom walls.[22] However, by the 1960s, the situation had improved rapidly. More and more families started living in single apartments, and the local authorities fixed the problems related to running water and sewage. Gradually, Maliq, which had reached a population of 3500 by the mid-1970s and exceeded 4000 in the late 1980s, started to take the shape of a small urban center.

The town of Maliq was an extension of the refinery, and its urban plan replicated the industrial organization of the work being carried out in the factory. The life of its inhabitants orbited around the factory, the town's administrative and cultural center, and the neighborhoods with houses and apartment buildings, all of which were placed along a single linear continuum.[23] Similar to an as-

---

22 On the lack of running water, AShV Korçë, F. 3/1, Komiteti i PPSh Qarku Korçë, 1957, Lista 8, d. 134, fl. 16. Minutes of the meeting of the Plenum of the ALP's Committee of Maliq. December 18, 1957. On cases of typhus, AShV Korçë, F. 3/4, Komiteti i PPSh Rrethi Maliq, 1957, Lista 10, d. 31, fl. 10. Report on the activity of the health institutions in the district of Maliq. On the diseases among workers and prolonged work hours, AShV Korçë, F. 3/4, Komiteti i PPSh Maliq, 1954, Lista 7, d. 17, fl. 19. Duties on the implementation of legality in favor of the workers. On the issue of conflicts, AQSh, F. 515, Ministria e Drejtësisë, 1959, d. 18, fl. 8. Memo on criminality and legality during the year 1958. March 19, 1959. On the lack of latrines, AShV Korçë, F. 3/2, Rrethi Korçë, 1953, Lista 9, d. 148, fl. 4. Report on the analysis of the work in the Party organization in the sugar combine in Maliq. On Hoxha admitting to the poor quality of buildings, AQSh, F. 14/AP, Komiteti i PPSh (OU), 1953, d. 5, fl. 70-71. Report "On the measures for the further raising of the standard of living of the working masses," given by Enver Hoxha at the meeting of the IX Plenum of the Central Committee of the ALP. December 24-25, 1953. On leaking roofs and damp walls, AShV Korçë, F. 3/4, Komiteti i PPSh Rrethi Maliq, 1956, Lista 9, d. 24, fl. 22-23. Minutes of the meeting of the Politburo of the ALP's Committee of Maliq. September 15, 1956. On the restroom windows, AQSh, F. 14/AP, Komiteti i PPSh (OU), 1953, d. 5, fl. 196. Minutes of the meeting of the IX Plenum of the Central Committee of the ALP. December 24-25, 1953.
23 On people living in barracks, AShV Korçë, F. 42, Komiteti Ekzekutiv i Komitetit të PPSh Maliq, 1971, d. 4, fl. 1. Report of Maliq's Executive Committee on the state of housing and the construction of dwellings with voluntary labor. On the solution of the problems of food and housing, AShV Korçë, F. 67, Kombinati i Sheqerit Maliq, 1962, d. 2, fl. 13. Report of the directory of the sugar combine on the fulfillment of the collective contracts during the year 1961. January 6, 1962. On running water and sewage, AShV Korçë, F. 3/1, Komiteti i PPSh Rrethi Korçë, 1970, Lista 26, d. 31, fl. 63. Memo concerning the urban development of the cities of Korça and Maliq. On the population of Maliq in 1975, AShV Korçë, F. 67, Kombinati i Sheqerit, 1975, d. 4, fl. 18-19. The history of the sugar combine

sembly line, the inhabitants of these new towns moved back and forth along this straight line for work, leisure, or to retreat to their houses. Mirroring how labor and space are divided according to specific roles and functions within a factory, the new town's spatial organization tended to segment space and the activities performed in it according to the principles of work, social activity, and family life. Each of these activities belonged to specific spaces along this axis.

The urban planning of Maliq, a city centered around an industrial enterprise, abided with factory logic. The industrial area was the workspace and was located at the extreme north of the settlement. Next to it was Block 3, the administrative, cultural, educational, and leisure section of the city. As in all dictatorships, education, culture, and leisure were under the stern guard of the political authorities. This principle determined the location of all these institutions in the central part of the town. The ALP and the Executive Committee, the house of culture, a theatre with 300 seats, and the 8-year school and gymnasium, the kindergartens, nurseries, and the infirmary all stood next to each other around a small central square. Blocks 1 and 2, which were located on the two sides of the main street of the town, were filled with shared one-floor houses. Finally, Block 4, which was located to the west of the central axis and was built later as the city expanded, had both state-owned apartment buildings and private houses.[24]

As for the villages, the government tried unsuccessfully to bring in families from the upland plains in the summer of 1945. The mountaineers did not respond to the call because of a fear of malaria, and only a few families agreed to settle.[25] Apparently, after this short-lived effort, the communists abandoned the idea. When the state farm was founded, its administration opted for seasonal workers from the surrounding villages. However, it turned out that it was impossible to find the necessary 1000 workers that the farm needed each season. The adverse living conditions in the farm dormitories, the poor food, and the low pay did not encourage the peasants to work there during the high season. The turnovers were so high that it was impossible for the administration to organize

---

of Maliq. On the population of Maliq in 1989, AShV Korçë, F. 42, Komiteti Ekzekuti i Komitetit të PPSh Maliq, 1989, Uncataloged files without number, Kutia 3397. Information on the problem of the unemployed work force in the city of Maliq.

24 On the organization of the town, AShV Korçë, F. 42, Komiteti Ekzekuti i Komitetit të PPSh Maliq, 1987, Uncataloged documents in files without number, Kutia 3398. Information on the regulatory plan of the town of Maliq, June 28, 1987. On the restaurants, shops, and bars, AShV Korçë, F. 67, Kombinati i Sheqerit, 1975, d. 4, fl. 18-19. The history of the Maliq sugar combine.

25 AShV Korçë, F. 3/1 PPSh Qarku Korçë, Lista 1, 1945, d. 14, fl. 59. Monthly Report of the ALP's Committee of Korça sent to the ALP's Central Committee. August 28, 1945.

CHAPTER 3

labor on the farm. One seasonal worker explained that the director of the farm even forced him to work on Sundays while he did not have a room to sleep in. In years when there was an abundant harvest, the peasants declined to work on the farm, and those few who dared to go did not meet the norms.[26]

The state farm's inability to supply the refinery became an object of grave concern for the ALP's Politburo. Regardless of the personal commitment that its director, Ilia Prifti, made to Enver Hoxha, the agricultural enterprise failed to attract seasonal workers and did not meet the state plan. The vast area of arable land combined with sugar beet's labor-intensive cultivation required the concentration of a large workforce. Additionally, the administration of the farm had a tough time finding a seasonal surplus labor force willing to harvest sugar beet.[27] The solution to this problem came in 1953. In consultation with the Minister of Agriculture, Hysni Kapo, a team of Soviet academics concluded that the only solution to labor scarcity was the establishment of permanent settlements and mechanization.[28] Kapo proposed the permanent settlement of 405 families on the farm to the Council of Ministers, and construction began that same year. On October 15, 1953, the Ministry of Construction introduced a plan and a timetable for the development of three rural settlements, each with 1500 hectares of arable land. In the mid-1960s, the state designated Drithas the village of the cereal,

---

26 On the solution of using seasonal workers, their refusal to work during abundant harvests, and the harsh living conditions at the state farm, AQSh, F. 14/AP, Komiteti i PPSh (OU), 1953, d. 36, fl. 34-39. Minutes of the meeting of the Politburo of the Central Committee. October 21, 1953; AQSh, F. 490, Këshilli i Ministrave, 1953, d. 183, fl. 1-4. Minutes and decisions of the Council of Ministers on the favorable treatment of the seasonal workers at the State Agricultural Farm of Maliq. October 27, 1953. On the harsh living conditions and low payment, AShV Korçë, F. 3/4, Rrethi Maliq, 1953, Lista 5, d. 39, fl. 1. Memorandum "On the problem of the State Agricultural Farm of Maliq." December 25, 1953; AQSh, F. 518, Ministria e Bujqësisë, 1953, d. 150, fl. 17. Memo of the Minister of Agriculture, Hysni Kapo, on the workforce at the Maliq farm. On the issue of bad food, AQSh, F. 14/AP, Komiteti i PPSh (STR), 1953, d. 10, fl. 4. Memo on the Maliq farm. May 6, 1953. On turnovers, AQSh, F. 490, Këshilli i Ministrave, 1954, d. 97, fl. 1. Memo on the situation at the State Agricultural Farm of Maliq and the measures that should be taken. March 24, 1954. On the complaints of the workers, AQSh, F. 515, Ministria e Drejtësisë, 1954, d. 4, fl. 2. Generalizations on crimes regarding the violation of work discipline during the first semester of the year 1954. December 14, 1954.
27 On the failure to attract seasonal workers, AShV Korçë, F. 3/1, Komiteti i PPSh Qarku Korçë, 1954, Lista 5, d. 56, fl. 11-15. Report on the campaign for the harvesting, weeding, and transportation of sugar beet. September 9, 1954. On the failure to convince the peasants to work at the state farm, AQSh, F. 14/AP, Komiteti i PPSh (OU), 1953, d. 5, fl. 168. Minutes of the meeting of the IX Plenum of the Central Committee of the ALP. December 24-25, 1953. On the need for concentrating a large work force at the state farm, AQSh, F. 490, Këshilli i Ministrave, 1953, d. 107, fl. 8. Memo on the situation at the Maliq farm.
28 AQSh, F. 490, Këshilli i Ministrave, 1953, d. 107, fl. 1. Minutes of the meeting of the Council of Ministers. September 30, 1953.

FIGURE 12. A new village in the reclaimed land of Maliq

Sheqeras the village of sugar, and Vreshtaz the village of vineyards. The real challenge, though, was not only building new houses and villages but also to find people who were willing to settle there.[29]

To entice the peasants, the director of the state farm proposed providing each family of new settlers with at least 2000 square meters for personal use as well as the installation of running water, telephone lines, and electricity. The government agreed with this practical scheme that intended to use material advantages as bait to attract the mountaineers to leave their hamlets and to move to the lowlands and participate in the building of socialism. On April 2, 1954, the Council of

---

29 The proposal of Hysni Kapo, AQSh, F. 490, Këshilli i Ministrave, 1953, d. 107, fl. 9. Memo on the situation at the Maliq farm. On the approval of the Council of Ministers for the permanent settlement of agricultural workers at the Maliq farm, *Ibid*, fl. 13–14. Measures for the improvement of the conditions at the Maliq farm. September 30, 1953. On the three sectors of the farm, AQSh, F. 490, Këshilli i Ministrave, 1953, d. 152, fl. 1. Memo of the Ministry of Construction for the construction of 95 buildings with 380 apartments at the Maliq farm. October 15, 1953; AQSh, F. 518, Ministria e Industrisë dhe Ndërtimit, 1953, d. 209, fl. 2. On constructions at the Maliq farm. December 21, 1953.

CHAPTER 3

Ministers approved Prifti's plan and provided financial rewards and mortgages to buy cattle for the families who moved in—although in some cases, the administration of the farm did not provide these to the newcomers.[30] The new inhabitants, who were mainly from the uplands of Korça, were from impoverished families. When the settlers arrived on the farm, they had almost nothing, and the administration supplied them with the most necessary items, such as sheets, blankets, beds, clothes, etc.[31] These incentives produced results. In 1957, around 1100 people were working and living on the farm. Each of them had a house, a private garden, a cow or five sheep, and poultry. Contrary to Nowa Huta, it was not the revolutionary fervor of propagandized youngsters that drove the peasants from the highlands to move to the plains of Maliq, nor was it the desire to break definitively with what they considered to be the dullness of rural life.[32]

Maliq also hosted the victims of ethnic cleansing in Greece, which makes this part of its story part of the traumas that afflicted societies between the Aegean and Baltic Seas during the twentieth century. Similar to Breslau, where the Polish state installed Poles expelled from Ukraine, in Maliq, the Tirana authorities settled Albanian migrants that the Greek army had forcefully evicted from their homes in 1949.[33] These migrants came from the eastern façade of the Gramos mountain range on the Greek side of the Albanian–Greek border, where, until World War II, there were fifty to sixty hamlets inhabited by Albanians: both Muslims and Orthodox Christians. This area became the very center of the Greek communist resistance. When the Greek army crushed the communists in 1949, it also expelled all the Albanian Muslims that inhabited the area. The Albanian-speaking Christians were not expelled because the Greek state conflated nationality with religion and considered them Greeks.[34]

---

30 The proposal of Ilia Prifti, AShV Korçë, F. 3/4, Rrethi Maliq, 1953, Lista 5, d. 39, fl. 1–3. Memorandum "On the problem of the State Agricultural Farm of Maliq." December 25, 1953. The approval of measures for the construction of houses, electrification, installation of telephone lines, running water, etc. at the Maliq state farm, AQSh, F. 490, Këshilli i Ministrave, 1954, d. 97, fl. 11. Some measures for the State Agricultural Farm of Maliq. April 2, 1954. On financial assistance and mortgages to the peasants that moved into the Maliq farm, AShV Korçë, F. 3/1, Komiteti i PPSh Qarku Korçë, 1954, Lista 5, d. 113, fl. 57. On the violation of laws and other irregularities at the State Agricultural Farm of Maliq. October 20, 1954.

31 On the provision of the families of the settlers with furniture, AShV Korçë, F. 3/4, Komiteti i PPSh Maliq, 1957, Lista 10, d. 26, fl. 8. Report on the improvement of the material conditions of the workers at the State Agricultural Farm of Maliq.

32 Lebow, *Unfinished Utopia*, 46–55.

33 On Breslau, see Thum, *Uprooted: How Breslau Became Wrocław*, 93–95.

34 On the difficult relations between Albania and Greece during the early stages of the Cold War era, Beqir Meta, *Tensioni greko-shqiptar: 1939–1949* [The Greek-Albanian tension: 1939–1949] (Tirana:

These uprooted Albanian speakers joined the ranks of the many other millions of victims of the numerous displacements that occurred in post-World War II Europe. After being expelled, they wandered across Albania for some years until, after hearing of the sugar refinery, they settled in Maliq.[35] Even today, after seven decades, some markers display their presence in Maliq. One of them is the coffee shop "Masllavica," the name of one of the hamlets destroyed in 1949. The coffee shop, which is located on the main boulevard of Maliq, is probably one of the last forms of the collective memory of a forgotten ethnic cleansing. It also shows how deracinating perpetrated by anti-communists supplied an industrial enterprise of a communist regime with a labor force.

After the difficulties of the first years, the initiative to encourage people to move to the farm paid off. In 1957, the state increased the minimum daily payment from ALL 80 to 100, while the maximum daily payment increased from ALL 130 to 136. When the agricultural workers surpassed their norms, their incomes were equal to those of industrial workers and state bureaucrats. Personal gardens further boosted their affluence. Gradually, the villages took shape based on the plan drawn by Projekti studio, which was founded in 1952 by a nucleus of Soviet and young Albanian architects who had studied in the Soviet Union. Similar to all new socialist towns, religious objects were absent. The centers of Maliq's new compact orthogonal settlements, which occupied an area of approximatively twenty-three hectares each, were dominated by administrative and social-cultural buildings.[36]

In 1959, a periodical boasted that the ALP built new villages in a place where once only fishermen with their boats could go. The fertile land that had once been covered by a swamp now buzzed with tractors and combines, it filled the granaries with cereals, and supplied the refinery with sugar beet.[37] This was the

---

Globus R, 2007); Beqir Meta, *Shqipëria dhe Greqia, 1949–1990: paqja e vështirë* [Albania and Greece, 1949–1990: The difficult peace] (Tirana: Globus R, 2007). On the human drama of the Greek Civil War, see the first-person account of William H. McNeill, *Greece: American Aid in Action, 1947–1956* (New York: Twentieth Century Fund, 1957).

35 Çelnik Jaupi, Informal interview by Artan Hoxha, Maliq, Albania, September 30, 2017.
36 On the improvement of the quality of life and the high salaries, AShV Korçë, F. 3/4, Komiteti i PPSh Maliq, 1957, Lista 10, d. 26, fl. 8-9. Report on the improvement of the material conditions of the workers of the State Agricultural Farm of Maliq. The salaries increased in this way: the daily payment of the workers of the first category increased from 80 to 100 lekë per day; the second category increased from 93 to 110 lekë; the third category from 109 to 122 lekë; and the fourth category increased from 130 to 136. On studio "Projekti," AQSh, F. 499, Ministria e Ndërtimit, 1956, d. 421, fl. 17-18. Memo of the Ministry of Construction on some urgent issues of urban planning in Albania.
37 "Atje ku më parë ishte këneta" [Where there used to be a swamp], *Për bujqësinë socialiste*, no. 8 (1959): 4–5.

example *par excellence* of the narrative: it showcased socialism's success in taming nature, spreading civilization and happiness where there had once been wilderness. As explained above, though, contrary to the mythology of the communist power apparatus, the construction of the refinery, and the new town and villages was the outcome of unanticipated circumstances.

In the immediate post-World War II period, the state authorities tried to bring to the plains people from the highlands, which was unsuccessful. However, they gave up on this plan as soon as they understood that few mountaineers were willing to move. In the end, it was the building of the sugar factory next to the Maliq gorge, fifteen kilometers away from Korça, that forced the state authorities to build a new small town next to it. In turn, the need to supply the refinery with sugar beet forced the administration to build villages and fill them with the necessary workforce. What started as a contingency, was used by the propaganda apparatus in retrospect and became another success story of Albanian socialist modernity. By the late 1950s, the inhabitants of the state farm earned and consumed more than any other peasants in the district—all thanks to the sugar industry.

Building Socialism, Spatializing Inequalities

Similar to its Soviet and Eastern European analogues, the Albanian socialist regime established professional hierarchies that defined a new social structure, the bottom of which held members of the cooperatives. Thus, in 1958, the annual income of the collective farms was ALL 19,720, while that of the workers was ALL 35,567. The uneven allocation of financial rewards and access to consumption also became visible in the annual income growth of peasants and workers. Thus, during 1958, workers' revenues increased by 11.1%—from ALL 32,015 to ALL 35,567—while those of the peasants increased by only 0.9%—from ALL 19,528 to ALL 19,720. Although the state rewarded the members of the agricultural cooperatives with industrial goods, their revenues were still lower than those of the workers. As a result, in the late 1950s, the urban population, which was approximately 316,000 people, purchased more than the 936,000 people who lived in the countryside.[38] The stipend provided to cooperative members was the sum of a basic monthly salary—much lower compared to that given to the workers and state bureaucrats—and the per capita distribution of the cooperative farm's an-

---

38   AQSh, F. 495, Komisioni i Planit të Shtetit, 1959, d. 134, fl. 21-22, 93, 116–117. Memo on the revenues per person of the peasantry.

nual income. The economic performance of the collective farms, which was critical for their members' earnings, depended on the type of crops that the State Planning Commission assigned them to cultivate, the soil quality, the climate, and other factors outside of the peasants' control. Thus, central planning, in combination with topography, pedology, climate, seeds, etc., produced inequalities among agricultural cooperatives.

How did all of these factors interplay with each other in Maliq? In what ways did they shape the spatial inequalities? Discussing the Soviet Union and Hungary, Neil Melvin and Iván Szelényi have already argued on the complexity of the social stratification of the socialist countryside and have questioned the validity of the concept of the "peasant class" in Soviet-type regimes.[39] Despite conforming their interpretations to the regime's tripartite division of society into peasants, workers, and technocrats, Albanian communist statisticians also recognized how such a division did not correspond to the mixed professional composition of the rural population. In the late 1950s, they realized that many families in the countryside had members that simultaneously fell into the categories of workers and clerks, who were employed in cooperatives, and that of private peasants. Socialist industrialization, rather than simplifying the spatial distribution of professions and classes, further intermingled them and complicated the social landscape.

In Maliq, the sugar industry made the socio-economic structure more intricate than it had been previously. Compared to the pre-World War II period, when almost all the inhabitants of the plains were peasants, after the building of the refinery in 1951, there were hundreds of workers, technicians, specialists, and vendors who interacted closely with the peasants.[40] As a result, by the 1950s, agriculture was not the only type of employment, and many families in the plains had a mixed professional composition. In addition, the intensification of the connection that the population of the plains had in economic sectors other than agriculture augmented the cash inflow of individual rural families and strengthened the threads that tied them to the market.

The nested spatial hierarchies of communist modernization became deeply pronounced in the fractures that divided Maliq's plains from the uplands of

---

39   Neil J. Melvin, *Soviet Power and the Countryside: Policy Innovation and Institutional Decay* (New York: Palgrave Macmillan, 2003), 133; Iván Szelényi, *Socialist Entrepreneurs: Embourgeoisement in Rural Hungary* (Madison, WI: University of Wisconsin Press, 1988).
40   AQSh, F. 495, Komisioni i Planit të Shtetit, 1959, d. 134, fl. 125. Memo on the realization of the salaries for the workers and clerks, and the revenues for the year 1959 and the expectation for the year 1960.

CHAPTER 3

Korça. The cooperatives in the highlands harvested an average of fifteen quintals of cereal per hectare, among the lowest in the country, while the plains yielded between forty-five to fifty quintals per hectare, among the highest in the country. As a consequence, the differences in the incomes between the peasants in the highlands and those in the plains of Maliq widened. For example, in 1970, the monthly average revenue per person in the countryside of the district of Korça was ALL 3265, while the average income in the uplands was ALL 2380.[41] This meant that the salaries in the lowland farms were far above the average and were much higher than those in the highlands. Concomitantly, the work in the latter was more time-consuming and backbreaking. In the meantime, in 1957, many agricultural workers at the Maliqi state farm earned record wages of ALL 6000 a month, an income comparable to that of the intelligentsia. If we count the increase in revenue produced in the Korça countryside as being 76% from 1960 to 1979, then the gap between the wages at the state farm and the collective farms, and especially in the uplands, widens even further.[42]

The electrification of the villages in the plains took place in tandem with the increase in income. In the late 1950s, the district of Korça had sixty-five electrified villages, a record for the entire country, and the bulk of them were located in the plateau.[43] By the early 1960s, all the villages in the plains had electricity as well as radios. In 1957, Korça's countryside had 325 radios, and in 1959, that num-

---

41 On the yield in the cooperatives of the uplands, AQSh, F. 14/AP, Komiteti i PPSh (OU), 1976, d. 96, fl. 22. Minutes of the meeting of the Secretariat of the ALP's Central Committee. September 21, 1976. On the yield of the agricultural enterprises in the plain of Maliq, AQSh, F. 14/AP, Komiteti i PPSh (OU), 1976, d. 96, fl. 20. Minutes of the meeting of the Secretariat of the ALP's Central Committee. September 21, 1976; AQSh, F. 490, Këshilli i Ministrave, 1982, d. 530, fl. 4. Speech of Prime Minister, Adil Çarçani, at a meeting of the Plasa cooperative, in Korça. September 18, 1982. On the differences in revenues between the lowlands and the uplands, AShV Korçë, F. 3/2, Komiteti i PPSh Rrethi Korçë, 1970, Lista 26, d. 53, fl. 2. Memo of the ALP's Committee of Korça on the increase in revenues of the collective farms in the uplands. March 20, 1970.

42 On the uplanders working more and earning little, AQSh, F. 498, Ministria e Bujqësisë, 1968, d. 90/4, fl. 44-46. Study on the prospective development of the agricultural sector in the district of Korça for the years 1970–1980. July 1968. On the wages of the agricultural workers of Maliq, AShV Korçë, F. 3/4, Komiteti i PPSh Maliq, 1957, Lista 10, d. 26, fl. 8-9. Report on the improvement of the material conditions of the workers of the Maliq state farm. On the growth of incomes of the rural population of Korça see Guxho, *Zhvillime në strukturën socialklasore në fshat*, 130–134.

43 On the number of electrified villages in the district of Korça, AShV Korçë, F. 3/1, Komiteti i PPSh Qarku Korçë, 1957, Lista 8, d. 25, fl. 26. Report on the artistic and cultural work in the district. On Korça holding the record for electrified villages, AShV Korçë, F. 3/2, Komiteti i PPSh Rrethi Korçë, 1959, Lista 15, d. 153, fl. 5. Report on the situation and perspectives of the countryside. On the concentration of the majority of the electrified villages in the plain of Korça, AShV Korçë, F. 3/2, Komiteti i PPSh Rrethi Korçë, 1961, Lista 17, d. 103, fl. 58-60. Table of the electrification of the villages in the district of Korça.

ber doubled to 655; the bulk of them were owned by members of the agricultural enterprises of the plains, who had higher incomes as well as electricity. Two decades later, all the families in the villages on the plains had radios, while at the state farm, where the houses had amenities similar to those of urban dwellers, a good portion of the families owned TV sets.[44] Upland villages, however, could not easily access these commodities and technologies.

The spatial organization of the villages of the plains was another critical factor that helped in their electrification. Before World War II, the rural communities on the Maliq plains did not comprise clustered settlements, but rather communities of households scattered across a vast area. The scattered plots and lack of roads forced many peasants to build their houses close to their land. On the other hand, the houses being so far removed from each other hampered electrification, sewer construction, running water, the building of schools and sanitary services, and a functional trade network of stores and other amenities.[45]

The communist regime was committed to using as much arable land as possible and to mechanizing agriculture and decided to discipline the peasants' constructions. In the early 1960s, the state imposed its monopoly on the management of the territory, and it prohibited the peasants from building anything without prior permission from the local authorities. Additionally, because the topography of the plains favored the formation of packed rural centers, the gov-

---

44 On the electrification of the villages of the plain of Maliq, AShV Korçë, F. 3/2, Komiteti i PPSh Rrethi Korçë, 1961, Lista 17, d. 103, fl. 58-60. Table of the electrification of the villages in the district of Korça. On the peasants of the plain possessing radios and TVs, AShV Korçë, F. 3/2, Komiteti i PPSh Rrethi Korçë, 1974, Lista 30, d. 69, fl. 31. Report of the Maliqi State Farm on the moral and political attitude of the workers of this enterprise; AQSh, F. 499, Ministria e Bujqësisë, 1955, d. 55/6, fl. 110. Report on the situation of the collective farms in the district of Korça. February 2, 1955. On the number of radios in the countryside of Korça in 1957, AShV Korçë, F. 3/1, Komiteti i PPSh Qarku Korçë, 1957, Lista 8, d. 25, fl. 26. Report on the artistic and cultural work in the district. On the number of radios in the countryside of Korça in 1959, AShV Korçë, F. 3/2, Komiteti i PPSh Rrethi Korçë, 1959, Lista 15, d. 107, fl. 8. Letter of the ALP's Committee of Korça on the cultural life in the countryside of the district. June 27, 1959. On the ownership of radios and TVs in the first half of the 1970s, AShV Korçë, F. 3/2, Komiteti i PPSh Rrethi Korçë, 1974, Lista 30, d. 69, fl. 31. Report of the State Farm Maliqi on the moral and political attitude of the workers of this enterprise. On the furnishing of the houses at the state farm, AShV Korçë, Bundle of uncataloged documents without a collection number, 1964, fl. 7. Report of the presidency of the Korça branch of the Union of Albanian Women on the measures for the improvement of the economic, social, and cultural conditions of the countryside. February 18, 1964.
45 On the scattered villages of the plain of Maliq, Vasilika Cicko, "Tipare të reja të vendbanimeve fshatare" [New features of rural settlements], in *Konferenca kombëtare e studimeve etnografike* [National conference of ethnographic studies] (Tirana: Akademia e Shkencave e RPSSH, 1977), 444. On the scattered villages and the difficulties in their modernization, AQSh, F. 495, Komisioni i Planit të Shtetit, 1960, d. 145, fl. 8-9. Report on the construction of dwellings in Albania since 1945.

ernment decided to transform the villages in the lowlands into clustered settlements.[46] In line with this project for the revamping of the countryside, Tirana ordered the spatial organization of the villages according to Hippodamian principles, with straight roads and orthogonal angles. In Korça, the local authorities, under the banner of the maximization of the exploitation of arable land that had been in place since the late 1950s, banned the unauthorized constructions in the countryside. Concurrently, many specialists from Tirana, many of whom were also students of the faculty of engineering, drew layouts for the villages of the plains. Soon, old settlements, such as Orman Pojan, Rëmbec, and Pojan, emerged as compact abodes based on a rectangular grid.[47]

It was no accident that these new plans targeted the villages where the collectivization of agriculture had advanced the furthest. In Albania, collectivization was in full swing, as was the case in other Eastern European countries. As a result, the collectivized area jumped from 14.5% of the arable land in 1955 to 85% in 1960.[48] Besides coercion, Tirana's authorities used soft strategies to convince the peasants to join the cooperatives by showing the alleged superiority of socialism and the benefits that could be derived from collectivization. The regime built 7-year schools, kindergartens, nurseries, health centers, and bakeries in the collectivized villages. The reconstruction of Rëmbec and Pojan, for example, had the clear purpose of enticing the peasants of Maliq to join the cooperatives. The sizable investments that the regime carried out in these model villages would showcase what socialism meant and how advantageous it was to integrate into the socialist sector of the economy.[49]

Besides their use for propaganda, the building of educational, health, and trade network services played crucial functions in the policy of Tirana's leadership to fragment the unity of the multifunctionality and autonomy of rural

---

46   Enver Faja and Isuf Sukaj, *Urbanistika dhe ndërtimet në fshat* [Urban planning and constructions in the countryside] (Tirana: Shtëpia Botuese e Librit Universitar, 1990), 78; Cicko, "Tipare të reja të vendbanimeve fshatare," 445.

47   On the commitment of the local authorities of Korça to maximize the use of arable land, AShV Korçë, F. 3/2, Komiteti i Rrethi Korçë, 1961, Lista 17, d. 2, fl. 12-13. Report on the collective farms in the district of Korça for the year 1960 and the tasks for their development. March 28, 1961. On the engineers and students that drafted the urban planning of the villages of the plain of Maliq, AShV Korçë, F. 3/2, Komiteti i PPSh Rrethi Korçë, 1960, Lista 16, d. 110, fl. 5. Memo on the cultural work in the district. May 14, 1960; AShV Korçë, F. 3/2, Komiteti i PPSh Rrethi Korçë, 1960, Lista 16, d. 104, fl. 1. Letter of the ALP's Central Committee sent to the ALP's local committees concerning the dispatching of cultural brigades to the countryside. June 8, 1960.

48   Guxho, *Zhvillime në strukturën socialklasore në fshat*, 20-21.

49   AShV Korçë, F. 3/2, Komiteti i PPSh Rrethi Korçë, 1960, Lista 16, d. 110, fl. 5. Memo on the cultural work in the district. May 14, 1960; Cicko, "Tipare të reja të vendbanimeve fshatare," 444-447.

households. In their houses, the peasants ate, slept, reproduced, gave birth, reared their children, worked, and died. With the maternities, nurseries, kindergartens, schools, collective farms, bakeries, stores, etc., Tirana's communist authorities broke this unity and, through many threads, connected the peasants to the outer world that lay outside the walls of their homes, especially with the state-run institutions. Besides its political mission, this network of state-controlled services played a prominent economic role.

At first, they were critical of women working in the cooperatives. The regime, however, eager to double its labor force in agriculture, had to pull the women out of the patriarchal household economy. Attaining this goal also meant breaking up the closed economy of the household to connect the peasants with the socialist market. If the women worked as wage laborers, it meant that they could neither raise their children nor prepare the bulk of their food or clothes themselves. For them to work in the socialist sector, the state would need to assist the women in the roles they had always played within the rural patriarchal household.

Building state networks for trade and education in the countryside was not merely an expression of the modern state's drive to interfere in the private sphere, regulate it, and monopolize the rearing of future generations. It is true that this web of state-led services, which was meant to integrate women within the socialist system, also underpinned the extension of the communist regime's power in the realm of the familial and intimate sphere. However, dotting the countryside with the reticle of preschool and trade establishments played an essential economic function. These services became especially crucial for the inclusion of women on the collective farms.

Cheap female labor was critical to the regime's finances and investment agenda because it allowed the state to save resources and to allocate them to industry. Such a mechanism perpetuated the simultaneous subordination of agriculture and peasant women to the secondary sector of the economy. The central authorities were especially interested in using women's labor in the most productive cooperatives. Additionally, when it came to the distribution of preschool institutions and trade networks, the state organs openly favored the collective farms that had high economic importance and where the female workforce was more needed. By 1961, there were 13 nurseries, 39 kindergartens, and 42 bakeries in the collective farms of Korça, with the majority of them distributed in the plains.[50]

---

50 AShV Korçë, F. 3/2, Komiteti i PPSh Rrethi Korçë, 1961, Lista 17, d. 25, fl. 115. Memo on work with the masses of the women in the countryside. August 16, 1961.

CHAPTER 3

In December 1961, while pursuing Tirana's orders, the ALP's Committee of Korça ordered the opening of nurseries and bakeries in all the large cooperatives in the district within the coming year. The peasant women who worked in the socialist economy would now buy their bread instead of baking it themselves at home.[51] The introduction and expansion of stores and childcare institutions were part of the goal of the ALP's leadership to transform the peasant families from economic units that were mainly oriented toward production into consumption-oriented social molecules.[52] In line with this goal, the regime struggled, not without success, to interrupt the domestic output of furnishings, clothes, foodstuffs, etc., and stimulated consumption over accumulation. It not only considered handicrafts to be a reflection of the mentality of private property but also as being responsible for detaching rural families from the market.

The establishment of trade and childcare institution networks and the introduction of new ways of feeding and dressing were a part of Tirana's social engineering of the countryside. Besides the ideological component that drove the "war against backward customs and superstitions," as the Albanian communist leadership used to call its civilizing mission in the countryside, there was also an essential economic element underpinning its cultural policy. According to the ALP structures, raising the cultural level of the peasantry also meant teaching them to manage their financial resources and to use their savings to expand the inventory of appliances, furniture, clothing, and other goods that made life cultured. In this way, the rural population would support domestic manufacturing. Korça's Democratic Front taught peasant couples to manage their incomes to buy blankets and linen; clothes for work, free time, and bedtime; dishware and utensils; and tables and chairs. It was in this context that the regime's organs started a wholesale attack against the home-made felt clothes that the peasants used for both work and their free time. The state's local branches considered felt to be unhygienic and urged the peasants to buy the wool, flannel, and cotton clothes that had been produced in the textile combine "Stalin" in

---

51 On the order for peasant women to buy bread in bakeries, AShV Korçë, F. 3/2, Komiteti i PPSh Rrethi Korçë, 1961, Lista 17, d. 8, fl. 55-56. Report of the ALP's Committee of Korça on its work for the implementation of the measures for the schooling and technical-professional education of women, and their rise in responsibility. December 21, 1961.

52 On the policy of the communist regime to transform the household from a production to a consumption unit, AShV Korçë, Bundle of uncataloged documents without a collection number, 1981, fl. 9. Some conclusions from a study of family psychology in the district of Korça and the problems that emerged. January 20, 1980.

Tirana. Contrary to felt, the propaganda apparatus stated, these industrial clothes were hygienic and healthy.[53]

Becoming cultured meant becoming good consumers who would support the development of national industry. In order to connect the peasants tightly to the market and to orient them toward consumption despite their low incomes, in 1957, the government decreased the prices of many market goods. In the meantime, the state authorities intensified their campaigns against the domestic production of clothing in the countryside.[54] The regime also ordered the reduction of the peasants' gardens from 500–700 square meters, as had been the norm, to only 300 square meters. By reducing the peasants' ability to produce their own food, the communist state sought to erode the economic base of the peasant household, increase the market dependency of the rural population, separate production from consumption, and, thus, expand the domestic market.[55]

The effect of these efforts, which aimed to break any form of self-sufficiency separating rural families from the market, was immense. Thus, the demand for items such as buckram, drapery, threads, pasta, shoes, towels, soap, and some of the most important foods related to cultured life, grew exponentially. For example, the number of finished goods purchased in the countryside between 1950 and 1958 more than doubled. The rural population bought wool, calico, flannel, velvet, thread, sweaters, socks, sweatshirts, sandals, and shoes from the markets. Before the establishment of socialism, these items were either unknown, unused, or home-made. Although at a lower level compared to the urbanites, the peasants also increased the range of foodstuffs bought from the state market, including items such as rice, sugar, oil, marmalade, macaroni, canned fish, and flour.[56]

---

53 AShV Korçë, Bundle of uncataloged documents without a collection number, 1961, fl. 4-6. Lecture of the Democratic Front of Korça on the improvement in the lifestyle in the countryside.

54 On the decrease in prices, AShV Korçë, F. 3/4, Komiteti i PPSh Rrethi Maliq, 1957, Lista 10, d. 1, fl. 20. Report of the First Secretary of the ALP's Committee of Maliq, Ilo Xega, at the Fourth ALP Conference in the district of Maliq. March 31, 1957. On the fight against the domestic production of clothing, AShV Korçë, Bundle of uncataloged documents without a collection number, 1961, fl. 4. Lecture of the Democratic Front of Korça on the improvement in the lifestyle in the countryside.

55 Cicko, "Tipare të reja të vendbanimeve fshatare," 444–447.

56 On the growth of incomes of the rural population in the district of Korça and the increase of its purchasing power, Guxho, *Zhvillime në strukturën socialklasore në fshat*, 130–134. On the decrease in the prices of industrial goods, Astrit Kallfa, *Arritje dhe probleme të ngushtimit të dallimeve thelbësore ndërmjet qytetit dhe fshatit* [Achievements and problems of the narrowing of the differences between town and countryside] (Tirana: Universiteti i Tiranës, 1984), 147. On the growth of demand for light industrial goods in the countryside of the region of Korça, AShV Korçë, F. 3/1, Komiteti i PPSh Qarku Korçë, 1957, Lista 8, d. 138, fl. 4. Report of the ALP's Committee of Maliq on the situation of trade in the district and the measures for its increase. September 9, 1957; AQSh, F. 495, Komisioni i Planit të Shtetit, 1959, d. 134, fl. 21-22. Statistics on the sale of goods to the working masses in the city, country-

CHAPTER 3

However, in the district of Korça, the effects of these policies that sought the creation of modern rural consumers were far from uniform. Indeed, they deepened topographic inequalities. The farmers of the plains of Maliq compensated for the reduction in their personal gardens with their salaries. By the mid-1960s, the rural population living on the plains was already using different clothes for work and for domestic use or leisure time. Urban fashion penetrated and dominated the rural dressing-style, and the peasants of Maliq began to buy their clothes in Korça. Shoes and rubber boots for winter replaced the traditional leather opinga, and velvet and cotton clothing displaced felt. Both men and women uncovered their heads, and caps and scarfs ceased being part of the peasants' attire, while young girls started keeping their hair short, similar to their urban peers.[57]

The agricultural cooperatives of the plains, which had high revenues and competed to become model collective farms, also played an important role in the regime's internal civilizing mission. For a collective farm to become a model farm meant that its members kept their houses clean, painted them with lime, furnished them with new furniture, especially with beds and tables, used individual dishes, built lavatories, and sealed their septic holes.[58] Cooperatives of the plains, such as that of Libonik, spent ALL 700,000 to buy cupboards, dishes, drinking glasses, blankets, sheets, etc., for its members.[59] However, this was not the case with the inefficient agricultural enterprises in the uplands. The mem-

---

side, and other categories of the population. On the increase in the number of confections bought in the countryside, AShV Korçë, F. 3/2, Komiteti i PPSh Rrethi Korçë, 1959, Lista 15, d. 65, fl. 17. Report on the role of consumer cooperatives in raising culture in the countryside. On foodstuff items bought in the countryside, AQSh, F. 495, Komisioni i Planit të Shtetit, 1959, d. 134, fl. 21-22. Statistics on the sale of goods to the working masses in the city, countryside, and other categories of the population.

57 On the use of different types of dresses, AShV Korçë, Bundle of uncatalogued documents without a collection number, 1964, fl. 18. Report of the presidency of the Korça branch of the Union of Albanian Women on the measures for improvement in the economic, social, and cultural conditions of the countryside. February 18, 1964. On the introduction of new attires and tastes, AShV Korçë, Bundle of uncataloged documents without a collection number, 1961, fl. 4. Lecture of the Democratic Front of Korça on improvement in the lifestyle of the countryside; AShV Korçë, Bundle of uncatalogued documents without a collection number, 1964, fl. 18-19. Report of the presidency of the Korça branch of the Union of Albanian Women on measures for improvement in the economic, social, and cultural conditions of the countryside. February 18, 1964; Andromaqi Gjergji, "Provë për një studim etnografik në kooperativën bujqësore "Shkëndia" (rrethi i Korçës)" [An essay on an ethnographic study of the collective farm Shkëndija (District of Korça)], *Etnografia shqiptare* [Albanian ethnography] 2, (1963): 96–98.

58 AShV Korçë, F. 3/1, Komiteti i PPSh Rrethi Korçë, 1957, Lista 8, d. 190, fl. 2. Letter of the ALP's Central Committee: "On a more cultured life in the countryside." October 14, 1957.

59 AShV Korçë, F. 3/4, Komiteti i PPSh Rrethi Maliq, 1957, Lista 10, d. 5, fl. 4. Report on the sanitary propaganda in the countryside. December 18, 1957.

bers of the latter, whose incomes were very low, had no alternative to counterbalance the reduction of their private plots.

It was economic inequality that hampered the ability of the uplanders to meet the regime's standard of "cultured life" rather than any form of alleged resistance to it. The local ALP organs, though, rather than reflecting on the structures that generated the slow pace of social and cultural transformations in the uplands, elaborated a narrative that made the highlands the "Other" of the lowlands, where people resisted change and did not embrace socialist culture. Inequality and a marginalized position vis à vis the administrative and regional economic centers soon unfolded at the discursive level as well. Korça's communist structures that were in charge of cultural policies juxtaposed the positive model of the plains of Maliq with the negative example of the uplands.

According to local ALP organs, in the plains, people used beds, while in the highlands, the people still slept on the ground and used the same rugs to cover themselves throughout the entire winter without washing them once.[60] When it came to eating, the rural population of the plains of Maliq ate in a cultured way, they ate at tables, sat in chairs, and used glasses, personal dishes, forks, and spoons. Once again, the uplands were the counterexample, where cultured eating was not making headway. Even in the 1960s, as this narrative goes, the uplanders still rejected the new ways of life and kept eating like their grandfathers.[61]

None of the local propagandists concluded that the uneven distribution of the state trade and services network, meant to alleviate women's work in the collective farms, amplified these intraregional inequalities. Despite the regime's goal to cover the entire countryside with preschool institutions and stores and use them for social engineering, the decision of December 1961 favored the most productive and largest collective farms, all located on the Korça plateau and in Maliq. The unprofitable cooperatives in the mountainous areas of the country remained marginal to these investments for a long time. The uneven allocation of these services increased the workload of women in the highlands sensibly, es-

---

60 AShV Korçë, Bundle of uncatalogued documents without a collection number, 1961, fl. 2. Lecture of the Democratic Front of Korça on improvement in the lifestyle of the countryside.
61 AShV Korçë, Bundle of uncatalogued documents without a collection number, 1961, fl. 6. Lecture of the Democratic Front of Korça on improvement in the lifestyle of the countryside. On drinking from the same glass in the uplands, AShV Korçë, Bundle of uncatalogued documents without a collection number, 1964, fl. 8 and 17. Report of the presidency of the Korça branch of the Union of Albanian Women on improvement in the economic, social, and cultural conditions of the countryside. February 18, 1964; AShV Korçë, Bundle of uncatalogued documents without a collection number, No year, fl. 3. Report of the Korça Women's Organization on a more cultured life in the countryside.

pecially in the 1960s, when collectivization reached the remotest areas. Patriarchy in the highlands was hard to eliminate as there was negligible state support for women, and the latter found themselves fulfilling their obligations on the collective farms and in their own homes simultaneously.

However, there was another set of nested inequalities within agriculture that also directly impacted the position and status of women between the state farms and the cooperatives. Thus, in 1959, in Korça's state farms, the largest of which was in Maliq, four women held the position of brigadier, and thirty-two others worked in the administration of these economic units. This might seem to be a negligible number, but by the late 1950s, only 190, or 5% of the total 3312 agricultural workers at the state farms were female, while they represented 19.7% of the farms' administration. The picture was different in the collective farms. In the same year, 42.2% of the cooperatives' workforce, 11,533 out of 27,221, was composed of females. Despite the considerable number of women working on the collective farms, there was only one female brigadier, along with seven more women working as accountants. The regime intervened to adjust the gendered imbalances that could be seen in the power distribution of the collective farms. In 1960, the ALP's leadership issued a decision that enforced the creation of social mobility opportunities for women and their participation in the commanding positions of the collective farms. Within the same year, four women were promoted to head or vice chair of the collective farms where they worked, while the number of accountants increased slightly, from seven to eleven.[62]

Education became a powerful tool for women in exploiting the opportunity structure of the socialist system and to ascend the bureaucratic and power apparatus. Rising within the ranks of administration and occupying important positions in either the industrial or agricultural sectors required a minimum level of professional education. The regime's efforts started producing results by the early 1960s. Thus, in 1961, in the entire district of Korça, there were 2423 women with 7-years of schooling, 567 with high school, and 78 women with a university degree. That same year, in the district's elementary schools there were 7197 girls,

---

62 On the number of women working in the administration and leading positions in the state farms and cooperatives, AShV Korçë, F. 3/2, Komiteti i PPSh Rrethi Korçë, 1959, Lista 15, d. 65, fl. 26-27. Memo on the work of the ALP's organization in the district of Korça for the rise of women in responsibility. September 9, 1959. On the ALP's order to promote women, AShV Korçë, F. 3/2, Komiteti i PPSh Rrethi Korçë, 1961, Lista 17, d. 13, fl. 27. Memo of the ALP's Committee of Korça on the schooling and technical-professional education of women and their promotion to positions with responsibility. January 24, 1961.

FIGURE 13. Young women working in the laboratory of the sugar factory of Maliq

2971 were studying in high schools, and 309 were at university. A generation of women accessed education and the opportunities that it opened for social mobility within the socialist context. Additionally, behind these optimistic figures of the ALP's statistics, there were broader spatial and social inequalities that determined women's careers that remained hidden.[63]

First, there was a sharp geographic unevenness in the quality of education. The best teachers worked in urban schools. Additionally, while the 7-year school in Maliq, which was famous in all the district for its electrical clock, running water, centralized heating, and fifteen very qualified teachers—two-thirds of the pedagogical staff in the area did not have the proper qualifications.[64] The distribution of competent and unqualified teachers in the Maliq area, which included villages from both the lowlands and uplands, was based on topographical lines. Some of the best 7-year schools in the Korça countryside were in the plains of

---

63 AShV Korçë, F. 3/2, Komiteti i PPSh Rrethi Korçë, 1961, Lista 17, d. 8, fl. 42. Report of the ALP's Committee of Korça concerning the measures for the schooling and technical-professional education of women and their rise in responsibility. December 21, 1961.
64 On the 7-year school of Maliq, Nesti Furrxhi, "Më e mira në rrethin e Korçës" [The best in the district of Korça], *Bashkimi*, July 1, 1959, 157 (4338): 3. On the underqualification of two thirds of the pedagogical staff in the Maliq area, AShV Korçë, F. 3/4, Komiteti i PPSh Rrethi Maliq, 1957, Lista 10, d. 62, fl. 3. Memo on the scientific and ideologic content of instruction in the elementary and 7-year schools.

Maliq, as was the case with those of the villages of Vashtëmi and Pirg.[65] No school from the highlands ever made its way to the top rankings.

The quality of education was strongly correlated to the uneven distribution of the skilled workforce. The bulk of the technocrats in the Korça region worked and lived in Maliq. By the second half of the 1970s, out of the 5100 employees of the state farm, there were 255 specialists with vocational school education and 74 with a university degree. Moreover, thanks to continuing education courses and part-time schools, the agricultural enterprises of the plain of Maliq had some of the most educated and qualified farmers in the entire country. Of the 25 engineers in the district of Korça, 15 worked in the town of Maliq, while 24 of the 64 agronomists and veterinarians in the region worked on the collective farms located on the plains. If we include doctors and teachers, then the number of those with a university degree increases considerably. Moreover, 900 peasants from the villages on the plain of Maliq worked in the combine for half the year.[66]

For all of these specialists with university degrees or vocational training, their good biographies, party membership, and loyalty, education were critical to their promotion. The ALP's leadership, which knew that loyalty without skills was not enough, ordered all of its members holding key administrative and economic positions within the power apparatus to attend various levels of professional ed-

---

65 AShV Korçë, F. 3/4, Komiteti i PPSh Maliq, 1957, Lista 10, d. 30, fl. 7. Information on the situation of state education in the district of Maliq.

66 On the number of engineers, agronomists, veterinarians, and agricultural technicians working in Maliq, AShV Korçë, F. 3/1, Komiteti i PPSh Qarku Korçë, 1958, Lista 9, d. 1, fl. 4. Memo concerning propaganda with a lecture on the region. January 15, 1958; AShV Korçë, F. 3/2, Komiteti i PPSh Rrethi Korçë, 1960, Lista 16, d. 115, fl. 8-13. List of specialists with a university degree in the agricultural sector in the district of Korça. December 17, 1960. On the number of people with a university education at the Maliq state farm, AQSh, F. 14/AP, Komiteti i PPSh (STR), 1978, d. 415, fl. 104. Report of the Ministry of Agriculture sent to the ALP's Central Committee on some problems for the development of the Maliq state farm. November 30, 1978. On the number of specialists with a vocational education at the Maliq state farm, AQSh, F. 14/AP, Komiteti i PPSh (STR), 1975, d. 814, fl. 36. Report on the work of the ALP's organization of the Maliq state farm for increasing the role of the communists and mobilizing forces for meeting the state plan. On the courses held at the Maliqi state farm for the qualification of the agricultural workers, AQSh, F. 14/AP, Komiteti i PPSh (STR), 1973, d. 546, fl. 5. Information on the education of the workers at the state farms of Maliq. On the level of education of the peasants of the plain of Maliq, AQSh, F. 14/AP, Komiteti i PPSh (OU), 1976, d. 99, fl. 2. Minutes of the meeting of the Secretaries of the ALP's Central Committee. October 1, 1976. On engineers and laboratory technicians, AQSh, F. 497, Ministria e Industrisë së Lehtë Ushqimore, 1977, d. 149, fl. 29. Study on the improvement of the processes of the cultivation, transportation, and processing of sugar beet. On the number of doctors, nurses, teachers, and specialized workers, AShV Korçë, F. 3/1, Komiteti i PPSh Qarku Korçë, 1958, Lista 9, d. 8, fl. 14. Information on the specialist staff in the locality of Maliq. On the number of peasants employed part-time at the combine, AShV Korçë, F. 3/2, Komiteti i PPSh Rrethi Korçë, 1952, Lista 8, d. 64, fl. 3. Report from the party control committee in the "November 8th" sugar combine in Maliq. October 7, 1952.

ucation. The training of this class of rulers required them to develop skills to lead, understand, and implement orders, and to perform the necessary functions within the structures of the socialist managerial state.[67] As a result, the groups that composed the backbone of the power structure and who also lived in the urban and industrial centers were those more tightly connected to education. In Bourdieu's terms, they developed a habitus that represented a set of dispositions constructed by the new white-collar group under socialism, where knowledge and education played a central role in their status and social standing.[68] As a consequence, the members of this professional group that emerged at the beginning of the regime's life started reproducing their privileged position within the society.[69] This was the communist power establishment, which the Montenegrin dissident Milovan Djilas christened in the 1960s as the "unperfect society," and which the historians Stephen Kotkin and Jan Gross have termed "uncivil society," clearly counterposing it to liberal civil society.[70]

Ironically, education, which was meant as an instrument of emancipation, became in practice one of the primary means for the preservation of access to the power structure and to the reproduction of social inequalities. The majority of the peasants and workers did not support their children going to the gymnasiums (preparatory high schools) or other professional schools but regarded them instead as part of the agriculture labor force. Based on the ALP structures realized in Maliq in 1980, those who invested more in the education of their children were clerks and technocrats.[71] This was reprehensible for an allegedly socialist state and society. Once the power structure reached maturity, many of its members realized that rather than blurring and eliminating class divisions, socialism indeed

---

67 On the education of clerks and cadres, AShV Korçë, F. 3/2, Komiteti i PPSh Rrethi Korçë, 1961, Lista 17, d. 4, fl. 9. Report on the work of the ALP's committee with the local councils of the district; AShV Korçë, F. 3/1, Komiteti i PPSh Qarku Korçë, 1958, Lista 9, d. 8, fl. 11-12. Report on the ideological education of the communists in the locality of Maliq; AShV Korçë, F. 3/1, Komiteti i PPSh Rrethi Maliq, 1958, Lista 11, d. 2, fl. 31. Memo concerning the communist cadres in the locality of Maliq for the year 1957.

68 On Bourdieu's formulation of habitus, see Pierre Bourdieu, *The Logic of Practice*, trans. Richard Nice (Stanford, CA: Stanford University Press, 1990), 52–65.

69 Historian Shannon Woodcock has also explored how the interplay of education and gender has reinforced privilege and power in communist Albania. For more, see Shannon Woodcock, *Life is War: Surviving Dictatorship in Communist Albania* (Bristol, UK: HammerOn Press, 2016).

70 Milovan Djilas, *The Unperfect Society: Beyond the New Class*, trans. Dorian Cooke (New York: Harcourt, Brace & the World, 1969). See also Milovan Djilas, *The New Class: An Analysis of the Communist System* (New York: Frederick A. Praeger, 1957). Stephen Kotkin, *Uncivil Society: 1989 and the Implosion of the Communist Establishment*, with contributions by Jan T. Gross (New York: Modern Library, 2010), 11–16.

71 AShV Korçë, Bundle of uncataloged documents without a collection number, 1981, fl. 34-36. Some conclusions from a study on family psychology in the district of Korça. January 20, 1980.

produced and reinforced them. Ironically, a political and economic system that claimed to represent an alliance of workers and peasants and ruled on their behalf ended up creating a vast bureaucratic apparatus to rule them instead.

The girls who went to study at university and who moved up to hold leadership positions overwhelmingly came from parents who worked as specialists and technocrats. They were from urban centers and the villages of the plains. Thus, their success, which appeared to demonstrate the regime's alleged success in flattening gender inequalities on the surface, expressed the fractures of multiple disparities that the regime's industrialization had produced. It exposed the differentiation of economically and administratively more privileged areas in the plains of Maliq from those areas comprising the uplands. The sugar industry and the important role it played in the regional and national economy was one of the primary structural factors that augmented the number and importance of the group of specialists and technocrats. It provided them with power and enhanced the opportunities for many of the girls from the plateau of Korça to pursue university studies. The social and spatial hierarchies mutually constituted, reinforced, and consolidated each other.

Love for the Plain

The industrialization of the plateau of Korça, where the sugar industry occupied a central role, created a regional economic system that constructed spatial inequalities. The plains and the cities of Maliq and Korça, represented the core area. The uplands became peripheral areas that orbited around the regional center located in the plains. Besides raw materials, the highlands supplied the industrial centers with a workforce. In the second half of the 1940s and in early 1950s, the communist regime had a hard time extracting a surplus workforce from the highlands. Thus, from 1945 to 1950, the urban population in the district of Korça grew meagerly from 24,602 to 27,447. However, by the end of the decade, the situation had radically changed. From 1945 to 1961, the total population of the district grew from 103,531 people in 1945 to 139,465 in 1960. The most dramatic increase was that of the urban population, which, by 1960, had jumped to 45,828, while the rural population grew from 78,929 to 93,637. It was not natural growth that almost doubled the urban population but rather rural migration, which explains the moderate rate of demographic increase in the countryside.[72]

---

72   On population growth in the district of Korça, AShV Korçë, F. 3/2, Komiteti i PPSh Rrethi Korçë, 1961, Lista 17, d. 103, fl. 64. The growth of the population in the district of Korça. On rural migra-

By the late 1950s, agriculture in Albania had lost its status as a profession, a process that, as Sheila Fitzpatrick has argued, took place in the Soviet Union during the 1930s.[73] In Korça, too, the state organs identified the widespread tendency, especially among many young men from the uplands, to seek jobs outside of agriculture and to move to towns, something that they noted with great concern.[74] In the 1980s, Anna Kutrzeba-Pojnarowa observed that scientific and technical changes had diluted the attachment of peasants to the land and agriculture.[75] According to her, the youth's disinterest in following their family tradition and working in the fields was especially strong in the villages close to industrial centers, where the young people preferred to pursue other modes of life. While this statement holds some truth to it, it also needs adjustment and further elaboration in the context of Maliq. The mechanization of agriculture indeed created surplus labor, while the industry soaked it up and introduced youth to the excitement of urban life. However, working in factories and living in shacks for long periods of time was not very exciting either.

Technological changes alone do not explain everything, especially in socialist systems, where political decisions had critical importance in understanding the steep increase in rural–urban migration. The state's strategy to subordinate agriculture to industry, the allocation of the bulk of the resources to the secondary sector, and the concentration of investments in the lowlands explain the estrangement of many Albanian peasants, especially uplanders, from agriculture. The regime's efforts to recover farming's lost prestige among the youth by explaining to them the alleged outstanding potential and perspectives that lay in the countryside were unsuccessful.[76] Instead, the only way to restrain the growing desire to move outside of agriculture would be to fix the structural imbalances between worker and peasant incomes. The regime neither leveled the differences

---

    tions as the major source of urban growth in the district of Korça, AShV Korçë, F. 3/2, Komiteti i PPSh Rrethi Korçë, 1961, Lista 17, d. 33, fl. 69-72. Report on the resolution of residency requests (*pasaportizim*) for the years 1960–1961. December 9, 1961.
73 Sheila Fitzpatrick, *Stalin's Peasants: Resistance and Survival in the Russian Village after Collectivization* (Oxford: Oxford University Press, 1994), 92–95 and 148–151.
74 AShV Korçë, F. 3/2, Komiteti i PPSh Rrethi Korçë, 1960, Lista 16, d. 63, fl. 4. Draft-report on the work of the ALP among the youth.
75 Anna Kutrzeba-Pojnarowa, "The Influence of the History of Peasantry on the Model of the Traditional Peasant Culture and the Mechanisms of its Transformations," in *The Peasant and the City in Eastern Europe: Interpreting Structures*, eds. Irene Portis Winner and Thomas G. Winner (Cambridge, MA: Schenkman Publishing Company, 1984), 94.
76 AShV Korçë, F. 3/2, Komiteti i PPSh Rrethi Korçë, 1960, Lista 16, d. 63, fl. 4. Draft-report on the work of the ALP among the youth.

CHAPTER 3

in incomes between farmers of cooperatives and state employees, nor did it improve rural infrastructure, resulting in many youngsters from the uplands migrating towards the core national or regional economic centers. Indeed, the uneven development was more convenient for the ALP regime. Raising the wages for the more than 60% of the national workforce employed on collective farms would be for too expensive for Tirana's meager coffers.

The migration of many youngsters from rural areas and the highlands to the urban and industrial centers in the lowlands panicked many communist cadres, whose majority, ironically, were of peasant backgrounds themselves. When the communists came into power, Albania had roughly 26,000 workers. The industrialization of the country swelled the latter's ranks. Thus, in 1960, there were 145,000 workers, and in 1982, that number had jumped to 550,000.[77] As explained above, the countryside was the pool from which the communist regime extracted the industrial workforce. In 1972, for example, half the workers in the Korça region were of peasant backgrounds. However, the large share of peasants among the ranks of the socialist working class was a source of concern for the local ALP Committee, which sounded the alarm.

In 1972, only 28% of the workers met the norm. According to the top cadres of Korça, the reason for this low performance lay in their origins. These newly made workers, the local party leadership complained, brought with them the backward mentality of the countryside, put their personal interests above that of the collectivity, and kept the work pace low. Moreover, the majority of them lacked any sense of self-improvement, and only a few of the workers from peasant backgrounds pursued professional qualifications. Such an attitude, concluded the ALP Committee of Korça, demonstrated that their petit bourgeoisie mentality conflicted with the socialist ethos of work.[78] These prejudices towards the peasants were by no means limited to the district of Korça alone. Officials of the Ministry of Justice, too, explained the alarming rate of turnover in industries on the high number of workers from rural backgrounds. Being freshly recruited,

---

77 On the increase in the number of workers in 1945 and 1960, Durmishi, *Punëtorët në Shqipëri (1945–1960)*, 81–119; On the number of workers in 1982, Harilla Papajorgji, *Struktura socialklasore a klasës sonë punëtore* [The social structure of our working class] (Tirana: 8 Nëntori, 1985), 68.
78 AShV Korçë, F. 3/2, Komiteti i PPSh Rrethi Korçë, 1972, Lista 28, d. 43, fl. 3-4. Report of the ALP's Committee of Korça regarding the fight it waged against the handicraft concept of work. February 26, 1972; AShV Korçë, F. 3/2, Komiteti i PPSh Rrethi Korçë, 1970, Lista 26, d. 6, fl. 3-4. Study of the ALP's Committee of Korça on the condition of the working class. January 13, 1970.

they argued, these workers lacked work-consciousness.[79] Nobody mentioned, though, the terrible living conditions and the arbitrary attitude of the administration of the industrial enterprises.

In all cases, party and state bureaucrats did nothing else but reiterate Enver Hoxha. In April 1949, the ALP's leader, announcing his support for Lenin, accused the peasants of being petit bourgeoisie who were against state control, regardless of capitalism and socialism. Two years later, in 1951, Mehmet Shehu reiterated the same conclusion and even stated that peasants were hampering the emergence of light industry.[80] All these statements expose the shallowness of the ALP regime's Leninist slogan of representing an alliance between the working class and the peasantry. Contrary to their public declarations, the ALP's cadres, similar to Lenin, distrusted the peasants and firmly believed that they opposed socialism.

In the eyes of the urban-based power holders, the peasants were corrupting socialism by ruralizing the working class. Keeping the peasants at a distance from the workers' centers was necessary for the socialist project. Thus, the ALP's power apparatus ideologically justified rural retention as desirable for the preservation of the purity of the working class. Reinstating clear-cut boundaries between workers and peasants became necessary, in the belief of the top Albanian communists. It simultaneously meant reinforcing the spatial inequalities by limiting access to the privileged areas and economic sectors. Indeed, the disparities between the city and countryside under communism expressed the spatial distribution of social hierarchies that were inherent to the model of the workers' state. Considering this a threat to socialism, the Albanian communist leadership constructed a scale of importance that subordinated the peasants to the workers. Additionally, despite its claims to obliterate the vertical and horizontal spatial inequalities, the Tirana regime's policies in fact both generated and preserved them.

In addition to the ideological anxieties related to the construction of socialism, there were also other important factors of an economic nature that concerned the Albanian communist leadership with respect to the growing levels of rural migration. First of all, the country's industry could not absorb all the

---

79   On the conclusions for the lack of the peasants' work conscience, AQSh, F. 515, Ministria e Drejtësisë, 1952, d. 5, fl. 16. Memo on crimes in 1952 in comparison to 1951.
80   On Hoxha's report, AQSh, F. 14/AP, Komiteti i PPSh (OU), 1949, d. 1, fl. 22-29. Report of Enver Hoxha given at the II Plenum of the ALP's Central Committee. April 28–30, 1949. On Mehmet Shehu's statement, AQSh, F. 14/AP, Komiteti i PPSh (OU), 1950, d. 16, fl. 11. Report of Mehmet Shehu given at the Plenum of ALP's Central Committee. August 11, 1950.

rural migrants. In 1961, unemployment in the urban centers of Korça district reached the figure of 4257 people, which alarmed the ALP's local organs. Moreover, the state authorities could not afford to build new apartments for them.[81] At this point, the central authorities decided to bring uncontrolled migration to a halt. To stop it, they devised a system of legal and administrative restrictions that were intended to fix people to their place of inhabitation and work, known as the *pashaportizimi*.[82]

Besides enforcing administrative barriers, the regime also started propaganda campaigns to convince the peasants not to leave their villages. In the region of Korça, the tendency towards migration was stronger among the uplanders, who targeted the regional urban centers and the plains of Maliq. The local organs of the regime organized campaigns among the highlanders to inculcate a love for their villages. Alas, despite the efforts of the ALP's regional structures, the will of the peasants from the mountain villages to migrate to the lowlands and the cities only grew stronger. Despite the state's measures, the living conditions for the uplanders remained much lower compared to those experienced by the lowlanders.

The constant increase in the productivity and revenue of the collective farms contrasted with the poor performance of the cooperatives in the highlands. The vertical disparities between the plains of Maliq and the surrounding hills and mountains kept growing.[83] In order to bypass the legal barriers, the uplanders pursued strategies that destabilized both the administrative restrictions and the puritan moral tenets of the regime. Although the state banned the buying of houses without prior permission, dozens of families settled without permission. The efforts of the ALP's local committees notwithstanding, many families bought their homes from the current owners without the prior approval of the state or-

---

81 On the increase in unemployment, AShV Korçë, F. 3/2, Komiteti i PPSh Rrethi Korçë, 1961, Lista 17, d. 107, fl. 1. Memo of the ALP's Committee of Korça regarding the problem of unemployment. November 24, 1961. On the lack of financial resources for housing, AShV Korçë, F. 3/2, Komiteti i PPSh Rrethi Korçë, 1961, Lista 17, d. 33, fl. 69-72. Report on the resolution of residency requests for the years 1960–1961. December 9, 1961.

82 On rural retention in Albania, Derek R. Hall, *Albania and the Albanians* (London: Pinter References, 1994), 67–68; Örjan Sjöberg, "Rural Retention in Albania: Administrative Restrictions on Urban-Bound Migration," *East European Quarterly* 7, no. 2 (1994): 205–234; Georges Frélastre, "Retention of the Rural Population in Eastern Europe," in *Staying On: Retention and Migration in Peasant Societies*, ed. José Havet (Ottawa: Ottawa University Press, 1988), 197–199.

83 AShV Korçë, Bundle of uncataloged documents without a collection number, 1983, fl. 17-18. Report of the Democratic Front of Korça on its activity to reinforce the unity between the Party and the people. July 11, 1983.

gans, moved in, and then asked for residency permits after the fact.[84] However, many people, especially the youth, pursued other, more efficient strategies that exploited legal loopholes to their advantage.

The right that partners had to transfer their wives or husbands transformed marriage into a privileged mechanism for migration, especially among young women from the highlands. Many young women refused the advances of the young men in their hamlets and sought to marry in the villages located on the plains of Maliq. There were cases when young women who were members of ALP organizations married men with anti-party pasts from the towns for the sole purpose of moving out of their villages. On one occasion, a twenty-three-year-old woman from a hamlet in Gora married a fifty-two-year-old man from Maliq. The local ALP council considered this arrangement unacceptable and did not allow them to marry. According to the communist authorities, this was a relationship that was based on "material interests" rather than on love. Even ALP members from Gora, Opar, and Gramsh did not show much love for their highland villages. Instead, they sought to marry their daughters in Maliq, Korça, or in the villages of the plains, which enraged the local communist leadership. As a result, by the late 1960s, many hamlets in the highlands had a considerable surplus of unmarried men. Facing the discrepancy between groom surpluses and bride shortages, many young men resorted to the old and glorious Albanian highland custom of wife abduction.[85]

Young men also used marriage as a strategy to move to town. As pointed out by a report from the ALP's Committee of Maliq that was prepared in 1988 with a pronounced nostalgia for the past: "It is an undeniable fact that it has been an Albanian custom that the bride goes to her husband's house after the wedding. Unfortunately, this beautiful tradition has started to decline."[86] The gender hi-

---

84 AShV Korçë, F. 3/2, Komiteti i PPSh Rrethi Korçë, 1961, Lista 17, d. 33, fl. 69-72. Report on the resolution of residency requests (*pashaportizimi*) for the years 1960–1961. December 9, 1961; AShV Korçë, F. 42, Komiteti Ekzekutiv i Komitetit të PPSh Maliq, 1988, uncatalogued files without a number (19), fl. 10, Kutia 3397. Conclusions regarding the increase in the population of Maliq. April 1, 1988.

85 On marriage with age differences and the bad example of the communists of Gora and Opar, AShV Korçë, F. 42, Komiteti Ekzekutiv i Komitetit të PPSh Maliq, 1988, uncatalogued files without a number, Kutia 3397. Conclusions regarding the increase in the population of Maliq. April 1, 1988. On the surplus of unmarried men, AShV Korçë, F. 3/2, Komiteti i PPSh Rrethi Korçë, 1974, Lista 30, d. 71, fl. 6-7. Opinions on marriages and divorces in the district of Korça. May 16, 1974; AShV Korçë, Bundle of uncatalogued documents without a collection number, 1981, fl. 39. Conclusions from a study on family psychology in the district of Korça. January 20, 1980. On the abduction of wives, AShV Korçë, F. 3/2, Komiteti i PPSh Rrethi Korçë, 1974, Lista 30, d. 69, fl. 74. Information on the moral and political attitude in the collective farms of the area of Gora-Moglica. November 14, 1974.

86 AShV Korçë, F. 42, Komiteti Ekzekutiv i Komitetit të PPSh Maliq, 1988, uncatalogued files without a number (19), fl. 5, Kutia 3397. Conclusions regarding the increase in the population of Maliq. April 1, 1988.

erarchies and norms related to the patriarchal household were under attack. For decades, the ALP had attacked the patriarchalism of the past. However, when it came to controlling peoples' movements, the communist cadres rediscovered the usefulness of some of the customs they had assaulted for years. Additionally, when the communist structures realized that patriarchalism established a rigid pattern of gender mobility, they considered parts of this tradition as beautiful. It is important to note that such an attitude not only demonstrates the communists' selective use of patriarchy, it also reveals that the ALP's power apparatus never entirely rejected the patriarchal gender hierarchies, and always tried to reinforce them in practice.

The Executive Committee of Korça took measures to enforce the "beautiful" custom and the hierarchy of gender relations. In 1984, it ordered the moving of male spouses to their wives' residences to be halted, and the local organs only approved female spouses to change residences. According to this rule only women could travel to live with their husbands, and not vice versa.[87] Notwithstanding the cadres' complaints and the state's orders, young men from the highlands continued searching for potential marriages that would allow them to move into the lowlands. Even the prevalent taboos did not restrain them from marrying older women, divorced women or women with children, women with physical anomalies, or even those with "bad morals". One of the most notorious cases was that of a young man from a village who married a woman eight years older than himself and who was previously divorced with three children. According to the party functionaries, this "scandalous" case demonstrated that this choice was not based on love but instead based on calculations to "win the city." Many of these men, once they obtained their new residence, divorced their spouse and married other women who were usually from their native village. To bring such a phenomenon to an end, the authorities in Maliq threatened that all newcomers would lose their residence if they separated from their wives.[88]

---

[87] On the order of the Executive Committee of Korça, AShV Korçë, F. 42, Komiteti Ekzekuti i Komitetit të PPSh Maliq, 1988, uncatalogued files without a number (19), fl. 8, Kutia 3397. Conclusions regarding the increase in the population of Maliq. April 1, 1988.

[88] On "scandalous" marriages and other strategies to move to the state farm, AShV Korçë, F. 42, Komiteti Ekzekuti i Komitetit të PPSh Maliq, 1988, uncatalogued files without number (19), fl. 8, Kutia 3397. Conclusions regarding the increase in the population of Maliq. April 1, 1988; Maliq Zambak Shënollari, informal interview with Artan Hoxha, Maliq, Albania, January 21, 2018; Perit Kume, informal interview with Artan Hoxha, Maliq, Albania, January 21, 2018. On the threat of the local authorities to oppose the residency of newcomers who divorced their wives, AShV Korçë, F. 42, Komiteti Ekzekuti i Komitetit të PPSh Maliq, 1988, uncataloged files without a number, Kutia 3397. Conclusions regarding the mechanical increase in the population of Maliq. April 1, 1988.

In communist Albania, opportunities had a topographical profile: employment opportunities were located in state enterprises in the lowlands, with these opportunities paying better than those on collective farms. There were fewer opportunities and lower pay in settlements that were at higher altitudes.[89] In Maliq, it was the sugar combine that created these opportunities. The refinery was at the center of a regional economic system that rewarded those who lived on the plain. This meant high salaries for the workers and the hundreds of peasants who worked there part-time, as well as relatively good remuneration on the state farm and on the other collective farms that supplied the refinery with sugar beet. The people of Maliq had greater resources and better access to the increasing range of market goods that were entering into people's lives. The failure to impose uniformity in material life, though, had a considerable impact. It laid bare the marginalization of large swaths of the population, especially those peoples inhabiting the uplands. In communist systems, exclusion not only took place along class lines, but along spatial lines as well. The closer one was to the state, the greater access one had to the benefits the power structure controlled and distributed. It was not only the social hierarchies that created identities in communist Albania, but also the distance from the state. The regime, with its bureaucratic allocation of resources, produced a series of spatial hierarchies, placing the highlands at the end of the remuneration scale. As the peasants of Gora used to say, "if you want to marry off your son, you need to find him a state job."[90]

The plains of Maliq were closer to state power. The sugar combine and the state farm were among the most prominent enterprises representing the presence of the state in the regional economy, as well as the privileges that were related to it. As in Manush Myftiu's story of the well, the sugar industry in the plains of Maliq consumed a large share of the capital that the central authorities allocated to the region. Those who were closer to this gravitational point benefited the most from a system that was based on the unequal distribution of resources that prioritized state employees. Additionally, these employees mainly comprised the inhabitants of the city of Maliq and the villages of the state farm. They were all newcomers and lived better than they did in the older communities of the plain and had a much better quality of life compared to the villages in the uplands that

---

89 On the inequalities of revenues in the Albanian countryside following the topography, see Lulzim Hana and Ilia Telo, *Tranzicioni në Shqipëri: arritje dhe sfida* [Transition in Albania: Achievements and challenges] (Tirana: Akademia e Shkencave të Shqipërisë, 2005), 50.
90 AShV Korçë, F. 3/2, Komiteti i PPSh Rrethi Korçë, 1974, Lista 30, d. 69, fl. 73-74. Information on the moral and political attitude on the collective farms of the area of Gora-Moglica. November 14, 1974.

they had left behind when they migrated. Even today, these people still take pride when they compare their life during communism to life in the other surrounding rural communities, where not all people are nostalgic for the past system. As we will see in the fifth chapter, in Maliq, too, people remember the communist era with strong doses of sentimentalism. Besides having a history, the memory of communism also has a geographical economy, and it is shaped, among others, by the spatial inequalities that it fostered.

CHAPTER 4

Maliq and the World

A Tapestry of Transnational Exchanges

Things, objects, and commodities, says Igor Kopytoff, have biographies, careers, and social lives in the same way that people do. They have a history, which should be conceived of as a diagram of motions, of people handing them to one another, and making different uses of them. In other words, societies construct objects as they construct people.[1] The history of sugar is made up of constant movements that connect the people who cultivate, process, and trade sugar cane and sugar beet with those who pour the final product into their cups of coffee and tea. Looking at a grain of sugar, the observer sees the vast global socioeconomic forces that shape the lives of those who produce it and the tastes of those who consume it. The links that connect the hard labor in the fields to the sweet pleasure of those who consume it contain transnational connections that tie the world into one single unit. To understand the links that sugar creates, it is necessary to investigate all levels of production, distribution, exchange, and consumption.[2]

---

1   Igor Kopytoff, "The Cultural Biography of Things: Commoditization as Process," in *The Social Life of Things: Commodities in Cultural Perspective*, ed. Arjun Appadurai (Cambridge: Cambridge University Press, 1986), 64–90.
2   This component of my analysis is based on the article of Arjun Appadurai, "Introduction: Commodities and the Politics of Value," in *The Social Life of Things*, 3–63. Another important work that stresses the relation between production, consumption, and larger social transformation is that of Sidney W. Mintz, *Sweetness and Power: The Place of Sugar in Modern History* (London: Penguin Books, 1985); Sidney W. Mintz, "Notes toward a Cultural Construction of Modern Foods," *Social Anthropology* 17, no. 2 (2009): 209–216; Ralph S. Hattox, *Coffee and Coffeehouses: The Origins of a Social Beverage in the Medieval Near East* (Seattle: Washington University Press, 1985). On the interplay between production, consumption, and transnational connections during socialism see Mary C. Neuburger, *Balkan Smoke: Tobacco and the Making of Modern Bulgaria* (Ithaca, NY: Cornell University Press, 2013); Paulina Bren and Mary C. Neuburger, eds., *Communism Unwrapped: Consumption in Cold War Eastern Europe* (Oxford: Oxford University Press, 2012); David Crowley and Susan E. Reid, eds., *Pleasures*

CHAPTER 4

If a single grain of sugar contains all this, what of its production site? What can we discover when we look at the development and history of such a site? What broader history do we find in the biography of a place like Maliq? These questions came to my mind one morning in the summer of 2016 when I was visiting Maliq. That morning, I sat with some locals on the porch of a coffee shop along the "Bonifikimi" (Reclamation) promenade under some tall pine trees next to a theater; an edifice of 1950's Soviet-style neoclassical construction. The fresh morning air, the scent of dew, coffee accompanied by a cigarette, and a thin column of grey smoke climbing into the air facilitated our conversation. We touched on many aspects of Maliq's past with great pleasure. My interlocutors enjoyed recalling their lives and merging them with the wider story of Albania's land of sugar.

The story of Maliq is also the story of the many transnational connections, encounters, and exchanges that have crossed Albania's borders. In the 1950s, families lived with teams of Soviet engineers and technicians who helped the Albanians build the sugar refinery. Those I spoke with explained the impact that these foreign specialists had on town life. Maliq, one local told me while taking a drag from his cigarette, was built from scratch and its initial inhabitants were illiterate or half-literate upland peasants. The Soviets, in his words, were "our window to the world" and "introduced the newly urbanized villagers to a new lifestyle and culture."[3] My interlocutors recalled the parties the Soviets organized every weekend—at which they taught the Albanians to dance the foxtrot (and even to make vodka). There, in the atmosphere created around the sugar factory, a new world was in the making, a world created by contacts, connections, exchanges, and lived experiences.

Besides the sugar refinery project, the Soviets also set the blueprint for the new industrial town. The legacy of communist Albania's romance with the USSR during the 1950s remains and is recorded in its buildings. Maliq's structures are not too dissimilar from those in many other small towns built after World War II in the Soviet sphere; they are texts written in brick and mortar that tell us how the town belonged to a much wider transnational cultural socialist space. The fa-

---

in *Socialism: Leisure and Luxury in the Eastern Bloc* (Evanston, IL: Northwestern University Press, 2010); Susan E. Reid and David Crowley, eds., *Style and Socialism: Modernity and Material Culture in Post-War Eastern Europe* (Oxford: Oxford University Press, 2000).

3   Festim Tomori, informal interview by Artan Hoxha, Maliq, Albania, July 20, 2016; Fredi Vangjeli, informal interview by Artan Hoxha, Maliq, July 20, 2016; Pandeli Prifti, informal interview by Artan Hoxha, Maliq, July 20, 2016; Piro Lazi, informal interview by Artan Hoxha, Tirana, November 11, 2017.

cades, urban planning, and architectural models are not, however, the only tokens of the expansion of Soviet influence to the shores of the Mediterranean. Although the sugar factory has long since closed, the architectonic legacy of the town and its identity remain largely intact. Unlike the large cities of post-Socialist Albania, Maliq did not experience a construction boom after the fall of communism and its face has remained largely unchanged. There are only a few new buildings: a seldom used mosque, an Orthodox church surrounded by willows, some villas, and a series of coffee shops.

Communist Albania's land of sugar connected the people who lived there to the world—and not only to the socialist world. In Maliq, Bulgarian, Romanian, Yugoslav, Italian, and Polish specialists worked in the combine to refine red sugar from Cuba. The farms of the plain cultivated selected strains of sugar beet imported from the USSR, Czechoslovakia, Hungary, East Germany, France, and the Netherlands. The combine had technology of Soviet, Bulgarian, Polish, Romanian, Yugoslav, West German, Italian, Belgian, and even Japanese provenance. Maliq emerges as a site where intersected pluri-directional influences weaved a texture with many threads from a myriad of places. What does this fabric of connections tell us about the most isolated and least developed socialist country in Europe?

Maliq's story is similar to that of the North Korean city of Hamhŭng and its vinalon factory. Pyongyang's xenophobic and isolationist regime has constructed a narrative about the development of its major chemical industry that supports the myth of self-reliance. Official North Korean propaganda claims that the idea of the establishment of the vinalon industry in Hamhŭng originated after the communist takeover and that the country developed this industry and rebuilt the city with its "own forces." However, as has been proven, the entire project started in the era of Japanese rule and developed with substantial foreign aid, especially from East Germany.[4] In 1953, at the height of the friendship between Tirana and Moscow, Enver Hoxha claimed that it was the Soviets who decided to build the sugar combine.[5] Like the vinalon city, the transformation of Maliq into the center of sugar production in Albania started in the interwar era. The Italians pushed the project further after invading Albania in 1939. Unlike

---

4   Cheehyung Harrison Kim, "North Korea's Vinalon City: Industrialism as Socialist Everyday Life," *positions: asia critique* 22, no. 4 (2014): 809–836.
5   AQSh, F. 14/AP (OU), 1953, d. 2, fl. 126. Report on the measures for the improvement and development of agriculture. March 2–3, 1953.

CHAPTER 4

Hamhŭng, though, Maliq became an intersection of technologies and knowledge generated on both sides of the Iron Curtain.

In 1945, Albania had no tradition and no expertise in sugar production. At no point during the communist period was it able to build the industrial infrastructure necessary to produce all the machinery and equipment for Maliq domestically. Building the entire sugar complex meant accumulating knowledge from outside the country and implementing it ex novo. During the forty years of operation, the sugar refinery of Maliq became a site where the communist regime used technology and expertise borrowed from both the Soviet bloc and the West. In many ways, Albania's dependency on capital, technology, knowledge, and expertise from more developed countries was similar to the experience of the new post-colonial states of the Global South. Countries like Kenya, Algeria, Syria, and Indonesia were locales of fierce competition between the two superpowers and their respective allies, each of whom advocated their own specific path to modernity.[6]

Even the Soviets considered Albania to be a country that shared many similarities with the Third World. Khrushchev, who did not divide the world into only East and West but also into the undeveloped South and developed North, applied the civilizational gradient to his smaller allies when he considered them hotheaded and irrational southerners. Although small, Albania had a disproportionate influence on the plans of the USSR's post-Stalinist elite and its quest for global supremacy. For the Soviet leadership, Albania, with its Muslim majority population, represented a model for the Third World and Muslim countries; a role that the Kremlin had, until then, reserved for its Caucasian and Central Asian republics. Through the southernmost member of the Soviet bloc, Moscow wanted to provide the new post-colonial states with living proof that socialism was the right developmental alternative for them.[7] However, the ALP leadership did not support these plans and eluded Soviet demands that the country play this role in the Kremlin's Middle Eastern diplomacy.

---

6   Lorenzini, *Global Development: A Cold War History*.
7   Elidor Mëhilli, "Globalized Socialism, Nationalized Time: Soviet Films, Albanian Subjects, and Chinese Audiences across the Sino-Soviet Split," *Slavic Review* 77, 3 (2018): 624; Elidor Mëhilli, *From Stalin to Mao*, 191–192; Elidor Mëhilli, "Defying De-Stalinization: Albania's 1956," *Journal of Cold War Studies* 13, no. 4 (2011): 12–13. On the role of Central Asia and the Caucasus in the Soviet diplomatic strategy of development, see Artemy M. Kalinovsky, *Laboratory of Socialist Development*, 19 and 201; Masha Kirasirova, "'Sons of Muslims' in Moscow: Soviet Central Asian Mediators to the Foreign East, 1955–1962," *Ab Imperio* 4 (2011): 106–132.

What the Soviets—and the Americans—did not understand about Albania and some other developing countries was that their similar recent history shaped their political and economic agendas. The political elites of these latecomers were committed to fast-track modernization and economic self-sufficiency. To paraphrase David Engerman's eloquent formulation: if for the superpowers development was a weapon of the Cold War, for the elites of the developing countries the Cold War was a weapon for achieving modernization.[8] The latter exploited the Cold War to extract expertise, technology, and funding from the competing blocs in order to pursue their own transformative projects, without, however, fulfilling the political demands tied to such aid—much to the frustration of their sponsors.[9] However, for the leaders of the Third World, development and autarky were not ends but instruments for the preservation of their political independence. The Soviet leadership would soon learn that the new elites of the decolonized world were unreliable, capricious, and ideologically unorthodox.[10] Hoxha had the same commitment to political independence and self-sufficiency as Ben Bella in Algeria, Syria's Ba'ath Party, and non-socialist leaders like Nasser, Nehru, Sukarno, and Nkrumah, who sought to modernize their countries using both American and Soviet financial and technological aid.[11]

Albania's historical experience was similar to that of other post-colonial Middle Eastern nation states: a state established from the ashes of the Ottoman Empire that was economically undeveloped and politically weak. Its more powerful neighbors, Yugoslavia, Greece, and Italy, had constantly threatened the country's independence. As can be gleaned from the behavior of Italy during World War II or Tito's Yugoslavia after the war, Albania was a space for expansion and control. In both cases, the political influence started with economic subordination.[12] For the Albanian communist leadership, the result was that

---

8   David C. Engerman, "Development Politics and the Cold War," *Diplomatic History* 41, no. 1 (2017): 18.
9   Corinna Unger, "Histories of Development and Modernization: Findings, Reflections, Future Research," H-Soz-Kult, 09.12.2010, <www.hsozkult.de/literaturereview/id/forschungsberichte-1130>, pp. 15–17.
10 See the contributions in the special issue of *Diplomatic History* 33, no. 3 (2009), which contextualize modernization of the Third World within the framework of the Cold War. See also Alessandro Iandolo, "The Rise and Fall of the 'Soviet Model of Development' in West Africa, 1957–64," *Cold War History* 12, no. 4 (2012): 683–704.
11 On the flirting of the Third World with both superpowers during the Cold War era, see Nathan J. Citino, "Modernization and Development," in *The Routledge Handbook of the Cold War*, eds. Artemy M. Kalinovsky and Craig Daigle (London: Routledge, 2014), 118–130.
12 On Yugoslavia's influence over Albania from 1944 to 1948, see Norman M. Naimark, *Stalin and the Fate of Europe: The Postwar Struggle for Sovereignty* (Cambridge, MA: Harvard University Press, 2019), 54–87; Ana Lalaj, "The Soviet-Yugoslav Break and Albania," *Studia Albanica* 39, no. 2 (2005): 123–127. On the complexity of Albanian-Italian relations during the interwar era, see *Historia e shq-*

economic development remained one of the most important constants of its policy. To attain this goal, even under the yoke of uncompromising Stalinism, Tirana engaged with both Western and Eastern partners. After breaking with Moscow, the ALP leadership had more room to set its own course without being liable to any external power center.

For Albania, as for the other countries of Eastern Europe, modernization was a global enterprise. It was not defined exclusively by one ideology. Modernization for them went beyond the academic debates over whether modernity was a Western liberal ideal or comprised the utilization of advanced technology under authoritarian indigenous institutions. Rather than through ideological orthodoxies and scruples, Hoxha and his associates approached this goal with the mundane calculations of *realpolitik*. In this sense, the ALP leadership's attitude toward modernization was similar to that of many leaders of post-colonial states, who did not worry so much about what exactly modern meant but rather what alternative suited them better.[13] Stalin himself did not see any contradictions when he identified socialism as a combination of American efficiency and Lenin's thought. The multiple exchanges that took place in Maliq also demonstrate how problematic the East–West divide is when it is dissociated from the North–South watershed. The boundaries between these spatial and conceptual categories are blurred, and the circulation, dissemination, and exchange of knowledge, technologies, people, capital, and models across space during the Cold War was multilateral and pluri-directional.

The Maliq project, as part of the ALP's development program, was part of this global trend of development that started before the ALP came to power. The latter simply inherited the baton and intensified the process. Development and socialism cannot be identified simply with steel mills and dams. Beyond

---

iptarëve gjatë shekullit XX [The history of the Albanians during the 20th century], vol. III (Tirana: Botime Albanologjike, 2020), 432–478. Alessandro Roselli, *Italy and Albania: Financial Relations in the Fascist Period* (London: I. B. Tauris, 2006).

13 On the debate on modernity and the Soviet experiment see, Michael David-Fox, "Multiple Modernities vs. Neo-Traditionalism: On Recent Debates in Russian and Soviet History," *Jahrbücher für Geschichte Osteuropas* 54, no. 4 (2006): 535–555; Terry Martin, "Modernization or Neo-Traditionalism? Ascribed Nationality and Soviet Primordialism," in *Stalinism: New Directions*, ed. Sheila Fitzpatrick (London: Routledge, 2000), 348–367; Yanni Kotsonis, "Introduction: A Modern Paradox – Subject and Citizen in Nineteenth- and Twentieth-Century Russia," in *Russian Modernity: Politics, Knowledge, Practices*, eds. David L. Hoffmann and Yanni Kotsonis (London: Routledge, 2000), 1–16; David L. Hoffmann, "European Modernity and Soviet Socialism," *Ibid*, 245–260; See also the articles of Shmuel Eisenstadt, Björn Wittrock, and Johann P. Aranson in the special issue of *Daedalus* dedicated to the topic of multiple modernities, where these authors have engaged with the problem of the modernity of the Soviet model and its experiment. For more see *Daedalus* 129, no. 1 (2000).

the heroic images of heavy industry, metallurgists working among the sparks of melted iron, or welders hanging on top of smokestacks, socialism is made up of more ordinary, less heroic images. After all, life under socialism was not that extraordinary. What is more important is that Maliq became a focal point of transnational transactions that saw the dissemination of new technologies, goods, ideas, forms of work organization, and lifestyles in Albania. What do these exchanges, links, and breaks that occurred in Maliq tell us about Albania, Eastern Europe, the Cold War, and the twentieth century? What hides beneath the story of the dissemination of knowledge and technologies across the East–West and North–South divides?

The transnational historiographic trend of recent decades has effectively decentralized nations, nation states, and/or superpowers from the focus of historical inquiry. Engaging with the human, cultural, and technological exchanges across the East–West and North–South divides, this scholarship has undermined the notion of the rigidity of borders and has questioned the validity of the metaphor of the "Iron Curtain." The complicated web of interactions across the ideological divide has raised doubts over the bipolar division of the world during the years of the Cold War and the alleged interruption of globalization during its first two decades.[14] In this context, some authors have called the fence

---

14 See Dragostinova, *The Cold War from the Margins*; Lorenzini, *Global Development: A Cold War History*; the forum "Beyond the Iron Curtain: Eastern Europe and the Global Cold War," *Slavic Studies* 77, no. 3 (2018): 684; Simon Mikkonen and Pia Koivunen, eds., *Beyond the Divide: Entangled Histories of Cold War Europe* (New York: Berghahn, 2015); Hyung-Gu Lynn, "Globalization and the Cold War," in *The Oxford Handbook of the Cold War*, eds. Richard H. Immerman and Petra Goedde (Oxford: Oxford University Press, 2013), 584–601; Patryk Babiracki and Kenyon Zimmer, eds., *Cold War Crossings: International Travel and Exchange across the Soviet Bloc, 1940s–1960s* (College Station, TX: Texas A&M University Press, 2014); Peter Romijn, Giles Scott-Smith, and Joes Segal, eds., *Divided Dreamworlds? The Cultural Cold War in East and West* (Amsterdam: Amsterdam University Press, 2012); Rana Mitter and Patrick Major, eds., *Across the Blocs: Exploring Comparative Cold War Cultural and Social History* (London: Frank Cass, 2004). On the Soviet Union, see Michael David-Fox, *Showcasing the Great Experiment: Cultural Diplomacy and Western Visitors to the Soviet Union, 1921–1941* (Oxford: Oxford University Press, 2015); Michael David-Fox, *Crossing Borders: Modernity, Ideology, and Culture in Russia and the Soviet Union* (Pittsburgh, PA: University of Pittsburgh Press, 2015). See the special issue of *Diplomatic History* 33, no. 3 (2009) dedicated to the Soviet bloc's efforts to influence and shape the modernization of the Global South. On the role of the perceptions created from exchanges, mobility, and information flows across the East-West divide see György Péteri, ed., *Imagining the West in Eastern Europe and the Soviet Union* (Pittsburgh, PA: University of Pittsburgh Press, 2010); Stephen Lovell, *The Shadow of War: Russia and the USSR, 1941 to the Present* (Oxford: Wiley-Blackwell, 2010), 287–313. For the technology transfer and circulation of scientific knowledge across the East-West divide see Besnik Pula, *Globalization under and after Socialism: The Evolution of Transnational Capital in Central and Eastern Europe* (Stanford, CA: Stanford University Press, 2018), 65–107; Sampsa Kaataja, "Expert Groups Closing the Divide: Estonian-Finnish Computing Cooperation Since 1960s," in *Beyond the Divide*, 101–120; Anssi Halmesvirta, "Hungary Opens Toward the

that cut Europe in half a "nylon curtain" or a "semipermeable membrane."[15] This study on Maliq will contribute to this thriving literature by focusing simultaneously on the intra- and inter-bloc movements of people and the exchange, interconnection, and dissemination of technology, knowledge, and ideas. My goal is to trace the multifaceted relation between the wider political orientation of Albania and its effect on East–West exchanges. This chapter will explore the links that connected Maliq with both competing blocs during the Cold War. While I do not deny the importance of the ideological framework and political expediency, my analysis broadens our field of vision by bringing other variables into the equation. I will argue that broader social dynamics were critical factors that, alongside and interwoven with ideologies and political factors, determined the exchanges and contacts of Hoxha's regime with countries within and outside the socialist bloc. The tapestry that was woven in Maliq includes both continuities and the contingent dynamics of flows in both the West–East and North–South directions.

Maliq and Its East–West Economy of Knowledge

The Albanian communists borrowed their sugar refinery project, and the idea of autarky that undergirded it, from the past. Since the early years of its rule, the ALP's leadership emphasized its commitment to achieving economic autonomy. In 1945, the Ministry of the Economy announced a series of priorities for Albanian industrial development, which argued that the building of an industrial complex would guarantee the country's independence from the caprices of

---

West: Political Preconditions for Finnish-Hungarian Cooperation in Research and Development in the 1960s and 1970s," *Ibid*, 150; Austin Jersild, "The Soviet State as Imperial Scavenger: 'Catch Up and Surpass' in the Transnational Socialist Bloc, 1950–1960," *American Historical Review* 116, no. 1 (2011), 109–132. On the attempts of the countries of the Soviet bloc in the 1970s, to modernize their economies with technology and capital borrowed from Western Europe, see Jan Winiecki, "Soviet-type Economies' Strategy for Catching-up through Technology Import—an Anatomy of Failure," *Technovation* 6, no. 2 (1987): 115–145; Morris Bornstein, *East-West Technology Transfer: The Transfer of Western Technology to the USSR* (Paris: OECD, 1985); Friedrich Levcik and Jiri Skolka, *East-West Technology Transfer: Study of Czechoslovakia* (Paris: OECD, 1984); Philip Hanson, *Trade and Technology Transfer in Soviet-Western Relations* (London: Macmillan Press, 1981); Angela Stent Yergin, *East-West Technology Transfer: European Perspectives* (London: SAGE Publications, 1980); Eugene Zaleski and Helgard Wienert, *Technology Transfer between East and West* (Paris: OECD, 1980).

15 On the definition of "nylon curtain," see György Péteri, "Nylon Curtain–Transnational and Transsystemic Tendencies in the Cultural Life of State-Socialist Russia and East-Central Europe," *Slavonica* 10, no. 2 (2004): 113–123; On the Iron Curtain as "semi-permeable membrane," see Michael David-Fox, "The Iron Curtain as Semi-Permeable Membrane: Origins and Demise of the Stalinist Superiority Complex," in *Cold War Crossings*, 14–39.

the international market. In a similar tone to that of the interwar era, the program stated that domestic manufacturing eliminated the need for imports, which drained domestic capital for the profit of foreign manufacturers and workers.[16] Industry was not the only sector influenced by such policies. The Albanian communist leader, echoing slogans and policies similar to those of Mussolini's "battaglia del grano" (battle for grain), stated that one of the principal goals of the party he led was self-sufficiency in cereals and other crucial foodstuffs. Lenin, too, used a similar slogan when he stated that the struggle for bread is the struggle for socialism.[17]

This was not limited to Albania alone. John Lampe and Marvin Jackson have questioned the dichotomy between the interwar era and the socialist period since the early 1980s. These authors argue that despite the apparent differences there are also significant continuities between these two periods. They give as examples the commitment of the political elites of Europe to economic self-sufficiency, state-owned enterprises, and restrictions on foreign capital both pre- and post-World War II. Such tendencies made their way into the socialist regimes of the Balkans during the Cold War era. The Balkans were not alone in this post-World War II era, as the drive for autarky also survived for many years in Spain, Portugal, and Ireland.[18]

One of the goals of the ALP was to domestically produce all the sugar that Albanians consumed. They stated this goal in 1945, and the State Planning Commission argued on different occasions that Albania had suitable climatic conditions to establish a sugar beet industry, and that the building of sugar factories would guarantee Albania's sugar self-sufficiency.[19] The communists did not need

---

16 AQSh, F. 494, Ministria e Ekonomisë, 1945, d. 131, fl. 42–43. Memo on Albanian industry.
17 On the ALP's plan for economic autarchy, AQSh, F. 14/AP (OU), 1947, d. 8, fl. 9. Minutes of the meeting of the ALP's Politburo concerning the draft of the five-year economic plan. March 6, 1947. On grain self-sufficiency, see the declaration of the Head of State Planning, Nako Spiru. AQSh, F. 14/AP (OU), 1947, d. 21, fl. 4. Minutes of the meeting of the ALP's Politburo on the directives of the first Five-Year Plan. July 5, 1947. For self-sufficiency in grain, sugar, sugar-beet, sunflower, cotton, and flax, etc. see AQSh, F. 14/AP (OU), 1948, d. 11, fl. 90. Report of the economic plan of the ALP's Politburo member, Gogo Nushi, presented to the First Congress of the ALP. November 13–14, 1948. On the use of Lenin's slogan, AQSh, F. 14/AP (OU), 1953, d. 2, fl. 8–10. Report of the Minister of Agriculture, Hysni Kapo, on measures for the improvement and development of agriculture. March 2–3, 1953.
18 On the Balkans, Lampe & Jackson, *Balkan Economic History*, 13; On Europe, Mark Mazower, *Dark Continent: Europe's Twentieth Century* (London: Penguin Books, 1998), 296–300.
19 On the establishment of the sugar industry, AQSh, F. 494, Ministria e Ekonomisë, 1945, d. 131, fl. 48. Memorandum on Albanian industry. On the goal of the State Planning Commission AQSh, F. 14/AP (STR), 1947, d. 330/10, fl. 30. Memo of the State Planning Commission prospective plan for the development of light industry; AQSh, F. 14/AP (STR), 1947, d. 330/14, fl. 2. Albanian industry during the Zog era and the goals of the economy after the liberation of the country.

to waste energy deciding where to establish their sugar industry. The Italians had left their blueprints and some of the buildings were nearly completed. The new Albanian authorities considered resuming the project in the plain of Korça in early 1946 when the reclamation of the swamp had not yet begun. In 1947, they sought help to complete it.[20]

The problem was finding the machinery and preparing the technical staff to use it. The ALP asked Yugoslavia for help. In late 1947, the communist authorities in Belgrade pledged to supply its southern neighbor with the necessary technical assistance to establish its sugar refinery with a capacity of 2000 tons of sugar per year. Yugoslav generosity, though, had its limits. The machinery Belgrade sent to Korça belonged to an old refinery from 1923 that had been out of service since 1933. When it was put to work in 1949, its capacity hardly reached 1500 tons a year.[21] The machinery was riddled with problems and inefficiencies. When the Yugoslavs left in the summer of 1948, in the throes of the break between Tirana and Belgrade after the Tito–Stalin split, the refinery was not yet operational.[22] The assembly restarted only after the arrival of Soviet specialists in late Autumn of 1948 and the factory started processing sugar in January of 1949.[23]

---

20 On the use of the Italian project, see AQSh, F. 498, Ministria e Bujqësisë dhe Pyjeve, 1945, d. 12, fl. 2-4. Memo on the ex-Albanian Joint-Stock Sugar Company (Korça). January 1, 1946; AQSh, F. 14/AP (STR), 1947, d. 330/10, fl. 11-12. Memo of the State Planning Commission on the five-year economic plan. On the cultivation of sugar beet "Rëndësia e madhe e Maliqit për ekonominë e vendit t'onë" [The great importance Maliq has for our economy], *Bashkimi*, June 11, 1946, 3.

21 On the Yugoslav pledge for the building of the sugar refinery, see "Raport informativ i Nako Spirut në plenum" [Report by Nako Spiru in the Plenum], in *Marrëdhëniet shqiptaro-jugosllave: 1945–1948: dokumente* [Albanian-Yugoslav relations, 1945–1946: documents], eds. Ndreçi Plasari and Luan Malltezi (Tiranë: DPA, 1996), 76. On the content of the deal and its flaws, see AQSh, F. 517, Ministria e Industrisë, 1948, d. 48, fl. 14. Report of the Ministry of Industry concerning the fulfillment by the Yugoslav government of its pledges to support Albanian industry; "Si e kanë sabotuar trockistat Jugosllavë ndërtimin e së parës fabrikë sheqeri" [How the Yugoslav Trotskyites sabotaged the construction of the first sugar refinery], *Puna* [Work], April 6, 1949 (221): 1; AQSh, F. 14/AP (STR), 1951, d. 451, fl. 2. Report of the Directory of Industry of the ALP's Central Committee on the Sugar Enterprise "Ali Kelmendi." October 15, 1951.

22 On July 1, 1948, only two days after COMINFORM's excommunication of Tito, Hoxha asked all the Yugoslav specialists to leave the country. James O'Donnell, *A Coming of Age: Albania under Enver Hoxha* (New York: University of Columbia Press, 1999), 27. On the Soviet-Yugoslav split and the role of Albania in it, see Mark Kramer, "Stalin, the Split with Yugoslavia, and the Soviet-East European Efforts to Reassert Control, 1948–1953," in *The Balkans in the Cold War*, ed. Svetozar Rajak et al. (London: Palgrave Macmillan, 2017), 29–64; Leonid Ia. Gibianskii, "The Soviet-Yugoslav Split and the Soviet Bloc," in *The Soviet Union and Europe in the Cold War, 1945–1953*, eds. Francesca Gori and Silvio Pons (London: Macmillan Press, 1996), 222–245.

23 On the progression of the work on the refinery under the leadership of the Yugoslavs, AQSh, F. 14/AP (STR), 1948, d. 225/1, fl. 1-3. Comments of the Council of Ministers on the sugar refinery brought from Yugoslavia; AQSh, F. 14/AP (STR), 1951, d. 451, fl. 2. Report of the Directory of Industry of the

At this point, the sugar industry became a broker of communication: a mirror that reflected the shift of alliances but also a symbol of the narrative of the heroic resistance of Hoxha's regime against foreign encroachment. As had become an established custom, stories of alleged economic sabotage followed the rupture of the political alliance. Tirana claimed that the Yugoslav technicians that had entered Albania to build the factory had consciously sabotaged it with the intention of inhibiting the construction of Albanian industry.[24] Hoxha and his closest associates used the sugar enterprise as a handloom to weave narratives that placed Albania within a transnational context of alliances and betrayals, of ruptured threads and new connections.

Moreover, the refinery was too small and did not produce enough sugar to meet domestic demand. For this reason, when Hoxha went to Moscow in the summer of 1947, he asked Vyacheslav Molotov to help his government build another sugar processing factory in the region of Korça. The Soviet Foreign Minister agreed to supply Albania with the necessary financial, technological, and logistical support.[25] Unlike the first refinery, Tirana built the new one from scratch close to the village of Maliq, near the Devoll gorge. Except for the building materials, all the equipment came from the Soviet Union. When Hoxha visited Moscow in March 1949, he asked Stalin to send specialists for the construction of the sugar refinery. The Soviet leader obliged him,[26] and the specialists arrived in late Autumn. Besides the Soviets, Romanian technicians also participated in the construction of the refinery in Maliq. Italian engineers and technicians, who had come to Albania after the war and had yet to leave the country, were also involved. Before the construction of the refinery in Maliq many of them had worked on the reclamation of swampland, while others had worked on the

---

ALP's Central Committee on the Sugar Enterprise "Ali Kelmendi." October 15, 1951. On the arrival of the Soviet specialists, AMPJ, 1948, d. 23, fl. 22-23. Letter of the Ministry of Industry on the urgent needs of the sugar refinery in Korça.

24 Dali Ndreu, "Si e kanë penguar dhe sa e kanë damtuar trockistat jugosllavë industrinë t'onë" [How the Yugoslav Trotskyites hindered and harmed our industry], *Bashkimi*, January 7, 1949, 2. Ironically, the author of this article, a high-ranking member of the ALP's Politburo and a prominent commander of the communist-led resistance during World War II, would be executed in 1956 for alleged cooperation with the Yugoslav secret services in toppling Hoxha from power.

25 AQSh, F. 14/AP (OU), 1947, d. 1, fl. 109. Protocol of the meeting of the ALP's Politburo. August 30, 1947; AMPJ, 1948, d. 23, fl. 24; AQSh, F. 14/AP (OU), 1947, d. 23, fl. 6. Minutes of the meeting of the ALP's Politburo. Report on the visit of the Albanian delegation to Moscow. July 27, 1947.

26 *Shqipëria në dokumentet e arkivave ruse* [Albania in the documents of the Russian archives], eds. Islam Lauka and Eshref Ymeri (Tiranë: Toena, 2006), doc. 3 (16), 216.

CHAPTER 4

FIGURE 14. Moments from the construction of the sugar factory of Maliq

processing factory in Korça.[27] Hence, Maliq became a crucible of encounters between representatives of opposite poles: the builders of socialism and the former builders of fascism all gathered in one place.

During the two years it took to construct the refinery, 92 Soviet specialists worked in Maliq in groups of 30. The Soviet fitters astonished the Albanians with the pace of their work to such a degree that there are still people in Maliq today who recall the Russians and their work ethic with awe. The innovations they brought with them in terms of work methods accelerated the pace of construction and compensated for the lack of a local labor force, which had previously hindered the project.[28] The results were spectacular. The construction site in Maliq received the Order of the Flag of the Council of Ministers and the Albanian director was so confident in his workers' newly learned skills that he planned to challenge two other major construction sites in the country to a competition.[29]

The Soviets not only helped to build the sugar factory but also helped to fill it with workers. The construction site became a school where the Soviet engineers

---

27 AQSh, F. 14/AP (STR), 1951, d. 451, fl. 4. Report of the Directory of Industry of the ALP's Central Committee. October 15, 1951; AQSh, F. 14/AP (STR), 1949, d. 669, fl. 21-22. Reports of the ALP's Committee of Korça regarding progress on the work of the sugar factory of Maliq. September 19 & 23, 1949.
28 On the Soviet team, AQSh, F. 14/AP (STR), 1951, d. 490, fl. 3. Memo of the Minister of Construction, Rapo Dervishi concerning the construction of the sugar refinery of Maliq. October 26, 1951; AQSh, F. 499, Ministria e Ndërtimit, 1951, d. 160, fl. 29. On the impression of the Soviet fitters on the locals, Fredi Vangjeli, informal interview by Artan Hoxha, July 20, 2016. On the scarcity of labor at the regional and national level and the failure of its total mobilization, AQSh, F. 14/AP (STR), 1949, d. 80, fl. 16. Protocol of the meeting of the Politburo of the ALP's Committee of Korça. December 27, 1949; AQSh, F. 14/AP (STR), 1950, d. 54, fl. 68-69. Minutes of the meeting of the Bureau of the ALP's Committee of Korça. February 28, 1950.
29 On the decoration, see AQSh, F. 14/AP (OU), 1951, d. 25, fl. 8. Report of the director of the sugar refinery on the progress of the work in Maliq, presented at the meeting of the ALP's Politburo. On competition with other enterprises, see *Ibid*, f. 44-45. Report of the analysis of the group of instructors of the ALP's Committee of Korça on the situation in Maliq. August 4–7, 1951.

taught courses on the use of machinery and prepared an entire generation of sugar specialists in the country.[30] The design bureau in Moscow also embarked on the construction of a small workers' town next to the refinery, and the specialists that came to build the industrial establishment also took care to supervise its construction. The Soviet chief engineer, Alexey Mikhailovich Goloborodko, personally took care of the decoration of the city and the planting of flowers and trees in its parks—those very pines under whose shade I drank coffee and talked about the Soviet expedition and the history of Maliq. As one journalist put it, Maliq was the offspring of the Albanian–Soviet relationship.[31]

Like all "civilizing missions," the relationship between the Soviet teachers and the Albanian pupils was also marked by differences. The former enjoyed the same privileges that the urban elites had experienced in the USSR since the 1930s and, ironically, reproduced the same pattern of distinction that the Italians had articulated vis-à-vis the Albanians during the interwar years.[32] In this corner of the Balkans, distinctions were not drawn along class lines but national identities. The Soviet specialists, whether engineers or technicians, experienced different treatment not only compared to Albanian workers and peasants but also to Albanian specialists. Reproducing patterns of colonial rule, the Soviets had separate living quarters and a special canteen supplied by the shops of Korça where the Albanians were not permitted to eat. The security measures heightened the divisions between technicians and toilers. The safety of the Soviets was a top priority, and the staff that served them in the canteen were all people with a good political background, while the Ministry of the Interior guarded their residence.[33]

---

30 AShV Korçë, F. 3/2, Komiteti i PPSh Rrethi Korçë, 1951, Lista 7, d. 212, fl. 2. Memo of the ALP's Committee of Korçë concerning the preparation of the cadres for the industrial sector. August 2, 1951; AQSh, F. 499, Ministria e Ndërtimit, 1951, d. 225/1, fl. 24. Correspondence between the Ministry of Construction and the Ministry of Industry on the construction of the sugar refinery of Maliq. October 3, 1951.

31 Jorgji Mihali, "Qyteti industrial, pjellë e miqësisë shqiptaro-sovjetike" [The industrial town, child of Soviet-Albanian friendship], *Bashkimi* 137 (4338), July 1, 1959, 3.

32 On the privileges of Italian workers and specialists in Albania during the interwar years, Misha, *Lëvizja punëtore në Shqipëri*, 270 & passim.

33 On class distinctions and benefits in the USSR in the 1930s, Sheila Fitzpatrick, "The Bolshevik Invention of Class: Marxist Theory and the Making of 'Class Consciousness' in Soviet Society," in *The Structure of Soviet History: Essays and Documents*, ed. Ronald Grigor Suny (Oxford: Oxford University Press, 2003), 173; Sheila Fitzpatrick, "Ascribing Class: The Construction of Social Identity in Soviet Russia," *The Journal of Modern History* 65, no. 4 (1993): 745–770. On the supply of the Soviet team, AQSh, F. 14/AP (OU), 1951, d. 25, fl. 46. Minutes of the meeting of the Politburo of the ALP's Central Committee. April 27, 1951; AQSh, F. 490, Këshilli i Ministrave, 1952, d. 1052, fl. 3. Information on the situation in the sugar combine of Maliq. On the Ministry of the Interior guarding their resi-

CHAPTER 4

According to the deal with Moscow, Tirana's authorities, besides their salaries, also had to pay for the Soviet technical team's travel tickets and provide them with furnished apartments, heat, electric light, food, and other industrial goods for personal use.[34] The Albanian authorities generally fulfilled these commitments and also supplied the Soviet technical staff with radios and games and placed cars at their disposal so that they could travel to Korça or the lake of Ohrid. Moreover, the Soviet chief engineer had at his disposal a GAZ car, a privilege that only the ALP's leading functionaries enjoyed.[35] He also had access to the army's commissary, which, during the hard postwar years, had the best goods. For the Albanians, all these wonders were forbidden, but the Soviet specialists still complained about their working and living conditions. They considered their experience in Maliq difficult and constantly complained, sometimes justifiably so, about the lack of a regular supply of vodka and the material deprivation they had to endure.[36] They were not satisfied with the food service or their supplies; neither were they impressed by the lack of workers, means of transportation, or technicians.[37]

The first expedition left after completing the building of the refinery, and a new one came to teach the Albanians how to use it. The new team of specialists changed its approach toward the Albanians. They were not there for a short period and had to live and work closely with the locals. There were no linguistic barriers between the Soviets and the Albanians anymore. A good part of the refinery's local personnel, recruited from the ranks of the workers that participated in the construction of the refinery, could speak Russian as they had been trained in the Soviet Union from 1949 to 1951.[38] Their status vis-à-vis the

---

dence, AQSh, F. 14/AP (OU), 1951, d. 25, fl. 14. Some issues discussed in the meeting of the Politburo of the ALP's Central Committee regarding the sugar combine of Maliq. April 27, 1951.

34 AQSh, F. 517, Ministria e Industrisë, 1950, d. 31, fl. 1-2. Agreement between the Albanian and Soviet governments on the payment of the Soviet technicians that will provide their technical expertise in Albania. September 21, 1950.

35 AQSh, F. 499, Ministria e Ndërtimit, 1951, d. 225, fl. 35. Memo of the Ministry of Construction concerning the building of industrial establishments.

36 On the supply of the Soviet chief engineer in the military commissary, AQSh, F. 14/AP (OU), 1951, d. 25, fl. 46. Minutes of the meeting of the Politburo of the ALP's Central Ccommittee. April 27, 1951. On the irregular supply of vodka, AQSh, F. 499, Ministria e Ndërtimit, 1951, d. 160, fl. 14. On material deprivations, AShV Korçë, F. 3/2, Rrethi Korçë, 1952, Lista 8, d. 187, fl. 1. The ALP's Central Committee instructions sent to the local party committees. August 7, 1952.

37 AQSh, F. 14/AP (OU), 1951, d. 25, fl. 46. Minutes of the meeting of the Politburo of the ALP's Central Committee. April 27, 1951. On the lack of workers, transportation, and technicians, AShV Korçë, F. 3/2, Rrethi Korçë, 1952, Lista 8, d. 187, fl. 1. The ALP's Central Committee instructions sent to the local party committees. August 7, 1952.

38 "Kombinati i sheqerit '8 Nëntori'" [The sugar combine "November 8th"] *Shqipëri-BRSS* [Albania-USSR], 10-11 (1951): 22.

Soviet technicians had changed. They were no longer simple toilers but specialists educated in the USSR. Moreover, the Soviets came with their families and the interactions between them and the locals were not limited to working time but extended well beyond. Their children socialized with Albanian children—one interviewee recalls playing with Volodya (Vladimir), the son of the Soviet chief engineer in the refinery.[39] It is these whom the people from Maliq still remember with nostalgia. They were not only introducing models of work but also lifestyles.

In the 1950s, Maliq became an access point for experiencing the Soviet Union first-hand. Besides the workers of the refinery, others went to the Soviet Union throughout the decade to learn new crafts, from driving tractors to welding with oxygen.[40] These exchanges with the Soviets impressed the Albanians to the point that many of them really believed in the superiority of Soviet science and technology. Almost all the communist cadres considered the Soviet Union to be the savior of Albania and the world. The West, in the minds of many Albanians, had lost its primacy in science and the locus of civilization had moved to the East, this time in the Third Rome. This belief took root in particular among local cadres and specialists, on whose shoulders the fulfillment of Tirana's plans sat. Soviet technology gave them the devices they needed to meet the state plan and overcome the endemic delays and inefficiencies as best they could.

This Stalinist superiority complex intoxicated the communist cadres of Maliq too, who fully embraced Soviet hegemony.[41] Here, like everywhere else in the country, the Albanian cadres worshipped the Soviets in the same way that the latter adored everything American during the interwar era. Now it was the turn of the Soviets to be in the position of superior beings that had the answer for everything.[42] In their endless reports and correspondence, the cadres of Maliq never stopped praising Soviet science, which they raised to the status of myth. Hekuran Arapi, a fitter who worked in Maliq, said to Enver Hoxha that the Party, with the help of the Soviet Union, had sweetened the future of the country like

---

39 Miçurin Hasko, informal interview with Artan Hoxha, Korça, December 2017.
40 Stavri Kamenica, "E ndjejmë vehten të lumtur" [We feel happy], *Bashkimi* 137 (4338), July 1, 1959, 3.
41 I have borrowed the term "Stalinist complex of superiority" from Michael David-Fox, "Rise of the Stalinist Superiority Complex," in David-Fox, in *Showcasing the Great Experiment*, 285–311.
42 On American idolatry in the Soviet Union of the interwar era, see Richard Stites, *Revolutionary Dreams: Utopian Vision and Experimental Life in the Russian Revolution* (Oxford: Oxford University Press, 1989), 145–164.

the sugar of Maliq.⁴³ Thoma Samara, the first director of the sugar factory, stated that Soviet technology was the most advanced in the world.⁴⁴ The belief in the superiority of everything Soviet was not merely a myth engineered for propagandist goals. It actually was a widely shared belief that captivated the minds of all layers of the communist hierarchy, from the top leadership all the way down to the cadres that stained their hands with grease. The press praised Soviet technology as the best in the world on an almost daily basis. When talking about Maliq, the press considered its machinery to be the crown jewel of the world's technology.⁴⁵ Translations of Soviet methods were widely used in Albania, such as the Kulikov construction method and chain plastering, and methods for the efficient use of machines and overhauling, such as those of Kursinov, Levchenko-Mukhanov, and Zhandarova-Agafanova, appeared everywhere.⁴⁶

Operating the factory was just one part of the process. Agriculture and the cultivation of sugar beet were also crucial to the refining of sugar. The Soviets and their scientific achievements made their presence felt even here. When the agronomist of the district of Korça talked about the declining yield of sugar beets, they referred to the practices applied in the Soviet Union as the example to follow. The proposal for a given method was supported by examples of its successful application in the Soviet Union. They also referred to Soviet literature to learn more about the growth process of sugar beet. Agricultural periodicals, such as *Socialist Agriculture*, translated pedagogical articles that provided examples of how the Soviet farms cultivated sugar beet. The Albanian cadres considered what they called "the Soviet experience" to be a model to mimic and a yard stick by which everything else should be measured.⁴⁷

---

43 "Bisedimi i shokut Enver Hoxha me delegacionin e punëtorëve të fabriksës së sheqerit 8 Nëndori" [The conversation of comrade Enver Hoxha with the sugar refinery workers' delegation], *Bashkimi*, November 2, 1951, 3.

44 "Fjala e drejtorit të fabrikës, Thoma Samara" [The speech of the director, Thoma Samara], *Zëri i Popullit*, November 3, 1948, 2.

45 "Kombinati i sheqerit '8 Nëntori" ["November 8ᵗʰ" sugar refinery], *Shqipëri-BRSS*, 10–11 (1951): 22. See also Hoxha, *Tharja e kënetës së Maliqit*, 219–229; Mëhilli, *From Stalin to Mao*, 119–125.

46 V. Ziu, "Kuadro të ardhëshme për industrinë tonë" [Future cadres of our industry], *Bashkimi*, June 4, 1953, 3; Nikolla Kallfa, "Pregatitemi për prodhimin e ri" [We are getting ready for new production], *Zëri i Popullit* 202 (1528), August 22, 1953; AQSh, F. 14/AP (STR), 1953, d. 113, fl. 4-6. Information on the use of Soviet methods in the industrial sector of Korça; AShV Korçë, F. 3/2, Komiteti i PPSh Rrethi Korçë, 1953, d. 135, Lista 9, fl. 1 & 4. Reports of the ALP's Committee of Korça on the personal example of the communist cadres in the building of socialism. July 21, 1953; AShV Korçë, F. 3/1, Komiteti i PPSh Qarku Korçë, 1954, Lista 5, d. 56, fl. 8. Information on the readiness of the sugar factory for the beginning of the 1953–1954 season.

47 On Soviet examples, see Nesti Çekani, "Shërbimet kulturale në panxhar-sheqerin" [The services to sugar beet], *Bashkimi*, May 14, 1954. On the provision with Soviet examples, see "Kombajni i vjeljes

Although Maliq was predominantly a point of exchange between Albania and the Soviet Union, it also weaved threads of connections with other socialist countries which helped the development of the sugar industry in Albania. In the context of the aid that the COMECON countries gave to Albania, Bulgaria agreed to supply its Balkan ally with the machinery for an alcohol factory in Maliq. Additionally, in 1959, a team of Bulgarian specialists came and worked in Maliq to help their Albanian comrades expand their light industry. Czechoslovak and East German specialists, who were sent by their respective governments to help Albania develop its sugar industry, also worked there. These specialists experimented with sugar beet and taught the Albanian technicians how to cultivate it. Members of the Soviet kolkhozes also came to Maliq. Their visits were part of a broader plan of exchanges, which Moscow implemented with the goal of popularizing the USSR in the states of the socialist bloc. The Soviet farmers visited the beet farms and taught the peasants of Maliq, who had just started collective farming, how to cultivate better sugar beet.[48]

Maliq not only became a destination for Soviet farmers and specialists but also for the USSR's leadership. In 1959, when Nikita Khrushchev visited Albania, he stopped at the state farm of Maliq, which was established on reclaimed land, and had lunch with its director, Ilia Prifti. Tirana's regime did not only want to showcase Maliq to its distinguished friend and benefactor; its sugar factory also demonstrated to its people and the world the transformation of the

---

së panxhar sheqerit" [Sugar beet harvesting combine], *Bujqësia socialiste*, 7 (1956): 29. On referring to Soviet literature, see Nesti Çekani, "Ta vjelim në kohë panxhar-sheqerin" [We should harvest sugar beets on time], *Për bujqësinë socialiste*, 8 (1955): 7–8. Translated Soviet articles, see N. Rozhnaçuk, "Nga eksperienca e kolkozianëve sovjetikë. Prodhonjësit e panxharit të sheqerit i plotësuan zotimet e tyre" [From the experience of the Soviet farmers. The producers of sugar beets fulfilled their commitments], *Bujqësia socialiste*, 3 (1955): 17–18. On praise for the Soviet experiences, V. Stralla, "Shërbimet kulturale dhe përdorimi i mjeteve të mekanizuara në bimën e panxhar-sheqerit" [The services and the use of mechanized means for the sugar beets], *Bashkimi*, May 13, 1956, 3; Llukan Tase, "Të hedhim bazat për rendimente të larta në panxhar sheqeri" [Let's lay the ground for higher yields of sugar beets], *Bujqësia socialiste*, 3 (1956): 15.

48 On the alcohol factory, AShV Korçë, F. 3/2, Komiteti i PPSh Rrethi Korçë, 1959, Lista 15, d. 160, fl. 6. Memo on the progress of the work for the construction of the alcohol factory in Maliq. August 8, 1959. For the courses of the Czechoslovak agronomist, AQSh, F. 490, Këshilli i Ministrave, 1952, d. 1052, fl. 9. Memo of the Ministry of Industry regarding the condition of the Maliqi sugar factory. February 22, 1952. On the experiment of the researcher from the DDR, AQSh, F. 498, Ministria e Bujqësisë, 1960, d. 79, fl. 3. Documentation concerning the development of a sugar beet culture in the People's Republic of Albania. On the visit of the members of the Soviet kolkhoz in Maliq, "Në fushën e panxharit" [In the field of sugar beets], *Shqipëri-BRSS*, 10-11(1951): 26. On the practice of exchanges of farmers between the USSR and the socialist countries, see Patryk Babiracki, "The Taste of Red Watermelon: Polish Peasants Visit Soviet Collective Farms, 1949–1952," *Cold War Crossings*, 40–77.

countryside during the ALP's era. In 1960, Tirana's authorities decided to use Maliq as an example of the socialist transformation of the countryside, and as a result the refinery, the state farm, and the cooperatives of the plain became destinations for foreign visitors, who occasionally arrived to see with their own eyes the socialist transformation of the plain.[49]

Exchanges were not limited to people. They included, besides machinery, sugar beet hybrids (Albania was not able to produce its own hybrids until well into the 1980s).[50] For this reason, the regime was forced to import prized seeds. The Albanians imported their first beet varieties from the Soviet Union, but during the 1950s they also started importing some from Czechoslovakia, the GDR, Poland, and Hungary. In the closing years of the decade, the seeds imported from these countries started to replace the Soviet seeds. Maliq became a laboratory where Albanians experimented with different seeds produced by socialist countries and tested the scientific achievements of the bloc. This situation gradually undermined the ubiquitous sense of Soviet scientific supremacy. The Albanian specialists soon realized that the varieties from Central European countries contained more sugar than the Soviet varieties. They started to openly argue for the superiority of the Czechoslovak, East German, and Hungarian hybrids and advocated their import.[51] By the end of the 1950s, the euphoria over and enthusiasm for Soviet science had been quelled among the agricultural specialists in Maliq as they started deconstructing the myth of Soviet scientific superiority that they had helped to construct. After the split with Moscow in 1961, Tirana imported all its elite seeds from the peoples' democracies of Central Europe.[52]

---

49 On Khrushchev's visit, S. Arrëza, "Korça pret miqt e dashur" [Korça welcomes dear friends], *Miqësia* [Friendship], 1959 (6). On the transformation of Maliq into a touristic destination, AShV Korçë, F. 3/2, Komiteti i PPSh Rrethi Korçë, 1960, Lista 16, d. 147, fl. 5 & 9. The centers to be visited by tourists during the year 1960; AMPJ, viti 1982, d. 1213, fl. 27. Information of the Committee for Cultural Relations at the Ministry of Foreign Affairs. March 31, 1982.

50 AQSh, F. 490, Këshilli i Ministrave, 1987, d. 357, fl. 1-9. Correspondence between the Prime Minister's Office, the Ministry of Agriculture, and the Ministry of Foreign Affairs regarding the allocation of funds for importing 100 tons of sugar beet seeds. April 3-October 12, 1987.

51 AQSh, F. 498, Ministria e Bujqësisë, 1958, d. 62/5, fl. 3. Memo on the activity of the Albanian delegation of the Commission for Economic and Technical-Scientific Cooperation in the Field of Agriculture and Food Industry during the year 1958. December 1958; Thoma Lolo, "Rezultatet e llojeve të panxhar sheqerit në konditat e vëndit tonë" [The results of different sugar beet strains in our country], *Buletini i Shekencave Bujqësore* [The Bulletin of Agricultural Sciences], 1 (1962): 58–66.

52 AQSh, F. 14/AP (STR), 1961, d. 184, fl. 3. Report on the cultivation and industrialization of sugar. February 2, 1961. For a concise overview of Albanian-Soviet relations and the split, see Elidor Mëhilli, "Enver Hoxha's Albania: Yugoslav, Soviet, and Chinese Relations and Ruptures," in *Routledge Handbook of Balkan and Southeast European History*, 448–450; Hamit Kaba, "Refleksione në politikën e

However, by the late 1960s there was a shift in the imports of hybrid seeds of sugar beet that became especially obvious by the early 1970s. During these years, Albania began to import sugar beet seeds from countries outside of the Soviet bloc, like Italy, West Germany, and the Netherlands.[53] By this time, the Albanian specialists had started arguing that the Czechoslovak hybrids were outdated and that they needed to move toward the polyploid seeds used in the West to increase yields.[54] The need to import more productive seeds pushed the communist regime to intensify its trade with the countries of Western Europe, and in the 1970s and 1980s Albania imported polyploid seeds from France and Denmark, respectively.[55] The import of seeds reflected a much broader shift in the orientation of Albanian trade from the early 1970s. Currency can serve as a compass that demonstrates the direction of the magnetic fields of influences and interactions. Even after the break with Moscow, throughout the 1960s and early years of the 1970s, the Albanians kept using the Soviet ruble as the basic currency for their international transactions and for estimating foreign trade. During the course of the 1970s, the ruble lost ground to the US dollar—although the ruble remained the staple currency for transactions between Tirana and the socialist bloc countries. By the 1980s, due to growing trade with the West, the US dollar had become the basic currency for estimating the cost of imports.

This shift is also traceable at the level of international trade. In the 1950s, Albania did more than 93% of its international trade with countries of the Soviet bloc and almost 97% with socialist countries.[56] In 1980, only 38.7% of the country's exports went to members of the Warsaw Pact, and only approximately 58% went to socialist countries. When it came to imports, where machinery and mechanical equipment were among the most important categories, in 1980 the share of the socialist countries was less than 55% of the total. The remainder of imports

jashtmë të shtetit shqiptar pas vdekjes së Stalinit" [Reflections on the foreign policy of the Albanian state after the death of Stalin], in Hamit Kaba, *Shqipëria në rrjedhën e Luftës së Ftohtë* [Albania in the course of the Cold War] (Tirana: Flamuri, 2017), 173–180.

53   AQSh, F. 495, Komisioni i Planit të Shtetit, 1972, d. 38, fl. 7. Information of the State Planning Commission on the cultivation of sugar beet. September 25, 1972.

54   AQSh, F. 14/AP (STR), 1979, d. 83, fl. 41. Information of the Ministry of Agriculture sent to the ALP's Central Committee on the cultivation and processing of sugar beet. November 13, 1979.

55   On the import of seeds from France AQSh, F. 490, Këshilli i Ministrave, 1977, d. 160, fl. 10. Minutes of the meeting of the Council of Ministers regarding the expansion of the processing capacity of the sugar factory of Maliq. November 23, 1977. On the import of seeds from Denmark, AShV Korçë, F. 67, Kombinati i Sheqerit, 1987, d. 85, fl. 1-3. Report of the sugar combine of Maliq regarding the progress of the cultivation of sugar beet. March 5, 1987.

56   *Anuari statistikor i Republikës Popullore të Shqipërisë 1960* [Statistical annuarium of the People's Republic of Albania 1960] (Tirana: Drejtoria e Statistikës, 1960), 240–241.

came from capitalist countries—mainly from Western Europe. During the 1980s, trade conducted with Italy and West Germany increased considerably.[57] By this time, in the context of *Ostpolitik* and *Osthandel*, inaugurated in 1969 by Willy Brandt, the FGR had become the main trading partner of socialist countries among the NATO members.[58] Such a shift was also reflected in its increasing level of trade and exchange with communist Albania. Over the ensuing years, Tirana entangled itself more and more with the Western-centered web of trade—but it never cut itself off from trade with the Soviet bloc. The socialist countries remained the main trading partners of Albania, not so much due to a preference for their products but because they accepted barter trade.

The magnitude of the shift in orientation was even more prominent in the realm of scientific and technological exchanges. The sugar industry is a case in point. In the 1960s, the Albanian technocrats, who shared the wider belief in the scientific revolution that had caught the imaginations of university-trained specialists, started looking in new directions.[59] This goal, however, was not unique to the ranks of specialists and found fervent support in the upper echelons of the regime. Under the surface of isolationism, the focus of the Albanian power apparatus shifted from scientific knowledge generated in socialist countries to that produced on the western side of the fence. By the end of the decade, the idea of socialist technological inferiority replaced that of the socialist technological superiority of the 1950s. The Albanian communists did not imagine East and West to be categories with a fixed hierarchical relationship with each other. The replacement of the East by the West as the center of technological progress also led to the Orientalization of Eastern Europe and the Balkans. This feeling did not take root only among researchers and scientists but also among the highest circles of the ALP.

Hysni Kapo, one of the most powerful leaders of the ALP, set the quota of sugar beet yields in direct competition with Greece and Yugoslavia, which he and his colleagues saw as direct competitors. While they accepted that an industrialized country like Italy would have higher yields, Kapo set as a realistic goal the surpassing of Albania's two Balkan neighbors in productivity. The constant comparison with Yugoslavia and Greece was a yardstick for the ALP's work. As a spe-

---

57 *Vjetari statistikor i vitit 1989* [Statistical annuarium of 1989] (Tirana: Drejtoria e Statistikës, 1989], 172–175.
58 Yergin, *East-West Technology Transfer*, 15–50.
59 On the wider belief in scientific revolution in Eastern Europe in the 1960s, Iván Szelényi, *Socialist Entrepreneurs: Embourgeoisement in Rural Hungary* (Madison, WI: The University of Wisconsin Press, 1988), 152–153.

cialist of the Ministry of Agriculture pointed out, comparisons with the achievements of its neighbors showed how much of a road Albania still had to travel.[60] Even the specialists in Maliq made similar comparisons. Considering the efficiency of sugar processing in the countries of Western Europe unattainable for the time being, they were ambitious enough to want to reach at least the level of productivity of the countries of Eastern Europe.[61] While accepting their inferiority compared to the West, they could not do the same with the East.

As David Crowley argues, any evocation of the West necessarily constituted a comment about the East.[62] By competing with the West, the socialist countries transformed the US and the capitalist bloc into the yardstick by which they measured their achievements. However, this was not so much the case with Albania. Propaganda and public rhetoric aside, for the ALP's leaders the real Other that served as the necessary counter-image to shape their self-perceptions were the countries of the socialist bloc and their Balkan neighbors, regardless of their socio-economic system. In the form of a nested Orientalism, the carriers of a very violent anti-Western and anti-imperialist discourse were ironically reproducing the hegemonic force of the West.[63] They were trying to identify themselves as developed not by surpassing the West—something the ALP's leadership knew was an impossible feat—but by outdoing the other socialist countries. For the Albanian modernizers, it was necessary to find their Other in Eastern and Southeastern Europe. The hierarchies they constructed, which placed the country above the socialist and Balkan states, would give meaning to their efforts to catapult Albania into the status of a modern European state.

Regardless of its special relationship with Mao's China and Beijing's consistent financial and technological aid, the Albanian communist leadership nurtured deep suspicions about their Chinese counterparts.[64] The persistence of Al-

---

60 AQSh, F. 490, Këshilli i Ministrave, 1977, d. 361, fl. 35. Report of the Ministry of Agriculture on the increase in the production of sugar beet. April 29, 1977.
61 AShV Korçë, F. 67, Kombinati i Sheqerit, 1980, d. 19, fl. 6. Some opinions of the specialists of the sugar combine regarding the construction of a new establishment for the processing of sugar beet. August 15, 1980.
62 David Crowley, "Paris or Moscow? Warsaw Architects and the Image of the Modern City in the 1950s," *Imagining the West*, 110; See also James Carrier, "Introduction," in *Occidentalism: Images of the West*, ed. James Carrier (Oxford: Clarendon Press, 1995), 1–32.
63 I have borrowed this term from the article of Milica Bakić-Hayden and Robert M. Hayden, "Nesting Orientalisms: The Case of Yugoslavia," *Slavic Studies* 54, no. 4 (1995): 917–931.
64 On Albanian-Chinese relations and the financial and technological aid Albania received from China, Gjon Boriçi, *Marrëdhëniet shqiptaro-kineze në Luftën e Ftohtë në Luftën e Ftohtë, 1956–1978* [Albanian-Chinese relations in the Cold War, 1956–1978] (Tirana: Geer, 2022). On the suspicions of Enver Hoxha and his closest associates concerning the Chinese communist leadership, Mëhilli, *From Stalin*

bania's eastward orientation after the break with the USSR did not mean, in the minds of the Albanian cadres, that the East preserved its position as the representative of history's destination. In their mental map of the late 1960s, divided by imaginary lines, filled with fluid meanings and hierarchies, the Albanians dethroned the East as the place of light and threw it again into the realm of backwardness. Such an axiological shift expressed the resentment they had vis-à-vis the peoples' democracies of Eastern Europe. Albania was the least industrialized country of the bloc, and its socialist allies considered it backward, primitive, and deeply Oriental, which continuously frustrated Tirana's leadership.[65] After Tirana's regime broke with the Soviet alliance, it had the freedom to draw a new map that loaded space with a different scale of values. The Albanian modernizers subverted the hierarchy they had constructed in the 1950s. This new map of geographical identities shows that although Albania broke with its Eastern European allies, they, along with its Balkan neighbors, remained the yardstick with which the ALP regime measured itself. Rather than the West, the ALP wanted to catch up with and overtake the East.

György Péteri has argued that the peoples' democracies built their identity around their antithesis, the Occident. The West was the necessary Other for the Soviet experiment and hence a critical component of socialist self-perception.[66] The Albanian case is somewhat more complicated. After the break with the Soviet bloc, in 1961, Tirana's regime did not construct its identity solely in competition with the capitalist West, as was the case with the other socialist states. The Albanian communists forged their understanding of self also from competition with Eastern Europe. It was very hard for the Albanians to escape from the specter of the Orient, which haunted them even under the umbrella of socialist internationalist brotherhood. The efforts to escape from it only reinforced the Orient further, which was projected onto others.

With the new turn toward Western Europe, the saviors for Albanian modernizers were not the technology and scientific achievements of the Soviet Union

---

to Mao, 211–225; Elidor Mëhilli, "Mao and the Albanians," in *Mao's Little Red Book: A Global History*, ed. Alexander C. Cook (Cambridge: Cambridge University Press, 2014), 165–184.

65 For more on the attitudes and reactions of specialists and technicians from East Central Europe who worked in Albania, see Elidor Mëhilli, "Socialist Encounters: Albania and the Transnational Eastern Bloc in the 1950s," *Cold War Crossings*, 107–133.

66 György Péteri, "The Occident Within—or the Drive for Exceptionalism and Modernity," *Kritika: Explorations in Russian and Eurasian History* 9, no. 4 (2008): 929–937. On the importance of the West in the self-understanding of the socialist regimes, see Michael David-Fox, "Conclusion: Transnational History and the East-West Divide," *Imagining the West*, 258–267.

or China but those of the liberal democracies. Although tightly controlled and diminished, the flux of people crossing state borders with Maliq as their point of departure or destination was never interrupted. The Ministry of Light Industry sent a Danish specialist to the sugar refinery to discuss issues regarding the technology of the sugar combine. The Dane promised to send his Albanian colleagues the blueprints of some necessary equipment so that the Albanians could produce them in the country.[67] In the late 1980s, after relations with their southern neighbor improved, a group of Greek specialists visited the combine of Maliq. The Albanians were especially eager to learn from Greece's experience because the two countries had a similar climate and the Greek sugar industry had shown great results.[68]

During the winter of 1979–1980, a small group of eleven Polish specialists and a German technician lived in Maliq. They were there to help the Albanians reconstruct the combine and assemble the machinery.[69] In the late 1970s, the Albanian government granted the Polish company Polimex-Cekop, which had built sugar refineries in Greece—a token of the pluri-directional circulation of technological exchanges across the East–West divide—the right to reconstruct the sugar combine of Maliq and double its processing capacities. The authorities in Tirana did not choose the Polish company for any ideological or technological preference. On the contrary, Italian, West German, and Danish firms took part in the competition and the Albanian government openly preferred their offers because it considered Western technology to be far superior to that of the Poles. The Albanian specialists were well aware that the technological level in the West was far more advanced than that of the Soviet bloc, including that of sugar beet processing.[70]

---

67 AShV Korçë, F. 67, Kombinati i Sheqerit, 1982, d. 8, fl. 11-12. Memo of the sugar combine of Maliq regarding conversations with the Danish specialist, E. J. B. Giese, on the problems of the processing of sugar beet. October 28, 1982.
68 AShV Korçë, F. 67, Kombinati i Sheqerit, 1988, d. 3, fl. 1-2. Information on the visit of the Greek specialist to Maliq. December 12, 1988.
69 On the Polish specialists, see AQSh, F. 497, Ministria e Industrisë së Lehtë Ushqimore, 1977, d. 209, fl. 1. Letter of the Ministry of Light Industry and Food concerning the Polish specialists that will work in expanding the processing capacity of the sugar factory of Maliq. April 9, 1977; AShV Korçë, F. 67, Kombinati i Sheqerit, 1980, d. 52, fl. 1. Letter of the Ministry of Light Industry and Food concerning the liquidation of the financial obligations of the foreign specialists. December 22, 1980. On the German specialist, *Ibid*, fl. 7. Letter of the directory of the sugar combine in Maliq concerning the liquidation of the bills of the Polish specialists. September 16, 1980.
70 AShV Korçë, F. 67, Kombinati i Sheqerit, 1980, d. 19, fl. 6. Some opinions of the specialists of the sugar combine in Maliq regarding the construction of a new establishment for the processing of sugar beet. August 15, 1980.

CHAPTER 4

From 1971, the Albanians used technology imported by the world-renowned West German company BMA to build a starch factory in the combine of Maliq. However, the Western companies wanted hard currency—something the Albanians did not have. Tirana wanted to buy the technology through barter trading, and because the Poles were willing to operate on these terms the government in Tirana was forced to choose Polimex.[71] However, the technology used for the reconstruction was not entirely Polish. The Albanians and the Polish company bought machinery from countries in both ideological camps for the reconstruction of the combine: the UK, Japan, Greece, Italy, Belgium, West Germany, Austria, East Germany, Czechoslovakia, Romania, Bulgaria, Yugoslavia, and China.[72] In 1987–1988, the Yugoslavs returned to the region of Korça after exactly 40 years. This time, they did not come to bring an old rusty refinery but to assemble two turbines for the power plant of Maliq.[73]

The foreign specialists that came to Albania after 1961 did not integrate into the local population's daily life as was the case in the 1950s. The regime took care to restrict any uncontrolled contact with foreigners. The Albanians were careful in their relations with the foreign specialists who came to reconstruct the sugar factory and avoided socializing with them after work. As an engineer recounts, when a Polish colleague asked him to go for a beer, he only accepted after asking for permission from the refinery's party secretary.[74] This was the height of the regime's xenophobic rhetoric. However, while considering all foreigners coming

---

71 On the construction of the starch factory with German technology, AShV Korçë, F. 67, Kombinati i Sheqerit, Pa vit, Kutia 680, viti 1994, d. 13, fl. pa numër. Study on the existing condition of the sugar combine of Maliq. December 9, 1994. On the Albanian preference for Western technology and the terms of the Western firms to trade with hard currency, AQSh, F. 497, Ministria e Industrisë së Lehtë Ushqimore, 1977, d. 148, fl. 97-98. Information concerning the steps that should be taken to conclude the work on expanding the processing capacity of the sugar combine. On the Polish firm establishing refineries in Greece, see AShV Korçë, F. 67, Kombinati i Sheqerit, 1988, d. 3, fl. 1-2. Information on the sugar combine regarding the visit of the Greek specialist to Maliq. December 12, 1988.
72 On British equipment, see AQSh, F. 490, Këshilli i Ministrave, 1979, d. 400, fl. 14. Information on the construction, assemblage, and expansion of the sugar combine in Maliq. On the machinery from the other countries, AQSh, F. 490, Këshilli i Ministrave, 1979, d. 400, fl. 30. Information on the expansion of the sugar combine in Maliq, AQSh, *Ibid*, fl. 43. Information on the materials of the sugar combine of Maliq; *Ibid*, fl. 64. Letter of the ALP's Committee of Korça on supplying the sugar combine of Maliq with machinery. March 3, 1979; *Ibid*, fl. 73-71. Information on the condition of the machinery and equipment for the sugar combine of Maliq. June 22, 1979.
73 AQSh, F. 490, Këshilli i Ministrave, 1986, d. 246, fl. 33. Proposal of the draft-idea for the installation of a turbine with a capacity of 35 tons/hour in the thermal power station of Maliq.
74 On the impact of the Poles, Piro Lazi, informal interview by Artan Hoxha, Tirana, November 11, 2017. On socialization with Polish colleagues, Miçurin Hasko, informal interview by Artan Hoxha, Korça, December 2017.

into the country as potential agents and taking care to keep them away from the Albanians as much as possible, the regime did not interrupt the movement of people. In fact, by the end of the 1970s there was an increase in such exchanges.

The most intense form of exchange was the visits of Albanian specialists to other countries. The technocrats were a driving force behind the new course of technological exchanges and orientations. They were crucial actors in constructing the new complex of Western technological superiority that pervaded Albania in the 1970s and 1980s. While the regime tried to keep the populace in quarantine, the technocrats negotiated change and innovation and mediated connections with the world, although under the strict supervision of the ALP. Indeed, the regime allocated the bulk of the funds dedicated to the buying of foreign scientific literature to the specialists of the industrial sector.[75] It is true that mobility and exchange during the two last decades of the communist era were far from the levels seen in the 1950s. However, the Albanian specialists did manage to preserve a degree of mobility when beyond state borders. In the early 1970s, they visited the hated and disengaged Yugoslavia, the revisionist and Catholic Poland, and marginal NATO-member France, where they witnessed the cultivation of sugar beet and seed selection and brought some back to experiment with in Maliq. Later that decade, the Ministry of Agriculture sent sugar beet specialists to Italy to learn from the experience of their neighbors in the Apennine peninsula.[76]

In the late 1970s, the specialists of the sugar combine of Maliq insisted that the government send specialists to West Germany, France, Belgium, Italy, Denmark, Austria, Poland, and Czechoslovakia. There, the Albanians could study the blueprints of foreign machinery so as to produce them at home. In 1980, a group of specialists at the Ministry of Agriculture prepared a report that advocated the same idea: they needed to follow the experience and achievements of countries with similar ecological conditions to Albania, such as Greece, Italy,

---

75 AQSh, F. 14/AP (STR), 1973, d. 215, fl. 1-8. Information of the Ministry of Education and Culture on the criteria that must be applied for the buying of foreign literature. April 29, 1973; *Ibid*, fl. 10-15. Criteria drafted by the Council of Ministers on the buying and distribution of foreign literature. June 20, 1973.

76 On the visit to France, Poland, and Yugoslavia, AQSh, F. 498, Ministria e Bujqësisë, 1973, d. 33, fl. 4-9. Report on some problems related to the seed and cultivation of sugar beet in Yugoslavia, Poland, and France. April 1973. On the need to replace the Czechoslovak hybrids with polyploid seeds, *Ibid*, fl. 18. Information on some problems related to the seed used for the cultivation of sugar beet. June 11, 1973. On the visit to Italy, AQSh, F. 14/AP (STR), 1979, d. 83, fl. 41. Information of the Ministry of Agriculture on the cultivation and processing of sugar beet. November 13, 1979.

CHAPTER 4

and France, but also in countries that had dissimilar climatic conditions like Belgium and Denmark, from a close distance. They proposed to send specialists to these countries to familiarize themselves with specific components of sugar beet cultivation.[77] None of these countries were socialist. These initiatives included a visit by a delegation from the combine of Maliq to Ankara in Turkey to attend an international seminar on the processing of sugar. During this visit, their Turkish colleagues gave them a full layout of the West German technology they used to produce refined sugar and white crystalline sugar. The chief engineer of the sugar combine, Llazar Plasa, who was part of the delegation, was very happy to find out the ways in which "Europe" dealt with the specific processes of sugar production. "Europe" here refers to Western European and German technology rather than Turkey.[78]

When the specialists of the sugar combine returned from their visit to Asia Minor, they were happy, partly because they were now armed with new European knowledge, but also because, to their satisfaction, everybody they met in Turkey, from the policemen in the airport to the workers of the sugar factories, knew of Enver Hoxha. The Turks identified Albania with its leader, and some of them compared Hoxha to Ataturk. To the delight of the Albanians, others said that the ALP leader was the heir of Mustafa Kemal.[79] The delegation brought back titles of books and journals that talked about sugar processing and asked the National Library to buy them. The visit was so successful that the regime sent other specialists to the annual exchanges in Turkey in 1982, 1985, and 1987.[80] The specialists of the sugar industry in Maliq and Korça were not iso-

---

[77] AQSh, F. 490, Këshilli i Ministrave, 1979, d. 401, fl. 10-11. Report of a group of specialists of the sugar combine in Maliq regarding the possibility of building a sugar factory with a processing capacity of 5000 tons per year. November 23, 1979; AQSh, F. 497, Ministria e Bujqësisë, 1980, d. 54, fl. 29-30. Report of the Ministry of Agriculture regarding the necessary measures for increasing the yield of sugar beet. October 10, 1980.

[78] AQSh, F. 497, Ministria e Industrisë së Lehtë Ushqimore, 1981, d. 557, fl. 22-23. Information of the Albanian delegation that took part in the training for the perfection of sugar processing held at the Institute of Sugar in Ankara, Turkey. February 8, 1982.

[79] On the copying of German technology in Turkey AQSh, F. 497, Ministria e Industrisë së Lehtë Ushqimore, 1981, d. 557, fl. 23-24. Information of the Albanian delegation that took part in the training for the perfection of sugar processing held at the Institute of Sugar in Ankara, Turkey. February 8, 1982. On Enver Hoxha, AShV Korçë, F. 67, Kombinati i Sheqerit, 1982, d. 8, fl. 5. Report of the director of the sugar combine of Maliq, Llazar Plasa regarding the application of the experience the Albanian delegation brought from their visit to Turkey. March 6, 1982.

[80] On the ordering of scientific books, see AQSh, F. 497, Ministria e Industrisë së Lehtë Ushqimore, 1981, d. 557, fl. 23-24. Information of the Albanian delegation that took part in the training for the perfection of sugar processing held at the Institute of Sugar in Ankara, Turkey. February 8, 1982. On sending delegations to Turkey, AShV Korçë, F. 67, Kombinati i Sheqerit, 1982, d. 27, fl. 1-5. Correspon-

lated from the broader scientific debates of the late 1960s, 1970s, and 1980s. For example, the directory of the sugar combine supported its arguments, in its reports to the Ministry of Light Industry, by referring to the contemporary scientific literature and experiences from around the world. In a meeting that the agronomist of the refinery had with the Minister of Light Industry, he again used the example of the practices used in the "world" to make his point and defend his work.[81] Using the concept of the "world" served as a formula of technological legitimation. The "world" (*bota*) was of course not the entire world. It was a metonym for the developed countries of Western Europe. Using the term "the West" was ideologically inexcusable and could cost one dearly. However, linguistic devices like "the world" could serve their purpose very well by not transgressing ideological orthodoxy.

In the early 1970s, the "world" (*bota*) entered Albanians' everyday vocabulary as a synonym for the West[82]—and they still deploy this term today in the same way. Expressions like "to do the things like the whole world" or "to become like the world" are widely used in reference to the goal of making Albania "European" and reflect frustration with this constantly moving target. Flattening the world to Western Europe and expanding the latter to the whole world demonstrates how the Albanians reinforced and reproduced, even during the Cold War and under Socialism, the Eurocentric conceptualization of the world. Indeed, the concept of Europe and its project for a united continent as a model for the world was not simply created by the members of the European Community. Rather than emerging exclusively from the centers of the industrial countries lo-

---

dence between the Ministry of Light Industry and Food and the sugar combine of Maliq for the candidates that the state will send outside of the country for specialization. Mat 5-6, 1982; AShV Korçë, F. 67, Kombinati i Sheqerit, 1985, d. 44, fl. 2. Correspondence between the Ministry of Light Industry and Food and the sugar combine of Maliq regarding the candidates that will be sent for training in Turkey. April 24–25, 1985; AShV Korçë, F. 67, Kombinati i Sheqerit, 1987, d. 14, fl. 1-4. Correspondence between the Ministry of Light Industry and Food and sugar combine of Maliq regarding the candidates that will participate in the course organized by UNIDO in Turkey. July 3–September 15, 1987.

81 AShV Korçë, F. 67, Kombinati i Sheqerit, 1984, d. 1, fl. 22. Memo of the sugar combine of Maliq regarding the loss of sugar content in beets during their harvest, transportation, storage, and processing. December 12, 1984; AQSh, F. 497, Ministria e Industrisë së Lehtë dhe Ushqimore, 1985, d. 7, fl. 17. Minutes of the meeting of the Collegium of the Ministry of Light Industry and Food on the problem of losses at the sugar combine in Maliq. June 29, 1985.

82 *Indoktrinimi komunist përmes kulturës, letërsisë dhe artit (dokumente historike). Vëllimi II (1969–1973)* [The communist indoctrination through culture, literature, and art (Historical Documents). Volume II (1969–1973)], eds. Beqir Meta, Afrim Krasniqi, and Hasan Bello (Tirana: Emal, 2019), 198–199, 203, 483 & 525. Sometimes, people made it clear that for them the "world" meant the West (*Ibid*, 525); while at other times they spoke openly in favor of the country to open up to the West (*Ibid*, 220).

cated on the west of the ideological fence, the construction of Europe has been a decentralized process in which the countries located at its fringes have also participated—including the less open socialist states of the continent.

The Albanian communist power structure reinforced the notion of Europe as a destination that would replace the past and emancipate the country from its Ottoman legacy. The efforts to become part of Europe are ongoing and this powerfully shapes the self-image of Albanians. In fact, in Albania the word *bota* is also used to refer to public opinion—the gaze of society and the community that forces individuals to conform to widely accepted norms. Sayings like "what the world will say" or "the world is watching" are related to the notions of honor, shame, and respectability that mirror the disciplining of the individual to the norms of society and define their place in it. In this sense, Western Europe also represents the gaze of the powerful—the source of standards and respect. It represents what W. E. B. Du Bois called the double-conscience: looking at oneself through the eyes of others.[83] In the first chapter of this book, I explained the importance of Europe's gaze to the way Albanian intellectuals and political elites defined themselves and their society, a phenomenon that has been present since the late 1800s when the national movement gained momentum. Ironically, the communists continued on this path and reinforced the set of expectations, images, beliefs, and feelings upon which the concept of Europe rests.

Many of the sugar beet specialists in Maliq, who read foreign journals and imported the debates to the microcosm of communist Albania's sugar land, sought radical changes in agricultural practices. In the debates with their more conservative colleagues, the innovators used as their slogan: "We cannot remain behind—the *world* [italics are mine] is moving forward."[84] In the 1970s, the Institute of Industrial Studies proposed that the State Planning Commission and the Ministry of Light Industry apply in Maliq the technologies introduced in the West since 1961. The countries of Central Europe, the report said, had used this technology since 1967 and it proposed to implement the achievements of the "world" in Albania as well.[85] Competition with the Soviet bloc and technological borrowing across the fence served as an argument for the Albanian special-

---

83 W. E. B. Du Bois, *The Souls of Black Folk* (Oxford: Oxford University Press, 2007), 8.
84 AShV Korçë, F. 3/2, Komiteti i PPSh Rrethi Korçë, 1973, Lista 29, d. 66, fl. 37. On some fundamental organizational and economic problems of the agricultural economies. February 27, 1973.
85 AQSh, F. 495, Komisioni i Planit të Shtetit, 1974, d. 20, fl. 1-4. Memo of the Institute of Industrial Studies concerning the reconstruction of the sugar combine of Maliq and the increase in the nutritional value of the dry pulp of sugar beet. February 9, 1974.

ist to ask for Albania to do the same. Without borrowing Western technology, the gap between the country and its socialist "others" would widen.

There was even more to it. In a masterful use of language, the deployment of the concept of the "world" collapsed any division of Europe into ideological camps that offered different and alternative forms of modernity. In fact, "world" devalued the socialist alternative, rejected the exclusivist rhetoric of the regime and its self-exclusionary discourse, and resisted and subverted it by using against its rhetoric one of the basic concepts of the modernizing ideology: the idea of progress, which the experts equated and essentialized with the West. "World" divested the ALP's discourse of development of any Cold War era ideological valence and integrated it into the ideology of a single worldwide path to progress. In other words, the Albanian technocrats had embraced the American theory of modernization by curiously reproducing under socialism the Western-centric set of hierarchies that this theory inspired. The West was the center of the world, and it offered the unique viable path to modernity, while others had to converge upon it. Progress legitimized the use of the "world's" experience; it allowed for not only the preservation of the connections but also the emulation of the European/Western model/s. By now, the Soviet myth had been squarely replaced by that of the West/Europe. The discourse of the technocrats about progress sought not only to borrow the technology but also the ideology that produced it.

As part of the orientation toward Western-generated knowledge and its growing circulation in the country, the researchers of the Agricultural Institute of Korça used the latest American scientific literature for the drainage of the plain of Maliq.[86] Although Hoxha considered the United States the generator of all the evils of the world and the main enemy of socialist Albania, the Albanian specialists, even in peripheries like Maliq, secretly devoured American publications on the production of sugar. Of course, the ties with Soviet literature were not abruptly cut off, especially in the face of the linguistic skills of the specialists of the sugar combine. The bulk of them were trained in the USSR or by the Soviet specialists who worked in Maliq during the 1950s.

Moreover, regardless of the continuous upgrading that the refinery went through, a substantial part of its technology was Soviet, and the instructions for the use of the machinery were in Russian. It was not easy for the specialists of Maliq to cut their ties with Soviet literature and science. Even in 1985, the

---

86   AQSh, F. 498, Ministria e Bujqësisë, 1980, d. 97, fl. 6-16. Report on the use of mathematical methods for the drainage of the plain of Korça.

specialists of the sugar combine kept using both old and recent literature that ranged from 1945 to 1984.[87] The Albanians kept accumulating research literature of varied provenance and used it for their own ends. In the 1970s and 1980s, Maliq became an intersection of technologies, influences, and languages coming from both blocs. In this way, during these decades of extreme isolationism of the communist regime Maliq was still a replica of what the Albanian territory had historically been, i.e., a crossroad of the monotheistic religions and their civilizations.

Growing contacts with both sides of the ideological divide also meant more linguistic skills, as the contemporary modern technology was not exclusively Western. Nevertheless, by this time there was a growing emphasis on the scientific contacts and achievements of the West, especially with the English-speaking world. By the 1980s, English started to replace Russian as a major tool for contact with the world. Now that the regime was sending its specialists for training in the West or countries with ties to the West, English became essential. Such a shift created serious problems as only one chemist in the sugar refinery knew the language of Shakespeare. The others knew the Russian of Lenin or the French of Balzac. In Maliq, the specialists started reacting to the linguistic barriers that hampered growing contact with English-written scientific forums and literature and began to adjust to the new situation. Many of them began to learn English and in the 1980s the combine subscribed to the very important British periodical *International Sugar Journal*.[88]

It is evident that during the early years of communist rule the specialists were more isolated because their experience was limited to that of the Soviet bloc. In the 1970s, with the growing orientation toward the West, the horizons of the technocrats widened, while the country was considered more isolated than ever.

---

87 On instructions in Russian for the use of machinery, Mira Carkanji, informal interview by Artan Hoxha, Tirana, June 2016; AQSh, F. 497, Ministria e Industrisë së Lehtë dhe Ushqimore, 1985, d. 7, fl. 3. Memo prepared by the specialists of the sugar combine of Maliq regarding the losses in weight and sugar content of sugar beet in the harvesting, storage, transportation, and processing. June 3, 1985.

88 On the growing importance of English and the knowledge of French and Russian, AShV Korçë, F. 67, Kombinati i Sheqerit, 1982, d. 27, fl. 1-2. Correspondence between the Ministry of Light Industry and Food and the sugar combine of Maliq on the candidates for training in the processing of sugar beet outside the country. April 24–May 6, 1982; AShV Korçë, F. 67, Kombinati i Sheqerit, 1985, d. 44, fl. 2. Correspondence between the Ministry of Light Industry and Food and the sugar combine of Maliq regarding the candidates that will be sent for training in Turkey. April 24–25, 1985. On the subscription to the British journal, AShV Korçë, F. 67, Kombinati i Sheqerit, 1987, d. 77, fl. 1. Correspondence between the directory of the sugar combine in Maliq and the export-import branch of the Enterprise for the Distribution of Books regarding the continuation of the combine's subscription to the periodical *International Sugar Journal*. July 1–9, 1987.

In the 1980s, the need to renovate the technology of the industrial establishments became critical, and Enver Hoxha gave instructions to upgrade the technology. The specialists embraced these directions with great zeal, including those of Maliq, where the technocrats, always quoting Hoxha, proposed a series of initiatives to renovate the combine and increase its productivity and efficiency. The renovation of technology meant, above all, an increase in contact and exchange of technology with the economically advanced countries of the West. Even for the production of other consumer goods related to sugar, e.g., jam and marmalade, the Albanians consulted West German literature.[89]

These shifts reflected the generational transformations in Maliq. The Western-oriented specialists were products of Albanian higher education who graduated in the 1970s and 1980s and, at least in the case of Maliq, were mostly in their late twenties or thirties. In the last decade of its existence, the regime started promoting a new generation of researchers and managers. By the mid-1980s, when Hoxha was at the end of his life, the central authorities clearly stated their goal of upgrading the technological infrastructure of the country's industry and rejuvenating the rank and file of the technocratic intelligentsia. Tirana's authorities sent many young specialists for training in Western Europe to update them with the latest technologies. In 1985, the Ministry of Light Industry and Food asked the sugar combine to send the names of specialists that would go to Turkey to attain professional qualifications, specifying that they had to be between 25 and 35 years old.[90] In the same way as it did in its early years, the regime deployed in its twilight years the master metaphor of the "old man"; this time, however, against itself. It paved the way for its use in the post-socialist era. Those who came to power after the collapse of communism simply recirculated a concept that had taken on a new life in the 1980s.

As knowledge and technology circulated in invisible but consistent ways, the commodities they produced and patterns of consumption changed accordingly.

---

89   On the proposal of Hoxha, AShV Korçë, F. 67, Kombinati i Sheqerit, 1982, d. 6, fl. 2. Memo on the expansion in the processing capacity of the sugar combine to 3000 tons of sugar beet per day. September 17, 1982. On the use of German literature on marmalade, AQSh, F. 497, Ministria e Industrisë së Lehtë dhe Ushqimore, d. 15, fl. 8. Minutes of the meeting of the Council of Ministers regarding the implementation of some measures for the better management of sugar and its byproducts. December 7, 1984.

90   AShV Korçë, F. 67, Kombinati i Sheqerit, 1985, d. 44, fl. 2. Request of the Ministry of Light Industry and Food sent to the sugar combine of Maliq regarding the candidates that will be sent for training in Turkey. April 19, 1985; AShV Korçë, F. 67, Kombinati i Sheqerit, 1987, d. 14, fl. 1. Request of the Ministry of Light Industry and Food sent to the sugar combine of Maliq regarding the candidates that will participate in the course organized by UNIDO in Turkey. July 3, 1987.

Producing goods and foods based on Western European literature also meant the importation of the habits and tastes related to the social, political, cultural, and economic contexts that created them. Technology is not free from ideology; it responds to the specific social, economic, and cultural context in which it is invented.[91] It can be an answer to existing needs or it can create needs within a particular ideological framework or *Weltanschauung*. It is not outside or independent of these factors. This was especially true in the context of the Cold War, when technology lost any claim of neutrality because it embodied the success of the cultural and political context that produced it.[92] When technology circulates, the ideology of the context that created it also moves with it. Of course, its implementation in another place does not have the same outcome as in the country of its origin, but it still triggers transformations and creates points of contact between different social contexts. As Yves Cohen argues, in the process of circulation there occurs a double transformation: that of the disseminated item and that of its receiver.[93] It is true that the Albanian communist regime tried to shape the imported technology to its own needs and integrate it within the larger fabric of its socialism. Yet, it could not totally alter the ideology that underpinned the technology it imported from Western Europe, and this became a link between ordinary Albanians and the world.

When the Albanian agronomists, engineers, and specialists of Maliq brought West German technological schemes to Albania or when the regime imported new polyploid or mono-germ seeds, they were either responding to similar needs to those that had created those technologies or, by borrowing them, they were introducing similar needs. With the end of the Stalinist complex of superiority, the diluting of the belief of Soviet technological supremacy, and the rise of the Western superiority complex, the Albanian communist regime and its technocrats were looking toward the West. However, with this machinery and other technologies the Albanians were also importing the ideology of the West, or at least components of it related to consumption. In the meantime, the Albanian communist regime started emphasizing the myth of self-reliance and quarantined the country because it was aware of the ideological power of the commodities of the West. What lies behind this paradox? Why did the ALP and the technocrats so desperately need to import technology in the first place? Tirana's

---

91   Bruno Latour, "Technology is Society Made Durable," *The Sociological Review* 38, S1 (1990): 110.
92   Lorenzini, *Global Development: A Cold War History*, 68.
93   Yves Cohen, "Circulatory Localities: The Example of Stalinism in the 1930s," *Kritika: Explorations in Russian and Eurasian History* 11, no. 1 (2010): 12–13.

communist regime was forced to seek technological solutions in the West because it had to solve challenges of a social and cultural nature. What challenges were Western technology supposed to fix?

Sugar Consumption and Cross-Border Exchanges

In 1954, an article published in the newspaper of the Albanian Democratic Front on the fifth anniversary of the sugar combine of Maliq boasted about the rise in the quality of life in Albania during the ten years of communist governance. This was especially true, the article claimed, for the countryside. The journalist used sugar consumption as a litmus test for his argument. Before World War II, Albanian peasants used sugar to make sweets only for important celebrations and daily access to such luxuries was only for wealthy speculators who did not work. After the establishment of communism, the consumption of sugar increased thanks to the care the ALP devoted to improve the living standards of the working masses and supply them with consumer goods.[94] Separating the argument from the ideological vocabulary and the regime's rhetoric, what remains true is that sugar consumption increased under communism. The trend had started in the interwar era, but the ALP's policies accelerated the process.

Sugar consumption took off in the 1950s. From 3900 tons of sugar sold in the market at the beginning of the decade, the number jumped to 15,000 tons by 1959, with a per capita consumption of 10 kg. In 1959, Maliq produced the bulk of the country's sugar—12,000 tons—and the country imported only 3000 tons. If the regime's leaders had any illusion that the country was headed toward self-sufficiency, they would very soon prove themselves wrong. The signs were there. The increase in consumption did not correspond to the population growth, which increased within the span of these ten years from 1.2 to 1.5 million. After the decrease caused by war and the post-World War II years, sugar consumption per capita more than doubled from 4.5 kg in 1950 to 10 kg per person in 1959.[95] By 1964, 1.8 million Albanians consumed 25,000 tons of sugar for an average of 13.9

---

94   Jorgji Mihali, "Industrija e jonë e sheqerit" [Our sugar industry], *Bashkimi*, 269 (2091), November 11, 1954, 3.
95   *Anuari statistikor i Republikës Popullore të Shqipërisë 1960* [Statistical annual of the People's Republic of Albania 1960] (Tirana: Drejtoria e Statistikës, 1960): on population, see p. 53; on domestic production of sugar p. 115; on sugar distribution in the market p. 229; on sugar imports pp. 268–269. On per capita sugar consumption in 1950–1959, AQSh, F. 495, Komisioni i Planit të Shtetit, 1959, d. 32, fl. 38. Study of the State Planning Commission on the standard of living of the population and the development of industry, agriculture, and culture in Albania.

kg per capita. Of all this sugar, Maliq processed only 14,000 tons, while the regime imported the remaining 11,000 tons from Cuba and Poland.[96]

The demand for sugar kept increasing. In the mid-1970s the pace of increase slowed and reached 14.2 kg/person while the total quantity of sugar consumed by the population and industry reached 33,000 tons. In 1980, the amount of sugar consumed in the country increased again to 42,700 tons and again in 1984 it jumped to almost 50,000 tons. Although the regime tried to keep the consumption per person below 14 kilograms per year, it could not control it. The diagram of consumption per head, according to a report by the Prime Minister's Office, kept increasing—from 15.9 kg/person in 1980 to 16.4 kg/person in 1984. By 1989, at the brink of the collapse of communism, when the population had exceeded 3.1 million, sugar consumption had increased to 19.4 kg per person.[97]

Albania had the lowest per capita consumption of sugar in Europe. In the mid-1970s, the annual per capita consumption in Yugoslavia was 29 kg, Bulgaria 33 kg, Hungary 38 kg, and Poland 44 kg; Greece's annual consumption per capita was 20 kg, Italy's 29 kg, West Germany's 37 kg, and Great Britain's 48 kg. Nevertheless, the increase of its use in Albania was impressive compared with that of the pre-World War II era or the beginning of the century. The country experienced a simultaneous increase in population and consumption, and both processes were interconnected. In the period that followed World War II, Albania had the highest rate of demographic growth in Europe. The country had a birth

---

[96] *Vjetari statistikor i Republikës Popullore të Shqipërisë 1965* [Statistical annual of the People's Republic of Albania 1965] (Tirana: Drejotria e Statistikës, 1965): on population, see p. 64; on the domestic production of sugar pp. 152–153; on sugar consumption p. 302; on imports p. 339.

[97] On the increase in sugar consumption, AQSh, F. 495, Komisioni i Planit të Shtetit, 1972, d. 38, fl. 7. Information of the State Planning Commission on the cultivation of sugar beet. September 25, 1972; On the total and per capita consumption in the mid-1970s; AQSh, F. 495, Komisioni i Planit të Shtetit, 1974, d. 20, fl. 17/1-18. Memo on the increase in the domestic production of sugar and the reduction of imports. October 8, 1974; AQSh, F. 495, Komisioni i Planit të Shtetit, 1975, d. 36, fl. 16. Memo concerning the meeting of sugar requirements for the years 1975–1977. On the total consumption of sugar in 1980 and 1984; AQSh, F. 495, Komisioni i Planit të Shtetit, 1981, d. 140, fl. 19-20. Memo of the State Planning Commission on the increase in the cultivation of industrial crops for meeting the needs of the country in fats, sugar, rice, and cotton for the seventh five-year plan. October 8, 1980. On per capita consumption in 1980 and 1984; AQSh, F. 490, Këshilli i Ministrave, 1984, d. 511, fl. 14. Study of the State Planning Commission sent to the Council of Ministers on the needs of the country's population for fats, sugar, and cotton and for the potential of meeting them through an increase in the intensification of agriculture. March 20, 1984. On per capita consumption in 1990 and sugar imports for 1989–1990, AQSh, F. 490, Këshilli i Ministrave, 1990, d. 314, fl. 14. Study of the State Planning Commission sent to the Prime Minister's Office concerning the fulfillment of the country's needs regarding fats, sugar, rice, cotton and the increase in tobacco production and its quality so as to balance the value of exports with imports. September 13, 1989. On population, *Vjetari statistikor i vitit 1989*, 17.

rate two to five times higher than that of the continent as a whole while experiencing a sharp decrease in natural deaths. These processes were an outcome of the improvement of sanitary services and the growth of calorific intake per capita, which leaped from 2500 calories per day in 1965 to 3160 in 1980. There occurred an expansion in the consumption of meat, dairy, fats (especially oil, either olive or industrial, and butter), and sugar. The State Planning Commission correctly anticipated that the demand for these goods would increase while observing a decrease in the consumption of wheat and bread, the traditional staples of the Albanian diet.[98]

Beyond the triumphalist declarations for the successes of the ALP, the demographic growth and expansion of consumption stirred anxieties among the communist planners. The communist regime introduced the global revolution of rising expectations to Albania.[99] However, the project of improving the living standards of the population presented Tirana's leadership with the daunting challenge of feeding a growing population that was progressively consuming more. Maliq failed to produce enough sugar to keep up with the explosive combination of a population boom and steep growth of per capita consumption. The combine refined 67 thousand tons of sugar between 1966 to 1970, and ten years later, between 1976 and 1980 it refined 83 thousand tons. The growing deficit forced the regime to increase annual imports from 14,600 tons in 1975 to 40,000 tons of sugar in 1988.[100] The increase in imports meant that precious hard currency was

---

98   On population growth, caloric intake, and the increase in the consumption of sugar, AQSh, F. 495, Komisioni i Planit të Shtetit, 1978, d. 51, fl. 4-7. Prognosis on the increase in population and per capita consumption in the future five-year plan up to the year 2000. February 4, 1978. On sugar consumption in the other countries of Europe, *Ibid*, fl. 40. Index of the State Planning Commission on the consumption of the principal consumer goods in some European countries; on the increase in life expectancy and population growth, see Arjan Gjonça, *Communism, Health and Lifestyle: The Paradox of Mortality Transition in Albania, 1950–1990* (Westport, CT: Greenwood Press, 2001), 59–107.

99   On the global pattern of the revolution of rising expectations, Lorenzini, *Global Development: A Cold War History*, 34.

100 On the problem of supplying the growing population with sugar, AQSh, F. 498, Ministria e Bujqësisë, 1968, d. 90/4, fl. 4. Study of the Ministry of Agriculture regarding the prospective development of agriculture in the district of Korça for the years 1970–1980. July 1968. On the quantity of sugar that the refinery of Maliq processed, AQSh, F. 495, Komisioni i Planit të Shtetit, 1981, d. 140, fl. 20-21. Memo of the State Planning Commission on the increase in the cultivation of industrial crops for meeting the needs of the country in fats, sugar, rice, and cotton for the seventh five-year plan. October 8, 1980. On sugar imports for 1974, AShV Korçë, F. 67, Kombinati i Sheqerit, 1983, d. 3, fl. 31. Study of a group of specialists of the sugar combine of Maliq sent to the Executive Committee of Korça regarding meeting the needs of the country with sugar through an increase in the processing capacity of the combine and the construction of a new sugar factory in Korça. November 30, 1983. On sugar imports in 1988, AQSh, F. 490, Këshilli i Ministrave, 1988, d. 600, fl. 8. Study on the expansion of the domestic capacities of sugar processing and the decrease of imports. March 22, 1988.

flowing out of the country. The issue of raising imports became even more acute with the stratospheric rise in sugar prices on the international market in the early 1970s, which, of course, also affected the capacity of the Albanian state to import either unprocessed or unrefined sugar. By this time, the communist authorities, who kept insisting on autarky, considered the issue of sugar to be a matter of national interest. The depression of the mid-1970s and the subsequent rise in prices further stiffened the Tirana leadership's resolve to produce all the sugar the population consumed domestically.[101]

The the regime's responses to the asymmetry between the slow increase in sugar production and the faster increase in consumption were multiple and not at all unique. The government tightened the belt to decrease sugar consumption in the country. It decided to stop the production of alcohol from sugar beet molasses and used maize molasses for this purpose instead. The government also decreased the production of pastries markedly for both the domestic market and for export. The continuous increase in sugar prices on the international market worried the government, and the State Planning Commission circulated at various times the idea of limiting the general use of sugar or, if necessary, its retail control.[102] All these measures of the government, which aimed at keeping the annual consumption per person below 14 kilograms, failed to give results and the figure kept rising. The power of the ALP met its limits, and its upper echelons faced pressures from below, which they could not tame.

Attempting to decrease consumption failed to give results. Eliminating imports meant above all increasing the processing capacity of the country's sugar industry and maximizing sugar beet and sucrose yields. In other words, this meant an increase in efficiency and an intensification of production. The problem became even more pressing due to the limited arable land that the country had at its disposal. It was these exigencies that forced the Tirana regime to intensify the technological and know-how borrowings from Western countries. Although

---

[101] On the increase in prices on the international markets, AQSh, F. 14/AP (STR), 1974, d. 871, fl. 14-15. Information on current world prices of some primary goods. November 25, 1974. On Tirana's resolve to attain autarky, AQSh, F. 14/AP (OU), 1976, d. 96, fl. 23-24. Minutes of the meeting of the Secretariat of the ALP's Central Committee. September 21, 1976; AQSh, F. 490, Këshilli i Ministrave, 1977, d. 345, fl. 95. Memo with technical and economic arguments for the expansion of the "November 8th" sugar factory.

[102] AQSh, F. 495, Komisioni i Planit të Shtetit, 1974, d. 20, fl. 17/1-18. Memo on the increase in the domestic production of sugar and the reduction of imports. October 8, 1974; AQSh, F. 495, Komisioni i Planit të Shtetit, 1981, d. 140, fl. 19-20. Memo of the State Planning Commission on the increase in cultivation of industrial crops for meeting the needs of the country in fats, sugar, rice, and cotton for the Seventh Five-year Plan. October 8, 1980.

Maliq never processed enough sugar to satisfy domestic demand, the efforts of the communist state to respond to the increase in consumption shaped its history. What do the many links recorded in Maliq reveal about the broader history of socialist Albania? In what ways are consumption, production, and connections with the outside world intertwined?

Industrialization and urbanization only partially explain the increase in sugar consumption. The urban population quadrupled from 238,000 in 1945 to 1.1 million in 1988.[103] However, this still only represented 35% of the total population until the collapse of the regime. There were apparent inequalities in sugar consumption between the urban and rural areas. In the 1960s, out of twenty-seven districts of the country, the eight that contained the major urban centers consumed almost 60% of the sugar in the country. For the entire decade of the 1950s, the urban population consumed more sugar than the countryside.[104] The growth of urban areas alone, however, cannot explain the steep increase in sugar consumption in the country. The rural population also increased its consumption of sugar. Thus, in 1961 the rural population consumed 132% more sugar than it did in 1956.[105]

The country experienced a substantial increase in per capita income both in the cities and in the countryside. Thus, in 1975 the income of the average Albanian was almost five-fold what it was in 1938—although workers had better salaries than members of the collective farms. In the meantime, the regime decreased prices several times.[106] The rise in incomes and fall in prices is very important for understanding the growth of consumption for it has to do with the purchasing power of the population and its ability to engage in financial transactions. How-

---

103 *Vjetari statistikor i Republikës Popullore të Shqipërisë 1964* [Statistical annual of the People's Republic of Albania 1964] (Tirana: Drejtoria e Statistikës, 1964), 61.

104 On sugar consumption, *Vjetari statistikor i Republikës Popullore të Shqipërisë 1963* [Statistical annual of the People's Republic of Albania 1963] (Tirana: Drejtoria e Statistikës, 1963), 260; *Vjetari statistikor i Republikës Popullore të Shqipërisë 1964*, 304; *Vjetari statistikor i Republikës Popullore të Shqipërisë 1965*, 305. On sugar consumption in urban and rural areas, AQSh, F. 495, Komisioni i Planit të Shtetit, 1959, d. 134, fl. 21. Index of the State Planning Commission on the sale of commodities in towns and villages.

105 Dervish Gjiriti, "Probleme të shpërndarjes së prodhimit dhe të nivelit të jetesës në fshat" [Problems of the distribution of production and the standard of living in the countryside] *Ekonomia popullore* [People's economy] 10, no. 6 (1963): 57.

106 On the increase in consumption and the decrease in prices, see AQSh, F. 495, Komisioni i Planit të Shtetit, 1959, d. 32, fl. 36-38. Study of the State Planning Commission on the standard of living of the population and the development of industry, agriculture, and culture in Albania. On the increase in incomes, Aristotel Pano, *Probleme të toerisë, të metodologjisë dhe të analizës së të ardhurave kombëtare të RPSSH* [Problems with the theory and methodology of the analysis of national incomes] (Tirana: Universiteti i Tiranës, 1982), 123–124.

ever, it does not necessarily follow that the increase in earnings translated into an increase in consumption. The latter depended on a host of factors that included connections with and independence from the market, tastes, and patterns of consumption. The increase in sugar consumption reflected a broader trend of the continuously growing demand of the population for fats, meat, fish, rice, apparel, furniture, etc. While the urban population had greater purchasing power compared to the rural population, the latter, especially in the lowlands, had been strongly integrated into the state market since the 1950s, which introduced new tastes and needs to the countryside.

By the end of the 1950s, there was a dramatic increase in the confections and clothes sold in the village market stores. Traditional costumes, with the exception of the older generation in the uplands, disappeared. In state stores, the peasants increasingly bought new furniture: radios, gramophones, sewing machines, beds, cupboards, sofas, and a record number of cooking wares that were becoming integral parts of rural households. The peasants made increasing purchases of sugar, macaroni, marmalade, oil, tomato sauce, rice, and army beefs. At a national level, the upbeat trend was especially conspicuous for sugar-based goods like marmalades and jams, the consumption of which, together with that of sugar, exceeded state plans. The continuous increase put the ALP leadership in a very difficult position vis-à-vis the population because the regime could not afford the expansion of the demand for commodities. As the Ministry of Agriculture pointed out in the late 1980s, the imports of foodstuff had almost tripled, creating a stress that the Albanian economy could not withstand.[107]

The new patterns of consumption were largely an outcome of the ALP's policies. The regime was a driving force that fostered economic, social, and cultural transformations that accelerated the expansion of consumption in Albania during the second half of the twentieth century. Its relentless and stubborn insistence on nationalizing agriculture and eradicating private property in the countryside broke the economic shell that had kept the household loosely connected to the market before. The rural population stopped being self-employed and

---

107 On the growth of consumption in the countryside during the 1950s, AShV Korçë, F. 3/2, Komiteti i PPSh Rrethi Korçë, 1959, Lista 15, d. 65, fl. 1-22. Report on the role of consumer cooperatives in the rise of culture in the countryside. On exceeding the consumption of sugar, jam, and marmalade, AQSh, F. 495, Komisioni i Planit të Shtetit, 1966, d. 122, fl. 1-2. Information on the fulfillment of the plan regarding sales in the socialist retail sector. March 14, 1967. On the statement of Qirjako Mihali, AQSh, F. 490, Këshilli i Ministrave, 1990, d. 314, fl. 29. Minutes of the meeting of the Council of Ministers regarding the fulfillment of the country's needs regarding fats, sugar, rice, cotton and the increase in tobacco production and its quality. March 9, 1990.

ended up employed with a salary. The so-called herding process (*tufëzimi*) and full collectivization eliminated all the animals and private plots, forcing the peasants to buy everything they needed at the state markets.[108] The communist state expropriated the peasants, transforming them into a free labor force. Detached from the means of production and with extremely limited property, the rural population produced very few commodities for personal consumption.

To quote Joseph Schumpeter, what capitalism's "creative destruction" had done in Western Europe since the late eighteenth century, the ALP did at an accelerated pace in the second half of the twentieth century under the banner of real socialism.[109] Like capitalism, the socialist regimes destroyed the old social structures and reconfigured them anew by pulling the whole society into the gravitational force of the market, with the difference that the latter was controlled by the state. The Soviet alternative, though, was not the only political project that relied on state intervention for the purpose of including isolated social pockets within the market. With the New Deal, the American government intervened through different forms of infrastructural investments to include in the market the poor rural South where largely self-sufficient households still prevailed well into the 1930s. In Western Europe, especially through the welfare state, the coalition between the state and the private sector and the constant interventionist policies of the governments expanded markets and brought about the European economic miracle.[110]

The Soviet model, which conceived the state as the single economic actor entitled to lead radical social transformations, represents the most extreme form of this twentieth-century global trend.[111] For the Marxist–Leninist leaders, the state was a deus ex machina for achieving in a short time what capitalism had achieved in more than 150 years. For them, socialism was simultaneously a shortcut and a gas pedal for going through the same process as the affluent capitalist countries

---

108 On Albanian agriculture during socialism, see Örjan Sjöberg, "'Any Other Road Leads to the Restoration of Capitalism in the Countryside': Land Collectivization in Albania," in *The Collectivization of Agriculture in Communist Eastern Europe*, 369–397; Derek Hall, *Albania and the Albanians* (London: Pinter Reference, 1994), 119–121. On the process of herding, Skënder Gjoleka, Marko Vangjeli, and Ago Nezha, *Për tufëzimin e bagëtive të oborreve kooperativiste* [On the herding of the cooperative gardens' livestock] (Tirana: Shtëpia e Propagandës Bujqësore, 1982).
109 Joseph Schumpeter, *Capitalism, Socialism and Democracy* (London: Routledge, 2003), 81–86.
110 Brent Cebul, "Creative Competition: Georgia Power, the Tennessee Valley Authority, and the Creation of a Rural Consumer Economy, 1934–1955," *The Journal of American History* 105, no. 1 (2018): 45–70.
111 On the economic impact of Social Democracy in Western Europe, Tony Judt, *Postwar: A History of Europe since 1945* (New York: Penguin Books, 2005), 360–389.

at a higher speed. György Péteri has argued that the socialist regimes suffered from the tension between their modernizing drive and the need they felt to avoid the blurring of distinctions with capitalist systems and create a genuine alternative to the latter. In the end, they did not solve this tension and the West's patterns and standards shaped them.[112]

Hoxha's regime was another case that carried this contradiction. Sticking to the Marxist scheme of splitting historical progress into stages and driven by the modernizers' heterochronic approach to time, whose goal was to intensify the pace of history and compensate for "lost time," the socialist regimes reproduced many of the patterns of the capitalist societies. Tirana's authorities did nothing other than create a proletariat that was detached from the means of production. The difference was that the employer was the state. Like capitalism, the policies of the Soviet systems created consumers. The original contribution of the Hoxha regime was that it transformed the peasants into salaried workers without moving them from the countryside. The rural population now largely depended on the market and the processed goods produced by the food industry and supplied by the state-controlled market. This process accelerated in the late 1960s with the Albanian "Cultural Revolution," which coincided with a steep increase in sugar consumption.[113]

Moreover, the regime's insistence on pulling women out of the familial economy and fully employing them either in the collectivist or state sector had an immense impact on the patterns of food consumption. Mothers were not at home anymore and had less time to prepare food for their children. The new forms of employment and the triumph of monetary forms of exchanges in the countryside hugely impacted the consumption patterns of the rural population, which converged on those of the cities—although without ever being identical. The employment of both parents outside the household imposed a specific rhythm and direction on the flow of time in everyday life. Now, it was the state bureaucracy that determined its rhythms and introduced its own conception and organiza-

---

112 György Péteri, "Introduction: The Oblique Coordinate Systems of Modern Society," in *Imagining the West*, 1–12. See especially pp. 8 and 12; Péteri, "Nylon Curtain," 113–123.

113 On the Cultural Revolution in Albania, see Miranda Vickers, *The Albanians: A Modern History* (London: I. B. Tauris, 1999), 193–201; *Historia e Partisë së Punës të Shqiërisë* [The history of the Albanian Labor Party] (Tirana: 8 Nëntori, 1981), 387–159; Peter Prifti, "Albania," in *The Communist States in Disarray 1965–1971*, eds. Adam Bromke and Teresa Rakowska-Harmstone (Minneapolis, MN: University of Minnesota Press, 1972), 198–220; Nicholas C. Pano, "Albania in the Sixties," in *The Changing Face of Communism in Eastern Europe*, ed. Peter A. Toma (Tucson, AZ: University of Arizona Press, 1970), 245–280.

tion of time, which is also reflected in the booming trade of personal watches in the countryside in the 1950s.[114] Working outside the household forced the peasants to buy the bulk of their commodities in the market, something that transformed their diet. Sugar became a standard staple of the average diet. It was not merely used for coffee and sweets but became a critical component in the diet of adults and especially children. Kids with a slice of bread spread with butter and sugar or with sugar and olive oil in hand became one of the most familiar images of socialist Albania, both in urban areas and the countryside.

The Albanian communist regime created the context for the penetration of new tastes and patterns of consumption because it reshaped the social fabric of the country. This gave a death blow to the old rural communities and forced them to depend on the market. Hoxha shattered the closed circle of the producers that consumed their own product. It was not possible anymore for the peasants to control the whole alimentary chain from production to consumption. The communists were the architects of these multilayered and profound transformations, which increased consumption to the point that undermined any effort of the regime to establish economic self-sufficiency in the principal commodities of everyday use. Sugar gained importance in the 1920s, but the communists made it extremely important for the entire society and not just some specific groups within it.

The extensive use of sugar forced the regime, which had not given up on its autarkic dreams, to look for technological solutions, only to see itself caught more and more in the web of international trade and transnational exchanges. The tension between the growing demand for sugar and the regime's drive for autarky transformed Maliq into an intersection of transnational exchanges of ideas, peoples, and technologies from the interwar era all the way to the collapse of communism. It was the growing pressure from below for sugar and the need to supply the population without giving up on the goal of self-sufficiency that made Maliq an access point to the world. The communist state established a higher degree of social cohesion within the country and created modern consumers only to see itself obliged to pursue not its own agenda but that of the people. When the communist regime did not meet the growing consumption demand of the population, the ALP lost its legitimacy.

---

114 AShV Korçë, F. 3/2, Komiteti i PPSh Rrethi Korçë, 1959, Lista 15, d. 65, fl. 17. Report on the role of consumer cooperatives in the rise of culture in the countryside.

CHAPTER 4

This chapter shows that in socialist systems, the dynamics of the transnational exchanges were not determined exclusively in and by the state. The dissemination of know-how and technology became entangled within the complexity of the domestic social, economic, and cultural transformations that were taking place in Albania. The communist regime accelerated the creation of the modern consumer in Albania, and in turn the latter forced the state to maintain its connections with the world and import technologies that produced commodities that responded to the tastes of its society. The final result was an energizing process that continuously reinforced itself and put Tirana's authorities in a fragile position vis-à-vis the consumers it had itself helped to create.

Once it had created them, the regime could not respond to the needs of these groups that were detached from any property and were entirely dependent on the market. Any effort to meet their needs, including the demand of the ALP leadership for a technological revolution in order to stand up to the "imperialist encirclement,"[115] deepened Tirana's dependence on the technologically more advanced North, either on the West or the East of the ideological divide. When we talk about isolationism, we should not only look at people who move across boundaries. Neither should we look merely at the connections of the country with the international railroad system or the bunker and siege mentality that it represents, whether or not the shops have the same outlook for decades prior, or other impressionistic depictions that construct an image of stagnation and isolation.[116]

Rather than relying exclusively on the visible signs, the analysis should investigate what takes place behind the façade. We should be careful not to conflate without much investigation the rhetoric, which often times is for public consumption, with the practices that take place behind the scenes. This was especially true for political systems that lacked transparency, like those based on the Soviet model. Thinking in terms of binaries like openness vs. closedness deprives the argument of the grey areas and the nuances of the complexities of social interactions and realities. For this reason, it is better to approach the policing of Albanian society and Tirana's efforts to reduce unmediated communication with

---

[115] "Vendim i Plenumit të Komitetit Qendror të PPSh 'Mbi punën e bërë dhe masat që duhen marrë për të shfrytëzimin e plotë të aftësive prodhuese në industrinë mekanike, për spcializimin dhe kooperimin e mëtejshëm të saj" [Decision of the III Plenum of the ALP's Central Committee "On the work done and the measures to be taken for the full exploitation of the productive capacities in mechanical industry, and for its further specialization and cooperation], October 14, 1967, *Dokumente kryesore te Partisë së Punës të Shqipërisë. Volume V. 1966–1970* [Main documents of the Albanian Labor Party. Volume V. 1966–1970] (Tirana: 8 Nëntori, 1974), 350–361.

[116] Elidor Mëhilli, "States of Insecurity," *The International History Review* 37, no. 5 (2015): 1051.

the world at large as an effort to tame and negotiate the transformation of the country. On the other hand, a multitude of unintended consequences were created by the many paradoxes that riddled socialist regimes. I would postulate that this is not only true for Hoxha's regime, but for the Soviet bloc as a whole.

During the Cold War era, Albania was the least open European country. However, it was not as isolated as it has generally been regarded. For a country that wanted to modernize, isolation was not an option. Albania was exposed to many invisible influences from around the world. The history of Maliq was framed by the constant multilevel and pluri-directional interactions of power relations, social forces, transnational cultural influences, and technological exchanges it had to negotiate and domesticate during its forty years of life. This flux of exchanges and cross-border movements blurred the boundaries between the national and the international, the foreign and the domestic. It also differentiates political rhetoric from practice—while unveiling a network of people connected through multiple sinews, from the local to the national, along with international webs of circulation of knowledge and technology. Maliq's history was shaped by one of the major contradictions of Hoxha's regime: the more it struggled to attain self-sufficiency, the more it was caught in the web of transnational exchanges and interactions.

Maliq was part of the different networks that connected multiple spatial levels, temporal units, and ideological actors. It was one of those connecting points between communist Albania and the world that, paradoxically, at the height of Albania's reduction of contacts with the world intensified the interactions and exchanges with it. Maliq was a contact point; a border site; a corridor of communication; and an intersection between Albania and the world. It also co-produced different myths and taxonomies and became a laboratory of different orders of knowledge and a testing ground for the nationalist and modernizing project of self-sufficiency. Maliq connected many actors and many other spaces across the ideological specter of a divided Europe. It is a history of variable geometries. It tells us not only the story of Albania but also that of the twentieth century, of communism, of the Cold War, of trans-European and global interactions, and of how they affected one corner of the Balkans.

CHAPTER 5

Communism and After: From Sugar to Ruins

Ruins and the Angel of History

Maliq, communist Albania's sugar capital, hides behind a screen of vegetation on the west of the highway that links Korça to Tirana. The first thing any visitor sees when they enter the town is what remains of the sugar refinery. In the northern part of the inhabited area, on the right side of the street and fenced in by a wall, there are roofless buildings with walls of red brick plastered and painted in yellow, vast round storage tanks that once held molasses, and a large concrete smokestack. These are the relics of the only sugar refinery Albania has ever built. The ruins, like the bare bones of a carcass, lie motionless. The tall chimney does not emit smoke anymore. Surrounded by yellow dust and the desolate brownish landscape of barren hills, it is quiet and lifeless. Like a grave stele, it reminds the stranger passing by that there used to be an industrial complex in this place.

When I visited the ex-sugartown in September of 2017, I walked through the factory. Its streets were empty, noiseless, and covered by the debris of the post-socialist juggernaut. It looked like Klee's Angelus Novus, the angel of history that flies with its back toward the future, had fluttered over the sugar refinery of Maliq.[1] Detritus of construction materials—and even fragments of inscriptions—accompany the visitor across the streets of the refinery. There was no activity, there were no people, and there was no more sugar; there was nothing but half-destroyed buildings, the baking sun, and the ceaseless scratching song of the cicadas. In the meantime, the Devoll River continues to flow indifferently by the side of the in-

---

[1] See Walter Benjamin's interpretation of Klee's painting in Walter Benjamin, "Theses on the Philosophy of History," in *Illuminations: Essays and Reflections*, ed. Hannah Arendt and trans. Harry Zohn (New York: Schocken Books, 2007), 253–264. More specifically pp. 257–258.

dustrial ruins, impassive to time and history. The small town, which the communist regime built as an appendage to the refinery, suffered the consequences. With the factory lying in rubble, Maliq's inhabitants did not have many opportunities to make a living. The collapse of socialism meant the end of their old security, while the future that lay ahead was uncertain. Adapting to a new world was hard.

A child of state-socialism, Maliq was marginalized in the wake of its collapse. Integrating into the global capitalism of the twenty-first century was not easy for this ex-mono-industrial small town. Shielded by a wall of trees, it remained almost invisible for years; a pocket outside the stream of people and capital that relentlessly buzzes along the highway. The fate of Maliq and its refinery is not unique. Albania has plenty of similar towns that the communist regime of Tirana built from scratch. Kukës, Poliçan, Patos, Selenicë, Memaliaj, Milot, Rubik, Gramsh, Ballsh, Cërrik, Laç, and Rrëshen are a small sample of such towns. These towns, built around now-closed single industries, fill today's Albania like a dense constellation of despair, pessimism, acute social problems, poverty, and mass emigration.

Albania has attracted more attention for its bunkers that closed it off from the world than for its factories and industries that connected it with this same world. More attention is paid to the differences than to the commonalities. Maliq's fate, on the other hand, replicates that of thousands of industrial establishments and towns across the socialist world. The space from Kamchatka to the Adriatic is not only unified by a socialist past, as reflected by the standard urban designs, five-story apartment buildings, and materials used in construction.[2] Regardless of the local specificities, the countries of this immense space also share many historical similarities in the post-socialist era. The ruins of abandoned factories and mills that fill the entire area once dominated for half a century by socialist systems comprise one of the most conspicuous features of the post-socialist landscape.

Akarmara, Pyramiden, Kadykchan, Ugolny Ruchei, Alykel, Norilsk, Vorkuta, and Anadyr are only some of the hundreds of dying industrial towns scattered across Russia. Empty factories and crippled industrial centers, from Elsterberg in East Germany to Pernik and Vidin in Bulgaria or Anina Noua, Brad, and Petrila in Romania, are shadows of what they were 32 years ago. These towns fill the map of Eastern and Central Europe and the ex-Soviet space. Once symbols

---

[2] See the argument of Stephen Kotkin on the unity of material culture, the Soviet phenomenon established across the Eurasian space, in Stephen Kotkin, "Mongol Commonwealth? Exchange and Governance across the Post-Mongol Space," *Kritika: Explorations in Russian and Eurasian History* 8, no. 3 (2007): 487–531, especially pp. 520–526.

of socialist industrialization, these towns are now undergoing a gradual death following the collapse of communism and the radical shrinking of their industries. The communities whose activities spun around these factories have paid a heavy toll. Litter and rust mark the decline of the industrial areas in the aftermath of socialism's collapse in many countries of Eastern Europe. While it is true that there are post-socialist success stories in this region with thriving industries, the truth is that a good part of the industrial establishments have closed down. The dystopian images of urban, industrial, environmental, and social ruin represent the end of an era and the tectonic shift that accompanied the crossing of the threshold into another age.[3]

The ruined images of Maliq's sugar refinery, which I visited in 2017, do not characterize the ex-socialist countries alone. They can also be found throughout Western Europe and North America with similar social devastation. Christopher Barzak, in a short story on Youngstown, Ohio, brilliantly expresses the tension between the past, the present, and the future that characterizes ex-industrial communities. It encapsulates the disruption that the closing of the mills have caused to the fabric of their social lives. Similar to Klee's Angelus Novus, Barzak states in his short story that he moves through time with his back to the future, and the wind of the motion blows his hair toward the past.[4] While these communities move toward an unknown future, they know for sure what they used to be in the past. The latter is the only stable reference point against the uncertain present and future.

Beginning in 1911, Georg Simmel used ruins as a lens to understand history. Based on the Hegelian dialectic of history, which conceived the World Spirit in struggle with Nature, its antithesis, Simmel saw ruins as their synthesis. According to him, the rubble is the point where nature and human civilization enter into symbiosis.[5] In other words, ruins are the markers of what history's progress has left behind. During the interwar era, Walter Benjamin paid due attention to rubble, which he considered symbolic of historical decadence.[6] The

---

3   On the designation of the deindustrialized areas of Eastern Europe as dystopian, see Eagle Glassheim, *Cleansing the Czechoslovak Borderlands: Migration, Environment, and Health in the Former Sudetenland* (Pittsburgh, PA: University of Pittsburgh Press, 2016).
4   Christopher Barzak, "The B&O, Crossroads of Time and Space," *Muse* 12 (2011): 6.
5   Georg Simmel, "Two Essays: The Handle, and The Ruin," trans. David Kettler, *Hudson Review* 11, no. 3 (1958): 379–385.
6   Walter Benjamin, "The Ruin," in *The Work of Art in the Age of Its Technological Reproducibility and Other Writings on Media*, ed. and trans. Michael W. Jennings, Brigid Doherty, and Thomas Y. Levin (Cambridge, MA: Harvard University Press, 2008), 179–186.

CHAPTER 5

European and global economic crises of the interwar period convinced the German philosopher that ruins were an outcome of capitalism's cyclical destructions, which debunked its supporters' claims of linear progress. Capitalism's destructive need for innovation left heaps of rubble behind, thus making yesterday look ancient. Benjamin's analysis has been central to the study of deindustrialization and its social impact.[7]

So far, many scholars have used ruins as a lens to explore the link between capitalism's "creative destruction" and the way it has affected industrial communities. Scholars have mainly focused on the American and British Rust Belts, two of the areas that have been hardest hit by the outsourcing of manufacturing and industry closure.[8] However, this has not been the case in the study of contemporary Europe, including its ex-socialist eastern regions.[9] The industrial ruins of the socialist era have attracted the attention of some historians, but the amount of work produced on them is still limited.[10] Many local scholars, who identify socialism as a violent "non-European" rupture of the "natural European" course of the history of their countries, have focused mainly on the interwar era and its modernist legacy, which they consider European.[11] On the other hand, they have

---

[7] Caitlin DeSilvey and Tim Edensor, "Reckoning with Ruins," *Progress in Human Geography* 37, no. 4 (2013): 468.

[8] The literature on deindustrialization is vast. I would single out Christian Wicke, Stefan Berger, and Joana Golombek, eds., *Industrial Heritage and Regional Identities* (London: Routledge, 2018); Steven High, Lachlan MacKinnon, and Andrew Perchard, eds., *Deindustrialized World: Confronting Ruination in Postindustrial Places* (Vancouver: UBC Press, 2017); See the forum "Crumbling Cultures," in *International Labor and Working-Class* 84 (2013): 1–153; Tim Edensor, *Industrial Ruins: Spaces, Aesthetics and Materiality* (Oxford: Berg, 2005); Tim Edensor, "The Ghosts of Industrial Ruins: Ordering and Disordering Memory in Excessive Space," *Environment and Planning D: Society and Space* 23, no. 6 (2005): 829–849; Jefferson Cowie and Joseph Heathcott, eds., *Beyond the Ruins: The Meaning of Deindustrialization* (Ithaca, NY: ILR Press, 2003).

[9] Stefan Berger and Christian Wicke, "Introduction: Deindustrialization, Heritage, and Representations of Identity," *The Public Historian* 39, no. 4 (2017): 10.

[10] Györgyi Németh, "Contested Heritage and Regional Identity in the Borsod Industrial Area in Hungary," in *Industrial Heritage and Regional Identities*, 95–118; David Kideckel, "Identity and Mining Heritage in Romania's Jiu Valley Coal Region: Commodification, Alienation, Renaissance," *Ibid*, 119–135; David Kideckel, "Coal Power: Class, Fetishism, Memory and Disjuncture in Romania's Jiu Valley and Appalachian West Virginia," *ANUAC* 7, no. 1 (2018): 67–88; Ilinca Păun Constantinescu, Dragoș Dascălu, and Cristina Sucală, "An Activist Perspective on Industrial Heritage in Petrila, a Romanian Mining City," *The Public Historian* 39, no. 4 (2017): 114–141; Anca Pusca, "Industrial and Human Ruins of Postcommunist Europe," *Space and Culture* 13, no. 3 (2010): 239–255; See also the forum "Ruins and Russian Culture," in *Slavic Review* 65, no. 4 (2006). Of especial importance are the articles of Andreas Schönle, "Ruins and History: Observations on Russian Approaches to Destruction and Decay," *Ibid*, 649–669; and Thomas Lahusen, "Decay or Endurance? The Ruins of Socialism," *Ibid*, 736–746.

[11] See for example the analysis on Romania of Oana Tiganea, "Modern Industrial Heritage in Romania: Extending the Boundaries to Protect the Recent Past," *Docomomo* 49 (2013): 82–85.

not identified the industrial ruins of the socialist era as part of the broader global modernist legacy of the twentieth century.

It is legitimate to ask what these industrial wastelands can tell us about the post-socialist transition from planned to market economies. Is there any connection between the abandonment of old industrial complexes across the Western and Eastern European countries? The cultural theorist Svetlana Boym has suggested that the ruins are remnants and reminders,[12] and the historian Peter Fritzsche has argued that although dilapidated, ruins are not obsolete. He considers them texts for constructing alternative historical trajectories.[13] What exactly are the industrial ruins and devastated communities across Eurasia remnants and reminders of? How can they help us to better understand and write an alternative history of post-socialist societies? In this chapter, I will try to answer these questions by looking at the wreckage of the Maliq factory as part of a broader history of the twentieth century that transcends the ontological capitalist–socialist divide. The rubble of the sugar refinery discloses that the economic organization and the function it played had become obsolete. The networks it was part of have now shifted and national borders and nation-based fixed capital have lost the importance they had held up until the end of the last century.

Building a Regional Integrated Economic Web

To understand the social impact of the closure of the sugar factory, it is first essential to analyze its importance for the communities of Maliq. As explained in the second and fourth chapters, the refinery was part of a national and transnational network of exchange that linked the region of Korça to Albania and Europe. The factory was also at the center of a regional web of economic units that ranged from coal mines to agriculture farms and other light industry plants, especially those for the processing of fruits.[14] All these enterprises either supplied the refinery or were supplied by it. Because of its regional and national importance from its establishment in 1951 to the moment of its collapse, the communist regime transformed the refinery into the largest integrated industrial complex in the country. The factory's expansion fostered the modernization and

---

12 Svetlana Boym, "Ruinophilia," in *The Off-Modern* (New York: Bloomsbery, 2017), 43–48.
13 Peter Fritzsche, "The Ruins of Modernity," in *Breaking Up Time: Negotiating the Borders between Present, Past and Future*, eds. Chris Lorenz and Berber Beverange (Göttingen: Vandenhoeck & Ruprecht, 2013), 64.
14 Kallfa, *Arritje dhe probleme të ngushtimit të dallimeve thelbësore ndërmjet qytetit dhe fshatit*, 52–53.

CHAPTER 5

FIGURE 15. Filling and weighing sacks of sugar

improvement of supporting economies, and its efficiency enabled the smooth operation of sugar processing. As a result, Maliq and all the economic enterprises linked to sugar production remained sites where the communist state continuously invested fixed capital.

During the five months of its initial operation starting in October 1951, it processed 600 tons of sugar beet per day. A small factory attached to the refinery processed the pulp from the sugar beet and produced 32 tons of fodder per day. The industrial establishment also had a thermal power plant (TPP) capable of generating 3000 kW per hour and a machine shop for annual maintenance of the refinery. With the constant increase in per capita consumption and continued demographic growth, by the end of the decade the regime decided to expand both the refinery's output and the range of items that it processed. In 1959, the refinery underwent a general reconstruction, which augmented the power of the TPP to 7000 kW/h, the processing volume of the refinery to 900 tons of sugar beet per day, and that of dry pulp to 64 tons per day. It also added two other workshops to the combine inventory: one for the production of leaven, which supplied the bakeries of the major cities of the country, and another for the production of carbonic gas, used for soft drinks.[15] The original project of the refinery also included an alcohol factory, which initially remained on paper because of a lack of necessary funds. The growing demand for drinks and the lucrative profits it could generate pushed the administration of the refinery to press the government to start its construction as soon as possible. Although the combine directory stated that the work was to begin in 1958, the factory's building, the capacity of which was 100 hectoliters/day, started only in 1959–1960. In 1971, the factory added to its list of production centers a starch factory with a processing capacity of 10 tons per day.[16]

In the 1970s, the factory was connected to the plain of Maliq through another important agricultural project—the Bovine Breeding Enterprise. The Ministry of Agriculture decided to establish a specialized farm in Maliq with a capacity of 5000 cows, which would help the government to fix the meat deficit it was facing due to population growth. The State Planning Commission argued that the construction in proximity to the sugar factory was necessary because 70% of the bovine fodder was composed of the dry pulp of sugar beet. This type of fodder lost its nutritional value during transportation. Thus, the solution was to construct a bovine complex close to the factory. The collective farms would supply the bovine farm with the remaining 30% of fodder.

In turn, the farms in the area were to use the cattle as a source of organic fertilizer in order to increase the productivity of the arable land of the plain.[17]

---

15   AShV Korçë, F. 67, Kombinati i Sheqerit, 1981, d. 41, fl. 13-15. Lecture on the occasion of the thirtieth anniversary of the sugar factory. October 26, 1981; AQSh, F. 496, Ministria e Industrisë dhe Minierave, 1972, d. 447, fl. 2. A study of the sugar factory "November 8th." February 16, 1972.
16   On the maximum yield, AQSh, F. 490, Këshilli i Ministrave, 1957, d. 857, fl. 9. Memo on the condition of production of the sugar factory of Maliq. On the average yield of the farms located in the plain of Maliq, AQSh, F. 14/AP (STR), 1977, d. 711, fl. 36. Report of the Ministry of Agriculture on the concentration and intensification of the cultivation of sugar beet in the district of Korça. April 6, 1977. The average yield of sugar beet in the plain of Koça was 36.5 tons per hectare, but it was reduced by the yield from other areas of the district that had less fertile and inadequate soil for sugar beet. For more, AQSh, F. 490, Këshilli i Ministrave, 1977, d. 361, fl. 39. Memo of the Council of Ministers on the increase in the production of sugar beet. June 4, 1977. On the building of the alcohol factory in 1959–1960, AShV Korçë, F. 67, Kombinati i Sheqerit, 1981, d. 41, fl. 13-15. Lecture on the occasion of the thirtieth anniversary of the sugar factory. October 26, 1981. Regarding the building of the leaven factory, AShV Korçë, F. 67, Kombinati i Sheqerit, 1983, d. 14, fl. 10. Study of a group of specialists of the sugar factory of Maliq regarding the necessity of building a new sugar factory for procuring the needs of the country for the years 1986–1990. August 1983. On the inventory of the factory in the 1970s, AShV Korçë, F. 3/2, Komiteti i PPSh Rrethi Korçë, 1961, Lista 27, d. 23, fl. 79. Memo on the prospects of the sugar factory in Maliq.
17   AQSh, F. 495, Komisioni i Planit të Shtetit, 1974, d. 28, fl. 7-10. Memo concerning the construction of an establishment for the breeding of bovine next to the sugar factory of Maliq; AQSh, F. 14/AP (STR),

CHAPTER 5

It emerged later that the study had many flaws, and that the factory could supply only 30% of the farm's needs, which sought fodder in other regions, thus increasing the costs of production considerably. To fix the shortcomings in supply, in the late 1970s the government increased the output capacity of the factory producing dry pulp. The industrial unit was updated with new technology to enrich the fodder with urea so as to increase its nutritional value by 40%. By this time, the authorities also started building a mechanical transporter for the fodder, which connected the factory to the bovine farm.[18]

In the 1970s, the increasing yields of the farms of the plain of Maliq created bottlenecks at the factory. The use of extra fertilizers and the allocation of more tractors and water sprinklers than anticipated gave extraordinary results.[19] In the late 1970s, the farms of the plain yielded between 50 and 70 tons of sugar beet per hectare, far exceeding the processing capacities of the factory. As a result, the factory stored the sugar beet for longer than optimal periods, and during this time the beets lost considerable amounts of their sucrose content. The refinery's lack of capacity pressed the farms to delay harvesting the beets, which then lost their properties as a result of freezing temperatures and rainfall. The management of the refinery asked the government for a new round of reconstruction and an expansion in its capacities. To support its demands, it estimated that the state had lost 4500 tons of sugar annually due to the factory's limited processing capabilities.[20]

1974, d. 817, fl. 45-48. Memo concerning the construction of an establishment for the breeding of bovine next to the sugar factory of Maliq.

18 On the enrichment of dry pulp with urea, AQSh, F. 497, Ministria e Industrisë së Lehtë Ushqimore, 1979, d. 180, fl. 1-9. Correspondence between the Ministry of Agriculture, the Ministry of Light Industry and Food, the Ministry of Construction, the State Planning Commission, etc. for the construction of a new line of production of dry pulp from sugar beet enriched with urea. March–July 1979. On the mechanical transporter between the dry pulp factory and the bovine farm, AQSh, F. 497, Ministria e Industrisë së Lehtë Ushqimore, 1979, d. 181, fl. 1-7. Correspondence between the Ministry of Light Industry and Food, the Ministry of Industry and Mines, and the executive committee of Korça regarding the construction of a mechanic transporter for the dry pulp. April–June 1979.

19 On the assignment of 3000 tons of additional fertilizer, AQSh, F. 14/AP (STR), 1977, d. 711, fl. 37-38. Report of the Ministry of Agriculture on the concentration and intensification of the cultivation of sugar beet in the district of Korça. April 6, 1977. On the allocation of 80 extra tractors, AQSh, F. 490, Këshilli i Ministrave, 1977, d. 74, fl. 27. Decision of the Council of Ministers on the expansion of the sugar factory and the thermal power station of Maliq. April 8, 1977. On the assignment of 85 extra sprinklers, AQSh, F. 14/AP (STR), 1978, d. 9, fl. 14. Information on the work and measures taken for the fulfillment of the state plan for the cultivation and collection of sugar beet. April 6, 1978.

20 On the yields on the farms of the plain of Maliq, AQSh, F. 495, Komisioni i Planit të Shtetit, 1979, d. 133, fl. 2-3. Analysis of the State Planning Commission concerning the results of the production of sugar beet for the year 1979. January 31, 1980. On the extended periods that the refinery has stored sugar beet, AQSh, F. 490, Këshilli i Ministrave, 1976, d. 73, fl. 3-4. Memo of the Ministry of Agriculture

FIGURE 16. Storage points of sugar beet

According to a memo prepared at the Maliq sugar factory on April 28, 1976, the doubling of the processing capacity of the industrial complex would limit the losses to only 3% of the total output, or 460 tons. The government, however, wanted to build a new refinery in the plain of Thumanë located north of Tirana. Until the end of World War II, a large bog covered this plain. After reclaiming it, the communist regime tried to make it economically useful, and the development of this reclaimed plain for the sugar industry had many supporters in Tirana. A new industrial complex would have been more efficient than rehauling the older refinery. However, financial constraints, in addition to the soil quality of the plain of Thumanë, which was not very suitable for the cultivation of sugar beet, forced the government to approve Maliq's proposal.[21]

The regime's empty coffers, the growing price of sugar on the international market, and increasing domestic consumption induced Tirana to listen to

---

and the Ministry of Light Industry and Food on the price of sugar beet. January 3, 1976. On the yearly sugar losses, AShV Korçë, F. 67, Kombinati i Sheqerit, 1975, d. 2, fl. 2-3. Memo on the reconstruction of the sugar factory of Maliq. March 29, 1975.

21 Debate concerning the reduction of losses from the expansion of the factory, AQSh, F. 497, Ministria e Industrisë së Lehtë Ushqimore, 1976, d. 198, fl. 28-34. General considerations on the main technical and economic indicators of the sugar factory of Maliq. On the financial constraints of the regime and the decision to expand the Maliq factory, AQSh, F. 495, Komisioni i Planit të Shtetit, 1974, d. 20, fl. 31. Memo on the increase in the domestic production of sugar.

CHAPTER 5

FIGURE 17. The refinery after its reconstruction in the late 1970s

Maliq. In fact, after discussions that involved specialists and workers of the factory, the combine directorate came up with concrete proposals to deal with a situation that had a national impact. Maliq responded to the concerns of the central authorities and provided them with solutions. It argued that the factory had the required space, existing infrastructure, and specialized workforce, along with a supply of water and coal. The reconstruction expanded not only the production capacity of the refinery itself, but also that of the carbonic gas, starch, and alcohol factories.[22]

The factory's expansion in 1978 did not fix the problem of losses, which were not limited to sugar alone but to the whole range of goods that the factory pro-

---

22 On the involvement of workers and specialists of the Maliq factory in the discussion about the potential expansion of the "November 8th" combine. AShV Korçë, F. 67, Kombinati i Sheqerit, 1975, d. 2, fl. 7-8. Memo on the reconstruction of the sugar factory of Maliq. December 27, 1975. On the arguments of the directory of the "November 8th" combine regarding the expansion of the sugar factory, AQSh, F. 497, Ministria e Industrisë së Lehtë Ushqimore, 1973, d. 150, fl. 3-7. Memo of the directory of the sugar combine in Maliq regarding the expansion of the processing capacities of the sugar factory. September 10, 1973. On the reconstruction of the factories of the combine, AQSh, F. 497, Ministria e Industrisë së Lehtë Ushqimore, 1979, d. 164, fl. 5. Address of the Minister of Light Industry and Food, Kristaq Dollaku, on the occasion of the completion of the reconstruction of the sugar factory in Maliq. November 5, 1979.

cessed. The combination of inadequate conservation and spillages during processing caused the loss of 370 tons of sugar a day—a total of 5000 tons a year. A debate over the causes of the losses ensued. According to the inspectors of the Ministry of Light Industry, the main reason was the low caloric power of the coal that the refinery's TPP (thermal power plant) used for its turbines. The thermal power plant used coal extracted from different mines in the Korça region, some of them located only a few kilometers away from Maliq. The problem was that their coal was of low quality, which was a matter of grave concern, because its low calorific power undermined the entire process of sugar extraction and generated losses. For the factory to work, it required fuel with a calorific power of 8000 kc/kg, while the coal from the mine at Mborje-Drenova, one of the principal suppliers of the refinery, emitted only 6600 kc/kg. The low quality required more coal, which then created a supply problem. The lack of suitable fuel to produce enough heat to process sugar effectively also paralyzed the production of animal fodder from sugar beet, causing losses to the agricultural economy.[23]

Another problem was the primitive working conditions in the coal mines of the Korça district. Very often the fuel arrived at the factory containing moisture, further decreasing its calorific power and lowering the quality of the sugar. In the 1950s, the directory of the refinery asked the government to take the necessary measures to improve the working conditions at these mines, modernize them, and increase their extractive capacities to fulfill the needs of Albania's only sugar factory. The factory management also asked the Prime Minister's Office to construct elevators, equip the mines with wagons, and to have horses replace human muscles for hauling them. It was not for the love or care of their workers but the need for better results that pressed them to make such requests. It was also for the sake

---

23 On the continuation of losses after the expansion of the factory, AShV Korçë, F. 67, Kombinati i Sheqerit, 1984, d. 20, fl. 20. Memo of the directory of the Maliq sugar factory regarding the fulfillment of the tasks of the first semester of the year 1984. June 22, 1984. On the loss of 5000 tons of sugar per year, AQSh, F. 490, Këshilli i Ministrave, 1984, d. 511, fl. 20. Study of the State Planning Commission sent to the Council of Ministers on the needs of the country's population for fats, sugar, and cotton. March 20, 1984. On the low calorific power of the coal, AQSh, F. 497, Ministria e Industrisë së Lehtë dhe Ushqimore, 1983, d. 132, fl. 3 and fl. 15. Information on the conclusion of the harvesting and processing season of sugar beet for the year 1982–1983. May 7, 1983. On the losses caused by the low calorific power of coal, AQSh, F. 14/AP (STR), 1953, d. 468, fl. 22–23. Memo on the situation of coal at the sugar factory in Maliq-Korça. August 11, 1953. On the calorific power of the coal in the region of Korça and the problems caused by the need to increase the supply, AQSh, F. 497, Ministria e Industrisë së Lehtë dhe Ushqimore, 1983, d. 132, fl. 15. Information on the conclusion of the harvesting and processing season of sugar beet for the year 1982–1983. On the problems that the low quality of coal has caused for the processing of fodder, AShV Korçë, F. 67, Kombinati i Sheqerit Maliq, 1954, d. 4, fl. 3. Memo on the financial condition of the sugar factory of Maliq.

CHAPTER 5

of productivity that the administration of the sugar factory asked the government to accelerate the work pace and expand from two shifts to three. It did not take long before the Prime Minister's Office ordered the fulfillment of these requests.[24]

The expansion of the factory in the 1960s and 1970s, combined with the low quality of coal from the Korça district, further increased the need for fuel. As a consequence, many of the region's mines entered the refinery's orbit. Still, the problem of the coal's low calorific power remained the Achilles' heel of the refinery. To remedy it, the government ordered the factory be supplied with coal from mines outside the region, but this created enormous problems for transportation and supply. Facing such circumstances, the government decided in the late 1980s to build a factory in Maliq for enriching the local coal.[25]

The investments in communist Albania's Sugarland did not end with the expansion of the factory's TPP and the enrichment of the fossil fuels it used. In the early 1980s, a shift occurred in the regime's economic priorities. In the last decade of the communist era, Tirana siphoned the bulk of its resources into light industry and agriculture.[26] It was no accident that this U-turn took place after the break with China in 1978. Once Albania lost Beijing's financial support, Tirana's communist regime focused more and more on intensifying and increasing the productivity of those economic sectors that would remedy the food and fiber problems the country was facing. This explains why, even in its most difficult financial years, the regime continued to invest in Maliq.

---

24 On coal with humidity, AShV Korçë, F. 67, Kombinati i Sheqerit Maliqit, 1953, d. 6, fl. 2. Memo on the extra-accountable costs of sugar. On the lobbying efforts of the directory of the sugar factory to modernize and accelerate the pace of work in the mines that supplied it with fuel, AQSh, F. 14/AP (STR), 1953, d. 468, fl. 22-23. Memo on the situation of coal in the sugar factory in Maliq-Korça. August 11, 1953. On the decision of the government to fulfill the sugar factory's requests, AQSh, F. 490, Këshilli i Ministrave, 1953, d. 686, fl. 1-2. Council of Ministers's order for the Mborje-Drenova mine realization to supply the sugar combine of Maliq with coal. July 23, 1953.

25 On the supply of the factory of Maliq from the new mines, AQSh, F. 497, Ministria e Industrisë së Lehtë Ushqimore, 1976, d. 197, fl. 23-24. Memo regarding the expansion of the TPP of the sugar factory of Maliq. June 11, 1976. On the low quality of coal, AQSh, F. 497, Ministria e Industrisë së Lehtë Ushqimore, 1976, d. 198, fl. 34. General considerations on the main technical and economic indicators of the sugar factory of Maliq. On the supply from mines located outside of the region of Korça, AQSh, F. 497, Ministria e Industrisë së Lehtë dhe Ushqimore, 1983, d. 132, fl. 4. Information on the harvesting and processing of sugar beet. On the decision to build a factory for enriching coal, AQSh, F. 490, Këshilli i Ministrave, 1988, d. 400, fl. 4. Memo of the Ministry of Energy regarding a site for dumping ashes from the Maliq TPP.

26 For more on this shift that took place in the 1980s, see Raymond Hutchings, "Albanian Industrialization: Widening Divergence from Stalinism," in *Industrialisierung und gesellschaftlicher Wandel in Südosteuropa*, ed. Roland Schönfeld (Munich: Südosteuropa-Gesellschaft, 1989), 109–124. On the allocation of resources on heavy industry from the 1950s to 1970s, see Adi Schnytzer, *Stalinist Economic Strategy in Practice: The Case of Albania* (Oxford: Oxford University Press, 1982).

It was in this context that in 1982 the factory directory raised the bar and asked for another round of reconstruction, which would expand the factory's processing capacity from 2000 to 3000 tons of sugar beet per day. The factory's director, Llazar Plasa, argued to the Executive Committee of Korça that such a volume of production would reduce the processing time for the sugar beets to only 100 days. Such a step, according to the factory's director, would save much of the sugar beet currently wasted through long storage or early harvesting.[27] The factory specialists couched their proposal to the government in the language of regionalization. They argued that the region would specialize in the production of sugar by concentrating the entire process there, from planting and processing to final preparation for the market. Such an alternative aligned with the directives of the Central Committee for the concentration and specialization of agriculture and industry. This proposal found strong support even in the Ministry of Light Industry, where the specialists considered increasing the capacity of the refinery as the only solution to the losses. In 1984, the Ministry decided to expand the processing capacity of the factory, designating 1987 as the year to start the project.[28] The lack of capital and the final demise of the regime left the project on paper.

There were also other projects which aimed at increasing the efficiency of the sugar industry and other sectors related to it. It is important to note that in its final years, the regime was very active in taking measures and initiatives to deal with the challenges facing communist Albania. It was not a passive or apathetic gerontocratic state, deprived of responses, energy, or imagination.[29] In the last

---

[27] AShV Korçë, F. 67, Kombinati i Sheqerit, 1982, d. 6, fl. 1-3. Memo on the expansion of the processing capacity of the sugar combine. September 17, 1982; AShV Korçë, F. 67, Kombinati i Sheqerit, 1983, d. 3, fl. 34-35. Study of a group of specialists of the sugar combine of Maliq about meeting the sugar needs of the country through an increase in the processing capacity of the factory and the building of a new sugar factory in Korça. November 30, 1983.

[28] On the letter sent to the government, AShV Korçë, F. 67, Kombinati i Sheqerit, 1983, d. 3, fl. 38-43. Study of a group of specialists of the sugar factory of Maliq regarding meeting the sugar needs of the country through an increase in the processing capacity of the factory and the building of a new sugar factory in Korça. November 30, 1983. On the support that the letter found in the Ministry of Light Industry, AQSh, F. 497, Ministria e Industrisë së Lehtë dhe Ushqimore, 1983, d. 133, fl. 31. Report of Shaqir Prizreni regarding the situation and measures for increasing the sugar content of sugar from beets; AQSh, F. 497, Ministria e Industrisë së Lehtë dhe Ushqimore, 1985, d. 7, fl. 17. Minutes of the meeting of the collegium of the Ministry of Light Industry on the problem of the losses of the sugar factory of Maliq. June 29, 1985. On the decision to expand the processing capacities of the sugar combine in 1987, AQSh, F. 497, Ministria e Industrisë së Lehtë dhe Ushqimore, 1984, d. 15, fl. 3. Memo of the Ministry of Light Industry and Food in relation to some measures for the better management of sugar and its byproducts.

[29] On gerontocracy as a feature of the last stages of the communist regimes in Eastern Europe, see Archie Brown, *The Rise and Fall of Communism* (New York: Harper Collins, 2009), 401–402.

decade of its existence, the ALP regime had not lost its belief in the future. On the contrary, the 1980s were a decade of uncommon debates, ideas, and projects, with the unusual involvement of specialists in discussions with the political power on providing viable alternatives. There was still the hope and belief that socialism was a viable alternative. Despite the deep economic crises and apparent paralysis, the regime and the entire apparatus of specialists and technocrats generated numerous projects to rejuvenate the economy and make it more productive and efficient. The regime kept believing in the future and planning for it. The last decade of the communist era was less heroic than the first years of socialist construction; there was no mud and water to reclaim, there were no mass mobilizations, and no red tape to cut. Nevertheless, there was neither a lack of dynamism nor a shortage of ideas or flexibility in the allocation of resources.

The government started to study the construction of a narrow-gauge rail system across the plain of Korça and the Devoll River to supply the factory with fuel and raw material. The central and local authorities had been toying with this plan since the late 1970s when increased yields and a lack of trucks exposed the problem of the transportation of sugar beet from the collecting centers to the factory. In the 1980s, the project reemerged with new vigor. It was divided into four stages and anticipated the building of multiple lines for a total length of 120 kilometers. This dense network would crisscross the entire plain and connect Maliq with the local mines and the damping field of Goçë, some kilometers to the west of Maliq in the highlands of Gora. The project of infrastructural improvement also included lines for the mechanical transportation of dry pulp between the bovine farm and the factory, as well as mechanized loaders for sugar beet at the collection centers.[30]

---

30   On the building of a narrow-gauge railway, AQSh, F. 490, Këshilli i Ministrave, 1987, d. 670, fl. 23–29. Study of a specialist from the Prime Minister's Office regarding the profitability of the use of narrow-gauge railways at the state farms of Maliq. June 29, 1987. On the designation of an area close to the village of Goçë as a dump site for ashes from the TPP of Maliq and Korça, AQSh, F. 490, Këshilli i Ministrave, 1988, d. 400, fl. 2-14. Correspondence and memos of the Ministry of Energy and the Council of Ministers for the designation of an area of 10.7 hectares in the village of Goçë as a dump site for ashes from the TPP of Maliq and Korça. October 10–November 16, 1988. On the problem of the transportation of sugar beet, AQSh, F. 490, Këshilli i Ministrave, 1977, d. 352, fl. 20–21. Information sent to the ALP's Central Committee on the situation regarding sugar beet yields in the district of Korça. February 3, 1977. On the project of the 1970s for the construction of a local network of railroads, AQSh, F. 490, Këshilli i Ministrave, 1977, d. 345, fl. 138. Memo regarding the estimates for the external facilities that will be built at the sugar factory of Maliq. On the emergence of the railroad projects in the 1980s, AQSh, F. 490, Këshilli i Ministrave, 1987, d. 670, fl. 34-39. Memo on the study of a specialist of the Prime Minister's Office regarding the construction of a narrow-gauge railway in the plain of Korça and the Devoll. On the mechanical loading and unloading of sugar beet at the collection cen-

Maliq's case of continuous renovation and investment with fixed capital fits into the pattern that Robert Allen described as occurring in the industrial investments of the Soviet Union during the last two decades of its existence. In his analysis, Allen argues that Moscow's allocation of resources to the reconstruction of old plants proved to be disastrous for its economy because it wasted capital for little gain. It was precisely what the large US corporations, with the federal government's consent, did not do with the Rust Belt. The USSR's rival shut down the old plants in the American industrial heartland and focused on new high-profit investments.[31] Allen, however, does not consider the simple fact that the socialist countries did not have the financial resources of the Western European market economies. For the USSR and its allies, it was more convenient to try to improve the industries they had rather than investing in new directions.

Allen, like most economists, leaves out of his analysis the social impact of these huge shifts. Jefferson Cowie and Joseph Heathcott have quite rightly argued that neutral or optimistic terms that economists use, like "downsizing," "restructuring," or "creative destruction," neglect the toll that the abandonment of old industries has had on many communities.[32] This reorientation of capital flows in the United States marked deep transformations in the networks of investment, production, and consumption, which gave many American firms the flexibility to extract profits in increasingly competitive markets. The adaptation of businesses to evolving circumstances came at a price, though. Foremost it signaled the end of the New Deal's arrangements between labor and investments in fixed capital, bringing to an end the illusion of capitalism's permanent stability.

The Soviet-type socioeconomic systems tried to fix capitalism's "creative destruction" and its drive to melt everything solid into air, as Marx put it. The communist regimes subordinated economic logic to political and ideological dictates—another factor that Allen's analysis does not take into account. However, the economic policies of the peoples' democracies were not an isolated phenomenon that took place only in the socialist oikumene. Instead, they were part of the broader interwar era critique of capitalism's constant mutability and the acute social tensions and inequalities it engendered. The New Deal, the welfare states,

---

ters, AQSh, F. 490, Këshilli i Ministrave, 1978, d. 379, fl. 141. Information regarding measures for the fulfillment of the quota of the state plan for the cultivation of sugar beet. August 19, 1978.

31 On Allen's argument of the reconstruction of the old plants, Robert C. Allen, *Farm to Factory: A Reinterpretation of the Soviet Industrial Revolution* (Princeton, NJ: Princeton University Press, 2003), 189–211.

32 Jefferson Cowie and Joseph Heathcott, "Introduction: The Meanings of Deindustrialization," in *Beyond the Ruins*, 1.

CHAPTER 5

and the economic policies of Fascist Italy and Nazi Germany all aimed at taming the free market and establishing the necessary stability to preserve the social cohesion needed for nations not to fall apart. As the world historian Diego Holstein has pointed out, in the aftermath of World War I, and especially after the Great Depression of 1929, the socioeconomic formula that combined nationalism with socialism triumphed to different degrees.[33]

The socialist regimes represented the most extreme version of a broader global anti-free market tide that had risen since the interwar era and refused to change its approach in the face of economic stagnation in the late 1960s, when the socioeconomic and political arrangements of the interwar era entered into a permanent crisis.[34] While the US, the UK, and other countries that orbited around the North Atlantic gravitational core abandoned the New Deal and Keynesian paradigm, transitioning to the new era of neoliberal globalization that dismantled the nation state and emphasized global interdependency, the socialist countries of Eastern Europe did not move in this direction. Ideological dogmatism came with the price of a lack of adaptability to new, unanticipated junctures. By the 1970s and 1980s, many industries in the socialist countries had entered into a permanent crisis of inefficiency. From the economic point of view, they had become liabilities in terms of assets. However, because political imperatives overshadowed financial ones, the socialist regimes got stuck in a spiral that ended with their final demise. In Eastern Europe, the Soviet-type regimes stuck to the Leninist project and remained deeply conservative and ideological, stripping them of the determination to undertake radical reforms, as was the case in post-Maoist China. As the historians Stephen Kotkin and Jan Gross have succinctly put it, the communist establishments of Eastern Europe were full of communists.[35] It was with the fall of state-socialism that the countries of the eastern part of Europe joined capitalist-led neoliberal globalism and gave up on the model that reconciled socialism with nationalism and tried to soften domestic and international inequalities.[36]

---

33 Diego Olstein, *A Brief History of Now: The Past and Present of Global Power* (London: Palgrave Macmillan, 2021), 159.

34 For an extensive critical exposition of this transition, see David Harvey, *The Condition of Postmodernity: An Enquiry into the Origins of Cultural Change* (Cambridge, MA: Blackwell, 1989), 121–197.

35 Kotkin and Gross, *Uncivil Society*, 32; Stephen Kotkin, "The Kiss of Debt: The East Bloc Goes Borrowing," in *The Shock of the Global: The 1970s in Perspective*, ed. Niall Ferguson et al. (Cambridge, MA: Harvard University Press, 2010), 91–93.

36 Charles S. Maier, "'Malaise': The Crisis of Capitalism in the 1970s," in *The Shock of the Global: The 1970s in Perspective*, 44–48; Holstein, *A Brief History of Now*, 160 & 201–207.

Maliq and Albania underwent the same global historical processes. As discussed in the first two chapters, for the Albanian political elites, during both the communist and interwar era, the sugar factory served above all as an instrument of nation-building. The ALP's leadership kept investing in Maliq to make it efficient and to give economic sustainability to its political objectives. This efficiency, though, depended very much on the state's support and elimination of any international competition. Once the post-socialist governments raised the shield of protectionism, the refinery of Maliq became exposed to the rationality of the free market, and its cold principles of efficiency based on profit. With the country fully committed to jumping into the globalized economy, with the state retreating from all economic intervention, and the nation state no longer the primary platform of development, the factory lost its political function. Once the country opened the gates to global market forces, all the regional and national economic circuits the sugar refinery belonged to melted away into thin air. This process was not limited to Maliq or Albania but belongs to a larger story that saw the reshuffling of the economic networks created after the end of World War II on both sides of the Iron Curtain. The next section will explain this process and its impact on Maliq in more detail.

The Fall of Communism and the Unraveling of the Web

The sugar refinery of Maliq did not long survive the collapse of communism, and in 1996 it closed forever. Unlike today's EU countries, where consumers use beet sugar mainly produced in the European Union, Albanians sweeten their coffee and prepare their pastries with cane sugar imported from Brazil, Columbia, and Panama. The fall of communism in Albania marked the end of the consumption of beet sugar. In the other ex-socialist countries of Eastern Europe, though, the sugar refineries survived for another decade. The protectionist policies of the post-socialist governments, and especially the EU shield of hefty subsidies for all sugar producers and the opening of its market to candidate countries, helped many of the sugar producers in Eastern Europe. However, this comfortable position did not last long.

In 2006, under pressure for greater efficiency, especially after opening its markets to foreign producers and increasing competition, the European Union started the process of restructuring the sugar industries. The EU reduced its subsidies and fixed prices and funneled them to only the principal producers, mainly located in the colder areas of the Baltic and the North Sea. The regional specialization of sugar production implemented by the EU—similar to what the ALP did in the context of the nation state—has favored only Poland among the countries of Eastern Europe. With this one exception, which is one of the leading producers of beet sugar in Europe—third behind Germany and France—the restructuring of the EU's sugar industry hit the ex-socialist countries very hard. As soon as they were exposed to free market rationality and a lack of state protection, many sugar refineries in Eastern Europe shut down. Bulgaria and Latvia lost their national sugar industries, and since 2006 they have become net importers, while the bulk of the factories in Hungary, Slovakia, and Lithuania have also closed down. However, the massive closing of sugar factories has also been the case for old members of the EU, like Italy, Portugal, Spain, Denmark, etc.[37]

In Albania, this process started earlier. With the collapse of communism, the whole economic system it had built for forty-five years unraveled. The state ceased to be the driving economic force, and the conceptualization of the nation as a cohesive and organic unit ended abruptly. State-led development fell under the hail of the aggressive critique of the ultra-modernists of market fundamentalism. The borders, which up to that moment had been real demarcation lines that carved in space the state's sovereignty and the application of national policies, stopped playing that role. With the post-socialist structural and institutional transformations, regional specialization and the entire web of local connections that supported spatial differentiation in the realm of production also collapsed. The breaking of the regional networks had another outcome: the dissolution of agricultural and industrial enterprises.

All post-socialist governments in Eastern Europe pursued a market liberalization agenda, which entered the political vocabulary under the name of shock therapy. Based on the growing popularity (if not effectiveness) of the policies developed to tackle the hyper-inflation crises in Latin America during the 1980s, shock therapy sought the elimination of the socialist past. Not too dissimilarly from the communists in the post-World War II years, who declared war against history and tried to erase it, the architects of post-communist transformations aimed at undoing the weight of the past. Obliterating every undesired trace of the past, either ethnic, cultural, material, institutional, or economic, has been a constant of the revolutionary changes perpetuated during the twentieth century in the countries that populate the area between the Baltic and the Adriatic Sea.

---

37 "Report of the High-Level Group on Sugar," July 5, 2019, pp. 9–10. Document downloaded to https://agriculture.ec.europa.eu/farming/crop-productions-and-plant-based-products/sugar_en#documents. Last accessed, September 18, 2022.

Part of the historical legacy that the post-socialist governments had to wipe out was the state's role in the economy. It was the high tide of the New Right economic policies and their popularity in the United States and Great Britain. The liberal market economies of these two countries provided the hegemonic examples to follow for the westernization of the countries of Eastern Europe. Through shock therapy, they offered a template for fast-track modernization that replaced the Soviet alternative by rejecting any form of state intervention in the economy.[38] As Tassilo Herschel has put it, the American model "became the only show in town."[39] On the other hand, the cooperative market economies, also known as Rhenish capitalism and best represented by the German model, which highlighted the state's role in coordinating the economy, did not have much appeal in the first years of the post-socialist era.

The goal of shock therapy's key ingredients—privatization, liberalization, and the opening of domestic markets—was to increase economic efficiency.[40] For the post-socialist governments, this recipe meant relinquishing any protectionism or financial support to commercial and industrial enterprises. Another essential component of the transition process was international trade, which the architects of the post-socialist economic transformation considered to be one of the primary means of underpinning the radical rejuvenation of the Eastern European economies.[41] The restructuring of state policies regarding production and trade exposed the enterprises of the ex-socialist countries to global market forces without any backing. It was very difficult for groups within the state apparatuses that wanted a more gradualist transformation to make their voices heard without being called communist—something that in the early 1990s almost everybody tried to avoid. In the aftermath of communism's collapse, neoliberalism supporters considered any form of statist economy a return to the socialist past.[42] Only in the course of the 1990s, after the bitter experiences of recession, deindustrialization, skyrocketing unemployment, and deterioration of economic con-

---

[38] On the neoliberal recipes of shock therapy and its implementations, see Jacek Kochanowicz, "A Moving Target or a Lost Illusion? East Central Europe in Pursuit of the West in Two Globalization Phases," in *Mastery and Lost Illusions: Space and Time in the Modernization of Eastern and Central Europe*, eds. Włodzimierz Borodziej, Stanislav Holubec, and Joachim von Puttkamer (Munich: De Gruyter Oldenbourg, 2014), 41–45.

[39] Tassilo Herrschel, *Global Geographies of Post-Socialist Transition: Geographies, Societies, Policies* (London: Routledge, 2007), 59.

[40] On the key ingredients of the neoliberal policies, Herrschel, *Global Geographies of Post-Socialist Transition*, 47.

[41] Herrschel, *Global Geographies of Post-Socialist Transition*, 63–64.

[42] Herrschel, *Global Geographies of Post-Socialist Transition*, 49.

ditions, did post-socialist governments roll back the state under the banner of "modernizing the state."[43]

As a result, not all the countries of Eastern Europe implemented the principles of shock therapy faithfully—something also reflected in the policies toward the sugar industry.[44] The Albanian post-socialist governments pursued one of the most robust liberalizing economic courses in Eastern Europe.[45] Interestingly enough, the country switched from the most representative hardliner of ideological orthodoxy to the most committed follower of the neoliberal principles of the free market. The zeal that the post-socialist elites professed toward the newly embraced credo, a characteristic of all the recently converted from one dogma to another, was not without rationale. Tirana's new leadership, eager to distance themselves from Enver Hoxha's legacy and model, ended up implementing shock therapy with great enthusiasm but without much reflection. In a short time, the myth of the miracle of market logic replaced that of socialism's central planning. The Albanian self-proclaimed anti-communist reformers fully committed themselves to erase everything "socialist."

As was the case in all these countries of Eastern Europe after the collapse of the Soviet-type regimes, the Albanian post-socialist political elites held the firm belief that only integration into the Western-centered global economy guaranteed development.[46] Ironically, Albania was the least prepared country among the members of the ex-socialist club for the dogmatic implementation of neoliberal recipes. As already mentioned above, shock therapy promoted a set of policies devised for the capitalist states of Latin America, which were already fully integrated into the Western-centered global economic system. As the practice demonstrated, the same prescriptions for radical and immediate transformations faced severe limitations when applied to the countries of Eastern Europe, which had just come out of the socialist experience. As Craig Young has argued, regardless of the desire to make the ex-Soviet bloc a tabula rasa, nei-

---

43 Herrschel, *Global Geographies of Post-Socialist Transition*, 69.
44 On the different paths of economic transformations in Eastern Europe after the collapse of communism, see Philipp Ther, *Europe since 1989: A History*, trans. Charlotte Hughes-Kreutzmüller (Princeton, NJ: Princeton University Press, 2016), 79–94.
45 On shock therapy in Albania, see Clarissa De Waal, *Albania Today: A Portrait of Post-Communist Turbulence* (London: I. B. Tauris, 2005); Elez Biberaj, *Albania in Transition: The Rocky Road to Democracy* (Boulder, CO: Westview Press, 1998).
46 On the widely shared belief that only integration in the capitalist global system guaranteed development, see Craig Young, "Marketisation, Democratisation and Inequality in Central Eastern Europe," in *Global Geographies of Post-Socialist Transition*, 79.

ther Western advisors nor post-socialist politicians could write off the socialist experience.[47]

Political scientist Besnik Pula has recently argued that the success of the transition to a market economy depended in no small part on the linkages that each of the Eastern European countries had established with the Western-centered capitalist system during the socialist era. By the 1970s, many of the countries of the Soviet bloc had borrowed capital and technology from Western European countries and engaged in an intense trade relationship with them. The goal of the communist elites of Eastern Europe was to improve their industrial base and liquidate the loans by exporting their finished goods to the West. In the end, these exchanges increased the socialist countries' dependence on the market democracies. According to Pula, the intense economic contacts with the liberal democracies established networks that proved to be useful for the countries of Eastern Europe after the fall of communism, when they were able to attract massive Western foreign direct investments.[48]

Although Albania increased its exchanges with Western European countries, the ALP kept itself at arm's length from any similar economic entanglement to that of its Eastern European analogues. If we follow Pula's line of argument, it means that when the communist regime collapsed, the country did not attract many Western investors because the ALP leadership had not integrated Albania's economy into the global capitalist system. Of course, there are other critical geostrategic factors too. The wars in ex-Yugoslavia kept many investors away from the country. The ailing economies of neighboring Greece and southern Italy did not help very much either. However, it is essential to note that the fact that Albania had not established links with the West similar to those of the Visegrad countries or Yugoslavia did not make the immediate transition into the free market a sage decision. The repercussions are apparent across the country, including in Maliq.

The opening of the borders would prove to be catastrophic for the sugar refinery. Indeed, the factory in Maliq had come into being precisely as a bulwark against international trade. As has already been analyzed in the first chapter, since the interwar era the principal argument for building a sugar factory in Albania had been to preserve much-needed hard currency from flowing outside of

---

47 Young, "Marketisation, Democratisation and Inequality in Central Eastern Europe," 76.
48 Besnik Pula, *Globalization under and after Socialism: The Evolution of Transnational Capital in Central Eastern Europe* (Stanford CA.: Stanford University Press, 2018).

the country. For the Albanian political elite to have a domestic sugar industry meant reducing their economic dependency on primary goods and reinforcing the country's fragile political independence. Since the interwar era, the sugar scheme was an industrial undertaking that had precise political functions.

The Albanian interwar era elites conceived of the Maliq sugar scheme as falling within the paradigm of the development of import-substituting-industries, which conflated industrialization with political independence. According to this paradigm, the creation of a national industrial base, which produced the majority of the goods consumed by the population, was the only means to preserve economic and political independence.[49] The communists inherited the same worldview as their predecessors and continued at a faster pace and with greater determination the project of industrialization and the assertion of national sovereignty. As was the case with their interwar era forerunners, the communist elite considered the nation state to be the central platform of social and economic modernization. Thus, the ALP's takeover did not mark a significant break with the interwar period regarding the link between economic development and political independence. In reality, the historical caesura did happen with the collapse of the communist regime, when the nation state lost its primacy as the primary vehicle of social and economic development. By this time, the new paradigm of development stopped considering industrialization and dependence as being contradictory.[50]

The implementation of shock therapy and the opening of the domestic market to international trade exposed how vulnerable an economic unit built on political premises, like Maliq's sugar industry, was to the rationality of the free market. However, the radical policies of Tirana's post-socialist governments in the early 1990s crippled even further the ability of the refinery to adapt to the new circumstances and be competitive. The first blow came with the Agrarian Reform implemented between June 1991 and October 1992. The neoliberal postmodern fragmentation of the arable land that started in the 1980s in Western Europe with the downsizing of plots and agricultural economies arrived in Eastern Europe in the 1990s under the banner of post-socialist restructuring.[51]

---

49 László Bruszt and Béla Greskovits, "Transnationalization, Social Integration, and Capitalist Diversity in the East and the South," *Studies in Comparative International Development* 44, no. 4 (2009): 414.
50 Bruszt and Greskovits, "Transnationalization, Social Integration, and Capitalist Diversity," 415.
51 On these processes in the Netherlands, see Joks Janssen and Luuk Knippenberg, "The Heritage of the Productive Landscape: Landscape Design for Rural Areas in the Netherlands, 1954–1985," *Landscape Research* 33, no. 1 (2008): 21–22.

Under pressure from Western governments, the majority of the Eastern European post-socialist governments implemented agrarian reforms. The goal was to scale down the size of the agricultural units to give them more flexibility, increase the productivity of the rural sector, and enhance their market-oriented activity. Soon, the architects of the economic transformations discovered that they had replaced large efficient agricultural enterprises with small farmers that could not compete on the global market. For many countries in Eastern Europe, these reforms marked a return to the pre-socialist period, where farmers had small and scattered plots. After realizing that the socialist regimes' collective farms were indeed productive and that the new private farmers were economically inefficient, the Eastern European governments started programs of land consolidation.[52] This was not the case with Albania, though.

Compared to their Eastern European analogues, the Albanian post-socialist reformers had a more radical and less flexible approach to the restructuring of the primary sector. They held the firm belief that large agricultural cooperatives were a cancer to efficiency.[53] Under the banner of "restructuring," they dismantled the entire economic structure inherited from the past without any regard for the social and economic repercussions. The agrarian reform that started in July of 1991 divided the arable land between 490,000 private farms, with an average size of 1 ha, and fragmented it into more than 1.9 million scattered plots. The Albanian government took pride in implementing the most radical distribution of land to private owners in all of Eastern Europe. In Hungary, Slovakia, and the Czech Republic, the post-socialist governments did not disband the collective farms that controlled half of the arable land until well into the 2000s; while in the ex-Soviet Republics, except for Russia, the agricultural farms controlled 84% of the arable land.[54] Ironically, the restructuring of

---

[52] Antoine Roger, "'Romanian Peasants' Into 'European Farmers'? Using Statistics to Standardize Agriculture," *Development and Change* 45, no. 4 (2014): 732–752; Jaroslav Janus and Iwona Markuszewska, "Land Consolidation–A Great Need to Improve Effectiveness. A Case Study from Poland," *Land Use Policy* 65 (2017): 143–153; Van Dijk, "Complications for Traditional Land Consolidation in Central Europe," 505–511; see also the essays on Bulgaria, Romania, Czech Republic, Hungary presented in the symposium organized by the FAO office for Europe and Asia "Land Fragmentation and Land Consolidation In CEEC: A Gate Towards Sustainable Rural Development in the New Millennium," held in Munich, February 25–28, 2002. http://www.fao.org/europe/events/detail-events/en/c/285102/.

[53] On the firm belief of dismantling the agricultural cooperatives as inefficient units, see, Gramoz Pashko, "The Albanian Economy at the Beginning of the 1990s," in *Economic Change in the Balkan States: Albania, Bulgaria, Romania, and Yugoslavia*, eds. Örjan Sjöberg and Michael L. Wyzan (London: Pinter Publishers, 1991), 136.

[54] Zvi Lerman, "Policies and Institutions for Commercialization of Subsistence Farms in Transition Countries," *Journal of Asian Economics* 15, no. 3 (2004): 462.

CHAPTER 5

agriculture undermined commercialization and efficiency. After the dissolution of the cooperatives, the majority of the peasants ended up becoming subsistence farmers. The small plots, mainly long strips of arable land, replaced the large parcels of the communist era. Simultaneously, the Albanian post-socialist governments liberalized domestic markets and opened the borders to international trade.[55]

The situation, which reminds one of Hegel's famous statement that history repeats itself twice, returned to what it had been before collectivization. With the dissolution of the cooperatives and the return of agriculture to subsistence farming, the peasants had been reduced in extremis to the cultivation of industrial cash crops. Their lack of liquid capital thinned peasant investments in farm assets to a minimum, while the state, loyal to the "hands-off" approach, did not intervene to help the newly made private farmers overcome the crisis.[56] The government did not even encourage the peasants to combine their plots and cooperate as private individuals in producing for mass markets, allowing them to remain extremely vulnerable to international competition. As a farmer from a village in the plain of Maliq told me, his storage was full of unsold crops and vegetables because those imported were cheaper and outpriced them.[57] Rather than helping the Albanian farmers to be more efficient, the free market favored those who were stronger and crippled those in a disadvantageous position. Since 1991, due to the principle of non-interventionism, no government has conceived pro-

---

55 On the post-socialist agrarian reform and the opening of the international borders to trade and movement of capital, see Azeta Cungu and Johan F. M. Swinnen, "Albania's Radical Land Reform," *Economic Development and Cultural Change* 47, no. 3 (1999): 605–619; Daniel Müller and Thomas Sikor, "Effects of Postsocialist Reforms on Land Cover and Land Use in South-Eastern Albania," *Applied Geography* 26, nos. 3-4 (2006): 176.

56 On the transformation of property relations in the Albanian post-socialist countryside, Johannes Stahl, *Rent from the Land: A Political Ecology of Postsocialist Rural Transformation* (London: Anthem Press, 2010). On the fragmentation of arable land, Thomas Sikor, Daniel Müller, and Johannes Stahl, "Land Fragmentation and Cropland Abandonment in Albania: Implications for the Roles of State and Community in Post-Socialist Land Consolidation," *World Development* 37, no. 8 (2009): 1411–1423; Daniel Müller and Darla K. Munroe, "Changing Rural Landscapes in Albania: Cropland Abandonment and Forest Clearing in the Postsocialist Transition," *Annals of the Association of American Geographers* 98, no. 4 (2008): 855–876; Harold Lemel and Albert Dubali, "Land Fragmentation," in *Rural Property and Economy in Post-Socialist Albania*, ed. Harold Lemel (New York: Berghahn Books, 2000), 109–125. On the orientation of agriculture toward self-consumption and the reduction in cultivation of cash crops, *Theory and Practice of Rural Development: Experiences in Albania*, ed. Vittorio Gallerani et al. (Roskilde, Denmark: Federico Caffé Center Publisher, 2004), 29. On the low investments in farm equipment, Severin Kodderitzsch, *Reforms in Albanian Agriculture: Assessing a Sector in Transition* (Washington DC: The World Bank, 1999), 6.

57 Qetsor Agolli, informal interview with Artan Hoxha, Vashtëmi, Albania, December 17, 2017.

grams of regional specialization, which would connect the peasants to broad markets and motivate them to establish voluntary cooperatives.

As was the case in the late 1940s and early 1950s, the peasants of Maliq in the 1990s were not interested in cultivating a labor-intensive crop like sugar beet and even less to sell it at fixed prices. The state, on the other hand, did not provide any subsidies for the private farmers to prompt them to continue cultivating sugar beet. In 1992, while the Albanian post-socialist governments stuck with dogmatic determination to the principle of non-interventionism, the European Community did not give up on supporting their sugar beet farmers financially. Although the EC reduced the price support system for sugar, which had been functioning since 1968, it compensated for it by introducing direct payments to farmers—the EU would end this form of support only in 2017. After the agrarian reform, Maliq's refinery had to deal with many individual farmers who sold sugar beet at market prices, increasing the costs of sugar substantially at a moment when the factory had to compete in a liberalized market.[58]

Besides the raw material, the integrated industrial complex of Maliq also had to struggle for energy. By the early 1990s, the local mines lost state financial support and shrunk their operations—some even closed. Of course, the low quality of their coal did not help them survive. Many miners lost their jobs. Stavri Prifti, whom I met almost every day during my research in Korça, used to work in one of these mines. Born in one of the villages of the plain of Maliq, he became a worker and moved to the city after having completed his military service. After the closing of the mines, he found himself jobless and with a family to feed. The employees of the Local State Archive of Korça (Arkvi Shtetëror Vendor, Korçë), almost all of them women, paid him to do the menial and heavy work they could not do, like moving heavy boxes packed with documents up and down the stairs. The archivists gave him "something" in exchange, which means a couple of dollars. Every day he wandered around the city in search of similar work. The face of this short, bald, toothless man, poorly dressed, stinking of alcohol and tobacco,

---

58   On the reconstruction of land property and the effects of the agrarian reform on the activity of the sugar refinery, AShV Korçë, F. 67, Kombinati i Sheqerit, Kutia 677, viti 1992, dosje pa numër, fletë pa numër. Memo of the director of the sugar factory, Petraq Stratobërdha concerning the perturbing problems for the cultivation of sugar beet for the year 1993. February 22, 1993; *Ibid*, fletë pa numër. Memo of the director of the sugar factory, Petraq Stratobërdha concerning the troubling problems with the cultivation of sugar beet and the sugar factory of Maliq, January 16, 1993. On EC/EU financial mechanisms for supporting sugar beet farmers, "EU sugar quota system comes to an end," EU press release on September 29, 2017. https://ec.europa.eu/commission/presscorner/detail/en/IP_17_3487. Last access, September 18, 2022.

transmitted to me an unambiguous message. Sometimes smiling and sometimes with eyes filled with tears, Stavri represented in flesh and bone the human rubble that testifies by its very presence the transition between different historical ages. This ruined man expressed with all his being a drama that started for him with upward mobility and ended with downfall and poverty.

The closing of the mines crippled the regular coal supply for the TPP, hampering the ability of the refinery to process the sugar beet that it bought from the peasants at increased prices. The difficulties with furnishing the sugar factory with energy and raw materials put it at a distinct disadvantage compared with its international competitors. There were climate and soil conditions that determined the location of the sugar factory. On the other hand, the plain of Maliq was not well connected with the coastal areas and ports. Transporting sugar beet and coal to the region of Korça was extremely expensive and not profitable. However, the primary concern of the Albanian authorities when they built the refinery was not the engaging in trade with the world, but in supplying the domestic market.

Although political goals drove the entire sugar scheme in Maliq, it does not mean that the ALP apparatus was blind to efficiency. As I have already explained in chapter 2, and in the previous section, the communist regime made continuous investments to increase the productivity of both the factory and the agricultural farms. However, the refinery's successful operation depended heavily on state protection and its monopoly over the domestic market. It was the protection provided by either national governments or the EU that saved the majority of the sugar refineries in Eastern Europe for more than a decade. Once Brussels decided to cut the subsidies and lift the tariffs, the bulk of the sugar factories closed because they could not compete on the international market. Due to the zeal to which the Albanian political class faithfully pursued the blueprint for shock therapy, Maliq's refinery underwent this process earlier and closed down before them.

With the opening of the borders, the emerging class of post-socialist merchants started importing cheap foreign sugar that outcompeted Maliq's in the domestic market. Just like the interwar era's demands for mercantilism, the string of directors that led the factory until 1996 appealed to the government to raise customs barriers and fend off Maliq's international competition.[59] The factory administra-

---

59 AShV Korçë, F. 67, Kombinati i Sheqerit, Kutia 680, viti 1994, d. 13, fletë pa numër. Letter of complaint of the director of the sugar factory, Ismail Venxha, on the problems that had emerged from the

tion even deployed Orientalist categories, pointing to the fact that the private merchants bought their sugar in the East, and that the quality of the merchandise was suspicious.[60] "East" and "bad quality" fell into the same box. The directors used the axiological ontologies of East–West geographies to point out the need for state protectionism against international competition. Writing from Maliq, they saw the new economic policies with different lenses. For them, opening the borders was not necessarily a good thing. Dividing the world into geographic hierarchies, where the West stood on top, they openly preferred the linking of the country only with the latter. Superior technologies and high quality came only from the West. However, opening the doors to international trade and lifting tariffs did not mean exchanges only with the West. Due to Albania's low purchasing power, local merchants traded with countries that the directors identified with the East who sold cheap goods of low quality. According to a number of refinery administrations, Maliq produced sugar of better quality. However, quality is expensive, and they called on the government to return to protectionist policies to defend both the Albanian consumer and the national sugar industry.

Maliq's refinery administration reminded its superiors in Tirana of the critical economic and social repercussions that the closing of the factory would have for both the country and the district. In a letter sent to the government, one of the directors said that the sugar industry is the "heavy industry of light industry" and that its protection was critical to the national economy. Even after the collapse of communism, heavy industry maintained its prestige and still served as a metaphor for something of great importance. The factory's directors argued that the entire town of Maliq depended on the sugar industry and that the operation of the refinery had not merely economic but also social importance.

The refinery administration countered the dominant paradigm of pure market efficiency with that of the social responsibility toward workers, especially in

---

    operation of the sugar factory in Maliq. November 24, 1994; *Ibid*, fletë pa numër. Study on the sugar factory of Maliq concerning the existing situation of the factory and its future. December 12, 1994; *Ibid*, fletë pa numër. Complaint of the alcohol factory regarding the lack of steam. June 15, 1994; AShV Korçë, F. 67, Kombinati i Sheqerit, Kutia 677, viti 1992, dosje pa numër, fletë pa numër. Memo of the director of the sugar factory, Petraq Stratobërdha concerning the troubling problems with the cultivation of sugar beet for the year 1993. February 22, 1993; *Ibid*, fletë pa numër, Minutes of the meeting between the directory of the sugar factory and the Inspectorate of State Control. November 10, 1992.

60 On the use of the East, AShV Korçë, F. 67, Kombinati i Sheqerit, Kutia 680, viti 1994, d. 13, fletë pa numër. Memo of the directory of sugar factory with some data on the operation of the establishment during the last five years and the prospects for the future. November 18, 1994; *Ibid*, fletë pa numër. Letter of complaint of the director of the sugar factory, Ismail Venxha, on problems that have emerged from the operation of the sugar factory of Maliq. November 24, 1994.

single-industry towns. According to the latter view, it was the state's duty to take care of the industrial community of Maliq. To ensure the state's protection, the directors of the sugar factory highlighted its importance to the local economy by pointing out the centrality of the refinery to the regional web of economic enterprises. They mentioned how the factory's operations gave work to the coal mines that supplied it. The social and economic impact of the sugar industry was significant because its tentacles stretched across all of Korça.[61]

These pleas were in vain, however. They did not affect Tirana's policies, which stuck to the full liberalization guidebook. In the 1990s, protectionism was not an option. The collapse of communism also meant the end of the large patriarchal state that intervened in the economy to keep society in its warm bosom and defend it from the sharp cold of international competition and market fluctuations. The sugar factory was now on its own, as was the community that depended on it. Despite their efforts, the refinery administration failed to obtain loans from the World Bank and the FAO. The refinery did not have many prospects for success in the global market. The possibility of entering into cooperation with Greek firms did not materialize, either.[62] In the new economic structure, the factory had no role in either the national or the international division of labor. To phrase it differently, the Maliq refinery decapitalized. Additionally, its locality was distanced from capital relations.[63]

After the factory stopped working, and as proof of Hugo's dictum that "time is a devourer; man, more so," groups close to the country's top political circles got their hands on the machinery and sold it for scrap. This phenomenon, which

---

[61] AShV Korçë, F. 67, Kombinati i Sheqerit, Kutia 677, viti 1992, dosje pa numër, fletë pa numër. Memo of the director of the sugar factory, Petraq Stratobërdha concerning the disturbing problems with the cultivation of sugar beet and the sugar factory of Maliq. January 16, 1993; AShV Korçë, F. 67, Kombinati i Sheqerit, Kutia 680, viti 1994, d. 13, fletë pa numer. Decision of the directory of the sugar factory of Maliq concerning the existence of the establishment. May 12, 1994; *Ibid*, fletë pa numër. Study of the sugar factory of Maliq concerning the existing situation of the factory and its future. December 12, 1994.

[62] On loans from the FAO and the World Bank, AShV Korçë, F. 67, Kombinati i Sheqerit, Kutia 680, Pa vit, dosje pa numër, fletë pa numër. Programs of meetings and reports on the negotiations with representatives of the FAO and the World Bank on potential loans for the modernization of the sugar factory of Maliq. July 13, 1992. On negotiations with Greek firms, AShV Korçë, F. 67, Kombinati i Sheqerit, Kutia 680, viti 1994, dosje13, fletë pa numër. Reports regarding negotiations with representatives of Greek sugar companies on cooperation with the sugar factory of Maliq. July 1994; AShV Korçë, F. 67, Kombinati i Sheqerit, Kutia 677, viti 1992, dosje pa numër, fletë pa numër. Request of the directory of the sugar factory of Maliq to the President of Albania, Sali Berisha, to lobby the FAO for the procurement of loans from this branch of the UN. June 24, 1992

[63] On this concept, see John Urry, "Social Relations, Space and Time," *Social Relations and Spatial Structures*, eds. Derek Gregory and John Urry (London: Macmillan, 1985), 26.

Tim Edensor calls "the stage of plundering," is now very pronounced in the ex-socialist countries.⁶⁴ Ironically, the refinery became useful to the national and international economy through its destruction, not through production but as a carcass. What the partisans of shock therapy proclaimed to be short-term pain for long-term gain did not come to fruition, at least not in Maliq. The belief in the wonders of markets as the regulators of all social ills soon came up against the harsh reality that no one-size-fits-all policy works. As Frederick Cooper wisely stated, the idea of development emerged in late colonial thinking because markets alone could not produce growth and welfare for everybody.⁶⁵ Additionally, Maliq, to use the Ralf Dahrendorf's metaphor on post-socialist restructuring, has not come out of the "valley of tears."⁶⁶

Maliq Today: Ruins, Marginalization and Memory

"Decay sits among fallen places" wrote Nathaniel Hawthorne one hundred and eighty-five years ago.⁶⁷ Visiting Maliq between 2016 and 2018, I understood that Hawthorne's assertion still holds true. Behind a large iron door closed with heavy chains, the industrial complex laid in ruins, deserted, emptied, like De Chirico's dreamlike paintings of desolate squares and urban landscapes frozen in time. Meanwhile, the news kept reporting every year about floods from the Devoll River taking over the plain of Maliq. At times, the water invaded the lowest points of the plain for months, causing the peasants immense material damages and great hardship. It looked to me as if time had reversed its course, that some force had turned back the hands of the watch to the pre-1945 era. As one journalist put it in modernist language, Maliq has gone "from nothing to nothing."⁶⁸ "Something" is related to production. Both the swamp and the ruins are "nothing" to this author.

---

64 Edensor, *Industrial Ruins*, 23–24. On the scrap fever in the ex-socialist countries, see for example on Russia, Anne White, *Small-Town Russia: Postcommunist Livelihoods and Identities: A portrait of the Intelligentsia in Achit, Bednodemyanovks and Zubstov, 1999–2000* (London: Routledge, 2003), 113. Another case is that of Romania. For more, see Kideckel, "Identity and Mining," 121; Kideckel, "Coal Power," 73–74.
65 Frederick Cooper, "Writing the History of Development," *Journal of Modern European History* 8, no. 1 (2010): 20.
66 Ralf Dahrendorf, "Europe's Vale of Tears," *Marxism Today*, May 1990, 18–23; Jeffrey D. Sachs, "Crossing the Valley of Tears in East European Reform," *Challenge* 34, no. 5 (1991): 26–31.
67 Nathaniel Hawthorne, "The Canal Boat," *The New-England Magazine* 9 (December 1835): 403.
68 Ben Andoni, "Maliqi, nga hiçi në hiç" [Maliq, from nothing to nothing], *Mapo* 216, February 13, 2011, 18–19. On the continuous floods of the plain, see second, third, and fourth parts of the TV re-

As Tim Edensor has observed, for those who have embraced the vision that space must have an evident function (be it production or as property), ruins are places where there is nothing. What predicates the usefulness or uselessness of space, he continues, are the investments and disinvestments.[69] In the eyes of all those who bear a utilitarian vision, Maliq was a swamp, which they considered "nothing," and had transitioned into ruins with no economic function. It had thus returned to "nothing." Everything is reduced to market usefulness, while the communities disappear or at best become an appendage. Their history, their past, and their present are invisible to those who do not live in Maliq. This is not true, however, for its inhabitants. To many of them, the transition to a market economy has not offered much by way of compensation; during my research I observed that the town of sugar was stuck in the past, when it used to have a specific economic role, an identity, and its own communitarian culture strongly related to the industry. The past, however, was and is still alive. The ruins remind Maliq's people of the loss of the place's function, of what they had that they have not been able to replace. The deserted industrial complex symbolized the new post-socialist spatial inequalities and the majority of the locals were disgruntled about the directions their lives had taken since the fall of the communist regime. As Stephen Crowley reminds us in his analysis contrasting the thriving Russian global cities of Moscow and Saint Petersburg to the hundreds of stagnating small and medium-sized mono-industrial towns, there is a geographical pattern to discontent.[70]

The collapse of communism in Eastern Europe and the transition to market economies made visible an uneven pattern of development between the countries of the ex-socialist bloc that mirrored their socialist legacies. The different degrees of integration into the global economy and its production and investment networks have generated acute regional disparities within Eastern European nation states. Maliq's marginalization reflected the new spatial hierarchies linked to the new circuits of the flow of capital and labor. Beginning the interwar era, the Albanian authorities constructed Maliq as a space with a specific function in the national economy. After the collapse of communism, the sugar

---

portage prepared by the journalist Rudina Xhunga, "Këneta." (Second part) https://www.youtube.com/watch?v=XY7ti3Kh4nA&t=189s; (Third https://www.youtube.com/watch?v=bkoqOvtxsA; (Fourth part) https://www.youtube.com/watch?v=VBi5gznDPqA&t=145s. Last access, September 18, 2022.
69 Edensor, *Industrial Ruins*, 8.
70 Stephen Crowley, "Global Cities versus Rustbelt Realities: The Dilemmas of Urban Development in Russia," *Slavic Review* 79, no. 2 (2020): 388–389.

land lost its privileged position and was now marginalized once again. The locked doors demonstrate Maliq's abandonment both symbolically and literally.

Stepping into the administration building, the only structure of the industrial establishment left intact from the devastation of the 1990s, I met Vera Begolli, the director of the ghost-factory. She sat at her table and showed me samples of sugar and molasses that the refinery used to produce. Those samples were all that was left from what Maliq's industry used to process. Everything was gone, including the establishment itself. With a real sense of trauma, Vera mourned the bygone days when the sugar industry operated. They were sweeter times. She lamented the loss of the community that had been built around the sugar industry, the long-gone routines and relationships. Vera was not alone. Everybody I met in Maliq had a deep sense of loss. The magnetic field the factory once created was now gone, and with it their north pole. Now the town has lost its raison d'être, the function for which it came into being. Along with communism, its spatial division of labor was over. The threads of regional interdependencies, which gave birth to the town, had unraveled. Maliq had disconnected and the town of sugar had lost its function. Nation-building ceased to be a priority for the post-socialist Albanian governments.

Vera's lament was not nostalgia, that feeling of longing for a past that never existed which people construct through juxtaposition with the present. The historian of deindustrialization, Steven High, criticizes the use of nostalgia for explaining how ex-industrialized communities recall their past. According to him, nostalgia depoliticizes the past. Additionally, and most importantly, he argues, when middle-class academics, carrying the brunt of their class, consider the memories of the past to be merely nostalgia, they belittle the attachment of workers to their cultural worlds. We should not assume, he advises, that ex-industrial communities imagine a world that never existed.[71] Indeed, the 2000s caused Vera's longing for a bygone past; it was the mourning of a community that the restructuring of the global economy had marginalized. It was also true that many times she and others in Maliq looked back upon the past with rose-colored glasses. However, this does not mean that the world that disappeared never existed.

The term *Ostalgie* has entered the daily and academic jargon of today's Germany. It means to lament about the past in the eastern districts that used to be part of the GDR. Not very accurately, *Ostalgie* reduces the recollection of the

---

71 Steven High and David W. Lewis, *Corporate Wasteland: The Landscape and Memory of Deindustrialization* (Ithaca, NY: ILR Press, 2007), 94.

past to a mere craving for the communist past—the East. Just because this feeling of loss is dominant in the most peripheral areas of the ex-GDR that have found themselves in a disadvantaged position following the new economic transformation, it does not follow that this is a phenomenon limited to the ex-socialist countries.[72] As different studies have shown, the ex-industrial communities in Western Europe and especially the US are areas where the past and its sense of stability still define peoples' identities and political outlook.[73] Additionally, above all, the past vis-à-vis the present highlights the feeling of abandonment. When talking about the abandoned Austrian textile industry, Andrea Komlosy states that for their workers, the ruined buildings "evoke memories of an industry that has moved to other places in the world."[74]

In 2017 and 2018, Vera still hoped that someday the factory would start working again. She talked about the Poles, who wanted to rebuild the refinery and reuse the plain of Maliq for cultivating sugar beet. However, the sugar was gone forever. The production of sugar belonged to the past. It was part of history, and her hopes would not materialize, especially after the restructuring of the EU's sugar industry. What to do with Maliq and its plain? How to use it? These were questions and puzzles that central and local authorities tried to answer. At the time I was doing my research, plans were circulating for the construction of a new TPP that would supply the region with energy by using the peat of the plain as fuel.[75]

Local politicians, too, were trying to find other ways to integrate the plain of Maliq into the global division of labor as a space with a specific economic function. Some of them advocated for the return of the swamp. Using environmentalist vocabulary and expressing the green sensibilities of the Western middle

---

72   On *Ostalgie* in the peripheral areas of the ex-GDR, see Herrschel, *Global Geographies of Post-Socialist Transition*, 62.

73   On memory and nostalgia in the industrial communities of Western Europe and North America, see, Linde Egberts, *Chosen Legacies: Heritage in Regional Identity* (London: Routledge, 2017), 138–201; Tim Strangleman, "'Smoke-stack Nostalgia,' 'Ruin Porn' or Working-Class Obituary: The Role and Meaning of Deindustrial Representation," *International Labor and Working-Class History* 84 (2013): 28; Sherry Lee Linkon and John Russo, *Steeltown USA: Work and Memory in Youngstown* (Lawrence, KS: University Press of Kansas, 2002).

74   Andrea Komlosy, "Austria and Czechoslovakia: The Habsburg Monarchy and Its Successor States," in *The Ashgate Companion to the History of Textile Workers, 1650–2000*, eds. Lex Heerma van Voss et al. (New York: Ashgate Publisher, 2010), 72–73.

75   On the offer of the Poles, Vera Begolli, informal interview with Artan Hoxha, Maliq, Albania, July 20, 2017. On the plans to build a TPP in Maliq and the reactions against it, https://www.youtube.com/watch?v=wlhrupIFkjU; https://www.youtube.com/watch?v=ffbUHeEeS_Y; https://www.youtube.com/watch?v=BAXBSfFIeK0. Last access, September 18, 2022.

classes, local political and non-political actors complained about the reclamation and the destruction it had caused to the regional ecology and biodiversity.[76] Those who made these claims dressed their narratives in the imposing and prestigious attire of German science. Many people I met, mainly state bureaucrats, claimed that during World War II, German scientists had explored the swamp of Maliq and concluded that it was a primary station for all the birds that migrated from Russia to Africa. According to them, the Germans estimated that more than 5000 birds stopped every day in Maliq before continuing their journey south. When asked whether or not they had seen the document, the answer was always no. When asked again who had told them about this study, the answer was either a dry "I heard it" or the juicier "I heard it is in the archives." Despite my persistence, I failed to find any trace of this study in the archives.

Beneath the environmentalist discourse, rather than the will to reclaim lost biodiversity, hid the logic of profits. The return of the swamp would help the local political circles to commodify the plain by transforming part of it into a hunting ground. Their main targets were foreign hunters from rich Western countries. The legend of the German study served to legitimize the return of the swamp—maybe with the hopes of making Maliq a station for migrating birds and, as a result, a profitable hunting ground. This initiative was just a demonstration of the efforts of the local authorities to integrate Maliq into the broader international economic system and global circuits of capital: not by processing sugar, but by providing entertainment, not for the members of the Politburo, as was the case during the communist era, but for foreign tourists who would bring in precious hard currency.

This project was part of the conversation on the region's future, which at that time remained disconcertingly unknown, uncomfortably dark, and anxiously poor. In the meantime, the people in Maliq tried to survive. Their strategies, not dissimilar from those of other ex-socialist countries, ranged from emigration to opening some small stores or businesses.[77] In the villages, the scattered and small plots were of little use to the farmers of the plain of Maliq, who found themselves

---

76 Ardit Konomi, informal interview with Artan Hoxha, Korça, Albania, September 28, 2017; Ilia V. Ballauri, "Ngjalat e Korçës dhe nami i tyre shumëshekullor" [The centuries-old renown Korça's eels], http://korcapedica.com/korca-encyclopedica/korca-encyclopedica-nr9/201-bkn-ngjalat-e-korces-dhe-nami-i-tyre-shumeshekullor.html. Last access, September 18, 2022.
77 White, *Small-Town Russia*; Dimitra Kofti, "Moral Economy of Flexible Production: Fabricating Precarity between the Conveyor Belt and the Household," *Anthropological Theory* 16, no. 4 (2016): 433–453; Michael Burawoy, Pavel Krotov, and Tatyana Lytkina, "Involution and Destitution in Capitalist Russia," *Ethnography* 1, no. 1 (2000): 43–65.

outcompeted in an open market. The fate of those who lived in the town was no brighter. According to the law, its population is urban and as a consequence has no right to own land. What can one do in a settlement that does not produce anything? Like all poor areas, Maliq has a redundant workforce that now supplies the labor-hungry wealthier centers with workers. Reproducing an established pattern in post-socialist Albania, many migrated to other cities in the country or to Western Europe or North America. Some left for good, while others returned to open a hotel or a small business. Vera, the last employee of the ghost factory, co-owns a cafeteria, "Grill 824," where 824 stands for Maliq's altitude above sea level.[78]

Behind Vera's rarely open office lies the bare skeleton of an industrial dinosaur that did not survive the seismic shift of systemic collapse. Like the megacreatures that millions of years ago dominated our planet, only to disappear at the strike of a meteor, so the sugar industrial complex of Maliq did not survive the twentieth century. Of all its chimneys, only the large, round, white stack of the TPP is still intact. It was silent and did not spew smoke out of its wide throat. The others have been destroyed, and the shattered bricks are spread across the ruins of the factory. Those smokestacks, powerful symbols of the shrines that forged modernity, which, according to Bruce Springsteen, reached "like the arms of God into a beautiful sky of soot and clay," had crumbled.

Other tall structures have appeared or reappeared in the area. Newly built belfries and minarets dot the plain, even where there was once a swamp. Ironically, communism opened the way for the religious resurgence of the twenty-first century. The belfries and minarets do not reach God with black smoke that paints the sky with dark colors as was the case during the communist era but do so with the surahs from the Quran and bell reverberations instead. The old gods are back, but in a new age. The mosques are markers of the global era, built with the oil money of the Arab countries that are now using the new wave of globalization to spread Mohammed's universal vision. Many of the Christian Orthodox

---

[78] On the emigration pattern, see Karl Kaser, "The History of the Family in Albania in the 20th Century: A First Profile," *Ethnologia Balkanica* 4 (2000): 55. On the agrarian post-socialist reform in Korça, Yllson Manoku, *Historia e bujqësisë dhe agropërpunimit në rajonin e Korçës* [The history of agriculture and agro-processing in the region of Korça] (Korça: Universiteti Fan Noli, 2009), 196–238. On the inefficiency of the scattered plots in the plain of Maliq, Zambak Shënollari, informal interview with Artan Hoxha, Maliq, Albania, January 21, 2018; Petrit Kume, informal interview with Artan Hoxha, Maliq, Albania, January 21, 2018; Qetsor Agolli, informal interview with Artan Hoxha, Vashtëmi, Albania, December 17, 2017; On the post-socialist strategies of survival in Maliq, Vera Begolli, informal interview with Artan Hoxha, Maliq, Albania, July 20, 2017.

FIGURE 18. The sugar factory of Maliq. September 2017

churches are built with the funds of the Greek government, which tirelessly insists on patronizing Orthodoxy for political leverage in Albania. The shrines create a new map of Maliq and fill it with new meaning. While the ALP regime used the factory to establish a homogeneous identity and claim its sovereignty over the national space, the global age is re-multiplying the identities; Maliq is a site of competing and multifaceted loyalties.

In the meantime, Korça district occupies the bottom of the ladder for poverty in Albania, and the new shrines do not alleviate it.[79] The periodic return of the swamp and religious pluralism does not mean merely a return to the past. The factory represented what the twentieth century stood for: integrated industrial complexes, enforced borders, territoriality, and efforts to build cohesive social entities with members that professed unambiguous loyalty and identity. Maliq's ruins represent the fading away of the twentieth century and territoriality, while documenting Albania's leap into a new age that Ulrich Beck has coined

---

[79] Ëngjëll Pere and Will Bartlett, "On the Way to Europe: Economic and Social Development in Albania," in *Western Balkan Economies in Transition: Recent Economic and Social Developments*, eds. Reiner Osbild and Will Bartlett (Cham, Switzerland: Springer, 2019), 84. For a socio-economic analysis of the district of Korça, see Dhimitër Doka, *Zhvillime socio-ekonomike dhe rajonale të Shqiërisë pas vitit 1990* [Regional socio-economic developments in Albania after 1990] (Potsdam: Universität Potsdam, 2005), 147–199.

the "risk society."[80] This transition has affected both the old Western market democracies and the ex-socialist countries of Eastern Europe. What the political scientists have called the post-socialist transition or transformation, has indeed been a departure from the model of the twentieth century and a convergence with the twenty-first century's "risk society."

However, a ray of hope has pierced Maliq's dark present. When I returned to Maliq in 2020, I found out that the local authorities had leased the sugar factory to an Albanian fish processing company, Rozafa, for a twenty-year period. The company distributes seafood all around the world, including Japan.[81] According to the agreement between the two entities, Rozafa will transform some of the buildings of the industrial establishment into seafood processing factories where some 500 people will work. In addition, the private company is going to build restaurants and make part of the area of the refinery an entertainment center. This project reminded me of Pittsburgh, Pennsylvania, where I had spent six years of my life. I recalled the metamorphoses of Homestead Steel Works, Waterworks, and Southside, which, from centers of steel production were transformed into huge malls and shopping centers. From loci of production, all these immense plants have now been transformed into spaces of mass consumption.

Somehow, Maliq has reconnected with the global network of capital, reproducing a pattern already known to me from my experience in North America. Cheap labor and low rent have facilitated the entire project. Seafood processed by the people of Maliq will be exported around Europe and all the way to the Far East, while the industrial area will become a center that will produce pleasure through fish consumption and various forms of recreation, especially for children, rather than through sweet substances. Once again, Maliq is undergoing a new form of regionalization, this time within the global framework of the spatial division of labor. Maliq does not play a role in nation-building anymore. Instead, it will become part of a huge network where it will specialize in the processing of seafood, while locally it will supply the market with the precious services of amusement and consumption. The nation, as the intermediary link between the local and the global, has somehow retreated from its previous prominent role.

---

80 On the twentieth century as the period of the rise and fall of territoriality, see Charles S. Maier, "Consigning the Twentieth Century to History: Alternative Narratives for the Modern Era," *American Historical Review* 105, no. 3 (2000): 807–831. On risk society, Ulrich Beck, "Varieties of Second Modernity and the Cosmopolitan Vision," *Theory, Culture & Society* 33, nos. 7–8 (2016): 257–270.

81 Lease contract between the Municipality of Maliq and the Rozafa Company for the use of the locale of the sugar factory of Maliq. No. repertoire 369, no. collection 175. November 11, 2020.

Will Maliq reinvent itself from a town of sugar into a town of fish and entertainment? Only time will tell. For the time being, Vera Begolli is not happy. She keeps trying to find a way to bring sugar production back. Other people share the same opinion but not the local politicians, who want to create new jobs and exploit any opportunity to attract investments. While some of the buildings of the industrial complex are being reconstructed, others lay ghostly silent, devastated, filled with countless bricks and tiles. How long they remain unused and when these immense structures will be useful to capital depends on the profitability of the first investments. Until then, the ruins will still be there, as witnesses of what Maliq used to be and reminders of what it may be again someday.

* * *

One of the major flaws in the theories of post-socialist transition has been the perception of both planned and market economies as fixed antithetical types. As a result, many scholars and politicians have imagined the "Europeanization" of the Eastern European countries as a movement between two fixed points. Not only are there various forms of capitalism and socialism, but more importantly the old liberal democracies have been going through economic transitions themselves since at least the 1970s. The erosion of the industrial base in some Western countries, especially in the US and the UK, and shifts in the networks of investment and production have created seismic social and economic transformations, which are similar to those taking place in many ex-socialist countries in Eastern Europe. What we see are similar transitional dynamics that have been taking place in both liberal and ex-socialist camps.

The effects of the wave of neoliberal transformations have been uneven across space, and scholars such as Smoki Musaraj, who studies the post-socialist economic transformation in Albania, have argued that there are multiple forms of neoliberalism that are construed by the interaction of a series of international and domestic factors.[82] Compared to market economies, in the ex-socialist bloc of Eastern Europe the range of structural changes has been much more profound because it is related to the collapse of the political system and the type of economic management. However, there are significant overlaps as well. For this reason, rather than speaking exclusively of a post-socialist transition we should talk

---

82 Smoki Musaraj, "Tales from Albarado: The Materiality of Pyramid Schemes in Postsocialist Albania," *Cultural Anthropology* 26, no. 1 (2011): 87–88.

CHAPTER 5

about a major transition taking place from Russia to the US that is related to the deep economic structural transformations related to the new wave of globalization. Deindustrialization has been one of its major characteristics. This process has hit those old industrial economies that opened their state borders wide to the flow of capital, goods, and people particularly hard. Countries that have not had a dogmatic approach to free trade have suffered fewer losses in their industrial base and have experienced less traumatic effects during this transition.

However, other factors have played important roles as well. In Eastern Europe, the Catholic countries of the northern tier have not deindustrialized. Thanks to their geographic location, their highly professional and cheap labor force, and higher rate of integration into the global capitalist system since the 1970s, they have attracted Western European direct investment. Because their economic development still depends on these investments, they are haunted by the prospect of Western-based companies moving their industrial establishments to the east.[83] The countries of the southern tier of Eastern Europe (those that belong to the Byzantine and Ottoman sphere) and the Orthodox states bordering Russia have fared less well. Albania's post-socialist history has been defined, among other things, by longue durée influences, geostrategic contexts where many divergent interests intersect, and broader regional dynamics that transcend state borders. However, aside from regional historical particularism, global processes, too, have shaped the history of this spot of the Balkans and that of Maliq's refinery. The end of the sugar scheme is not merely a post-socialist drama, but is also the story of the collapse of the developmental strategy based on the nation state as the primary platform of modernization. With the demise of the ALP, Albania entered into the Western-centered global economy. With such a leap, the sugar industry lost the role it had played for decades.

With the passing of communism, both simple people acting spontaneously and the new post-socialist authorities overthrew the monuments to Enver Hoxha and Stalin that filled the main squares of Albanian cities. Shortly after, they closed the majority of the industrial plants. Albania now is full of pedestals without monuments and lifeless concrete skeletons. A world came to an end, and with it also the symbols that glorified it: monuments and factories. However, while the downing of Stalin's and Hoxha's busts signaled the end of socialism, the ruins of Maliq also mark the conclusion of the dreams of making Albania an in-

---

83 Andreas Nölke and Arjan Vliegenthart, "Enlarging the Varieties of Capitalism: The Emergence of Dependent Market Economies in East Central Europe," *World Politics* 61, no. 4 (2009): 695.

dustrial country with a self-sufficient economy. Bruce Springsteen once stated that one place "can embody the hopes and failures of the nation. It could be any place."[84] In Albania, Maliq embodies the hopes and failures of its age; the sacrifices the era of progress demanded and the tragedies it caused. The ruins and their contentious memories represent the burying of the past's hopes under the rubble of history's continuous earthquakes—much like Stavri Prifti's life.

The recollection of the past takes on greater importance in the face of mass disillusionment with what replaced socialism. Rather than a hard object, memory is a soft subject, like the watches in Dali's "La persistencia de la memoria." It is malleable and shaped, among other things, by the reality of the present. In Albania's ex-land of sugar, many people do not applaud the end of the sugar era. On the contrary, many of them long for its return. This is visible in the Maliq municipality's coat of arms: the sugar factory's smokestacks spilling white smoke into the blue sky are its central symbols. Although gone for good, the refinery still defines the identity of the small town. Not only that, but in the hall of the municipality there is a large painting depicting a heroic image of peasants and young men and women reclaiming the swamp. The prisoners and the use of forced labor do not appear in the tableau, proving once again how selective we are in the way we approach the past in order to construct our present upon it.

This is not some irrational feeling or a demonstration of the power of the communist discourse internalized by people who dislike liberalism's pantheon of values. What I saw in Maliq was not too different from the craving of the American blue-collar workers for the 1950s–1960s. The outsourcing of industries or their closing, especially in the small and medium-sized single-industry towns, has affected many people equally, in the American Rust Belt and North England, in the Carpathian and Ural Mountains, and in the Russian Far East. Maliq is one of these places—just one dot on a map punctuated by hundreds of other similar sites.

However, the landscape of ruin is not merely an outcome of the capitalist storm, of its creative destruction that leaves in its wake heaps of rubble, as Walter Benjamin and many scholars with left-wing leanings are prone to suggest. The ruins are not only an outcome of impersonal forces outside human control. After all, capitalism is a set of social relationships, and human actors are not powerless. The ruins are also a result of political decisions based on paradigm shifts and ideological factors. The European industrial core, called the Blue Banana, which

---

84 "The Boss Pays a Call to a Princeton Classroom," *Chronicle of Higher Education*, January 12, 2001, 37.

covers north-east Italy, Germany, the Low Countries, and north-east France, has not de-industrialized. It is in fact the economic engine of the EU. Brussels' policies to defend their entrepreneurs and workers are an example of political agency that contests any conclusion that points the finger at abstract systems.

The countries of Eastern Europe that avoided shock therapy and took a less dogmatic approach had much smoother and less traumatic social and economic transformations. Today Poland, Slovakia, the Czech Republic, and Slovenia are economically sound, outperforming older EU members like Greece, Portugal, and Italy's southern regions. The success stories of this group of ex-socialist countries, though, are also related to their integration into the European Union. The latter process has been critical for these countries to redefine the nation state and the strategies of development in the twenty-first century.[85] With its shield of subsidies, protectionism, and flow of investments, the EU has provided its eastern members with a powerful developmental platform that has successfully replaced the nation state. While the post-socialist transformation has been painful, the gains from the market economy, on the other hand, have overshadowed by far the losses and healed the scars.

In the early 1980s, Foucault contended that the system of the social-democratic welfare state in Western Europe and North America, which was at the core of the post-World War II Western European order, gave people more security but at the same time made them more dependent on the system.[86] Instead of an impersonal system exerting its power and controlling people's lives, as Foucault claims, the welfare state was indeed a response to pressures coming from below. In the face of a rising tide of democratization in Western societies and the emergence of mass politics in the twentieth century, governments did not have the luxury, as they had in the preceding century, of enduring market fluctuations.[87] Political pressures from unemployment, decreased wages, and rising prices forced many Western governments to step up and take measures to save their economic and political orders. The capitalist system created the preconditions for its own demise and only the reforms that established the alliance between labor and capital saved it.

---

85 Young, "Marketisation, Democratisation and Inequality in Central Eastern Europe," 76.
86 Michel Foucault, "The Risks of Security," in *Essential Works of Foucault*, vol. 3, *Power*, ed. James D. Faubion (New York: New Press, 2001), 368; Ivan T. Berend, "Foucault and the Welfare State," *European Review* 13, no. 4 (2005): 551–556.
87 Eric Helleiner, "Economic Nationalism as a Challenge to Economic Liberalism? Lessons from the 19th Century," *International Studies Quarterly* 46, no. 3 (2002): 317.

When, in the 1970s, to quote Henri Lefebvre, the flow of capital triumphed over the fixities, the alliance broke.[88] The factories outsourced away from those places where labor organizations raised the costs of production and constrained efficiency. Thus, it was not the modern state's choice and intention that made people dependent on it. It was the latter's vulnerability to market fluctuations and their mass participation in politics that forced European governments to provide the people with security. Thus, the state softened people's dependence on the market by taking over some responsibilities and making them partially dependent on its services. The now-closed factories once symbolized the security of livelihood. From sites of social conflicts, they became sites of social order. With their disappearance, conflicts resurfaced. The social and economic destitution in the deindustrialized towns has made them dens of discontent and political revolt. The people living there contemplate the end of the age that created them and realize that their future is going in a direction they cannot control.

Socialism represented the most radical solution to the conflicts that were reigning between the late nineteenth and early twentieth century. Rather than try to bridge the conflict, the socialist regimes decided to solve it unilaterally at the expense of private capital. However, as was also the case with Albania, the countries of Eastern Europe had a very small industrial base, which the communists, in pursuit of development, decided to expand. In the eyes of many Eastern European communists, the Soviet model was an alternative for development without the social conflicts allegedly inherent to capitalism. With their imposing presence, the mills and factories marked the presence of the working class and their alleged political order and state. Industrialization and the creation of large working classes, though, proved to be detrimental to the communist regimes in the era of economic stagnation. The process of working-class formation detached many young peasants from their largely self-sufficient rural households and made them dependent on wage labor and market supply. It was precisely this dependence that made the workers a disruptive and anti-systemic force in the economic stagnation of the late 1970s and 1980s. The fall of communism did not solve the problems for all the workers of Eastern Europe. The consequent deindustrialization transformed the urban centers affected by the closing of the industrial complexes into hubs of political radicalization—and criminality, too, which made them not very different from their British and American kin.

---

88 Henri Lefebvre, "The Worldwide and the Planetary," in *State, Space, World*, 202.

CHAPTER 5

The reactions to the end of industry are different. Some people vote with their feet and emigrate. Others, as is the case in the UK and the US, vote for populist–nationalist political programs that promise the return of the alliance between capital and labor and of the responsibility of investors toward the communities that depend on them. Oliver Kühschelm has rightly argued that the close connection between nationalism and industrialization has shaped the meaning of deindustrialization. The lost industries have also become an object of profound political importance because outsourcing has created the feeling that the nation is being hollowed out.[89] It is no accident that the ex-industrial communities and workers have been susceptible to nationalist discourse and economic protectionism, or, in other instances, to far-left populists who promise them a socialist utopia. History, though, keeps plowing toward the future, harvesting victims and sowing victors.

Maliq's history narrates the story of an enterprise that the last century created and the current one has thrown away. Its factory used to be an instrument of social and spatial inclusion. Its ruins represented, until lately, exclusion. Like a recess screened by a wall of trees, Maliq remains off the highway that connects Tirana with Korça. Once a buzzing town, for decades it has been a quiet place, loaded with memories recollected by the fading generation of sugar workers and chiseled into the factory's silent ruins. Yet the future is open. After three decades of trauma and marginalization, private capital has found its way to Maliq. Hope is gradually returning and the people of Maliq, while craving for the past, have faith that soon they will be on the side of history's victors rather than that of the losers, as has been the case thus far.

---

89 Oliver Kühschelm, "Nationalizing Consumption: Products, Brands, and Nations," in *Nationalism and the Economy: Explorations into a Neglected Relationship*, eds. Stefan Berger and Thomas Fetzer (Budapest: Central European University Press, 2019), 179.

Epilogue

In the late 1980s, my grandmother, Aneta Naçi, an ALP member who had just retired, and her neighbor, Ana Mihali, a schoolteacher, met every afternoon for the most important ritual of the day. On their Albanian-made Iliria TV, they watched the American soap operas *Santa Barbara* and *The Bold and the Beautiful* broadcast from Italy. My hometown, Fier, which the Venetians used during the Middle Ages as a trade fair—whence its name is derived, fiera—is situated only a few kilometers from the southeastern shores of the Adriatic Sea. With the heel of the Apennine boot slightly more than seventy nautical miles away, the broadcasts of the Italian television stations could easily be received. Despite the communist authorities' jamming, people always invented new antennas that received the signals coming from the other side of the Adriatic. To return to my grandmother, although she and her neighbor did not understand Italian, they knew all the names of all the characters of the two serials, from Eden and Cruz to Brooke, Ridge, Eric, and Stephanie. I still remember the Hercules-like faces of Ronn Moss and Adolfo Martinez, for whom both women nurtured a particular sympathy. They commented with passion on all the scandals, love affairs, and betrayals that took place in the bosom of the Capwell and Forrester dynasties.

Just like the Christian Church, which, since Gregory the Great's era, has used pictures to teach the Christian message to the illiterate masses, the serials' iconography succeeded in conveying powerful messages without the need for any linguistic medium. In Albania and the other communist countries located along the Iron Curtain, TV became a new church, and the images coming from the capitalist side of Europe hit the communist regimes' claims right in the heart. In my grandma's living room emerged a nexus of synchronic and diachronic linkages that diluted Cold War polarities, imagined imperialist or historical enemies, and ideological orthodoxies. The regime's cynical propaganda and vapid fantasies about Albania as a socialist fortress under imperialist siege evaporated. At that moment, in that place, none of the women were thinking of irreconcilable differences with America or the systemic antagonism with capitalism.

A key component of my grandma and her neighbor's daily ritual was the sweetened Turkish coffee that both women sipped from porcelain china cups decorated with red roses and green leaves. The shortage of sugar and coffee troubled them very much because it jeopardized their sacred daily custom of watching the soap operas. On the other hand, the soap operas highlighted their misery and the failure of socialism to live up to its promises. In 1957, in his monumental book *Oriental Despotism*, Karl Wittfogel wrote that "many anxieties darken the path of life; but perhaps none is as devastating as the insecurity created by polarized total power."[1] My grandma's path in life was not insecure because of the alleged total power of the communist regime but by the shortages that the regime created. The images from Italian television stations made the scarcities of the 1980s even less bearable. After watching the daily series and the commercials that accompanied them, the two women discussed Albania's empty shops and rationed food while comparing their poor standard of living with the fabulous affluence they saw on the screen. They had no way of knowing whether the images coming from the US and Western Europe were embellished or not. Entangled between the dreamworld of capitalism and the discredited regime's propaganda, they felt disappointed with their poverty. Their disillusionment was quite a leap for them. Both women belonged to the generation that embraced communism in the aftermath of World War II and participated in its construction. They believed in the ability of the system implemented in the Soviet Union to deliver the promise of prosperity. Forty years later, though, they, like many others, understood very well that this was not the case anymore. The projections coming from the western side of the Iron Curtain buried the communist regime's claims of building an earthly utopia. On the contrary, they seemed to suggest that the liberal democracies had achieved a utopia of plenty.

In 1951, the American sociologist David Riesman proposed to bomb the Soviet Union and other socialist countries with American appliances and commodities in his famous satirical essay "The Nylon War". According to Riesman, the gadgets and machines would show the Soviet people the superiority of Ameri-

---

[1] Karl A. Wittfogel, *Oriental Despotism: A Comparative Study of Total Power* (New Haven, CT: Yale University Press, 1957), 155.

can life and the peaceful intentions of the USA.[2] In Albania, the success of the Western democracies' soft power came to fruition in the late 1970s and 1980s with the TV revolution and the incessant bombardment of Albanian society with commercials and Hollywood movies. The electromagnetic waves emitted from Italy indeed brought the wonders of capitalism into the houses of Albanians, showing them how shockingly poor and alienated they were due to the communist regime.

The failure to meet consumers' growing needs had fatal repercussions for the Albanian communist regime. Ironically, the economic stagnation of the 1970s and 1980s coincided with the mass introduction of television. Located on the border between the Eastern and Western blocs, Albania was exposed to broadcasts coming from both sides, which had tremendous political effects. Television brought Albanians into direct contact with embellished images emanating from Western Europe without the mediation of the regime. Moving from one extreme that depicted capitalism as nightmarish and dystopian to another that came through movies and commercials that made it seem like the realization of utopia caused shock and awe. Discovering their relative poverty compared to the societies living in the liberal democracies made the scarcities of the 1980s less tolerable for my grandmother and her neighbor. This was also the case for many other Albanians. The latter did not crave political freedom and a multiparty system but were rather more concerned with practical matters. The restrictions on consumption and the comparatively low standards of living alienated the regime from my grandmother, her neighbor, as well as hundreds and thousands of other Albanians.

From the complaints I heard in my grandma's living room, I discovered that the sugar we consumed, contained in 1 kg packages of thick brown paper, was refined in Maliq. Learning of Maliq's existence was intrinsically linked to the ambiguous balance sheet of the communist era. On the one hand, the ALP's regime transformed a plain once covered by a swamp into an important part of the Albanians' daily lives. The sugar Maliq processed made its way into every home in the country. However, the anxiety and discomfort that filled my grandma's living room showed that the refinery's output could not meet the growing demand of the population, thus leaving people without the necessary quantity of the sweet substance. The failure of the communist regime to keep up with con-

---

2   David Riesman, "The Nylon War," in *Abundance for What? And Other Essays* (New York: Doubleday & Co., 1964), 67–75.

sumption and deliver on its promise of prosperity eroded the foundations of its power much more than the craving for political freedom and pluralism. It was the lack of goods like sugar that struck the ALP's legitimacy at its heart. The Maliq project was an important component of Tirana's Soviet-type program of building socialism, and in this history we can trace the fruitless efforts to make Albania self-sufficient and a garden of felicity. The entire sugar scheme aimed to establish the conditions for the country's prosperity without relying on international markets. Maliq's failure to produce enough sugar, however, demonstrated, like many other industrial enterprises around the country, that self-sufficiency and affluence were chimeras.

* * *

Should we consider the entire Maliq scheme, which was part of the ALP's modernizing program, a failure? Is it fruitful to use such a rigid taxonomy that simplifies complex historical processes, which comprised wide-ranging social, economic, cultural, and environmental transformations? Using the binaries of failure and success, and top–down imposition versus bottom–up resistance obfuscates the importance of communist modernization, its broad ramifications, and long-lasting effects. Defining the outcomes of the developmental programs of the Soviet-type regimes in absolute terms means that we overlook their nuances and impact on Eastern European societies. We need to better define what failure and success mean in human history and to be more aware when using such terms.

In his book *Seeing Like a State*, James C. Scott argues that the schemes of improvement driven by the ideology of progress and what he calls "authoritarian high modernist vision," indeed, failed. Scott identifies these projects, which aimed to discipline and mold social and natural life, as an expression of technocratic, anti-democratic rule. It is important to note that Scott used the singular rather than the plural for the guiding vision of all these programs that sought to engineer both society and nature. He integrated the modernizing projects under one single denominator, regardless of the socio-economic systems and the ideological allegiance of the ruling elites that implemented them. Thus, Maliq's transformation emerges as part of a large process that includes within it trends that do not spring exclusively from Soviet-type regimes. Additionally, he uses the notion of failure indiscriminately for all schemes. According to him, these projects failed due to resistance from common people or nature, which did not conform to the technocrats' blueprints and rationales. In other words, the tension between centralized bureaucratic management and grassroots democracy resulted in the triumph of the latter.[3]

I agree with Scott in so far as he transcends the Cold War East–West dichotomy and identifies shared precepts and concepts of how to organize and regulate the human and natural world. As seen in this study, the communists took the Maliq project from their predecessors. The ALP's leadership took the baton and implemented it using a new institutional, political, and economic framework. At the same time, the communist transformation of Maliq was connected diachronically and synchronically with similar enterprises in Europe in the years following World War II. Regardless of the ruling ideology, all European governments of the era started programs to build new societies.

However, my work departs from Scott's conclusion when it comes to his use of failure and resistance. The issue here should not be reduced exclusively to whether or not the ALP's regime had a blueprint or how local conditions modified it. While the Albanian communist regime did not meet all its targets and did not create an egalitarian utopia, it transformed Maliq forever. First of all, it is important to note that the houses built with adobe and roofs of hay disappeared. Malaria disappeared and a network of schools and clinics covered all the villages. Although floods sometimes spread over the arable land, they did not threaten the villages and peasant households. For local people, these transformations were a much more important issue than any other argument regarding arrogant state intervention or the modification of the landscape. Indeed, the peasants raised their voices for more state intervention. As they very well knew, only the state's resources and expertise could guarantee the maintenance of the drainage system.

The Maliq scheme did not pit the rural population against technocrats. Many peasants supported the transformation of the plain because they saw it as a chance to improve their lot in life. If the rural population resisted the reclamation project during the interwar era, it was not because the village population resisted a plan that wanted to regulate and order their lives according to a logic that did not fit local circumstances. There were efforts by the Maliqi Company to use the draining of the swamp as a justification to appropriate peasant property, which is what triggered the conflict. Additionally, if the reclamation was never completed, this was due to a lack of funds and not because of any resistance. When

---

3   Scott, *Seeing Like a State*.

the communists restarted the project in 1946, the peasants did not resist. The use of the iron fist only partially explains why the rural population did not revolt. Less than fifteen years after the reclamation, the majority of the youth in the surrounding highlands wanted to move to the plain, and closer to the state authorities, because they saw greater opportunities for a better life there than in the economically peripheral mountain hamlets. The population of the area participated in the project that transformed a quagmire into Albania's center of sugar. Not only did they not resist; they joined forces with the technocrats and the communist bureaucratic apparatus to modernize the plain and the country. Indeed, the majority of technicians and specialists emerged from their ranks. Rather than tensions between antagonistic groups with diverging agendas, in Maliq I discovered cooperation and symbiosis.

A similar debate has taken place regarding the building of the Soviet system. Moshe Lewin, while exploring the rapid urbanization and industrialization of the Soviet Union during the 1930s, considered the mass of "backward" peasants that flooded the Soviet cities and the modernizing Bolshevik bureaucracy as two clashing civilizations. According to Lewin, the Soviet system took shape out of this tension that juxtaposed Stalin and his supporters, who wanted to modernize the country at break-neck speed, and an unresponsive and even resistant peasantry.[4] In his book *Magnetic Mountain*, where he analyzed everyday life in the steel town of Magnitogorsk, Stephen Kotkin rejected Lewin's claim and defined Stalinism as a civilization. By using the singular, Kotkin argued that Stalinism was not merely an imposition from above that generated conflict between the communist power apparatus, committed to modernizing the Soviet Union, and its backward-looking society. Instead, the Stalinist system was an outcome of both the power apparatus and society. Inspired by Michel Foucault's discursive analysis, Kotkin analyzed the language that people used in their daily lives and observed the emergence of a new subjectivity, which reproduced the regime's discourse of power. Thus, normal people became autonomous agents of Bolshevik power and enabled the Soviet regime to pervade all spheres of social activity.[5] Hence, rather than a clear-cut distinction between state and society, Kotkin saw a continuum.

---

[4] Moshe Lewin, *The Making of the Soviet System: Essays in the Social History of Interwar Russia* (New York: Pantheon, 1985), 258–285.
[5] Kotkin, *Magnetic Mountain*.

The works of Kotkin and Lewin, however, focus on industrial towns, where they see the locus of the forging of Soviet modernity. Conceiving the Soviet model in exclusively urban terms, they see the countryside as alien, not only in terms of having made no contribution to the construction of Soviet power but also as being in direct conflict with it. The rural population is depicted as an ocean of barbarity that is civilized only when it migrates to the cities and gets involved in industrial processes. Their stance does not differ much from the literature on collectivization that sees this process as a war between the communist state's grandiose plans and the peasantry's insistence on preserving its smallholdings. The reality, however, is more complex. The rural population did not always come into conflict with the regime and its program, but many times embraced and supported it, contributing to the building of a real socialist model. The countryside was an important site of system building, where the broad infrastructural, economic, cultural, and social transformations were not a violent imposition of the vision of an urban-based communist power.

Maliq was no exception. With a sugar refinery as the beating heart of a regional economic system, both Maliq's landscape and the social structure of the communities that lived on the plain underwent profound changes. It was not merely the emergence of a new subjectivity that allowed the ALP's power structure to disseminate and reinforce its power. Without diminishing the importance of ideological reproduction at the everyday level, the Soviet-type regimes also had to back up their claims for a better future by providing tangible proof. Likewise, they created real opportunities for people to move upward on the social ladder and improve their living standards. It is not an accident that the popular support for the communist regimes fell with the economic decline of the 1970s and 1980s. In Maliq, the sugar industry represented these new opportunities by creating space for many people to advance their position and status. Participating in the transformation of the plain into Albania's land of sugar was advantageous. Using the sugar industry as a platform to increase revenues and increase the opportunities for themselves and their families, the peasants of Maliq took part in the system-building. For this reason, it is important not only to celebrate how local actors and factors transmuted the center's blueprints and how these simple people without a voice made history but also to focus on those who embraced the projects of modernization and tied their fate to it. The latter were not a small minority of highly educated technocrats; many peasants supported modernization. When communism imploded, neither the plain nor its population were the same anymore.

Epilogue

Thus, the Manichean and simplistic failure/success approach does not help us to understand the implications and the impact of the broad and deep transformations that took place in Maliq during the communist era. However, the failure/success dichotomy has been the dominating modus operandi in the years following the collapse of the Soviet-type regimes. In the early 1990s, MTV relentlessly played the British band *Pet Shop Boys*' superhit *Go West*. Showing the Statue of Liberty, its video showed ex-communist subjects the path to the historical destiny of freedom and progress. "Going West" meant dismantling everything that would connect the ex-socialist countries to an allegedly bad East and failures, including the Maliq scheme. This process came to be known as shock therapy, and some of its most important tenets were the immediate privatization of the state economic sector, the extreme minimization of state intervention in the economy, and the opening of borders to the global market. These were thought to be the remedies for the deficiencies of socialist inefficiencies, while little attention was paid to the social repercussions. However, on the ground, in Albania's land of sugar, people who invested their energies and lives in the sugar industry found themselves redundant and their work considered useless.

To understand the problem that the people in Maliq are facing today, we should first comprehend the communist past, which shaped the area; not by evaluating it as a failure but looking at it as a major transformation that radically changed the local history forever. This is not only the case for the ex-land of sugar. The latter's history is the history of many large projects of modernization intended for both economic development and socio-cultural transformations. Whether or not the modernizing schemes met the elite's initial agenda is less important than grasping their social, economic, and cultural impacts. We should not forget that behind these developmental projects there were not only people at the top but also people at the bottom, who poured talent, sweat, and hope into them. We can understand the current world by studying what these people accomplished in their lives, because today we stand on their shoulders.

* * *

Many years after the fall of communism, every time I visited my other grandmother, Ferasete Hoxha—who also used to be an ALP member—she prepared me Turkish coffee sweetened with imported Brazilian sugar. Afterward, she filled two small glasses with liquor and, to complete the full range of the most important psychoactive substances that shape the modern world, each of us lit up a cigarette and inhaled nicotine while chatting. Ferasete did not like to talk about the present. She continuously tried to come to terms with the age in which she happened to live and strove to give meaning to her life. Looking at the dilapidated world that she participated in the construction of, my grandmother grappled with the past and struggled to understand whether or not what she fought for was worth it. Ferasete stared at the past, without complaining. Now the scarcity was just a bitter memory. After the dividing curtain had been lifted, she had had the opportunity to know what realities hid behind the TV screens, the soap operas, and the commercials. Other things concerned her. In an age when everything moves very quickly, she used the ritual of the coffee not to contemplate a forbidden world of affluence but to retell the past. She constantly rebuilt the latter's ruins and brought back a nuanced version of it to show me that there were things from her era that one should be proud of and that her life could teach me something. She belonged to a generation that struggled to industrialize the country, learn professions that nobody knew of before 1945, live better than their parents, and send their children to university. Additionally, and more importantly, those who took over the lead after the demise of communism had all been educated in that Albania, which, for better or worse, her generation had built. When communism fell, the country was not a tabula rasa.

My two grandmothers' stories, before and after the fall of communism, came to my mind that early September morning in 2017 when I headed to the archive of Korça. I was traveling in a cherry-red passenger van across the plain of Maliq. One reminded me of the disappointment with communism's promised land and the other of what came after it. At that moment, I grasped the complexity of the communist legacy. The memory of the scarcities showed the expectations communism created but did not live up to; the attempts to reevaluate the past and the insistence on not calling it a failure impelled me not to forget the work that was put into chasing the vision of a socialist utopia. I realized how much Maliq represents my grandmothers' lives and experiences. Today, while the promise of change appears on the horizon, the sugar capital of communist Albania is still a ghost of what it used to be. Maliq was once considered the "America in the home," the land of hopes where the vision of development materialized. Today it is a beautiful yet hapless place; it is sugarless and is no longer the buzzing industrial town it used to be. While in the third decade of the twenty-first century it is on the brink of changing its identity, Sugarland's story shows how, in this part of Europe, development remains an elusive target that keeps slipping away, leaving behind amputated projects, unfulfilled expectations, and continuous disillusionment that is often accompanied by fresh dreams. In Maliq, we can explore the implementation of the utopian projects of the nineteenth- and twentieth-century revolutionary elites—and the shattered dreams they left behind. I, for one, think it is worth telling Sugarland's story. It illustrates how we head toward the future while walking over history's ruins. The twenty-first century is very different from its predecessor, and yet the present still stands over the past's rubble. If neglected, the ruins may cause long-term historical consequences—if they have not done so already.

Bibliography

PRIMARY SOURCES

Archival Sources

AQSh—Arkivi Qendror i Shtetit (Central State Archive):
    Collections created between 1912 and 1945:
        Fondi 51 Sami Frashëri (Personal Collection of Sami Frashëri)
        Fondi 125 Kryesia e Republikës (Presidency of the Republic)
        Fondi 143 Koleksion Dokumentesh (Collections of Documents)
        Fondi 146 Parlamenti (Parliament)
        Fondi 149 Kryeministria (Prime Minister's Office)
        Fondi 150 Oborri Mbretëror (Royal Court)
        Fondi 151 Ministria e Punëve të Jashtme (Ministry of Foreign Affairs)
        Fondi 152 Ministria e Punëve të Brendshme (Ministry of the Interior)
        Fondi 155 Ministria e Drejtësisë (Ministry of Justice)
        Fondi 161 Mëkëmbësia e Përgjithshme (General Vicegerent of the Italian King in Albania)
        Fondi 163 Legata Italiane (Legation of Italy)
        Fondi 171 Ministria e Ekonomisë (Ministry of the Economy)
        Fondi 172 Ministria e Bujqësisë (Ministry of Agriculture)
        Fondi 177 Ministria e Punëve Botore (Ministry of Infrastructure)
        Fondi 178 Ministria e Financave (Ministry of Finances)
        Fondi 179 Banka Kombëtare (National Bank)
        Fondi 179/5 Banka Kombëtare Dega Korçë (National Bank, Korça branch)
        Fondi 188 Zyra e Statistikave (Office of Statistics)
        Fondi 317 Prefektura e Korçës (Prefecture of Korça)
        Fondi 319/12. Komuna e Maliqit (Commune of Maliq)
        Fondi 991 Kompania Anonime Maliqi (Maliqi Joint-Stock Company)
    Collections created between 1945 and 1990:
        Fondi 14/AP Arkivi i PPSh (ALP Archive)
        Fondi 489 Presidiumi i Kuvendit Popullor (Presidency of the Parliament)
        Fondi 490 Këshilli i Ministrave (Council of Ministers)
        Fondi 494 Ministria e Ekonomisë (Ministry of the Economy)
        Fondi 495 Komisioni i Planit të Shtetit (State Planning Committee)
        Fondi 496 Ministria e Industrisë dhe Minierave (Ministry of Industry and Mines)
        Fondi 497 Ministria e Industrisë Ushqimore (Ministry of Food Industry)
        Fondi 498 Ministria e Bujqësisë (Ministry of Agriculture)

Bibliography

    Fondi 499 Ministria e Ndërtimit (Ministry of Construction)
    Fondi 515 Ministria e Drejtësisë (Ministry of Justice)
    Fondi 517 Ministria e Industrisë (Ministry of Industry)
    Fondi 518 Ministria e Industrisë së Ndërtimit (Ministry of Construction and Industry)
AShV Korçë—Arkivi Shtetëror Vendor Korçë (State Local Archive of Korça)
    Fondi 3/1 Komiteti i PPSh, Qarku Korçë (ALP Committee of the Region of Korça)
    Fondi 3/2 Komiteti i PPSh, Rrethi Koçë (ALP Committee of the District of Korça)
    Fondi 3/2 Komiteti i PPSh, Nënprefektura e Qendrës (ALP Committee of the Vice Prefecture of Korça)
    Fondi 3/4 Komiteti i PPSh, Maliq (ALP Committee of Maliq)
    Fondi 3/901 Komiteti i PPSh, Kantjeri Maliq (ALP Committee of the Construction Site of Maliq)
    Fondi 42 Komiteti Ekzekutiv i Maliqit (Executive Committee of Maliq)
    Fondi 51 Komiteti Ekzekutiv i Korçës (Executive Committee of Korça)
    Fondi 67 Kombinati i Sheqerit, Maliq (Sugar Combine, Maliq)
AMPJ—Ministria e Punëve të Jashtme (Ministry of Foreign Affairs), 1920–1990
AMPB—Ministria e Punëve të Brendshme (Ministry of the Interior), 1945–1990
AIH—Arkivi i Institutit të Historisë (Archive of the Institute of History)
National Archives, College Park

Published Documents and Resources

Anuari statistikor i Republikës Popullore të Shqipërisë 1960 [Statistical annual of the People's Republic of Albania 1960]. Tirana: Drejtoria e Statistikës, 1960.

Dokumenta kryesore të Partisë së Punës të Shqipërisë. Volume II, 1949–1956 [Main documents of the Albanian Labor Party. Volume II. 1949–1956]. Tirana: Shtëpia Botuese e Librit Politik, 1972.

Dokumente kryesore të Partisë së Punës të Shqipërisë. Volume V, 1966–1970 [Main documents of the Albanian Labor Party. Volume V. 1966–1970]. Tirana: Shtëpia Botuese e Librit Politik, 1972.

Indoktrinimi komunist përmes kulturës, letërsisë dhe artit (dokumente historike). Vëllimi II (1969–1973) [The communist indoctrination through culture, literature, and art (historical documents). Volume II (1969–1973)]. Edited by Beqir Meta, Afrim Krasniqi and Hasan Bello. Tirana: Emal, 2019.

Marrëdhëniet shqiptaro-jugosllave 1945–1948: dokumente [Albanian-Yugoslav relations, 1945–1946: documents]. Edited by Ndreçi Plasari and Luan Malltezi. Tiranë: DPA, 1996.

Lauka, Islam and Eshref Ymeri, eds. *Shqipëria në dokumentet e arkivave ruse* [Albania in the documents of the Russian archives]. Tiranë: Toena, 2006.

Relacion i Bilançit më 31 Dhetuer 1938 paraqitun Mbledhjes së Përgjithëshme të Aksionistavet më 10 Qershor 1939 [Report on the balance sheet for the year 1938 presented at the meeting of the shareholders held on june 10, 1939]. Tirana: Banka Kombëtare e Shqipnis, 1939.

Relacion i Bilançit më 31 Dhetuer 1936 paraqitun Mbledhjes së Përgjithëshme të Aksionistavet më 7 Maj 1937 [Report on the balance sheet for the year 1936 presented at the meeting of the shareholders held on May 7, 1937]. Tirana: Banka Kombëtare e Shqipnis, 1937.

Bibliography

Selenica, Teki. *Shqipria më 1927* [Albania in 1927]. Tirana: Tirana, 1928.

Selenica, Teki. *Shqipria më 1923* [Albania in 1923]. Tirana: Ministria e P. Mbrendshme, 1923.

Statistika Importatjon – Exportatjone vjetës 1921 e Shtetit Shqyptár [Statistics of the Albanian state on imports and exports for the year 1921]. Shkodra: Ministrija e Financavet, 1922.

Statistika Tregtare e Importacjon – Eksportacjon-it prej 1 Kallnuerit deri më 31 Dhetuer 1926 [Commercial statistics on imports and exports for the year 1926]. Tirana: Ministria e Financavet, 1927.

Statistikë e Tregtis së Jashtëme: Viti 1935 [Statistics on foreign commerce for the year 1935]. Tirana: Ministria e Financavet, 1936.

Statistikë e Tregtis së Jashtëme: Viti 1928 [Statistics on foreign commerce for the year 1928]. Tirana: Ministria e Financavet, 1929.

Statistikë e Tregtis së Jashtëme: Viti 1927 [Statistics on foreign commerce for the year 1927]. Tirana: Ministria e Financavet, 1928.

Vjetari statistikor i Republikës Popullore të Shqipërisë 1965 [Statistical annual of the People's Republic of Albania 1965]. Tirana: Drejotria e Statistikës, 1965.

Vjetari statistikor i Republikës Popullore të Shqipërisë 1964 [Statistical annual of the People's Republic of Albania 1964]. Tirana: Drejotria e Statistikës, 1964.

Vjetari statistikor i Republikës Popullore të Shqipërisë 1963 [Statistical annual of the People's Republic of Albania 1963]. Tirana: Drejotria e Statistikës, 1963.

Vjetari statistikor i vitit 1989 [Statistical annuarium of 1989]. Tirana: Drejtoria e Statistikës, 1989.

Press Organs

Before 1945
- *Gazeta e Korçës* [The Korça gazette]
- *Koha* [Time]
- *Posta e Korçës* [Korça's mail]
- *Rilindja e Arbënisë* [The reawakening of Albania]
- *Shqipëria e Re* [New Albania]
- *Zëri i Korçës* [The voice of Korça]
- *Zëri i Popullit* [The people's voice] (Not the future press organ of the ALP)

After 1945
- *Bashkimi* [Unity]
- *Bujqësia socialiste* [Socialist agriculture]
- *Buletini i Shekencave Bujqësore* [The bulletin of agricultural sciences]
- *Buletini Teknik* [Technical bulletin]
- *Miqësia* [Friendship]
- *Për bujqësinë socialiste* [On socialist agriculture]
- *Përpara* [Forward]
- *Puna* [Work]
- *Shqipëri-BRSS* [Albania-USSR]
- *Zëri i Popullit* [The people's voice]
- *Zëri i rinisë* [The youth's voice]

Bibliography

SECONDARY SOURCES

"150 years of water correction in Jura: a pioneering enterprise." Accessed December 2018.
Abrams, Fred C. *Modern Albania: From Dictatorship to Democracy in Europe*. New York University Press, 2015.
Adanir, Fikret. "Semi-Autonomous Provincial Forces in the Balkans and Anatolia." In *The Cambridge History of Turkey*. Vol. 3, *The Later Ottoman Empire, 1603–1839*, edited by Suraiya N. Faroqhi, 157–185. Cambridge: Cambridge University Press, 2006.
Adas, Michael. "'Moral Economy' or 'Contested State'?: Elite Demands and the Origins of Peasant Protest in Southeast Asia." *Journal of Social History* 13, no, 4 (1980): 521–546.
Agnew, John, Michael Shin and Paul Richardson. "The Saga of the 'Second Industrial Divide' and the History of the 'Third Italy': Evidence from Export Data." *Scottish Geographical Journal* 121, no. 1 (2005): 83–101.
Albania (Geographical Handbook Series). London: Naval Intelligence Office, 1945.
Albert, Christian, Hendrik Vogel, Torsten Hauffe, and Thomas Wilke. "Sediment core fossils in ancient Lake Ohrid: testing for faunal change since the Last Interglacial." *Biogeosciences* 7, no. 11 (2010): 3435–3443.
Albert, Christian, and Thomas Wilke. "Ancient Lake Ohrid: biodiversity and evolution." *Hydrobiologia* 615, no. 1 (2008): 103–140.
Alexander, Catherine. "The Factory: Fabricating the State." *Journal of Material Culture* 5, no. 2 (2000): 177–195.
Alexopoulos, Golfo, "The Ritual Lament: A Narrative of Appeal in the 1920s and 1930s." *Russian History/Histoire Russe* 24, nos. 1–2 (1997): 117–129.
Allen, Robert C. *Farm to Factory: A Reinterpretation of the Soviet Industrial Revolution*. Princeton, NJ: Princeton University Press, 2003.
Amar, Tarik Cyril. "Sovietization as a Civilizing Mission in the West." In *The Sovietization of Eastern Europe: New Perspectives on the Postwar Period*, edited by Balázs Apor, Péter Apor, and E. A. Rees, 29–45. Washington DC: New Academia Publishing, 2008.
Andela, Gertruda M. *Kneedbaar landschap, kneedbaar volk. De heroïsche jaren van de ruilverkavelingen in Nederland*. Bossum: THOTH, 2000.
Anderson, Benedict. *Imagined Communities: Reflections on the Origin and Spread of Nationalism*. London: Verso, 2006.
Andoni, Ben. "Maliqi, nga hiçi në hiç" [Maliq, from nothing to nothing]. Mapo 216, February 13, 2011.
Andrea, Zhaneta. *Kultura ilire e tumave në pellgun e Korçës* [The Illyrian culture of Korça's Basin Tumuli]. Tirana: Akademia e Shkencave e RPSSh, 1985.
Andrea, Zhaneta. "Kultura e tumave të pellgut të Korçës dhe vendi i saj në Ballkanin juglindor" [The Illyrian culture of Korça's Basin Tumuli and its place in Southeastern Balkans]. In *Kuvendi I i studimeve ilire* [The first convention of the Illyrian studies], 163–174. Tirana: Akademia e Shkencave e RPSSh, 1974.
Angjeli, Kristaq. "Mbi kuptimin e mënyrën socialiste të jetesës" [On the meaning of the socialist way of life]. In *Konferenca kombëtare e studimeve etnografike* [The national conference of ethnographic studies], 453–457. Tirana: Akademia e Shkencave e RPSSH, 1977.

Bibliography

Appadurai, Arjun. "Introduction: Commodities and the Politics of Value." In *The Social Life of Things: Commodities in Cultural Perspective*, edited by Arjun Appadurai, 3–63. Cambridge: Cambridge University Press, 1986.

Aranson, Johann P. "Communism and Modernity." *Daedalus* 129, no. 1 (2000): 61–90.

Architettura, 14 (2006).

Arnold, Thomas Clay. "Rethinking Moral Economy." *American Political Science Review* 95, no. 1 (2001): 85–95.

Ashta, Anton. *Malarja në Shqipni* [Malaria in Albania]. Tirana: Botim i Universitetit Shtetnor të Tiranës, 1961.

Auderset, Juri and Peter Moser. "Mechanisation and Motorisation: Natural Resources, Knowledge, Politics and Technology in 19th- and 20th-century Agriculture." In *Agriculture in Capitalist Europe, 1945–1960: From Food Shortages to Food Surpluses*, edited by Carin Martiin, Juan Pan-Montojo, and Paul Brassley, 145–164. London: Routledge, 2016.

Austin, Dan and Sean Doerr. *Lost Detroit: Stories Behind the Motor City's Majestic Ruins*. Charleston, SC: The History Press, 2010.

Babiracki, Patryk, and Kenyon Zimmer, eds. *Cold War Crossings: International Travel and Exchange across the Soviet Bloc, 1940s–1960s*. College Station, TX: Texas A&M University Press, 2014.

Bairoch, Paul. "Les trois révolutions agricoles du Monde développé: rendements et productivité de 1800 à 1985." *Annales. Economies, sociétés, civilizations* 44, no. 2 (1989): 317–353.

Baker, Graeme and Peter Taylor. "Feudalism and the 'Southern Question' (AD 1500 to the Present)." In *A Mediterranean Valley: Landscape Archaeology and Annales History in the Biferno Valley*, edited by Graeme Baker, 286–307. London: Leicester University Press, 1995.

Bakić-Hayden, Milica. "Nesting Orientalisms: The Case of Former Yugoslavia." *Slavic Review* 54, no. 4 (1995): 917–931.

Bakić-Hayden, Milica and Robert M. Hayden. "Orientalist Variations on the Theme 'Balkans': Symbolic Geography in Recent Yugoslav Cultural Politics." *Slavic Review* 51, no. 1 (1992): 1–15.

Banac, Ivo and Katherine Verdery. *National Character and National Ideology in Interwar Eastern Europe*. New Haven, CT: Yale Center for International Area Studies, 1995.

Barca, Stefania. "A 'Natural' Capitalism: Water and the Making of the Italian Industrial Landscape." In *Nature and History in Modern Italy*, edited by Marco Armiero and Marcus Hall, 215–230. Athens, OH: Ohio University Press, 2010.

Bartlett, Will. "Economic Change in Yugoslavia: From Crisis to Reform." In *Economic Change in the Balkan States: Albania, Bulgaria, Romania and Yugoslavia*, edited by Örjan Sjöberg and Michael L. Wyzan, 32–46. London: Pinter Publishers, 1991.

Barzak, Christopher. "The B&O, Crossroads of Time and Space." *Muse* 12 (2011): 6.

Bassin, Mark. "'I Object to Rain that is Cheerless': Landscape Art and the Stalinist Aesthetic Imagination." *Ecumene* 7, no. 3 (2000): 313–336.

Bauerkämper, Arnd. "The Collectivization of Agriculture in Southeastern Europe." In *The Routledge Handbook of Balkan and Southeast European History*, edited by John P. Lampe and Ulf Brunnbauer, 431–438. London: Routledge, 2021.

Bauman, Zygmunt. *Modernity and the Holocaust*. Ithaca, NY: Cornell University Press, 1989.

Bibliography

Beck, Ulrich. "Varieties of Second Modernity and the Cosmopolitan Vision." *Theory, Culture & Society* 33, nos. 7–8 (2016): 257–270.

Belba, Arben. *Gjeografia e sektorit terciar në rajonin e Korçës* [The geography of the tertiary sector of the economy in the region of Korça]. Dissertation for the title of Doctor of Sciences defended in the Department of Geography. University of Tirana, 2013.

Bell, Wilson T. "One Day in the Life of Educator Khrushchev: Labor and *Kul'turnost'* in the Gulag Newspapers." *Canadian Slavonic Papers* 46, nos. 3–4 (2004): 289–313.

Belmecheri, Soumaya, Tadeusz Namiotko, Christian Robert, Ulrich von Grafenstein, and Dan L. Danielopol. "Climate controlled ostracod preservation in Lake Ohrid (Albania, Macedonia)." *Palaeogeography, Palaeoclimatology, Palaeoecology*, 277 (2009): 236–245.

Benjamin, Walter. "The Ruin." In *The Work of Art in the Age of Its Technological Reproducibility and Other Writings on Media*. Edited and translated by Michael W. Jennings, Brigid Doherty, and Thomas Y. Levin. Cambridge, MA: Harvard University Press, 2008.

Benjamin, Walter. "Theses on the Philosophy of History." In *Illuminations: Essays and Reflections*. Edited by Hannah Arendt. Translated by Harry Zohn. New York: Schocken Books, 2007.

Berend, Ivan T. and Bojan Bugaric. "Unfinished Europe: Transition from Communism to Democracy in Central and Eastern Europe." *Journal of Contemporary History* 50, no. 4 (2015): 768–785.

Berend, Ivan T. "What is Central and Eastern Europe?" *European Journal of Social Theory* 8, no. 4 (2005): 401–416.

Berend, Ivan T. "Foucault and the Welfare State." *European Review* 13, no. 4 (2005): 551–556.

Berend, Ivan T. "The Failure of Economic Nationalism: Central and Eastern Europe before World War II." *Revue économique* 51, no. 2 (2000): 315–322.

Berger, Mark T. "From Nation-Building to State-Building: The Geopolitics of Development, the Nation-State System and the Changing Global Order." *Third World Quarterly* 27, no. 1 (2006): 5–25.

Berger, Mark T. "Decolonisation, Modernisation and Nation-Building: Political Development Theory and the Appeal of Communism in Southeast Asia, 1945–1975." *Journal of Southeast Asian Studies* 34, no. 3 (2003): 421–448.

Berger, Stefan, Christian Wicke, and Jana Golembek. "Burdens of Eternity? Heritage, Identity, and the 'Great Transition' in the Ruhr." *The Public Historian* 39, no. 4 (2017): 21–43.

Berger, Stefan and Christian Wicke. "Introduction: Deindustrialization, Heritage, and Representations of Identity." *The Public Historian* 39, no. 4 (2017): 10–20.

Bernhard, Patrick. "Hitler's Africa in the East: Italian Colonialism as a Model for German Planning in Eastern Europe." *Journal of Contemporary History* 51, no. 1 (2016): 61–90.

Bernhard, Patrick. "Borrowing from Mussolini: Nazi Germany's Colonial Aspirations in the Shadow of Italian Expansionism." *The Journal of Imperial and Commonwealth History* 41, no. 4 (2013): 617–63.

Biberaj, Elez. *Albania in Transition: The Rocky Road to Democracy*. Boulder, CO: Westview Press, 1998.

Biggs, David A. *Quagmire: Nation-Building and Nature in the Mekong Delta*. Seattle: University of Washington Press, 2010.

Bibliography

Blackbourn, David. *The Conquest of Nature: Water, Landscape and the Making of Modern Germany.* New York: W. W. Norton, 2006.

Blanchot, Maurice, and Susan Hanson. "Everyday Speech." *Yale French Studies* 73 (1987): 12–20.

Bo Frandsen, Steen. "'The War We Prefer': The Reclamation of the Pontine Marshes and the Fascist Expansion." *Totalitarian Movements and Political Religions* 2, no. 3 (2001): 69–82.

Bodenschatz, Harald, Piero Sassi, and Max Welch Guerra, eds. *Urbanism and Dictatorship: A European Perspective.* Basel: Birkhäuser Verlag & Bauverlag, 2015.

Bodenschatz, Harald. "Urbanism and Dictatorship: Expanding Spaces for Thought!" In *Urbanism and Dictatorship: European Perspectives*, edited by Harald Bodenschatz, Piero Sassi, and Max Welch Guerra, 15–26. Gütersloh, Berlin-Basel: Bauverlag & Birkhäuser, 2013.

Booth, William J. "A Note on the Idea of the Moral Economy." *American Political Science Review* 87, no. 4 (1993): 949–954.

Bordon, Amandine, Odile Peyron, Anne-Marie Lézine, Simon Brewer, and Eric Fouache. "Pollen-inferred Late-Glacial and Holocene climate in southern Balkans (Lake Maliq)." *Quaternary International* 200, nos. 1–2 (2009): 19–30.

Boriçi, Gjon. *Marrëdhëniet shqiptaro-kineze në Luftën e Ftohtë, 1956–1978* [The Albanian-Chinese relations during the Cold War, 1956–1978]. Tirana: Geer, 2022.

Bornstein, Morris. *East-West Technology Transfer: The Transfer of Western Technology to the USSR.* Paris: OECD, 1985.

Bourcart, Jacques. *Shqipëria dhe shqiptarët.* Translated by Asti Papa. Tirana: Dituria, 2004.

Bourdieu, Pierre. *The Logic of Practice.* Translated by Richard Nice. Stanford, CA: Stanford University Press, 1990.

Boym, Svetlana. "Ruinophilia," In *The Off-Modern.* New York: Bloomsberry, 2017.

Brain, Stephen. *Song of the Forest: Russian Forestry and Stalinist Environmentalism, 1905–1953.* Pittsburgh, PA: University of Pittsburgh Press, 2011.

Bren, Paulina, and Mary C. Neuburger, eds. *Communism Unwrapped: Consumption in Cold War Eastern Europe.* Oxford: Oxford University Press, 2012.

Breuer, Stefan. "The Denouements of Civilization: Elias and Modernity." *International Social Science Journal* 43, no. 2 (1991): 401–416.

Brown, Archie. *The Rise and Fall of Communism.* New York: Harper Collins, 2009.

Brown, Kate. *Dispatches from Dystopia: Histories of Places Not Yet Forgotten.* Chicago: University of Chicago Press, 2015.

Brown, Kate. *Plutopia: Nuclear Families, Atomic Cities, and the Great Soviet and American Plutonium Disasters.* Oxford: Oxford University Press, 2013.

Brown, Kate. *A Biography of No Place: From Ethnic Borderland to Soviet Heartland.* Cambridge, MA: Harvard University Press, 2004.

Brown, Kate. "Gridded Lives: Why Kazakhstan and Montana are Nearly the Same Place." *American Historical Review* 106, no. 1 (2001): 17–48.

Brunnbauer, Ulf. "'The Town of the Youth': Dimitrovgrad and Bulgarian Socialism." *Ethnologica Balcanica* 9 (2005): 91–114.

Brusilovskaia, Lidiia. "The Culture of Everyday Life during the Thaw." *Russian Studies in History* 48, no. 1 (2009): 19–29.

Bibliography

Bruszt, László, and Béla Greskovits. "Transnationalization, Social Integration, and Capitalist Diversity in the East and the South." *Studies in Comparative International Development* 44, no. 4 (2009): 411–434.

Bujqësia në Republikën Popullore Socialiste të Shqipërisë [Agriculture in the People's Socialist Republic of Albania]. Tirana: 8 Nëntori, 1982.

Bungo, Makensen. *Këneta e vdekjes* [The swamp of death]. Tirana: Pheonix, 1996.

Burawoy, Michael, Pavel Krotov, and Tatyana Lytkina. "Involution and Destitution in Capitalist Russia." *Ethnography* 1, no. 1 (2000): 43–65.

Burdett, Charles. "The Other Spaces of Fascist Italy: The Cemetery, the Prison and the Internal Colony," In *Journey through Fascism: Italian Travel Writing between the Wars*. New York: Berghahn Books, 2007.

Byrne, Jeffrey James. "Our Own Special Brand of Socialism: Algeria and the Contest of Modernities in the 1960s." *Diplomatic History* 33, no. 3 (2009): 427–447.

Calhoun, Craig. "The Infrastructure of Modernity: Indirect Social Relationships, Information Technology, and Social Integration." In *Social Change and Modernity*, edited by Hans Haferkamp and Neil J. Smelser, 205–236. Berkley, CA: University of California Press, 1992.

Calhoun, Craig. "Indirect Relationships and Imagined Communities: Large-Scale Integration and the Transformation of Everyday Life." In *Social Theory for a Changing Society*, edited by Pierre Bourdieu and James S. Coleman, 95–112. Boulder, CO: Westview Press, 1991.

Caprotti, Federico. "Scipio Africanus: Film, Internal Colonization and Empire." *Cultural Geographies* 16, no. 3 (2009): 381–401.

Caprotti, Federico and Maria Kaïka. "Producing the Ideal Fascist Landscape: Nature, Materiality, and the Cinematic Representation of Land Reclamation in the Pontine Marshes." *Social and Cultural Geography* 9, no. 6 (2008): 613–614.

Caprotti, Federico. *Mussolini's Cities: Internal Colonialism in Italy, 1930–1939*. Youngstown, NY: Cambria Press, 2007.

Carrier, James G. "Moral Economy: What's in a Name?" *Anthropological Theory* 18, no. 1 (2018): 18–35.

Carrier, James G., ed. *Occidentalism: Images of the West*. Oxford: Calderon Press, 1995.

Casanova, Pablo Gonzalez. "Internal Colonialism and National Development." *Studies in Comparative International Development* 1, no. 4 (1965): 2–37.

Caselli, Gian Paolo and Grid Thoma. "The Albanian Economy during World War II and the First Attempt at Planning." *Journal of European Economic History* 34, no. 1 (2005): 93–119.

Cebul, Brent. "Creative Competition: Georgia Power, the Tennessee Valley Authority, and the Creation of a Rural Consumer Economy, 1934–1955." *The Journal of American History* 105, no. 1 (2018): 45–70.

Ceka, Neritan. *Ilirët* [The Illyrians]. Tirana: Ilar, 2001.

Ceka, Neritan, and Muzafer Korkuti. *Arkeologjia: Greqia – Roma – Iliria* [Archaeology: Greece - Rome - Illyria]. Tirana: ShBLU, 1998.

Charter, Melville. "Albania, Europe's Newest Kingdom." *The National Geographic Magazine* 59, no. 2 (1931): 131–182.

Bibliography

Chirot, Daniel. "Theories and Realities: What are the Causes of Backwardness?" In *Cores, Peripheries, and Globalization: Essays in Honor of Ivan T. Berend*, edited by Peter Hanns Reil and Balázs A. Szelényi, 63–72. Budapest: CEU Press, 2011.

Chirot, Daniel. "Ideology, Reality, and Competing Models of Development in Eastern Europe between the Two World Wars." *Eastern European Politics and Societies* 3, no. 3 (1989): 378–411.

Cicko, Vasilika. "Tipare të reja të vendbanimeve fshatare" [Features of the new rural settlements] In *Konferenca kombëtare e studimeve etnografike* [The national conference of ethnographic studies], 443–451. Tirana: Akademia e Shkencave e RPSSH, 1977.

Citino, Nathan J. "Modernization and Development." In *The Routledge Handbook of the Cold War*, edited by Artemy M. Kalinovsky and Craig Daigle, 118–130. London: Routledge, 2014.

Clark, Katerina. *Petersburg: Crucible of Cultural Revolution*. Cambridge, MA: Harvard University Press, 1995.

Clayer, Nathalie. *Në fillimet e nacionalizmit shqiptar: Lindja e një kombi me shumicë myslimane në Europë* [At the beginnings of Albanian nationalism: The birth of Muslim-majority nation in Europe]. Translated by Artan Puto. Tirana: Përpjekja, 2012.

Cohen, Deborah, and Maura O'Connor. "Introduction: Comparative History, Cross-National History, Transnational History—Definitions." In *Comparison and History: Europe in Cross-National Perspective*, edited by Deborah Cohen and Maura O'Connor, ix-xxiv. New York: Routledge, 2004.

Cohen, Yves, "Circulatory Localities: The Example of Stalinism in the 1930s." *Kritika: Explorations in Russian and Eurasian History* 11, no. 1 (2010): 11–45.

Constantinescu, Ilinca Păun, Dragoș Dascălu, and Cristina Sucală, "An Activist Perspective on Industrial Heritage in Petrila, a Romanian Mining City." *The Public Historian* 39, no. 4 (2017): 114–141.

Contending with Stalinism: Soviet Power and Popular Resistance in the 1930s. Edited by Lynne Viola. Ithaca, NY: Cornell University Press, 2002.

Cooke, Philip. "Keeping to the High Road: Learning, Reflexivity and Associative Governance in Regional Economic Development." In *The Rise of the Rustbelt: Revitalizing Older Industrial Regions*, edited by Philip Cooke, 231–245. London: UCL Press, 1995.

Cooper, Frederick. "Writing the History of Development." *Journal of Modern European History* 8, no. 1 (2010): 5–21.

Cooper, Frederick. *Decolonization and African Society: The Labor Question in French and British Africa*. Cambridge: Cambridge University Press, 1996.

Corboz, André. "The Land as Palimpsest." *Diogenes* 31, no. 121 (1983): 12–34.

Courtwright, David T. *Forces of Habits: Drugs and the Making of the Modern World*. Cambridge, MA: Harvard University Press, 2001.

Cowie, Jefferson, and Joseph Heathcott, eds. *Beyond the Ruins: The Meaning of Deindustrialization*. Ithaca, NY: ILR Press, 2003.

Creed, Gerald W. *Domesticating Revolution: From Socialist Reform to Ambivalent Transition in a Bulgarian Village*. University Park, PA: Pennsylvania University Press, 1998.

Crowley, David. "Paris or Moscow? Warsaw Architects and the Image of the Modern City in the 1950s." In *Imagining the West in Eastern Europe and the Soviet Union*, edited by György Péteri, 105–130. Pittsburgh, PA: University of Pittsburgh Press, 2010.

Crowley, David and Susan E. Reid, eds. *Pleasures in Socialism: Leisure and Luxury in the Eastern Bloc*. Evanston, IL: Northwestern University Press, 2010.

Crowley, Stephen. "Global Cities versus Rustbelt Realities: The Dilemmas of Urban Development in Russia," *Slavic Review* 79, no. 2 (2020): 365–389.

Crush, Jonathan. "Introduction: Imagining Development." In *Power of Development*, edited by Jonathan Crush, 1–21. London: Routledge, 1995.

Cungu, Azeta and Johan F. M. Swinnen. "Albania's Radical Land Reform." *Economic Development and Cultural Change* 47, no. 3 (1999): 605–619.

Çami, Muin. *Shqipëria në rrjedhat e historisë, 1912–1924* [Albania through the currents of history]. Tirana: Onufri, 2007.

Çami, Muin. *Shqiptarët dhe francezët në Korçë: 1916–1920* [The Albanians and the French in Korça: 1916–1924]. Tirana: Dituria, 1999.

Çami, Muin. *Shqipëria në marrëdhëniet ndërkombëtare (1914–1918)* [Albania in international Affairs (1914–1918)]. Tirana: Akademia e Shkencave e RPS të Shqipërisë, 1987.

Dahrendorf, Ralf. "Europe's Vale of Tears." *Marxism Today*, May 1990, 18–23.

David, Thomas, and Elisabeth Spilman. "Liberal Economic Nationalism in Eastern Europe during the First Wave of Globalization (1860–1914)." In *Cores, Peripheries, and Globalization: Essays in Honor of Ivan T. Berend*, edited by Peter Hanns Reil and Balázs A. Szelényi, 113–126. Budapest: CEU Press, 2011.

David-Fox, Michael. *Crossing Borders: Modernity, Ideology, and Culture in Russia and the Soviet Union*. Pittsburgh, PA: University of Pittsburgh Press, 2015.

David-Fox, Michael. *Showcasing the Great Experiment: Cultural Diplomacy and Western Visitors to the Soviet Union, 1921–1941*. Oxford: Oxford University Press, 2015.

David-Fox, Michael. "The Iron Curtain as Semi-Permeable Membrane: Origins and Demise of the Stalinist Superiority Complex." In *Cold War Crossings: International Travel and Exchange across the Soviet Bloc, 1940s–1960s*, edited by Patryk Babiracki and Kenyon Zimmer, 14–39. College Station, TX: Texas A&M University Press, 2014.

David-Fox, Michael. "Introduction: Entangled Histories in the Age of Extremes." In *Fascination and Enmity: Russia and Germany as Entangled Histories, 1914–1945*, edited by Michael David-Fox, Peter Holquist, and Alexander M. Martin, 1–12. Pittsburgh, PA: University of Pittsburgh Press, 2012.

David-Fox, Michael. "Conclusion: Transnational History and the East-West Divide." In *Imagining the West in Eastern Europe and the Soviet Union*, edited by György Péteri, 258–267. Pittsburgh, PA: University of Pittsburgh Press, 2010.

David-Fox, Michael. "Multiple Modernities vs. Neo-Traditionalism: On Recent Debates in Russian and Soviet History." *Jahrbücher für Geschichte Osteuropas* 54, no. 4 (2006): 535–555.

David-Fox, Michael. "What Is Cultural Revolution?" *The Russian Review* 58, no. 2 (1999): 181–201.

Davies, Thom. "A Visual Geography of Chernobyl: Double Exposure." *International Labor and Working-Class History* 84 (2013): 116–139.

Davis, Natalie Zemon. *The Return of Martin Guerre*. Cambridge, MA: 1983.

De Tocqueville, Alexis. *The Old Regime and the Revolution*. Translated by John Bonner. New York: Harper & Brothers, 1856.

De Vivo, Filippo. "Prospect or Refuge? Microhistory, History on the Large Scale." *Cultural and Social History* 7, no. 3 (2010): 387–397.

De Waal, Clarissa. *Albania Today: A Portrait of Post-Communist Turbulence*. London: I. B. Tauris, 2005.

Deák, István. "How to Construct a Productive, Disciplined, Monoethnic Society: The Dilemma of East Central European Governments, 1914–1956." In *Landscaping the Human Garden: Twentieth-Century Population Management in a Comparative Framework*, edited by Amir Weiner, 205–217. Stanford, CA: Stanford University Press, 2003.

Della Rocca, Roberto Morozzo. *Nazione e religione in Albania*. Lecce: Besa, 2000.

Denèfle, Michelle, Anne-Marie Lézine, Eric Fouache, and Jean-Jacques Dufaure. "A 12,000-Year Pollen Record from Lake Maliq, Albania." *Quaternary Research* 54, no. 3 (2000): 423–432.

Deringil, Selim. "The Ottoman Origins of Kemalist Nationalism: Namik Kemal to Mustafa Kemal." *European History Quarterly* 23, no. 2 (1993): 165–191.

Dervishi, Kastriot. *Burgjet dhe kampet e Shqipërisë komuniste*. Tirana: Instituti i Studimit të Krimeve dhe Pasojave të Komunizmit, 2015.

DeSilvey, Caitlin, and Tim Edensor. "Reckoning with Ruins." *Progress in Human Geography* 37, no. 4 (2013): 465–485.

Dixon-Gough, Robert. "The Role of Land Consolidation and Land Readjustment in Modern Society." In *The Role of the State and Individual in Sustainable Land Management*, edited by Robert W. Dixon-Gough and Peter C. Bloch, 159–176. Aldershot, VT: Ashgate, 2006.

Djilas, Milovan. *The Unperfect Society: Beyond the New Class*, translated by Dorian Cooke. New York: Harcourt, Brace & the World, 1969.

Djilas, Milovan. *The New Class: An Analysis of the Communist Systems*. New York: Frederick A. Praeger, 1957.

Dobrenko, Evgeny, and Eric Naiman. *The Landscape of Stalinism: The Art and Ideology of Soviet Space*. Seattle: Washington University Press, 2003.

Doevendans, Kees, Hans Lörzing, and Anne Schram. "From Modernist Landscapes to New Nature: Planning of Rural Utopias in the Netherlands." *Landscape Research* 32, no. 3 (2007): 333–354.

Dohan, Michael R. "The Economic Origins of Soviet Autarky 1927/1928–1934." *Slavic Review* 35, no. 4 (1976): 603–635.

Doka, Dhimitër. *Zhvillime socio-ekonomike dhe rajonale të Shqipërisë pas vitit 1990* [Regional socio-economic developments in Albania after 1990]. Potsdam: Universität Potsdam, 2005.

Douglas, Mary, and Baron Isherwood. *The World of Goods: Towards an Anthropology of Consumption*. London: Routledge, 1996.

Dowling, Timothy C. "Stalinstadt/Eisenhüttenstadt: A Model for (Socialist) Life in the German Democratic Republic, 1950–1968." Dissertation defended at Tulane University, 1999.

Dragostinova, Theodora K. *The Cold War from the Margins: a Small Socialist State on the Global Cultural Scene*. Ithaca, NY: Cornell University Press, 2021.

Dragostinova, Theodora K., and Małgorzata Fidelis. "Beyond the Iron Curtain: Eastern Europe and the Global Cold War: Introduction." *Slavic Review* 77, no. 3 (2018): 577–587.

Dragostinova, Theodora K. "Studying Balkan State-Building: From the 'Advantages of Backwardness' to the European Framework." *European History Quarterly* 48, no. 4 (2018): 708–713.

Dragostinova, Theodora K. "The 'Natural Ally' of the 'Developing World': Bulgarian Culture in India and Mexico." *Slavic Review* 77, no. 3 (2018): 661–684.

Dragostinova, Theodora K. *Between Two Motherlands: Nationality and Emigration among the Greeks of Bulgaria, 1900–1949*. Ithaca, NY: Cornell University Press, 2011.

Draskoczy, Julie S. *Belomor: Criminality and Creativity in Stalin's Gulag*. Boston: Academic Studies Press, 2014.

Dudek, Frantisek. "The Crisis of the Beet Sugar Industry in Czechoslovakia." In *The World Sugar Economy in War and Depression 1914–1940*, edited by Bill Albert and Adrian Graves, 36–46. London: Routledge, 1988.

Dunham, Vera S. *In Stalin's Time: Middleclass Values in Soviet Fiction*. London: Cambridge University Press, 1976.

Durmishi, Demir. *Punëtorët në Shqipëri (1945–1960)* [Workers in Albania (1945–1960)]. Tetovo, North Macedonia: Album, 2001.

Dyrmishi, Demir. "Fshatarësia si burim për shtimin e radhëve të klasës punëtore" [Peasantry as a source of the numerical growth of the working class]. *Studime historike* [Historical studies] 25, no. 2 (1988): 47–48.

Dufaure, Jean-Jacques, Eric Fouache, and Michelle Denèfle. "Tectonics and geomorphological evolution: the example of the Korçë basin (Albania)." *Géomorphologie: relief, processus, environnement* 5, no. 2 (1999): 111–128.

Edelman, Marc. "Bringing the Moral Economy Back into the Study of 21st-Century Transnational Peasant Movements." *American Anthropologist* 107, no. 3 (2005): 331–345.

Egberts, Linde. *Chosen Legacies: Heritage in Regional Identity*. London: Routledge, 2017.

Egro, Dritan. *Historia dhe ideologjia: një qasje kritike studimeve osmane në historiografinë modern shqiptare (nga gjysma e dytë e shekullit XIX deri sot)* [History and ideology: A critical approach to Ottoman studies in the Albanian historiography (from the second half of the 19th century to our day)]. Tirana: Maluka, 2007.

Eisenstadt, Shmuel. "Multiple Modernities." *Daedalus* 129, no. 1 (2001): 1–29.

Ekbladh, David. *The Great American Mission: Modernization and the Construction of an American World Order*. Princeton, NJ: Princeton University Press, 2010.

Ekbladh, David. "'Mr. TVA': Grass-Roots Development, David Lilienthal, and the Rise and Fall of the Tennessee Valley Authority as a Symbol for U.S. Overseas Development, 1933–1973." *Diplomatic History* 26, no. 3 (2000): 335–374.

Ekonomia politike (socializmi) [Political economy (socialism)]. Tirana: Akademia e Shkencave të Shqipërisë, 1981.

Elias, Norbert. "Technization and Civilization." *Theory, Culture, and Society* 12, no. 3 (1995): 7–42.

Elias, Norbert. *The Civilizing Process: Sociogenetic and Psychogenetic Investigations*. Translated by Edmund Jephcott. Oxford: Blackwell Publishing, 2000.

Edensor, Tim. "The Ghosts of Industrial Ruins: Ordering and Disordering Memory in Excessive Space." *Environment and Planning D: Society and Space* 23, no. 6 (2005): 829–849.

Bibliography

Edensor, Tim. *Industrial Ruins: Spaces, Aesthetics and Materiality.* Oxford: Berg, 2005.

Engelstein, Laura. "Culture, Culture Everywhere: Interpretations of Modern Russia, across the 1991 Divide." *Kritika: Explorations in Russian and Eurasian History* 2, no. 2 (2001): 363–393.

Engerman, David C. "Development Politics and the Cold War." *Diplomatic History* 41, no. 1 (2017): 1–19.

Ertola, Emanuele. "The Italian Fascist Settler Empire in Ethiopia, 1936–1941." In *The Routledge Handbook of the History of Settler Colonialism*, edited by Edward Cavanagh and Lorenzo Veracini, 263–276. London: Routledge, 2017.

Etges, Andreas. "Theoretical and Historical Reflections on Economic Nationalism in Germany and the United States in the Nineteenth and Early Twentieth Centuries." In *Nationalism and the Economy: Explorations into a Neglected Relationship*, edited by Stefan Berger and Thomas Fetzer, 87–98. Budapest: Central European University Press, 2019.

Faja, Enver, and Isuf Sukaj. *Urbanistika dhe ndërtimet në fshat* [Urban planning and constructions in the countryside]. Tirana: Shtëpia Botuese e Librit Universitar, 1990.

Faludi, Andreas. "The "Blue Banana" Revisited." *European Journal of Spatial Development*, Refereed Article No. 56 (2015): 1–23.

Fierza, Gjon. "Pyjet, kullotat dhe Shërbimi Pyjor i Shqipërisë në vështrimin historik" [Forests, pastures, and the Albanian Forest Service: A historical overview]. In *Pyjet dhe Shërbimi Pyjor Shqiptar në vite* [Forests and the Albanian Forest Service through the years], edited by Gjon Fierza, Kolë Malaj, and Janaq Mele, 23–80. Tirana: Graphic Line-01, 2013.

Findley, Carter Vaughn. "The Tanzimat." In *The Cambridge History of Turkey*. Vol 4, *Turkey in the Modern World*, edited by Reşat Kasaba, 11–37. Cambridge: Cambridge University Press, 2008.

Fischer, Bernd J., ed. *Balkan Strongmen: Dictators and Authoritarian Rulers of Southeast Europe*. West Lafayette, IN: Purdue University Press, 2007.

Fischer, Bernd J. *Albania at War, 1939–1945*. West Lafayette, IN: Purdue University Press, 1999.

Fischer, Bernd J. "Albanian Nationalism in the Twentieth Century." In *Eastern European Nationalism in the Twentieth Century*, edited by Peter F. Sugar, 25–34. Washington DC: American University Press, 1995.

Fischer, Bernd J. *King Zog and the Struggle for Stability in Albania*. New York: Columbia University Press, 1984.

Fishta, Iljaz, and Veniamin Toçi. *Ekonomia e Shqipërisë në vitet e para të ndërtimit socialist 1944–1948* [Albanian economy in the first years of socialist construction 1944–1948]. Tirana: Akademia e Shkencave të RPSSH, 1984.

Fishta, Iljaz, and Veniamin Toçi. *Gjendja ekonomike e Shqipërisë në vitet 1912–1944, prapambetja e saj, shkaqet dhe pasojat* [Albania's economic condition in the years 1912–1944, its backwardness, causes, and repercussions]. Tirana: 8 Nëntori, 1983.

Fitzpatrick, Sheila, and Alf Lüdtke. "Energizing the Everyday: On the Breaking and Making of Social Bonds in Nazism and Stalinism." In *Beyond Totalitarianism: Stalinism and Nazism Compared*, edited by Michael Geyer and Sheila Fitzpatrick, 266–301. Cambridge: Cambridge University Press, 2009.

Bibliography

Fitzpatrick, Sheila. "The Bolshevik Invention of Class: Marxist Theory and the Making of 'Class Consciousness' in Soviet Society." In *The Structure of Soviet History: Essays and Documents*, edited by Ronald Grigor Suny, 164–176. Oxford: Oxford University Press, 2003.

Fitzpatrick, Sheila. *Stalin's Peasants: Resistance and Survival in the Russian Village after Collectivization*. Oxford: Oxford University Press, 1994.

Fitzpatrick, Sheila. "Ascribing Class: The Construction of Social Identity in Soviet Russia." *The Journal of Modern History* 65, no. 4 (1993): 745–770.

Fitzpatrick, Sheila. "Becoming Cultured: Socialist Realism and the Representation of Privilege and Taste." In *The Cultural Front: Power and Culture in Revolutionary Russia*. Ithaca, NY: Cornell University Press, 1992.

Fitzpatrick, Sheila. *Everyday Stalinism: Ordinary Life in Extraordinary Times: Soviet Russia in the 1930s*. Oxford: Oxford University Press, 1999.

Fitzpatrick, Sheila. "The Great Departure: Rural-Urban Migration in the Soviet Union, 1929–1933," In *Social Dimensions of Soviet Industrialization*, edited by William G. Rosenberg and Lewis H. Siegelbaum, 15–40. Bloomington, IN: Indiana University Press, 1993.

Fitzpatrick, Sheila. "'Middle Class Values' and Soviet Life in the 1930s," in *Soviet Society and Culture: Essays in Honor of Vera S. Dunham*, edited by Terry L. Thompson and Richard Sheldon, 20–38. Boulder, CO: Westview Press, 1988.

Fouache, Eric, Stéphane Desruelles, Michel Magny, Amandine Bordon, Cécile Oberweiler, Céline Coussoth, Gilles Touchais, Petrika Lera, Anne-Marie Lézine, Lionel Fading, and Rébecca Roger. "Palaeogeographical reconstructions of Lake Maliq (Korça Basin, Albania) between 14,000 BP and 2000 BP." *Journal of Archaeological Science* 37, no. 3 (2010): 525–535.

Fouache, Eric, Jean-Jacques Dufaure, Michelle Denèfle, Anne-Marie Lézine, Pétrika Léra, Frano Prendi, and Gilles Touchais. "Man and environment around lake Maliq (southern Albania) during the Late Holocene." *Vegetation History and Archaeobotany* 10, no. 2 (2001): 79–86.

Foucault, Michel. "Afterword: The Subject and Power." In *Michel Foucault: Beyond Structuralism and Hermeneutics*, edited by Hubert L. Dreyfus and Paul Rabinow, 208–226. Chicago: Chicago University Press, 1983.

Foucault, Michel. "Different Spaces." In *Essential Works of Foucault, 1954–1984*. Vol. 2, *Aesthetics, Method, and Epistemology*, edited by James D. Faubion, 175–186. New York: The New York Press, 1998.

Foucault, Michel. *Discipline and Punish: The Birth of the Prison*, Translated by Alan Sheridan. New York: Vintage Books, 1991.

Foucault, Michel. "Governmentality." In *The Foucault Effect: Studies in Governmentality*, edited by Graham Burchell, Colin Gordon, and Peter Miller, 87–104. Chicago: Chicago University Press, 1991.

Foucault, Michel. "Of Other Spaces." In *Heterotopia and the city: Public space in a postcivil society*, edited by Michiel Dehaene and Lieven De Cauter, 13–30. London: Routledge, 2008.

Foucault, Michel. "'Omnes et Singulatim': Toward a Critique of Political Reason." In *Essential Works of Foucault, 1954–1984*. Vol 3, *Power*, edited by James D. Faubion, 298–325. New York: New Press, 2001.

Bibliography

Foucault, Michel. "Right of Death and Power over Life." In *The Foucault Reader*, edited by Paul Rabinow, 258–272. New York: Pantheon Books, 1984.

Foucault, Michel. *The Archaeology of Knowledge and the Discourse of Language*. Translated by Alan M. Sheridan Smith. New York: Vintage Books, 2010.

Foucault, Michel. "The Politics of Health in the Eighteenth Century." In *Power/Knowledge: Selected Interviews and Other Writings 1972–1977*, edited by Colin Gordon, 166–182. New York: Pantheon Books, 1980.

Foucault, Michel. "The Risks of Security." In *Essential Works of Foucault*. Vol 3, *Power*, edited by James D. Faubion, 365–381. New York: New Press, 2001.

Frank, Andre Guder. *ReORIENT: Global Economy in the Asian Age*. Berkeley, CA: University of California Press, 1998.

Frélastre, Georges. "Retention of the Rural Population in Eastern Europe." In *Staying On: Retention and Migration in Peasant Societies*, edited by José Havet, 197–212. Ottawa: Ottawa University Press, 1988.

Fritzsche, Peter and Jochen Hellbeck. "The New Man in Stalinist Russia and Nazi Germany." In *Beyond Totalitarianism: Stalinism and Nazism Compared*, edited by Michael Geyer and Sheila Fitzpatrick, 302–341. Cambridge: Cambridge University Press, 2009.

Fritzsche, Peter. "The Ruins of Modernity." In *Breaking Up Time: Negotiating the Borders between Present, Past and Future*, edited by Chris Lorenz and Berber Bevernage, 57–68. Göttingen: Vandenhoeck & Ruprecht, 2013.

Fuller, Mia. "Tradition as a Means to the End of Tradition: Farmers' Houses in Italy's Fascist-Era New Towns." In *The End of Tradition?*, edited by Nezar Alsayyad, 171–186. London: Routledge, 2004.

Gallerani, Vittorio, Meri Raggi, Antonella Samoggia, and Davide Viaggi, eds. *Theory and Practice of Rural Development: Experiences in Albania*. Roskilde, Denmark: Federico Caffé Center Publisher, 2004.

Gatrell, Peter, and Boris Anan'ich. "National and Non-National Dimensions of Economic Development in Nineteenth- and Twentieth-Century Russia." In *Nation, State and the Economy in History*, edited by Alice Teichova and Herbert Matis, 219–236. Cambridge: Cambridge University Press, 2003.

Gawrych, George W. *The Crescent and the Eagle: Ottoman Rule, Islam and the Albanians, 1874–1913*. London: I. B. Tauris, 2006.

Gebhardt, Stephan, Heiner Fleige, and Rainer Horn. "Shrinkage processes of a drained riparian peatland with subsidence morphology." *Journal of Soils and Sediments* 10, no. 3 (2010): 484–493.

Geertz, Clifford. "Deep Play: Notes on the Balinese Cockfight." In *The Interpretation of Cultures*. New York: Basic Books, 1973.

Gellner, Ernest. *Nationalism*. London: Weidenfeld & Nicolson, 1997.

Gellner, Ernest. *Nations and Nationalism*. Ithaca, NY: Cornell University Press, 1983.

Ghirardo, Diane. *Building New Communities: New Deal America and Fascist Italy*. Princeton, NJ: Princeton University Press, 1989.

Ghobrial, John-Paul A. "Introduction: Seeing the World like a Microhistorian." *Past and Present* 242, Supplement 14 (2019): 1–22.

Gibianskii, Leonid Ia. "The Soviet-Yugoslav Split and the Soviet Bloc." In *The Soviet Union and Europe in the Cold War, 1945–1953*, edited by Francesca Gori and Silvio Pons, 222–245. London: Macmillan Press, 1996.

Giddens, Anthony. "Time and Social Organization." In *Social Theory and Modern Sociology*. Stanford, CA: Stanford University Press, 1987.

Giddens, Anthony. "Time, Space, Social Change." In *Central Problems in Social Theory: Action, Structure and Contradiction in Social Analysis*. London: Palgrave Macmillan, 1979.

Ginzburg, Carlo. "Microhistory: Two or Three Things That I Know about It." In *Threads and Traces: True, False, Fictive*. Translated by Anne and John Tedeschi, Los Angeles: University of California Press, 2012.

Ginzburg, Carlo. *The Cheese and the Worms: The Cosmos of a Sixteenth-century Miller*. Translated by John and Anne Tedeschi. Baltimore: The Johns Hopkins University Press, 1992.

Ginzburg, Carlo, and Poni, Carlo. "The Name and the Game: Unequal Exchange and the Historiographic Marketplace." In *Microhistory and the Lost People of Europe*, edited by Edward Muir and Guido Ruggiero, 1–10. Translated by Eren Branch. Baltimore: Johns Hopkins University Press, 1991.

Ginzburg, Carlo. "Morelli, Freud and Sherlock Holmes: Clues and Scientific Method." *History Workshop* 9 (1980): 5–36.

Gjergji, Andromaqi. *Mënyra e jetesës në shekujt XIII-XX: përmbledhje studimesh* [The Way of Life through the Thirteenth to the Twentieth Centuries: A Collection of Studies]. Self-published, Tirana, 2002.

Gjergji, Andromaqi, Abaz Dojaka, and Mark Tirta. "Ndryshime në mënyrën e jetesës së fshatarësisë së sotme" [Transformations in today's peasantry way of life]. *Etnografia shqiptare* [Albanian Ethnography] 14 (1984): 5–33.

Gjergji, Andromaqi. "Ndryshimet e mëdha në mënyrën e jetesës në fshat dhe prirjet e zhvillimit në të ardhmen" [The great transformations in the life of the countryside and future tendencies of development]. In *Konferenca kombëtare për problemet e ndërtimit socialist* [The national conference on the problems of socialist construction], 330–335. Tirana: Akademia e Shkencave e RPSSH, 1979.

Gjergji, Andromaqi. "Provë për një studim etnografik në kooperativën bujqësore 'Shkëndia' (rrethi i Korçës)" [An essay on an ethnographic study of the collective farm Shkëndija (District of Korça)]. *Etnografia shqiptare* [Albanian ethnography] 2 (1963): 99–103.

Gjergji, Bashkim. *Revistat kulturore në rrjedhën e viteve '30* [Cultural journals in the course of the 1930s]. Tirana: Afërdita & Panteon, 1999.

Gjoleka, Skënder, Marko Vangjeli, and Ago Nezha. *Për tufëzimin e bagëtive të oborreve kooperativiste* [On the herding of the cooperative gardens' livestock]. Tirana: Shtëpia e Propagandës Bujqësore, 1982.

Gjonça, Arjan. *Communism, Health and Lifestyle: The Paradox of Mortality Transition in Albania, 1950–1990*. Westport, CT: Greenwood Press, 2001.

Glassheim, Eagle. *Cleansing the Czechoslovak Borderlands: Migration, Environment, and Health in the Former Sudetenland*. Pittsburgh, PA: University of Pittsburgh Press, 2016.

Godart, Justin. *Ditarët shqiptarë, marsi 1921- dhjetor 1951* [Albania Diaries, March 1921 - December 1951]. Translated by Asti Papa. Tirana: Dituria, 2008.

Goffman, Erving. *The Presentation of Self in Everyday Life*. Edinburgh: University of Edinburgh Press, 1956.

Good, David F. "The State and Economic Development in Central and Eastern Europe." In *Nation, State and the Economy in History*, edited by Alice Teichova and Herbert Matis, 133–158. Cambridge: Cambridge University Press, 2003.

Gorky, Maxim. "On the music of the Gross." In *Articles and Pamphlets*. Moscow: Foreign Languages Publishing House, 1950.

Götz, Norbert. "'Moral Economy': Its Conceptual History and Analytical Prospect." *Journal of Global Ethics* 11, no. 2 (2015): 147–162.

Gramsci, Antonio. "Americanism and Fordism." In Antonio Gramsci, *Selections from the Prison Notebooks*, edited by Quentin Hoare and Geoffrey Nowell Smith. New York: International Publishers, 1971.

Grzywna, Antoni. "The degree of peatland subsidence resulting from drainage of land." *Environmental Earth Sciences* 76, no. 16 (2017): 559.

Gurova, Ol'ga. "The Life Span of Things in Soviet Society." *Russian Studies in History* 48, no. 1 (2009): 47.

Guxho, Naun. *Zhvillime në strukturën socialklasore në fshat* [Developments in the Social Class Structure of the Countryside. Tirana: 8 Nëntori, 1985.

Guy, Nicola. *The Birth of Albania: Ethnic Nationalism, the Great Power of World War I and the Emergence of Albanian Independence*. London: I. B. Tauris, 2012.

Halfin, Igal. "Stalinist Confessions in an Age of Terror: Messianic Times at the Leningrad Communist Universities." In *Utopia/Dystopia: Conditions of Historical Possibility*, edited by Michael D. Gordin, Helen Tilley, and Gyan Parkash, 231–249. Princeton, NJ: Princeton University Press, 2010.

Halfin, Igal. "From Darkness to Light: Student Communist Autobiography during NEP." *Jahrbücher für Geschichte Osteuropas* 45, no. 2 (1997): 210–236.

Hall, Derek R. *Albania and the Albanians*. London: Pinter References, 1994.

Hall, Derek R. "Albania." In *Planning in Eastern Europe*, edited by Andrew H. Dawson, 35–65. London: Croom Helm, 1987.

Halliday, Jon, ed. *The Artful Albanian: the Memoirs of Enver Hoxha*. London: Chatto & Windus, 1986.

Halmesvirta, Anssi. "Hungary Opens toward the West: Political Preconditions for Finish-Hungarian Cooperation in Research and Development in the 1960s and 1970s." In *Beyond the Divide: Entangled Histories of Cold War Europe*, edited by Simon Mikkonen and Pia Koivunen, 138–150. New York: Berghahn, 2015.

Hanioğlu, M. Şükrü. *A Brief History of the Late Ottoman Empire*. New Jersey, NJ: Princeton University Press, 2008.

Hardeveld, Henk van, et al. "Supporting collaborative policy process with a multi-criteria discussion of costs and benefits: The case of soil subsidence in Dutch peatlands." *Land Use Policy* 77 (2018): 425–436.

Harley, John B. "Maps, Knowledge, and Power." In *The Iconography of Landscape: Essays on the Symbolic Representation, Design and Use of Past Environments*, edited by Denis Cosgrove and Stephen Daniels, 277–312. Cambridge: Cambridge University Press, 1988.

Hammond, Nigel G. L. "Illyris, Epirus and Macedonia in the Early Iron Age." In *The Cambridge Ancient History*. Vol. 3, Part I, *The Prehistory of the Balkans, the Middle East and the Aegean World, Tenth to Eighth Centuries BC*, edited by John Boardman, I. E. S. Edwards, N. G. L. Hammond, and E. Sollberger, 619–656. Cambridge: Cambridge University Press, 1982.

Hana, Lulzim, and Ilia Telo. *Tranzicioni në Shqipëri: arritje dhe sfida* [Transition in Albania: Achievements and challenges]. Tirana: Akademia e Shkencave të Shqipërisë, 2005.

Hann, Chris. "Moral(ity and) Economy: Work, Workforce, and Fairness in Provincial Hungary." *European Journal of Sociology* 59, no. 2 (2018): 225–254.

Hann, Chris "Moral Economy." In *The Human Economy: A Citizen's Guide*, edited by Keith Hart, Jean-Loise Laville, and Antonio David Cattani, 187–198. Cambridge: Polity Press, 2010.

Hann, Chris. "Fast Forward: The Great Transformation Globalized." In *When History Accelerates: Essays on Rapid Social Change, Complexity and Creativity*, edited by Chris M. Hann, 1–19. London: Athlone Press, 1994.

Hanson, Philip. *Trade and Technology Transfer in Soviet-Western Relations*. London: Macmillan Press, 1981.

Haraway, Donna. "A Cyborg Manifesto: Science, Technology, and Socialist-Feminism in the Late Twentieth Century." In *Simians, Cyborgs, and Women: The Reinvention of Nature*. New York: Routledge, 1991.

Harris, Grace Gredys. "Concepts of Individual, Self, and Person in Description and Analysis." *American Anthropologist* 91, no. 3 (1989): 599–612.

Harris, Steven. "In Search of 'Ordinary' Russia: Everyday Life in the NEP, the Thaw, and the Communal Apartment." *Kritika: Explorations in Russian and Eurasian History* 6, no. 3 (2005): 583–614.

Hart, Keith and Vishnu Padayachee. "Development." In *The Human Economy: A Citizen's Guide*, edited by Keith Hart, Jean-Louis Laville, and Antonio David Cattani, 51–62. Cambridge: Polity, 2010.

Harvey, David. *The Condition of Postmodernity: An Enquiry into the Origins of Cultural Change*. Oxford: Blackwell, 1989.

Hattox, Ralph S. *Coffee and Coffeehouses: The Origins of a Social Beverage in the Medieval Near East*. Seattle: Washington University Press, 1985.

Hawthorne, Nathaniel. "The Canal Boat." *The New-England Magazine* 9 (December 1835): 398–409.

Hellbeck, Jochen. "Everyday Ideology: Life During Stalinism." *Mittelweg 36*, no. 1 (2010).

Hellbeck, Jochen. "Fashioning the Stalinist Soul: The Diary of Stepan Podlubnyi, 1931–1939." In *Stalinism: New Directions*, edited by Sheila Fitzpatrick, 77–116. London: Routledge, 2000.

Hellbeck, Jochen. "Self-Realization in the Stalinist System: Two Soviet Diaries of the 1930s." In *Russian Modernity: Politics, Knowledge, Practices, 1800–1950*, edited by David L. Hoffmann and Yanni Kotsonis, 221–242. London: Palgrave Macmillan, 2000.

Hellbeck, Jochen. "Speaking Out: Languages of Affirmation and Dissent in Stalinist Russia." *Kritika: Explorations in Russian and Eurasian History* 1, no. 1 (2000): 71–96.

Hellbeck, Jochen. "Working, Struggling, Becoming: Stalin-Era Autobiographical Texts." *The Russian Review* 60, no. 3 (2001): 340–359.

Helleiner, Eric. "Economic Nationalism as a Challenge to Economic Liberalism? Lessons from the 19th Century." *International Studies Quarterly* 46, no. 3 (2002): 307–329.

Bibliography

Herment, Laurent. "Tractorization: France, 1945–1955." In *Agriculture in Capitalist Europe, 1945–1960: From Food Shortages to Food Surpluses*, edited by Carin Martiin, Juan Pan-Montojo, and Paul Brassley, 185–205. London: Routledge, 2016.

Herrschel, Tassilo. *Global Geographies of Post-Socialist Transition: Geographies, Societies, Policies*. London: Routledge, 2007.

Hessler, Julie. "Cultured Trade: The Stalinist Turn towards Consumerism." In *Stalinism: New Directions*, edited by Sheila Fitzpatrick, 182–209. London: Routledge, 2000.

Hetherington, Kevin. *Badlands of Modernity: Heterotopia and Social Ordering*. London: Routledge, 1997.

Herzfeld, Michael. "Political Optics and the Occlusion of Intimate Knowledge." *American Anthropologist* 107, no. 3 (2005): 369–376.

High, Steven, Lachlan MacKinnon, and Andrew Perchard, eds. *Deindustrialized World: Confronting Ruination in Postindustrial Places*. Vancouver: UBC Press, 2017.

High, Steven. "Beyond Aesthetics: Visibility and Invisibility in the Aftermath of Deindustrialization." *International Labor and Working-Class History* 84 (2013): 140–153.

High, Steven, and David W. Lewis. *Corporate Wasteland: The Landscape and Memory of Deindustrialization*. Ithaca, NY: ILR Press, 2007.

Hilaire-Pérez, Liliane, and Catherine Verna. "Dissemination of Technical Knowledge in the Middle Ages and the Early Modern Era: New Approaches and Methodological Issues." *Technology and Culture* 47, no. 3 (2006): 536–540.

Hirschman, Albert O. "The Rise and Decline of Development Economics." In *The Essential Hirschman*, edited by Jeremy Adelman. Princeton, NJ: Princeton University Press, 2013.

Historia e Partisë së Punës të Shqipërisë [The history of the Albanian Labor Party]. Tirana: 8 Nëntori, 1981.

Historia e popullit shqiptar. Vëll. 1, Ilirët, Mesjeta, Shqipëria nën Perandorinë Osmane [The history of the Albanian people. Volume 1. The Illyrians, the Middle Ages, Albania under the Ottoman Empire]. Tirana: Toena: 2002.

Historia e popullit shqiptar. Vëll. 2, Rilindja Kombëtare: vitet 30-të shek. XIX-1912 [The history of the Albanian people. Volume 2. The National Awakening: 1830s-1912]. Tirana: Toena, 2002.

Historia e Shqipërisë. Vëll. 2, Vitet 30 të shek. XIX-1912 [The history of Albania. Volume 2. 1830s-1912]. Tirana: Akademia e Shkencave të RPS të Shqipërisë, 1984.

Historia e Shqipërisë. Vëll. 3, 1912–1944 [The history of Albania. Volume 3. 1912–1944]. Tirana: Akademia e Shkencave të RPS të Shqipërisë, 1984.

Historia e Shqipërisë. Vëll. 4, 1944–1975 [The history of Albania. Volume 4. 1944–1975]. Tirana: Akademia e Shkencave të RPS të Shqipërisë, 1983.

Historia e Shqipërisë. Vëll. 3, Shqipëria nën sundimin feudalo ushtarak otoman (1506–1839) [The history of Albania. Volume 3. Albania under the feudal military Ottoman rule (1506–1839)]. Tirana: Universiteti Shtetëror i Tiranës, 1961.

Historia e shqiptarëve gjatë shekullit XX. Vëll. 3 [The history of the Albanians during the 20th century. Volume 3]. Tirana: Botime Albanologjike, 2020.

Hobsbawm, Eric J. *The Age of Extremes: A History of the World, 1914–1991*. New York: Vintage Books, 1996.

Hodge, Joseph Morgan. "Writing the History of Development (Part 1: The First Wave)." *Humanity: An International Journal of Human Rights, Humanitarianism, and Development* 6, no. 3 (2015): 429–463.

Hodge, Joseph Morgan. "Writing the History of Development (Part 2: Longer, Deeper, Wider)." *Humanity: An International Journal of Human Rights, Humanitarianism, and Development* 7, no. 1 (2016): 125–174.

Hoeksema, Robert J. "Three Stages in the History of Land Reclamation in the Netherlands." *Irrigation and Drainage* 56, S1 (2007): 113–126.

Hoffman, David L. *Stalinist Values: The Cultural Norms of Soviet Modernity, 1917–1941*. Ithaca, NY: Cornell University Press, 2003.

Hoffmann, David L. "European Modernity and Soviet Socialism." In *Russian Modernity: Politics, Knowledge, Practices*, edited by David L. Hoffmann and Yanni Kotsonis, 145–260. London: Routledge, 2000.

Holquist, Peter. "Violent Russia, Deadly Marxism? Russia in the Epoch of Violence, 1905–21." *Kritika: Explorations in Russian and Eurasian History* 4, no. 3 (2003): 627–652.

Hooijer, A., S. Page, J. Jauhiainen, W. A. Lee, X. X. Lu, A. Idris, and G. Anshari. "Subsidence and carbon loss in drained tropical peatlands." *Biogeosciences* 9, no. 3 (2012): 1053–1071.

Horváth, Sándor. *Stalinism Reloaded: Everyday Life in Stalin-City, Hungary*. Translated by Thomas Cooper. Bloomington, IN: Indiana University Press, 2017.

Hospers, Gert-Jan. "Restructuring Europe's Rustbelt: The Case of the German Ruhrgebiet." *Intereconomics* 39, no. 3 (2004): 147–156.

Hoxha, Artan R. *Tharja e kënetës së Maliqit dhe ndërtimi i regjimit komunist në periferi të Shqipërisë* [The reclamation of the swamp of Maliq and the building of the communist regime in the periphery of Albania]. Tirana: Onufir, 2021.

Hoxha, Artan R. "Exploiting and Conserving: Forests, Nation, and Strategies of Development in 20th-Century Albania." *Ekonomska i ekohistorija/Economic-and Ecohistory* 14, no. 1 (2018): 145–167.

Hoxha, Enver. *Titistët: shënime historike* [Titoistes]. Tirana: 8 Nëntori, 1982.

Hoxha, Enver. "Fjala e mbajtur në Kongresin e Parë të Kooperativave Bujqësore" [Speech held in the First Congress of the Collective Farms]. In *Vepra* [Works] 6. Tirana: Naim Frashëri, 1971.

Hoxhallari, Rezarta. *Trashëgimia natyrore e qarkut të Korçës dhe menaxhimi turistik i saj* [Natural heritage of Korca district and its touristic management]. Dissertation for the defense of the title of Doctor of Sciences, Department of Geography, University of Tirana, 2016.

Hutchings, Raymond. "Albanian Industrialization: Widening Divergence from Stalinism." In *Industrialisierung und gesellschaftlicher Wandel in Südosteuropa*, edited by Roland Schönfeld, 109–124. Munich: Südosteuropa-Gesellschaft, 1989.

Iandolo, Alessandro. "The Rise and Fall of the 'Soviet Model of Development' in West Africa, 1957–64." *Cold War History* 12, no. 4 (2012): 683–704.

Idrizi, Idrit. *Herrschaft und Alltag im albanischen Spätsozialismus (1976–1985)*. Munich: De Gruyter Oldenburg, 2019.

Bibliography

Iordachi, Constantin, and Arnd Bauerkämper, eds. *The Collectivization of Agriculture in Communist Eastern Europe: Comparison and Entanglements*. Budapest: CEU Press, 2014.

Iordachi, Constantin. "From Imperial Entanglements to National Disentanglement: The 'Greek Question' in Moldavia and Wallachia, 1611–1863." In *Entangled Histories of the Balkans: National Ideologies and Language Policies*, edited by Roumen Daskalov and Tchavdar Marinov, 67–148. Leiden: Brill, 2013.

Iordachi, Constantin, and Dorin Dobrincu, eds. *Transforming Peasants, Propriety and Power: The Collectivization of Agriculture in Romania, 1949–1962*. Budapest: CEU Press, 2009.

Iordachi, Constantin, and Katherine Verdery. "Conclusions." In *Transforming Peasants, Propriety and Power: The Collectivization of Agriculture in Romania, 1949–1962*, edited by Constantin Iordachi and Dorin Dobrincu, 455–472. Budapest: CEU Press, 2009.

Iordachi, Constantin. "'Entangled Histories:' Re-thinking the History of Central and Southeastern Europe from a Relational Perspective." *Regio – Minorities, Politics, Society*, English edition 7, no. 1 (2004): 113–147.

Isaacman, Allen F., and Barbara S. Isaacman. *Dams, Displacement, and the Delusion of Development: Cahora Bassa and Its Legacies in Mozambique, 1965–2007*. Athens, OH: Ohio University Press, 2013.

Ivetic, Egidio. *Le guerre balcaniche*. Milan: Il Mulino, 2007.

Jajeśniak-Quast, Dagmara. "Nowa Huta, Eisenhüttenstadt and Ostrava-Poruba in Early State Socialism: The Proletarianization and Ruralization of New Cities." In *Mastery and Lost Illusions: Space and Time in the Modernization of Eastern and Central Europe*, edited by Włodzimierz Borodziej, Stanislav Holubec, and Joachim von Puttkamer, 121–138. Munich: De Gruyter Oldenbourg, 2014.

Janssen, Joks, and Luuk Knippenberg. "The Heritage of the Productive Landscape: Landscape Design for Rural Areas in the Netherlands, 1954–1985." *Landscape Research* 33, no. 1 (2008): 1–28.

Janus, Jaroslav, and Iwona Markuszewska. "Land Consolidation—A Great Need to Improve Effectiveness. A Case Study from Poland." *Land Use Policy* 65 (2017): 143–153.

Jashiku, Ermira. *Vlerësimi dhe menaxhimi i risqeve natyrore dhe antropogjene në rethin e Korçës dhe të Devollit* [The evaluation of natural and anthropogenic risks in the districts of Korça and Devoll]. Dissertation for the defense of the title of Doctor of Sciences, Department of Geography, University of Tirana, 2016.

Jelavich, Barbara. *Russia's Balkan Entanglements 1804–1914*. Cambridge: Cambridge University Press, 1991.

Jelavich, Barbara, and Charles Jelavich. *The Establishment of the Balkan National States, 1804–1920*. Seattle: Washington University Press, 1977.

Jelavich, Barbara and Charles Jelavich, eds. *The Balkans in Transition: Essays on the Development of Balkan Life and Politics since the Eighteenth Century*. Hamden, CT: Archon Books, 1963.

Jersild, Austin. "The Soviet State as Imperial Scavenger: 'Catch Up and Surpass' in the Transnational Socialist Bloc, 1950–1960." *American Historical Review* 116, no. 1 (2011), 109–132.

Bibliography

Josephson, Paul R. *Industrialized Nature: Brute Force Technology and the Transformation of the Natural World*. Washington, DC: Island Press, 2002.

Jowitt, Kenneth. "The Sociocultural Basis of National Dependency in Peasant Countries." In *Social Change in Romania, 1860–1940: A Debate on Development in a European Nation*, edited by Kenneth Jowitt, 1–30. Berkeley, CA: University of California Press, 1978.

Judt, Tony. *Postwar: A History of Europe Since 1945*. New York: Penguin Books, 2005.

Juneja, Monica, and Margrit Pernau. "Lost in Translation? Transcending Boundaries in Comparative History." In *Comparative and Transnational History: Central European Approaches and New Perspectives*, edited by Heinz-Gerhard Haupt and Jürgen Kocka, 105–129. New York: Berghahn Books, 2012.

Jürgenson, Evelin. "Land Reform, Land Fragmentation and Perspectives for Future Land Consolidation in Estonia." *Land Use Policy* 57 (2016): 34–43.

Kaataja, Sampsa. "Expert Groups Closing the Divide: Estonian-Finnish Computing Cooperation since the 1960s." In *Beyond the Divide: Entangled Histories of Cold War Europe*, edited by Simon Mikkonen and Pia Koivunen, 101–120. New York: Berghahn, 2015.

Kaba, Hamit. "Refleksione në politikën e jashtme të shtetit shqiptar pas vdekjes së Stalinit" [Reflections on the foreign policy of the Albanian state after the death of Stalin]. In *Shqipëria në rrjedhën e Luftës së Ftohtë* [Albania in the course of the Cold War], 173–180. Tirana: Flamuri, 2017.

Kaelble, Hartmut. "Between Comparison and Transfers—and What Now? A French-German Debate." In *Comparative and Transnational History: Central European Approaches and New Perspectives*, edited by Heinz-Gerhard Haupt and Jürgen Kocka, 33–38. New York: Berghahn Books, 2012.

Kafadar, Cemal. *Between Two Worlds: The Construction of the Ottoman State*. Berkeley, CA: University of California Press, 1995.

Kagon, Robert H., and Arthur P. Molella. *Invented Edens: Techno-Cities of the Twentieth Century*. Cambridge, MA: MIT Press, 2008.

Kaika, Maria. "Dams as Symbols of Modernization: The Urbanization of Nature between Geographical Imagination and Materiality." *Annals of the Association of American Geographers* 96, no. 2 (2006): 276–301.

Kaika, Maria. *City of Flows: Modernity, Nature, and the City*. London: Routledge, 2005.

Kalinovsky, Artemy M. *Laboratory of Socialist Development: Cold War Politics and Decolonization in Soviet Tajikistan*. Ithaca, NY: Cornell University Press, 2018.

Kallfa, Astrit. *Arritje dhe probleme të ngushtimit të dallimeve thelbësore ndërmjet qytetit dhe fshatit* [Achievements and problems of the narrowing of the differences between town and countryside]. Tirana: Universiteti i Tiranës, 1984.

Kamenica, Marko. *Përmirësimi ujor i tokave në Shqipëri, 1946–1980* [The hydric improvement of soils in Albania, 1946-1980]. Tirana: Marin Barleti, 2013.

Kamenica, Marko. *Ulja vertikale e tokave torfike të bonifikuara të Maliqit* [Vertical depression of the reclaimed peatland of Maliq]. Tirana: Ministria e Arsimit dhe Shkencës.

Karaiskaj, Gjerak, and Petrika Lera. "Fortifikimet e periudhës së pare të hekurit në pellgun e Korçës" [The fortifications of the Early Iron Age in the Basin of Korça] In *Kuvendi I i studimeve ilire* [The first convention of the Illyrian studies], volume I, 163–273. Tirana: Akademia e Shkencave e RPSSh, 1974.

Kaser, Karl. "The History of the Family in Albania in the 20th Century: A First Profile." *Ethnologia Balkanica* 4 (2000): 45–57.

Kaya, Ibrahim. *Social Theory and Later Modernities: The Turkish Experience*. Liverpool: Liverpool University Press, 2004.

Keeler, Murray E., and Dimitrios G. Skuras. "Land Fragmentation and Consolidation Policies in Greek Agriculture." *Geography* 75, no. 1 (1990): 73–76.

Kelly, Catriona. "Ordinary Life in Extraordinary Times: Chronicles of the Quotidian in Russia and the Soviet Union." *Kritika: Explorations in Russian and Eurasian History* 3, no. 4 (2002): 631–651.

Kelly, Catriona, and Vadim Volkov. "Directed Desires: *Kul'turnost'* and Consumption." In *Constructing Russian Culture in the Age of Revolution, 1881–1940*, edited by Catriona Kelly and David Shepherd, 291–313. Oxford: Oxford University Press, 1998.

Khalid, Adeeb. "Backwardness and the Quest for Civilization: Early Soviet Central Asia in Comparative Perspective." *Slavic Review* 65, no. 2 (2006): 231–251.

Kideckel, David. "Identity and Mining Heritage in Romania's Jiu Valley Coal Region: Commodification, Alienation, Renaissance." In *Industrial Heritage and Regional Identities*, edited by Christian Wicke, Stefan Berger, and Joana Golombek, 119–135. London: Routledge, 2018.

Kideckel, David. "Coal Power: Class, Fetishism, Memory and Disjuncture in Romania's Jiu Valley and Appalachian West Virginia." *ANUAC* 7, no. 1 (2018): 67–88.

Kideckel, David A. *The Solitude of Collectivism: Romanian Villagers to the Revolution and Beyond*. Ithaca, NY: Cornell University Press, 1993.

Kim, Cheehyung Harrison. "North Korea's Vinalon City: Industrialism as Socialist Everyday Life." *positions: asia critique* 22, no. 4 (2014): 809–836.

Kirasirova, Masha. "'Sons of Muslims' in Moscow: Soviet Central Asian Mediators to the Foreign East, 1955–1962." *Ab Imperio* 4 (2011): 106–132.

Kochanowicz, Jacek. "A Moving Target or a Lost Illusion? East Central Europe in Pursuit of the West in Two Globalization Phases." In *Mastery and Lost Illusions: Space and Time in the Modernization of Eastern and Central Europe*, ed. by Włodzimierz Borodziej, Stanislav Holubec, and Joachim von Puttkamer, 31–50. Munich: De Gruyter Oldenbourg, 2014.

Kocka, Jürgen. *Capitalism: A Short History*. Translated by Jeremiah Riemer. Princeton, NJ: Princeton University Press, 2016.

Kocka, Jürgen, and Heinz-Gerhard Haupt. "Comparison and Beyond: Traditions, Scope, and Perspective of Comparative History." In *Comparative and Transnational History: Central European Approaches and New Perspectives*, edited by Heinz-Gerhard Haupt and Jürgen Kocka, 1–30. New York: Berghahn Books, 2012.

Kodderitzsch, Severin. *Reforms in Albanian Agriculture: Assessing a Sector in Transition*. Washington, DC: The World Bank, 1999.

Kofti, Dimitra. "Moral Economy of Flexible Production: Fabricating Precarity between the Conveyor Belt and the Household." *Anthropological Theory* 16, no. 4 (2016): 433–453.

Koka, Viron. *Rrymat e mendimit politiko-shoqëror në Shqipëri në vitet 30 të shekullit XX* [The social-political currents in Albania during the 1930s]. Tirana: Akademia e Shkencave të RPS të Shqipërisë, 1985.

Bibliography

Komlosy, Andrea. "Austria and Czechoslovakia: The Habsburg Monarchy and Its Successor States." In *The Ashgate Companion to the History of Textile Workers, 1650–2000*, edited by Lex Heerma van Voss, Els Hiemstra-Kuperus, and Elise van Nederveen Meerkerk, 43–74. New York: Ashgate Publisher, 2010.

Konitza, Faik. *Albania: The Rock Garden of Southeastern Europe*. London: I. B. Tauris, 2012.

Kopytoff, Igor. "The Cultural Biography of Things: Commoditization as Process." In *The Social Life of Things: Commodities in Cultural Perspective*, edited by Arjun Appadurai, 64–90. Cambridge: Cambridge University Press, 1986.

Korkuti, Muzafer. *Parailirët, ilirët, arbërit: histori e shkurtër* [Pre-Illyrians, Illyrians, and Albanians: A brief history]. Tirana: Toena, 2003.

Kosicki, Piotr H. "The Catholic 1968: Poland, Social Justice, and the Global Cold War." *Slavic Review* 77, no. 3 (2018): 638–660.

Kotsonis, Yanni. "Introduction: A Modern Paradox—Subject and Citizen in Nineteenth- and Twentieth-Century Russia." In *Russian Modernity: Politics, Knowledge, Practices*, edited by David L. Hoffmann and Yanni Kotsonis, 1–16. London: Routledge, 2000.

Kotkin, Stephen. *Uncivil Society: 1989 and the Implosion of the Communist Establishment*. With contributions by Jan T. Gross. New York: Modern Library, 2010.

Kotkin, Stephen. "The Kiss of Debt: The East Bloc Goes Borrowing." In *The Shock of the Global: The 1970s in Perspective*, edited by Niall Ferguson, Charles S. Maier, Erez Manela, and Daniel J. Sargent, 80–93. Cambridge MA: The Belknap Press of Harvard University Press, 2010.

Kotkin, Stephen. "Mongol Commonwealth?: Exchange and Governance across the Post-Mongol Space." *Kritika: Explorations in Russian and Eurasian History* 8, no. 3 (2007): 487–531.

Kotkin, Stephen. "Modern Times: The Soviet Union and the Interwar Conjuncture." *Kritika: Exploration in Russian and Eurasian History* 2, no. 1 (2001): 111–164.

Kotkin, Stephen. *Magnetic Mountain: Stalinism as a Civilization*. Berkeley, CA: University of California Press, 1995.

Kozlova, Natalia. "The Diary as Initiation and Rebirth: Reading Everyday Documents of the Early Soviet Era." In *Everyday Life in Early Soviet Russia: Taking the Revolution Inside*, edited by Christina Kiaer and Eric Naiman, 282–298. Bloomington, IN: Indiana University Press, 2006.

Kramer, Mark. "Stalin, the Split with Yugoslavia, and the Soviet-East European Efforts to Reassert Control, 1948–1953." In *The Balkans in the Cold War*, edited by Svetozar Rajak, Konstantina E. Botsiou, Eirini Karamouzi, and Evanthis Hatzivassiliou, 29–64. London: Palgrave Macmillan, 2017.

Krylova, Anna. "Soviet Modernity: Stephen Kotkin and the Bolshevik Predicament." *Contemporary European History* 23, no. 2 (2014): 167–192.

Krylova, Anna. "The Tenacious Liberal Subject in Soviet Studies." *Kritika: Explorations in Russian and Eurasian History* 1, no. 1 (2000): 119–146.

Kumar, Krishan. *From Post-Industrial Society to Post-Modern Society: New Theories of the Contemporary World*. London: Blackwell, 2005.

Kutrzeba-Pojnarowa, Anna. "The Influence of the History of Peasantry on the Model of the Traditional Peasant Culture and the Mechanisms of its Transformations." In *The Peas-

ant and the City in Eastern Europe: Interpreting Structures, edited Irene Portis Winner and Thomas G. Winner, 85–98. Cambridge, MA: Schenkman Publishing Company, 1984.

Kühschelm, Oliver. "Nationalizing Consumption: Products, Brands, and Nations." In *Nationalism and the Economy: Explorations into a Neglected Relationship*, edited by Stefan Berger and Thomas Fetzer, 163–188. Budapest: Central European University Press, 2019.

Lahusen, Thomas. "Decay or Endurance? The Ruins of Socialism." *Slavic Review* 65, no. 4 (2006): 736–746.

Lalaj, Ana. "The Soviet-Yugoslav Break and Albania." *Studia Albanica* 39, no. 2 (2005): 123–127.

Lampe, John R. *Balkans into Southeastern Europe, 1914–2004: A Century of War and Transition*. London: Palgrave Macmillan, 2014.

Lampe, John R., and Marvin R. Jackson. *Balkan Economic History, 1550–1950: From Imperial Borderlands to Developing Nations*. Bloomington, IN: Indiana University Press, 1982.

Lampe, John R., and Mark Mazower. *Ideologies and National Identities: The Case of Twentieth-Century Southeastern Europe*. Budapest: CEU Press, 2004.

"Land Fragmentation and Land Consolidation in CEEC: A Gate towards Sustainable Rural Development in the New Millennium," Munich, February 25–28, 2002. Accessed November 2018. http://www.fao.org /europe/events/detail-events/en/c/285102/.

Lanero, Daniel, and Lourenzo Fernandez-Prieto. "Technology Policies in Dictatorial Contexts: Spain and Portugal." In *Agriculture in Capitalist Europe, 1945–1960: From Food Shortages to Food Surpluses*, edited by Carin Martiin, Juan Pan-Montojo, and Paul Brassley, 165–184. London: Routledge, 2016.

Lash, Scott, and John Urry. *The End of Organized Capitalism*. London: Polity Press, 1987.

Latour, Bruno. *We Have Never Been Modern*. Translated by Catherine Porter. Cambridge, MA: Harvard University Press, 1993.

Latour, Bruno. "Where are the Missing Masses? The Sociology of a Few Mundane Artifacts." In *Shaping Technology/Building Society: Studies in Sociotechnical Change*, edited by Wiebe E. Bijker and John Law, 225–254. Cambridge, MA: MIT Press, 1992.

Latour, Bruno. "Technology is Society Made Durable," *The Sociological Review* 38, S1 (1990): 103–131.

Laszlo-Herbert, Mark. "The Construction and Transformation of Socialist Space in the Planned Cities of Stalinstadt and Sztálinváros," Dissertation defended at the University of Toronto, 2016.

Lebow, Katherine. *Unfinished Utopia: Nowa Huta, Stalinism, and Polish Society, 1949–1956*. Ithaca, NY: Cornell University Press, 2013.

Lebow, Katherine A. "Revising the Political Landscape: Nowa Huta, 1949–1957." *City & Society* 11, nos. 1–2 (1999): 165–184.

Lefebvre, Henri. *State, Space, World: Selected Essays*. Edited by Neil Brenner and Stuart Elden. Minneapolis: University of Minnesota Press, 2009.

Leifeld, J., M. Müller, and J. Fuhrer. "Peatland subsidence and carbon loss from drained temperate fens." *Soil Use and Management* 27, no. 2 (2011): 170–176.

Bibliography

Lemel, Harold and Albert Dubali. "Land Fragmentation." In *Rural Property and Economy in Post-Socialist Albania*, edited by Harold Lemel, 109–125. New York: Berghahn Books, 2000.

Lera, Petrika. "Vendbanimi Prehistorik i Podgories" [The prehistoric settlement of Podgoria]. In *Korça. Almanak* 2, 145–153. Tirana: 8 Nëntori, 1977.

Lerman, Zvi. "Policies and Institutions for Commercialization of Subsistence Farms in Transition Countries." *Journal of Asian Economics* 15, no. 3 (2004): 462.

Leskaj, Bujar. *Muzat e qëndresës: nëpër libra të kryqëzuar* [The muses of resistance: through crucified books]. Tirana: Geer, 2011.

Levcik, Friedrich, and Jiri Skolka. *East-West Technology Transfer: Study of Czechoslovakia*. Paris: OECD, 1984.

Levi, Giovanni. "Frail Frontiers?" *Past and Present* 242, Supplement 14 (2019): 37–49.

Levi, Giovanni. "On Microhistory." In *New Perspectives on Historical Writing*, edited by Peter Burke, 93–113. University Park, PA: Pennsylvania State University Press, 1992.

Lewin, Moshe. *The Making of the Soviet System: Essays in the Social History of Interwar Russia*. New York: Pantheon, 1985.

Lewis, Archibald R. "The Closing of the Medieval Frontier, 1250–1350." *Speculum* 33, no. 4 (1958): 475–483.

Lézine, A-M, U. von Grafenstein, N. Andersen, S. Belmecheria, A. Bordon, B. Caron, J.-P. Cazet, et al. "Lake Ohrid, Albania, provides an exceptional multi-proxy record of environmental changes during the last glacial-interglacial cycle." *Palaeogeography, Palaeoclimatology, Palaeoecology* 287 (2010): 116–127.

Li, Tania Murray. "Governmentality." *Anthropologica* 49, no. 2 (2007): 275–281.

Li, Tania Murray. "Beyond 'the State' and Failed Schemes." *American Anthropologist* 107, no. 3 (2005): 383–392.

Linkon, Sherry Lee, "Narrating Past and Future: Deindustrialized Landscapes as Resources." *International Labor and Working-Class History*, no. 84 (2013): 38–54.

Linkon, Sherry Lee, and John Russo. *Steeltown USA: Work and Memory in Youngstown*. Lawrence, KS: University Press of Kansas, 2002.

Linoli, Antonio. "Twenty-six Centuries of Reclamation and Agricultural Improvement on the Pontine Marshes." In *Integrated Land and Water Resources Management in History*, edited by Christoph Ohlig, 27–55. Siegburg: DWHG, 2005.

Livezeanu, Irina. *Cultural Politics in Greater Romania: Regionalism, Nation Building & Ethnic Struggle, 1918–1930*. Ithaca, NY: Cornell University Press, 1995.

Lolo, Thoma. "Rezultatet e llojeve të panxhar sheqerit në konditat e vëndit tonë" [The results of different sugar beet strains in our country]. *Buletini i Shkencave Bujqësore* [The bulletin of agricultural sciences] 1 (1962): 58–66.

Lorenzini, Sara. *Global Development: A Cold War History*. Princeton, NJ: Princeton University Press, 2019.

Lovell, Stephen. *The Shadow of War: Russia and the USSR, 1941 to the Present*. Oxford: Wiley-Blackwell, 2010.

Lubonja, Fatos. "Blloku (pa nostalgji)" [Blloku (without nostalgia)]. *Përpjekja*, no. 24 (2007), 11–31.

Bibliography

Lüdtke, Alf. "The Appeal of Exterminating 'Others': German Workers and the Limits of Resistance." *Journal of Modern History* 64, [Supplement], 4 (1992): S46-S67.

Lüdtke, Alf. "Introduction: What Is the History of Everyday Life and Who Are Its Practitioners." In *The History of Everyday Life: Reconstructing Historical Experiences and Ways of Life*, edited by Alf Lüdtke, 3–40. Translated by William Templer. Princeton, NJ: Princeton University Press, 1989.

Lynn, Hyung-Gu. "Globalization and the Cold War." In *The Oxford Handbook of the Cold War*, edited by Richard H. Immerman and Petra Goedde, 584–601. Oxford: Oxford University Press, 2013.

Macmillan, Margaret. *Paris 1919: Six Months that Changed the World*. New York: Random House, 2002.

Maier, Charles S. "Consigning the Twentieth Century to History: Alternative Narratives for the Modern Era." *The American Historical Review* 105, no. 3 (2000): 807–831.

Maier, Charles S. "'Malaise': The Crisis of Capitalism in the 1970s." In *The Shock of the Global: The 1970s in Perspective*, edited by Niall Ferguson, Charles S. Maier, Erez Manela, and Daniel J. Sargent, 25–48. Cambridge MA: The Belknap Press of Harvard University Press, 2010.

Manoku, Yllson. *Historia e bujqësisë dhe agropërpunimit në rajonin e Korçës* [The history of agriculture and agro-processing in the region of Korça]. Korça: Universiteti Fan Noli, 2009.

Martin, Terry. "Modernization or Neo-Traditionalism? Ascribed Nationality and Soviet Primordialism." In *Stalinism: New Directions*, edited by Sheila Fitzpatrick, 348–367. London: Routledge, 2000.

Marx, Karl, and Frederick Engels. *The Communist Manifesto*. London: Martin Lawrence, 1930.

Massey, Doreen. "Questions of Locality." *Geography* 78, no. 2 (1993): 142–149.

Masters, Bruce. "Christians in a Changing World." In *The Cambridge History of Turkey*. Vol. 3, *The Later Ottoman Empire, 1603–1839*, edited by Suraiya N. Faroqhi, 186–206. Cambridge: Cambridge University Press, 2006.

Maul, Daniel. "'Help Them Move the ILO Way': The International Labor Organization and the Modernization Discourse in the Era of Decolonization and the Cold War." *Diplomatic History* 33, no. 3 (2009): 387–404.

Mauss, Marcel. *The Gift: The Form and Reason for Exchange in Archaic Societies*. Translated by W. D. Halls. London: Routledge, 2002.

Mazower, Mark. *Governing the World: The History of an Idea, 1815 to the Present*. New York: Penguin Books, 2012.

Mazower, Mark. *Dark Continent: Europe's Twentieth Century*. London: Penguin Books, 1998.

Mazower, Mark. *Salonica, City of Ghosts: Christians, Muslims and Jews, 1430–1950*. New York: Alfred A. Knopf, 2005.

Mazower, Mark. *The Balkans: A Short History*. New York: The Modern Library, 2002.

Mazurek, Małgorzata. "Polish Economists in Nehru's India: Making Science for the Third World in an Era of De-Stalinization and Decolonization." *Slavic Review* 77, no. 3 (2018): 588–610.

McCannon, John. "Tabula Rasa in the North: The Soviet Arctic and Mythic Landscapes in Stalinist Popular Culture." In *The Landscape of Stalinism: The Art and Ideology of Soviet Space*, edited by Evgeny Dobrenko and Eric Naiman, 241–260. Seattle: Washington University Press, 2003.

McLuhan, Marshall. *Understanding Media: The Extension of Man*. Cambridge, MA: MIT Press, 1994.

McNeill, John R. *Something New Under the Sun: An Environmental History of the Twentieth-Century World*. New York: W. W. Norton, 2000.

McNeill, John R., and William H. McNeill. *The Human Web: A Bird's-Eye View of World History*. New York: W. W. Norton & Company, 2003.

McNeill, William H. *Greece: American Aid in Action, 1947–1956*. New York: Twentieth Century Fund, 1957.

Melvin, Neil J. *Soviet Power and the Countryside: Policy Innovation and Institutional Decay*. New York: Palgrave Macmillan, 2003.

Menkshi, Edlira. *Trashëgimia kulturore në funksion të zhvillimit social-ekonomik të qarkut Korçë* [Cultural heritage as a function of the socio-economic development of Korça's district]. Dissertation for the defense of the title of Doctor of Sciences, Department of Geography, University of Tirana, 2014.

Meta, Beqir. *Shqipëria dhe Greqia, 1949–1990: paqja e vështirë* [Albania and Greece, 1949–1990: The difficult peace]. Tirana: Globus R, 2007.

Meta, Beqir. *Tensioni greko-shqiptar: 1939–1949* [The Greek-Albanian tension: 1939–1949]. Tirana: Globus R, 2007.

Mëhilli, Elidor. "Defying De-Stalinization: Albania's 1956." *Journal of Cold War Studies* 13, no. 4 (2011): 4–56.

Mëhilli, Elidor. "Enver Hoxha's Albania: Yugoslav, Soviet, and Chinese Relations and Ruptures." In *Routledge Handbook of Balkan and Southeast European History*, edited by John R. Lampe and Ulf Brunnbauer, 447–455. London: Routledge, 2021.

Mëhilli, Elidor. *From Stalin to Mao: Albania and the Socialist World*. Ithaca, NY: Cornell University Press, 2017.

Mëhilli, Elidor. "Globalized Socialism, Nationalized Time: Soviet Films, Albanian Subjects, and Chinese Audiences across the Sino-Soviet Split." *Slavic Review* 77, no. 3 (2018): 611–637.

Mëhilli, Elidor. "Mao and the Albanians." In *Mao's Little Red Book: a Global History*, edited by Alexander C. Cook, 165–184. Cambridge: Cambridge University Press, 2014.

Mëhilli, Elidor. "Socialist Encounters: Albania and the Transnational Eastern Bloc in the 1950s." In *Cold War Crossings: International Travel and Exchange across the Soviet Bloc, 1940s-1960s*, edidet by Patryk Babiracki and Kenyon Zimmer, 107–133. College Station, TX: Texas A&M University Press, 2014.

Mëhilli, Elidor. "States of Insecurity." *The International History Review* 37, no. 5 (2015): 1037–1058.

Mikkonen, Simo, and Pia Koivunen, eds. *Beyond the Divide: Entangled Histories of Cold War Europe*. New York: Berghahn, 2015.

Mile, Ligor K. *Çështje të historië agrare shqiptare: fundi i shek. XVIII – vitet 70 të shek. XIX* [Issues of the Albanian agrarian history: The end of the XVIII century through the 1870s]. Tirana: Akademia e Shkencave e RPSSh, 1984.

Bibliography

Mile, Ligor. *Zejtaria fshatare shqiptare gjaë Rilindjes Kombëtare* [Albanian rural handicraft during the national awakening]. Tirana: Marin Barleti, 2001.

Millon, Henry A. "Some New Towns in Italy in the 1930s." In *Art and Architecture in the Service of Politics*, edited by Henry A. Millon and Linda Nochlin, 326–341. Cambridge, MA: MIT Press, 1978.

Mintz, Sidney. *Sweetness and Power: The Place of Sugar in Modern History*. London: Penguin Books, 1985.

Mintz, Sidney. "Notes toward a Cultural Construction of Modern Foods." *Social Anthropology* 17, no. 2 (2009): 209–216.

Misha, Kristaq. *Lëvizja punëtore në Shqipëri* [The workers' movement in Albania]. Tirana: Naim Frashëri, 1970.

Mitko, Thimi. "Topografi e Korçës" [Topography of Korça]. In *Thimi Mitko. Vepra* [Works], edited by Qemal Haxhihasani. Tirana: Akademia e Shenkcave e RPSSH, 1981.

Mitter, Rana, and Patrick Major, eds. *Across the Blocs: Exploring Comparative Cold War Cultural and Social History*. London: Frank Cass, 2004.

Moore Jr., Barrington. *Social Origins of Dictatorship and Democracy: Lord and Peasant in the Making of the Modern World*. Boston: Beacon Press, 1966.

Morukov, Mikhail. "The White Sea–Baltic Canal." In *The Economics of Forced Labor: The Soviet Gulag*, edited by Paul R. Gregory and Valery V. Lazarev, 151–162. Stanford, CA: Hoover Institution Press, 2003.

Mouzelis, Nicos P. *Politics in Semi-periphery: Early Parliamentarism and Late Industrialization in the Balkans and Latin America*. London: Macmillan, 1986.

Muçaj, Agim. *Lufta e fshatarësisë shqiptare kundër shfrytëzimit çifligaro-borgjez (1925–1939) dhe qëndrimi i klasave ndaj saj* [The struggle of the Albanian peasantry against feudal-bourgeois exploitation (1925–1939) and the attitude of the classes towards it]. Tirana: Shtëpia e Librit Universitar, 1990.

Mungiu-Pippidi, Alina, and Wim Van Meurs, eds. *Ottomans into Europeans: State and Institution-Building in South Eastern Europe*. New York: Columbia University Press, 2010.

Murray, Robin. "Fordism and Post-Fordism." In *New Times: The Changing Face of Politics in the 1990s*, edited by Stuart Hall and Martin Jacques, 38–53. London: Lawrence & Wishart, 1990.

Musaj, Fatmira. *Gruaja në Shqipëri (1912–1939)* [The woman in Albania (1912–1939)]. Tirana: Akademia e Shkencave e RSh, 2002.

Musaraj, Smoki. "Tales from Albarado: The Materiality of Pyramid Schemes in Postsocialist Albania." *Cultural Anthropology* 26, no. 1 (2011): 84–110.

Muzaka, Gjon. *Memorje* [Memories]. Translated by Dhori Qiriazi. Tirana: Toena, 1996.

Müller, Daniel, and Darla K. Munroe. "Changing Rural Landscapes in Albania: Cropland Abandonment and Forest Clearing in the Postsocialist Transition." *Annals of the Association of American Geographers* 98, no. 4 (2008): 855–876.

Müller, Daniel, and Thomas Sikor. "Effects of Postsocialist Reforms on Land Cover and Land Use in South-Eastern Albania." *Applied Geography* 26, nos. 3–4 (2006): 175–191.

Naçi, Nuçi. *Korça edhe katundet e qarkut* [Korça and the villages of its county]. Korça: Dhori Koti, 1923.

Bibliography

Naiman, Eric. "On Soviet Subjects and Scholars Who Make Them." *The Russian Review* 60, no. 3 (2001): 307–315.

Naimark, Norman M. *Stalin and the Fate of Europe: The Postwar Struggle for Sovereignty.* Cambridge, MA: Harvard University Press, 2019.

Nelson, Robert L. "The Fantasy of Open Space on the Frontier: Max Sering from the Great Plains to Eastern Europe." In *German and United States Colonialism in a Connected World: Entangled Empires*, edited by Janne Lahti, 41–62. London: Palgrave Macmillan, 2021.

Nelson, Robert L. "Review Essay: Emptiness in the Colonial Gaze: Labor, Property, and Nature." *International Labor and Working-Class History* 79 (2011): 161–174.

Nelson, Robert L. "From Manitoba to the Memel: Max Sering, Inner Colonization, and the German East." *Social History* 35, no. 4 (2010): 439–457.

Nelson, Robert L. "The *Archive for Inner Colonization*, the German East, World War One." In *Germans, Poland, and Colonial Expansion to the East: 1850 through the Present*, edited by Robert L. Nelson, 65–94. New York: Palgrave Macmillan, 2009.

Németh, Györgyi. "Contested Heritage and Regional Identity in the Borsod Industrial Area in Hungary." In *Industrial Heritage and Regional Identities*, edited by Christian Wicke, Stefan Berger, and Joana Golombek, 95–118. London: Routledge, 2018.

Neuburger, Mary C. *Balkan Smoke: Tobacco and the Making of Modern Bulgaria.* Ithaca, NY: Cornell University Press, 2013.

Neuburger, Mary C. *The Orient Within: Muslim Minorities and the Negotiation of Nationhood in Modern Bulgaria.* Ithaca, NY: Cornell University Press, 2004.

Ngjela, Spartak. *Përkulja dhe rënia e tiranisë shqiptare, 1957–2010* [The decline and fall of the Albanian tyranny], vol. 2. Tirana: UET Press, 2012.

Nonaj, Visar. *Albaniens Schwerindustrie als zweite Befreiung?: 'Der Stahl der Partei' als Mikrokosmos des Kommunismus.* Munich: De Gruyter Oldenburg, 2021.

Nölke, Andreas, and Arjan Vliegenthart. "Enlarging the Varieties of Capitalism: The Emergence of Dependent Market Economies in East Central Europe." *World Politics* 61, no. 4 (2009): 670–702.

O'Donnell, James. *A Coming of Age: Albania under Enver Hoxha.* New York: University of Columbia Press, 1999.

O'Malley, Pat, Shearing Clifford, and Lorna Weir. "Governmentality, Criticism, Politics." *Economy and Society* 26, no. 4 (2006): 501–517.

O'Malley, Pat. "Indigenous Governance." *Economy and Society* 25, no. 3 (1996): 310–326.

Offe, Claus. "The Utopia of the Zero-Option: Modernity and Modernization as Normative Political Criteria." *Praxis International* 7, no. 1 (1987): 1–24.

Olstein, Diego. *A Brief History of Now: The Past and Present of Global Power.* London: Palgrave Macmillan, 2021.

Olstein, Diego. *Thinking History Globally.* London: Palgrave Macmillan, 2015.

Opingari, Gaqo. "Aspekte të hidrografisë së rrethit të Korçës: Karakteristikat e përgjithshme të hidrografisë" [Aspects of the district of Korça hydrography: The general characteristics of hydrography]. In *Korça. Almanak* [Korça. Almanac] 2, 127–132. Tirana: 8 Nëntori, 1977.

Osokina, Elena A. "Economic Disobedience under Stalin." In *Contending with Stalinism: Soviet Power and Popular Resistance in the 1930s*, edited by Lynne Viola, 170–200. Ithaca, NY: Cornell University Press, 2002.

Bibliography

Osterberg-Kaufmann, Norma. "Albania." In *Constitutional Politics in Central Eastern Europe: From Post-Socialist Transition to the Reform of Political Systems*, edited by Anna Fruhstorfer and Michael Hein, 333–358. Wiesbden: Springer VS, 2016.

Osterhammel, Jürgen. "A 'Transnational' History of Society: Continuity or New Departure?" In *Comparative and Transnational History: Central European Approaches and New Perspectives*, edited by Heinz-Gerhard Haupt and Jürgen Kocka, 39–51. New York: Berghahn Books, 2012.

Packard, Randall M. *The Making of a Tropical Disease: A Short History of Malaria*. Baltimore: John Hopkins University Press, 2007.

Palomera, Jaime, and Theodora Vetta. "Moral Economy: Rethinking a Radical Concept." *Anthropological Theory* 16, no. 4 (2016): 413–432.

Pano, Aristotel. *Probleme të teorisë, të metodologjisë dhe të analizës së të ardhurave kombëtare të RPSSH* [Problems with the theory and methodology of the analysis of national incomes]. Tirana: Universiteti i Tiranës, 1982.

Pano, Nicholas C. "Albania in the Sixties." In *The Changing Face of Communism in Eastern Europe*, edited by Peter A. Toma, 245–280. Tucson, AZ: University of Arizona Press, 1970.

Papajorgji, Harilla. *Struktura socialklasore a klasës sonë punëtore* [The social structure of our working class]. Tirana: 8 Nëntori, 1985.

Pashko, Gramoz. "The Albanian Economy at the Beginning of the 1990s." In *Economic Change in the Balkan States: Albania, Bulgaria, Romania, and Yugoslavia*, edited by Örjan Sjöberg and Michael L. Wyzan, 128–146. London: Pinter Publishers, 1991.

Păun Constantinescu, Ilinca, Dragoș Dascălu, and Cristina Sucală. "An Activist Perspective on Industrial Heritage in Petrila, a Romanian Mining City." *The Public Historian* 39, no. 4 (2017): 114–141.

Pere, Ëngjëll, and Will Bartlett. "On the Way to Europe: Economic and Social Developments in Albania." In *Western Balkan Economies in Transition: Recent Economic and Social Developments*, edited by Reiner Osbild and Will Bartlett, 73–88. Cham, Switzerland: Springer, 2019.

Peckham, Robert Shannan. "Internal Colonialism: Nation and Region in Nineteenth-century Greece." In *Balkan Identities: Nation and Memory*, edited by Maria Todorova, 41–59. New York: New York University Press, 2004.

Pejo, Pali. *Lufta e Partisë së Punës të Shqipërisë për ndërtimin e bazës ekonomike të socializmit* [The struggle of the Labor Party of Albania for the construction of the economic base of socialism]. Tirana: 8 Nëntori, 1974.

Peltonen, Matti. "What is Micro in Microhistory?" In *Theoretical Discussions of Biography: Approaches from History, Microhistory, and Life Writing*, edited by Hans Renders and Binne de Haan, 105–118. Leiden: Brill, 2014.

Peltonen, Matti. "Clues, Margins, and Monads: The Micro-Macro Link in Historical Research." *History and Theory* 40, no. 3 (2001): 347–359.

Pennacchi, Antonio. *Fascio e martello: Viaggio per le città del duce*. Rome: Laterza, 2008.

Perchard, Andrew. "'Broken Men' and 'Thatcher's Children': Memory and Legacy in Scotland's Coalfields." *International Labor and Working-Class History* 84 (2013): 78–98.

Perica, Vjekoslav. *Balkan Idols: Religion and Nationalism in Yugoslav States*. Oxford-New York: Oxford University Press, 2002.

Bibliography

Péteri, György, ed. *Imagining the West in Eastern Europe and the Soviet Union*. Pittsburgh, PA: University of Pittsburgh Press, 2010.

Péteri, György. "Introduction: The Oblique Coordinate Systems of Modern Society." In *Imagining the West in Eastern Europe and the Soviet Union*, edited by György Péteri, 1–12. Pittsburgh, PA: University of Pittsburgh Press, 2010.

Péteri, György. "The Occident Within—or the Drive for Exceptionalism and Modernity." *Kritika: Explorations in Russian and Eurasian History* 9, no. 4 (2008): 929–937.

Péteri, György. "Nylon Curtain—Transnational and Transsystemic Tendencies in the Cultural Life of State-Socialist Russia and East-Central Europe." *Slavonica* 10, no. 2 (2004): 113–123.

Pietrykowski, Bruce. "Beyond the Fordist/Post-Fordist Dichotomy: Working Through 'The Second Industrial Divide'." *Review of Social Economy* 57, no. 2 (1999): 177–198.

Phillips, Jim. "Deindustrialization and the Moral Economy of the Scottish Coalfields, 1947 to 1991." *International Labor and Working-Class History* 84 (2013): 99–115.

Pipa, Arshi. "Kanal." In *The Walls behind the Curtain: East European Prison Literature, 1945–1990*, edited by Harold B. Segel, 24–25. Pittsburgh: University of Pittsburgh Press, 2012.

Pittaway, Mark. "Creating and Domesticating Hungary's Socialist Industrial Landscape: From Dunapentele to Sztálinváros, 1950–1958." *Historical Archaeology* 39, no. 3 (2005): 75–93.

Pllumi, Zef. *Rrno vetëm për me tregue* [Live only to narrate]. Shkodër: Botime Françeskane, 2006.

Popkin, Samuel. "The Rational Peasant: The Political Economy of Peasant Society." *Theory and Society* 9, no. 3 (1980): 411–471.

Poqueville, François. *Në oborrin e vezirit të Janinës* [In the court of the Vizier of Ioannina]. Translated by Ismail Hoxha. Tirana: Horizont, 1999.

Prendi, Frano. "La civilization prehistorique de Maliq." *Studia Albanica* 1 (1966): 255–280.

Prendi, Frano. "The Prehistory of Albania." In *The Cambridge Ancient History*. Vol. 3, part I, *The Prehistory of the Balkans, the Middle East and the Aegean World, Tenth to Eighth Centuries*, edited by John Boardman, I. E. S. Edwards, N. G. L. Hammond, and E. Solberger, 187–237. Cambridge: Cambridge University Press, 1982.

Prifti, Kristaq. *Lidhja shqiptare e Pejës: lëvizja kombëtare, 1896–1900* [The Albanian league of Peja: The national movement, 1896–1900]. Tirana: Akademia e Shkencave të RPS të Shqipërisë, 1984.

Prifti, Peter. "Albania." In *The Communist States in Disarray 1965–1971*, edited by Adam Bromke and Teresa Rakowska-Harmstone, 198–220. Minneapolis: University of Minnesota Press, 1972.

Priore, Michael J., and Charles Sabel. *The Second Industrial Divide: Possibilities for Prosperity*. New York: Basic Books, 1984.

Pulaha, Selami. *Prona feudale në tokat shqiptare: shek. XV–XVI* [Feudal property in Albanian lands: 15th–16th centuries]. Tirana: Akademia e Shkencave të RPSSH, 1988.

Pula, Besnik. *Globalization under and after Socialism: The Evolution of Transnational Capital in Central and Eastern Europe*. Stanford, CA: Stanford University Press, 2018.

Bibliography

Pula, Besnik. "Becoming Citizens of Empire: Albanian Nationalism and Fascist Empire, 1939–1943." *Theory and Society* 37, no. 6 (2008): 567–596.

Pusca, Anca. "Industrial and Human Ruins of Postcommunist Europe." *Space and Culture* 13, no. 3 (2010): 239–255.

Putnam, Lara. "Daily Life and Digital Reach: Place-based Research and History's Transnational Turn." In *Theorizing Fieldwork in the Humanities: Methods, Reflections, and Approaches to the Global South*, edited by Shalini Puri and Debra A. Castillo, 167–182. New York: Palgrave Macmillan, 2016.

Putnam, Lara. "The Transnational and the Text-Searchable: Digitized Sources and the Shadows They Cast." *The American Historical Review* 121, no. 2 (2016): 383–402.

Puto, Arben. *Historia diplomatike e çështjes shqiptare, 1878–1926* [The diplomatic history of the Albanian question]. Tirana: Albin, 2003.

Puto, Arben. *Çështja shqiptare në aktet ndërkombëtare të periudhës së imperializmit: përmbledhje dokumentesh me një vështrim historik* [The Albanian question in the international proceedings of the age of imperialism: document collection with a historical overview], volume II. Tirana: 8 Nëntori, 1984.

Puto, Arben. *Pavarësia e Shqipërisë dhe Diplomacia e Fuqive të Mëdha (1912–1914)* [Albanian independence and Great Powers diplomacy (1912–1914)]. Tirana: 8 Nëntori, 1976.

Quataert, Donald. *The Ottoman Empire, 1700–1922*. Oxford: Oxford University Press, 2005.

Rago, Paolo. *Tradizione, nazionalismo e comunismo nell'Albania contemporanea*. Rome: Nuova Cultura, 2011.

Redner, Harry. "The Civilizing Process—According to Mennell, Elias and Freud: A Critique." *Thesis Eleven* 127, no. 1 (2015): 95–111.

Reid, Susan E. "Who Will Beat Whom? Soviet Popular Reception of the American National Exhibition in Moscow, 1959." In *Imagining the West in Eastern Europe and the Soviet Union*, edited by György Péteri, 194–236. Pittsburgh, PA: University of Pittsburgh Press, 2010.

Reid, Susan E. "Khrushchev Modern: Agency and Modernization in the Soviet Home." *Cahiers du Monde Russe* 47, nos. 1–2 (2006): 227–268.

Reid, Susan E. "The Khrushchev Kitchen: Domesticating the Scientific-Technological Revolution." *Journal of Contemporary History* 40, no. 2 (2005): 297–298.

Reid, Susan E. "Cold War in the Kitchen: Gender and De-Stalinization of Consumer Taste in the Soviet Union under Khrushchev." *Slavic Review* 61, no. 2 (2002): 211–252.

Reid, Susan E., and David Crowley, eds. *Style and Socialism: Modernity and Material Culture in Post-War Eastern Europe*. Oxford: Oxford University Press, 2000.

Reinkowski, Maurus, and Gregor Thum, eds. *Helpless Imperialists: Imperial Failure, Fear and Radicalization*. Göttingen: Vandenhoeck und Ruprecht, 2013.

Repishti, Sami. *Nën hijen e Rozafës: Narrativë e jetueme* [Under the shadow of Rozafa: A lived story]. Tirana: Onufri, 2004.

Rhodes, James. "Youngstown's 'Ghost'? Memory, Identity, and Deindustrialization." *International Labor and Working-Class History*, 84 (2013): 55–77.

Ribot, Jesse C., and Nancy Lee Peluso. "A Theory of Access." *Rural Sociology* 68, no. 2 (2013): 153–181.

Bibliography

Richter, Ralph. "Industrial Heritage in Urban Imaginaries and City Images: A Comparison between Dortmund and Glasgow." *The Public Historian* 39, no. 4 (2017): 65–84.

Rieber, Alfred J. "Colonizing Eurasia." In *Peopling the Russian Periphery: Borderland Colonization in Eurasian History*, edited by Nicholas Breyfogle, Abby Schrader, and Willard Sunderland, 265–280. London: Routledge, 2009.

Riesman, David. "The Nylon War." In *Abundance for What? And Other Essays*. New York: Doubleday & Co. 1964.

Roberts, Neil and Jane Reed. "Lakes, Wetlands, and Holocene Environmental Change." In *The Physical Geography of the Mediterranean*, edited by Jamie Woodward, 255–286. Oxford: Oxford University Press, 2009.

Roger, Antoine. "'Romanian Peasants' into 'European Farmers'? Using Statistics to Standardize Agriculture." *Development and Change* 45, no. 4 (2014): 732–752.

Rognes, Jørn, and Per Kåre Sky. "Mediation in the Norwegian Land Consolidation Courts." Working Paper 14, North America Series, Land Tenure Centre. Madison, WI: University of Wisconsin-Madison, 1998.

Romijn, Peter, Giles Scott-Smith, and Joes Segal, eds. *Divided Dreamworlds? The Cultural Cold War in East and West*. Amsterdam: Amsterdam University Press, 2012.

Rose, Nikolas, Pat O'Malley, and Mariana Valeverde. "Governmentality." *Annual Review of Law and Social Science* 2 (2006): 83–104.

Roselli, Alessandro. *Italy and Albania: Financial Relations in the Fascist Period*. London: I. B. Tauris, 2006.

Roucek, Joseph S. *Balkan Politics: International Relations in No Man's Land*. Stanford, CA: Stanford University Press, 1948.

Ruder, Cynthia A. *Building Stalinism: The Moscow Canal and the Creation of the Soviet Space*. London: I. B. Tauris, 2018.

Ruder, Cynthia A. *Making History for Stalin: The Story of Belomor Canal*. Gainsville, FL: University Press of Florida, 1998.

Rugg, Dean S. "Communist Legacies in the Albanian Landscape." *Geographical Review* 84, no. 1 (1994), 59–73.

Rusi, Deko, and Zyhdi Pepa. *Mbi zgjidhjen komplekse të ndërtimit të socializmit në fshat në RPS të Shqipërisë* [On the complex solution of the socialist construction in the countryside]. Tirana: Universiteti i Tiranës "Enver Hoxha," 1986.

Rusi, Deko. *Transformimi socialist i Bujqësisë së RPSh* [The socialist transformation of agriculture in the People's Republic of Albania]. Tirana: Universiteti Shtetëror i Tiranës, 1962.

Saba, Andrea Filippo, ed. *Angelo Omodeo. Vita, progetti, opere per la modernizzazione. Una raccolta di scritti*. Roma-Bari: Laterza, 2005.

Sabel, Charles. *Works and Politics: The Division of Labor in Industry*. Cambridge: Cambridge University Press, 1982.

Sachs, Jeffrey D. "Crossing the Valley of Tears in East European Reform." *Challenge* 34, no. 5 (1991): 26–31.

Salleo, Ferdinando. *Albania. Un regno per sei mesi*. Palermo: Sellerio Editore, 2000.

Samuelson, Lennart. *Tankograd: The Formation of a Soviet Company Town: Cheliabinsk, 1900s-1950s*. London: Palgrave Macmillan, 2011.

Sanjust, Paolo. "Le città di fondazione del periodo fascista in Sardegna." In *Atlante delle città fondate in Italia dal tardomedioevo al Novecento. Italia centro-meridionale e insulare*, edited by Aldo Casamento. Bologna: Kappa, 2013.

Scaini, Maurizio. "Utopia and Fascist Foundation Cities. The Case of Torviscosa." *Dada* 1 (2012): 301–324.

Schivelbusch, Wolfgang. *Tastes of Paradise: A Social History of Spices, Stimulants, and Intoxicants*. Translated by David Jacobson. New York: Pantheon Books, 1992.

Schivelbusch, Wolfgang. *Three New Deals: Reflections on Roosevelt's America, Mussolini's Italy, and Hitler's Germany, 1933–1939*. Translated by Jefferson Chase. New York: Metropolitan Books, 2006.

Schmitt, Carl. *The Concept of the Political*. Translated by George Schwab. Chicago: University of Chicago Press, 2007.

Schmitt, Oliver Jens. *Shqiptarët: Një histori midis Lindjes dhe Perëndimit*. Translated by Ardian Klosi. Tiranë: T & K, 2012.

Schönle, Andreas. "Ruins and History: Observations on Russian Approaches to Destruction and Decay." *Slavic Review* 65, no, 4 (2006): 649–669.

Schumpeter, Joseph. *Capitalism, Socialism and Democracy*. London: Routledge, 2003.

Schnytzer, Adi. *Stalinist Economic Strategy in Practice: The Case of Albania*. Oxford: Oxford University Press, 1982.

Schwander-Sievers, Stephanie, and Bernd J. Fischer, eds. *Albanian Identities: Myth and History*. Bloomington, IN: Indiana University Press, 2002.

Scott, James C. *Domination and the Arts of Resistance: Hidden Transcripts*. New Haven, CT: Yale University Press, 1990.

Scott, James C. "Hegemony and the Peasantry." *Politics and Society* 7, no. 3 (1977): 267–296.

Scott, James C. "Protest and Profanation: Agrarian Revolt and the Little Tradition. Part I." *Theory and Society* 4, no. 1 (1977), 1–38.

Scott, James C. "Protest and Profanation: Agrarian Revolt and the Little Tradition. Part II." *Theory and Society* 4, no. 2 (1977): 211–246.

Scott, James C. "Revolution in the Revolution: Peasants and Commissars." *Theory and Society* 7, nos. 1/2 (1979): 97–134.

Scott, James C. *Seeing Like a State: How Certain Schemes to Improve Human Condition Have Failed*. New Haven, CT: Yale University Press, 1998.

Scott, James C. *The Moral Economy of the Peasant: Rebellion and Subsistence in Southeast Asia*. New Haven, CT: Yale University Press, 1976.

Scott, James C. *Weapons of the Weak: Everyday Forms of Peasant Resistance*. New Haven, CT: Yale University Press, 1985.

Scott, Joan W. "The Evidence of Experience." *Critical Inquiry* 17, no. 4 (1991): 773–797.

Segel, Harold B., ed. *The Walls behind the Curtain: East European Prison Literature, 1945–1990*. Pittsburgh, PA: University of Pittsburgh Press, 2012.

Sharafutdinova, Gulnaz. "Was There a 'Simple Soviet' Person? Debating the Politics and Sociology of 'Homo Sovieticus'." *Slavic Review* 78, no. 1 (2019): 173–195.

Shkurti, Spiro. "Sprovë për klasifikimin e parmendave shqiptare" [Essay for the classification of Albanian plows]. *Etnografia Shqiptare* [Albanian ethnography] 13 (1983): 101–139.

Bibliography

Shpuza, Gazmend. *Kryengritja Fshatare e Shqipërisë së Mesme, 1914–1915* [The peasant uprising of Central Albania, 1914–1915]. Tirana: Akademia e Shkencave e RPS të Shqpërisë, 1986.

Sikor, Thomas, and Christian Lund. "Access to Property: A Question of Power and Authority." *Development and Change* 40, no. 1 (2009): 1–22.

Sikor, Thomas, Daniel Müller, and Johannes Stahl. "Land Fragmentation and Cropland Abandonment in Albania: Implications for the Roles of State and Community in Post-Socialist Land Consolidation." *World Development* 37, no. 8 (2009): 1411–1423.

Silajdzic, Haris. *Shqipëria dhe ShBA në arkivat e Uashingtonit* [Albania and the USA in the Washington Archives]. Translated by Xhelal Fejza. Tirana: Dituria, 1999.

Simmel, Georg. "Two Essays: The Handle, and The Ruin." Translated by David Kettler. *Hudson Review* 11, no. 3 (1958): 379–385.

Simpson, Brad. "Indonesia's 'Accelerated Modernization' and the Global Discourse of Development, 1960–1975." *Diplomatic History* 33, no. 3 (2009): 467–486.

Sjöberg, Örjan. "'Any Other Road Leads Only to the Restoration of Capitalism in the Countryside': Land Collectivization in Albania." In *The Collectivization of Agriculture in Communist Eastern Europe: Comparison and Entanglements*, edited by Constantin Iordachi and Arnd Bauerkämper, 369–397. Budapest-New York: CEU Press, 2014.

Sjöberg, Örjan. *Rural Change and Development in Albania*. Boulder, CO: Westview Press, 1991.

Sjöberg, Örjan. "Rural Retention in Albania: Administrative Restrictions on Urban-Bound Migration." *East European Quarterly* 28, no. 2 (1994): 205–234.

Sjöberg, Örjan, and Michael L. Wyzan, eds. *Economic Change in the Balkan States: Albania, Bulgaria, Romania and Yugoslavia*. London: Pinter Publishers, 1991.

Smardon, Richard C. *Sustaining the World's Wetlands: Setting Policy and Resolving Conflicts*. New York: Springer, 2009.

Smith, Neil. *Uneven Development: Nature, Capital, and the Production of Space*. Athens, GA: University of Georgia Press, 1990.

Snowden, Frank M. *The Conquest of Malaria: Italy, 1900–1962*. New Haven, CT: Yale University Press, 2006.

Soja, Edward W. "The Spatiality of Social Life: Toward a Transformative Retheorisation." In *Social Relations and Spatial Structures*, edited by Derek Gregory and John Urry, 90–127. London: Macmillan, 1985.

Sorensen, Diana. "Alternative Geographic Mappings for the Twenty-First Century." In *Territories and Trajectories: Cultures in Circulation*, edited by Diana Sorensen, 13–31. Durham-London: Duke University Press, 2018.

Sowerwine, Jennifer C. "Territorialization and the Politics of Highland Landscapes in Vietnam: Negotiating Property Relations in Policy, Meaning and Practice." *Conservation and Society* 2, no. 1 (2004): 97–136.

Speich, Daniel. "The Kenyan Style of 'African Socialism': Developmental Knowledge Claims and the Explanatory Limits of the Cold War." *Diplomatic History* 33, no. 3 (2009): 449–466.

Stahl, Johannes. *Rent from the Land: A Political Ecology of Postsocialist Rural Transformation*. London: Anthem Press, 2010.

Bibliography

Starr, S. Frederick. "Visionary Town Planning during the Cultural Revolution." In *Cultural Revolution in Russia, 1928–1931*, edited by Sheila Fitzpatrick, 207–240. Bloomington, IN: Indiana University Press, 1978.

Steele, Jonathan. "Xenophobic Albania is Not Likely to Change," *The New York Times*. May 18, 1975, E3.

Stewart-Steinberg, Suzanne. "Grounds for Reclamation: Fascism and Postfascism in the Pontine Marshes." *Differences: A Journal of Feminist Cultural Studies* 27, no. 1 (2016): 94–142.

Stites, Richard. *Revolutionary Dreams: Utopian Vision and Experimental Life in the Russian Revolution*. Oxford: Oxford University Press, 1989.

Stoll, Steven. *The Fruits of Natural Advantage: Making the Industrial Countryside in California*. Berkeley, CA: University of California Press, 1998.

Strangleman, Tim, James Rhodes, and Sherry Linkon. "Introduction to Crumbling Cultures: Deindustrialization, Class, and Memory." *International Labor and Working-Class History* 84 (2013): 7–22.

Strangleman, Tim. "'Smokestack Nostalgia,' 'Ruin Porn' or Working-Class Obituary: The Role and Meaning of Deindustrial Representation." *International Labor and Working-Class History* 84 (2013): 23–37.

Sufian, Sandra M. *Healing the Land and the Nation: Malaria and the Zionist Project in Palestine, 1920–1947*. Chicago: The University of Chicago Press, 2007.

Sulstarova, Enis. *Arratisje nga lindja: orientalizmi shqiptar nga Naimi te Kadareja* [Escaping from the Orient: Albanian Orientalism from Naim Frashëri to Ismail Kadare]. Tirana: Dudaj, 2006.

Swain, Nigel. "Eastern European Collectivization Campaigns Compared, 1945–1962." In *The Collectivization of Agriculture in Communist Eastern Europe: Comparison and Entanglements*, edited by Constantin Iordachi and Arnd Bauerkämper, 497–534. Budapest: CEU Press, 2014.

Swire, Joseph. *Albania: The Rise of a Kingdom*. New York: Abe Book, 1971.

Swyngedouw, Erik. "Modernity and Hybridity: Nature, *Regeneracionismo*, and the Production of the Spanish Waterscape." *Annals of the Association of American Geographers* 89, no. 3 (1999): 443–465.

Swyngedouw, Erik. "Technonatural Revolutions: The Scalar Politics of Franco's Hydro-Social Dream for Spain, 1939–1975." *Transactions of the Institute of British Geographers* 32, no. 1 (2007): 9–28.

Szelényi, Iván. *Socialist Entrepreneurs: Embourgeoisement in Rural Hungary*. Madison, WI: University of Wisconsin Press, 1988.

Szelényi, Ivan. "The Rise and Fall of the Second Bildungsbürgertum." In *Cores, Peripheries, and Globalization: Essays in Honor of Ivan T. Berend*, edited by Peter Hanns Reil and Balázs Szelényi, 166–178. Budapest: CEU Press, 2011.

Szporluk, Roman. *Communism and Nationalism: Karl Marx versus Friedrich List*. Oxford: Oxford University Press, 1988.

Tabak, Faruk. "Economic and Ecological Change in the Eastern Mediterranean, c. 1550–1850." In *Cities of the Mediterranean: From the Ottomans to the Present Day*, edited by Biray Kolluoğlu and Meltem Toksöz, 23–37. London: I. B. Taurus, 2010.

Bibliography

Taylor, Charles. "Two Theories of Modernity." In *Alternative Modernities*, edited by Dilip Parameshwar Gaonkar, 172–196. Durham, NC: Duke University Press, 2001.

Ther, Philipp. "Comparison, Cultural Transfers, and the Study of Networks: Towards a Transnational History of Europe." In *Comparative and Transnational History: Central European Approaches and New Perspectives*, edited by Heinz-Gerhard Haupt and Jürgen Kocka, 204–225. New York: Berghahn Books, 2012.

Ther, Philipp. *Europe since 1989: A History*. Translated by Charlotte Hughes-Kreutzmüller. Princeton, NJ: Princeton University Press, 2016.

Thëngjilli, Petrika. *Historia e popullit shqiptar, 395–1831* [The history of the Albanian people, 395–1831]. Tirana: Toena, 2004.

Thomo, Pirro. *Korça: urbanistika dhe arkitektura* [Korça: Urban planning and architecture]. Tirana: Akademia e Shkencave të Shqipërisë, 2002.

Thompson, Edward P. "The Moral Economy of the English Crowd in the Eighteenth Century." *Past & Present* 50, no. 1 (1971): 76–136.

Thompson, Edward P. "The Moral Economy Reviewed," In *Customs in Common*. London: Penguin Books, 1993.

Thornes, John. "Land Degradation." In *The Physical Geography of the Mediterranean*, edited by Jamie Woodward, 563–582. Oxford: Oxford University Press, 2009.

Thum, Gregor. "Seapower and Frontier Settlement: Friedrich List's American Vision for Germany." In *German and United States Colonialism in a Connected World: Entangled Empires*, edited by Janne Lahti, 17–39. London: Palgrave Macmillan, 2021.

Thum, Gregor. *Uprooted: How Breslau Became Wrocław during the Century of Expulsions*. Translated by Tom Lampert and Allison Brown. Wrocław: Via Nova, 2011.

Tiganea, Oana. "Modern Industrial Heritage in Romania: Extending the Boundaries to Protect the Recent Past." *Docomomo* 49 (2013): 82–85.

Tilly, Charles. *Big Structures, Large Processes, Huge Comparisons*. New York: Russell Sage Foundation, 1984.

To, Phuc Xuan. "State Territorialization and Illegal Logging: The Dynamic Relationships between Practices and Images of the State in Vietnam." *Critical Asian Studies* 47, no. 2 (2015): 229–252.

Todorova, Maria. *Imagining the Balkans*. Oxford: Oxford University Press, 2009.

Todorova, Maria. "The Trap of Backwardness: Modernity, Temporality, and the Study of Eastern European Nationalism." *Slavic Review* 64, no. 1 (2005): 161.

Todorova, Maria, ed. *Balkan Identities: Nation and Memory*. New York: New York University Press, 2004.

Trentin, Massimiliano. "Modernization as State Building: The Two Germanies in Syria, 1963–1972." *Diplomatic History* 33, no. 3 (2009): 487–505.

Unger, Corinna. "Histories of Development and Modernization: Findings, Reflections, Future Research." H-Soz-Kult, 09.12.2010, www.hsozkult.de/literaturereview/id/forschungsberichte-1130.

Urry, John. "Social Relations, Space and Time." In *Social Relations and Spatial Structures*, edited by Derek Gregory and John Urry, 20–48. London: Macmillan, 1985.

Vandergeest, Peter, and Nancy Lee Peluso. "Territorialization and State Power in Thailand." *Theory and Society* 24, no. 3 (1995): 385–426.

Bibliography

Van Dijk, Terry. "Complications for Traditional Land Consolidation in Central Europe." *Geoforum* 38, no. 3 (2007): 505–511.

Van Hardeveld, H. A., P. P. J. Driessen, P. P. Schot, and M. J. Wassen. "Supporting collaborative policy process with a multi-criteria discussion of costs and benefits: The case of soil subsidence in Dutch peatlands." *Land Use Policy* 77 (2018): 425–436.

Veracini, Lorenzo. "Italian Colonialism through the Settler Colonial Lens." *Journal of Colonialism and Colonial History* 19, no. 3 (2018): no page numbers.

Verdery, Katherine, and Gail Kligman. *Peasants under Siege: The Collectivization of Romanian Agriculture, 1949–1962*. Princeton, NJ: Princeton University Press, 2011.

Verdery, Katherine. *The Vanishing Hectare: Property and Value in Postsocialist Transylvania*. Ithaca, NY: Cornell University Press, 2003.

Verdery, Katherine. *National Ideology under Socialism: Identity and Cultural Politics in Ceaușescu's Romania*. Berkeley, CA: University of California Press, 1991.

Vickers, Miranda. *The Albanians: A Modern History*. London: I. B. Tauris, 2001.

Viola, Lynne. *Peasant Rebels under Stalin: Collectivization and the Culture of Peasant Resistance*. Oxford: Oxford University Press, 1996.

Viola, Lynne. *The Best Sons of the Fatherland: Workers in the Vanguard of Collectivization*. Oxford: Oxford University Press, 1989.

Visi, Ligor. "Ndërmarrja Bujqësore e Maliqit, ekonomi e madhe e prodhimit socialist." In *Konferenca kombëtare për problemet e ndërtimit socialist*, 269–278. Tirana: Akademia e Shkencave e RPSSH, 1979.

Volkov, Vadim. "The Concept of *Kul'turnost'*: Notes on the Stalinist Civilizing Process," *Stalinism: New Directions*, edited by Sheila Fitzpatrick, 210–230. London: Routledge, 2000.

Von Eschen, Penny. "Locating the Transnational in the Cold War." in *The Oxford Handbook of the Cold War*, edited by Richard H. Immerman and Petra Goedde, 451–468. Oxford: Oxford University Press, 2013.

Wagner, Bernd, André F. Lotter, Norbert Nowaczyk, Jane M. Reed, Antje Schwalb, Roberto Sulpizio, Veruschka Valsecchi et al. "A 40,000-year record of environmental change from ancient Lake Ohrid (Albania and Macedonia)." *Journal of Paleolimnology* 41 (2009): 407–430.

Wallerstein, Immanuel. *World-Systems Analysis: An Introduction*. Durham and London: Duke University Press, 2004.

Weber, Eugene. *Peasants into Frenchmen: The Modernization of Rural France, 1870–1914*. Stanford, CA: Stanford University Press, 1976.

Weiner, Amir. "Nature, Nurture, and Memory in a Socialist Utopia: Delineating the Socio-Ethnic Body in the Age of Socialism." *The American Historical Review* 104, no. 4 (1999): 1114–1155.

Weiner, Annette B. *Inalienable Possessions: The Paradox of Keeping-While-Giving*. Berkeley, CA: University of California Press, 1992.

Weitz, Eric D. "Racial Politics without the Concept of Race: Reevaluating Soviet Ethnic and National Purges." *Slavic Reviews* 61, no. 1 (2002): 1–29.

Werner, Michael, and Bénédicte Zimmermann. "Beyond Comparison: *Histoire Croisée* and the Challenge of Reflexivity." *History and Theory* 45, no. 1 (2006): 30–50.

Bibliography

White, Anne. *Small-Town Russia. Postcommunist Livelihoods and Identities: A portrait of the Intelligentsia in Achit, Bednodemyanovks and Zubstov, 1999–2000*. London: Routledge, 2003.

Winiecki, Jan. "Eastern Europe: Challenge of 1992 Dwarfed by Pressures of Systems Decline." *Außenwirtschaft* 44, nos. 3/4 (1989): 345–365.

Winiecki, Jan. "Soviet-type Economies' Strategy for Catching-up through Technology Import—an Anatomy of Failure." *Technovation* 6, no. 2 (1987): 115–145.

Witowski, Gregory R. "Collectivization at the Grassroots Level: State Planning and Popular Reactions in Bulgaria, Romania, Poland, and the GDR, 1948–1960." In *The Collectivization of Agriculture in Communist Eastern Europe: Comparison and Entanglements*, edited by Constantin Iordachi and Arnd Bauerkämper, 467–496. Budapest: CEU Press, 2014.

Witowski, Gregory R. "On the Campaign Trail: State Planning and Eigen-Sinn in a Communist Campaign to Transform the East German Countryside." *Central European History* 37, no. 3 (2004): 400–422.

Wittfogel, Karl A. *Oriental Despotism: A Comparative Study of Total Power*. New Haven, CT: Yale University Press, 1957.

Wittrock, Björn. "Modernity: One, None, or Many? European Origins and Modernity as a Global Condition." *Daedalus* 129, no. 1 (2000): 31–60.

Wolff, Larry. *Inventing Eastern Europe: The Map of Civilization on the Mind of the Enlightenment*. Stanford, CA: Stanford University Press, 1994.

Woodcock, Shannon, *Life is War: Surviving Dictatorship in Communist Albania*. Bristol, UK: HammerOn Press, 2016.

Wright, Donald R. *The World and a Very Small Place in Africa: A History of Globalization in Niumi, the Gambia*. New York: M. E. Sharpe, 1997.

Yergin, Angela Stent. *East-West Technology Transfer: European Perspectives*. London: SAGE Publications, 1980.

Zaleski, Eugene, and Helgard Wienert. *Technology Transfer between East and West*. Paris: OECD, 1980.

Zanello, Francesca, Pietro Teatini, Mario Putii, and Giuseppe Gambolati. "Long term peatland subsidence: Experience study and modelling scenarios in the Venice coastland." *Journal of Geophysical Studies* 116, F4 (2011): 1–14.

Index

Adriatic, 2, 16, 32–33, 35–36, 60–61, 196, 212, 237
Africa, 60–61, 72, 127
African empire, 57
Agolli, Dritëro, 111
Akarmara, 196
Albania/Albanians 1, 4, 6, 10–11, 13–16, 18–22, 31–36, 39, 41–45, 47–48, 56–65, 67, 70, 73–74, 79, 84–85, 93–94, 97–108, 111, 114–119, 127, 132, 143–144, 149, 153–155, 157–159, 161, 166–172, 174–179, 182–188, 191–193, 195–196, 199, 205–207, 211–212, 214–215, 217, 228–229, 231–233, 235, 237–238, 240, 245
Albanian Communist Party (see also, ACP), 5–6, 65, 73, 113
Albanian Labor Party (see also, ALP), 65, 67–68, 73, 80, 84, 88–90, 93, 95, 97–102, 107–108, 110, 113–115, 119, 123–124, 127, 134, 137–141, 144–148, 154, 156, 158–160, 164, 168, 170–172, 175–176, 179, 182–183, 185–186, 188–189, 191–192, 208, 211, 215–216, 220, 229, 232, 237, 239–241, 243–244
Alexander, Catherine, 93
Algeria, 154–155
Allen, Robert, 207
Alykel, 196
Amadei, Pompeo, 45–46, 48, 59
Americanism, 17
Anadyr, 196
Anatolia, 35
Andela, Gertruda, 105
Anderson, Benedict, 97
AninaNoua, 196

Ankara, 176,
Apennine Peninsula, 175, 237
Apollonian, 68
Arabic, 24, 53
Arapi, Hekuran, 165
Armée d'Orient, 33–34,
Asia, 12, 16, 60, 78, 114, 154, 176
Ataturk, Mustafa Kemal, 176
Austria (see also, Austro-Hungary), 31–33, 35, 60, 76, 174–175, 226

Balkans, 8, 12–16, 18–20, 26, 31–33, 35–36, 45, 60–61, 72, 105, 113, 159, 163, 167, 170–172, 193, 232
Ballsh, 196
Baltic Sea, 72, 111, 126, 211–212,
Balzac, Honoré de, 180
Barzak, Christopher, 197
Bauman, Zygmunt, 58
Beck, Ulrich, 229
Begolli, Vera, 225, 231
Beijing, 171, 206
Belgium/Belgian, 153, 174–176
Belgrade, 160
Ben Bella, Ahmed, 155,
Benjamin, Walter, 97, 197–198, 233
Bilisht, 88
Bitola (see also, Monastir), 25, 31
Blloku, 110, 111
Blue Banana, 233
Brad, 196
Brazil, 211, 244
Brown, Kate, 116
Breslau/Wrocław, 15–16, 85, 126
British, 9, 60, 180, 198, 235, 244
Budapest, 72

287

Index

Bulgaria/Bulgarian, 15, 31, 167, 174, 184, 210
Bulgarian Empire, 3
Buzzati, Dino, 84
Byzantine Empire, 3, 232

Cahora Bassa dam, 72
Cangonj (pass of), 2
Carpathian Mountains, 233
Catholic/Catholicism, 175, 232
Caucasus/Caucasian, 154
Central Eastern Europe/Central Europe, 15, 25, 59, 72, 168, 178, 196
Central Powers, 32
Cërrik, 196
Chelyabinsk, 73, 119
China/Chinese, 171–174, 206, 210, 238
Christianity, 3, 7, 23–26, 126, 229, 237
Ciano, Galeazzo (see also Count Ciano), 60
Clark, Katerina, 95
Cohen, Yves, 182
Cold War, 9, 15, 19, 76, 95, 103, 155–159, 177, 179, 182, 193, 237, 241
Columbia, 211
COMECON (the Council of Mutual Economic Assistance), 79, 167
Conference of Ambassadors in London (1912–1913), 31
Constantine (King of Greece), 33
Cooper, Frederick, 223
Cowie, Jefferson, 209
Croatian, 76
Crowley, David, 171
Crowley, Stephen, 224
Cuba, 153, 184
Czech Republic, 217, 234
Czechoslovakia/Czechoslovak, 43–44, 72, 83, 153, 167–169, 174–175
Çërrava (hills of), 2

Dahrendorf, Ralf, 223
Dali, Salvador, 233
De Cauter, Lieven, 111

Dehaene, Michiel, 111
Denmark/Danish, 169, 176, 212
Devoll (basin/plateau), 2, 161
Devoll (river), 2, 24, 27, 36–37, 56, 77, 80, 195, 208, 223
Dionysian, 68
Djilas, Milovan, 110, 141
Dragostinova, Theodora, 14–15
Drithas, 124
Dry Mountain, 1–2
Du Bois, William E. B., 178
Dunavec (river), 63, 77
Dunham, Vera, 115

East Berlin, 72
Eastern Europe/Eastern European, 11–12, 14, 16–21, 36, 44–45, 61, 69, 72–73, 79, 95, 100, 109, 128, 132, 156–157, 171–172, 197, 199, 210–217, 220, 224, 230–232, 234–235, 240
East Germany/GDR, 17–18, 72, 79, 95, 100–111, 128, 132, 153, 168, 172, 174, 196, 199, 213, 215, 217, 224–226, 231, 240
Edensor, Tim, 223
Eisenhüttenstadt, 72
Egypt, 27, 29, 49, 61
Elsterberg, 196
Eneolithic, 3
Engerman, David, 155
England, 29, 61, 233
Entente Cordiale, 32
Estonia, 105
Etges, Andreas, 41–42
Ethiopians, 61
Evangjeli, Pandeli, 51
Europe, 3, 7, 10–12, 19, 21, 29–30, 34, 44, 46, 53, 57, 58–59, 68, 71, 76, 85, 103, 105–106, 153, 158, 171, 176–179, 184, 193, 198, 210, 212, 230, 237, 241, 245
European Community/EC, 177, 219
European Union/EU, 211, 219–220, 234
Europeanization, 231
European Concert, 31–32, 35

Index

Fascism/fascist, 30, 45, 57–63, 68, 70–72, 105, 117, 119, 162, 210
First Balkan War, 31
Fitzpatrick, Sheila, 115, 143
FAO (Food and Agriculture Organization), 222
Foucault, Michel, 87, 234, 242
France, 29, 33–35, 38–39, 47–48, 60–61, 63, 73, 96, 104, 108, 153, 169, 175–176, 180, 212, 234
Franco, Francisco, 58, 71
Frank, Andre Gunder, 115
Frashëri, Maliq, 53
Frashëri, Mehdi, 47

Germany/German, 5, 29, 31–33, 37, 60–61, 65, 72, 85–86, 104, 173, 176, 198, 210, 212–213, 225, 227, 234
Giddens, Anthony, 98
Global South, 154
Goçë, 208
Godart, Justin, 38
Goffman, Erving, 110
Goloborodko, Alexey Mikhailovich, 163
Gora (highland of), 1–2, 4, 24, 147, 149, 208
Gramsh, 147, 196
Great Britain, 60, 184, 213
Greco-Italian War, 65
Greece/Greeks, 25, 31–33, 35, 49, 71, 105, 126, 155, 170, 173–175, 184, 215, 222, 234
Gregory the Great, 237
Gross, Jan, 141, 210
Grove of Pheasants, 109, 110–111

Habsburg, 31–33, 60
Hamhŭng 153–154
Harley, John B. 111
Hawthorne, Nathaniel 223
Heathcott, Joseph 209
Herschel, Tassilo 213
High, Steven 225
Hobsbawm, Eric 14

Holquist, Peter 73
Hollywood 239
Holstein, Diego 210
Hoover Dam 109
Horváth, Sándor 116
Hoxha, Enver 11, 34, 80, 88, 91, 100, 102, 107, 111, 119, 122, 153, 155–156, 161, 165, 176, 179, 181, 190–191, 232
Hoxha, Ferasete 244–245
Hugo, Victor, 222
Hungary/Hungarian, 31, 33, 35, 39, 61, 72, 129, 153, 168, 184, 212

Illyrian Kingdom, 3
Indonesia, 154
Iron Curtain, 11, 21, 68, 103, 105, 108, 154, 157, 211, 237, 238
Islam/Islamization, 3, 23, 24
Istanbul, 24–25, 26, 30
Italy/Italian, 31–35, 42, 45, 46, 57, 58, 61, 63–65, 68, 71, 119, 155, 169–170, 174–175, 184, 210, 212, 215, 234, 237–238, 239

Jackson, Marvin, 159
Jakova, Tuk, 88, 102,
Japan/Japanese, 153, 174, 230
Jura, 68, 71
Jews, 25

Kadykchan, 196
Kalinovsky, Artemy, 16
Kamchatka, 196
Kapo, Hysni, 88, 90, 124, 170
Kenya, 154
Keynesianism, 104
Këllëzi, Abdyl, 107
Khrushchev, Nikita, 154, 167
Klee, Paul, 195, 197
Koleka, Spiro, 71, 87
Kopytoff, Igo,r 151
Korça (city), 1, 4, 7, 8, 15, 17, 21, 23, 25–26, 27, 30–31, 33–36, 39–40, 45, 48, 51–52, 63–65, 70, 76, 80, 84, 88–89, 92, 99,

289

Index

106, 126, 128, 130, 132–134, 136–137, 139–140, 142–144, 146–148, 160–164, 174, 176, 179, 195, 199, 205, 207, 219–220, 222

Korça (district), 23, 25, 32–33, 41–42, 118, 130, 166, 206, 229, 236, 245

Korça (plain/plateau), 1, 2, 23, 24, 26, 27, 37–38, 42, 48, 63, 64, 108, 137–138, 142, 160, 208

Kotkin, Stephen, 17, 141, 210, 242–243

Kotta, Kostandin, 51

Kremlin, 154

Kukës, 196

Kutrzeba-Pojnarowa, Anna, 143

Kühschelm, Oliver, 236

Lampe, John R., 13, 159

Latin America, 212, 214

Latvia, 212

League of Nations, 47

Lefebvre, Henri, 96, 99, 115, 235

Lenin, Vladimir Ilyich, 145, 156, 159, 180, 189, 210

Leshnicë, 54

Lewin, Moshe, 242

Libya/Libyans, 61

Lithuania, 212

Littoria, 57–59

London, 31–32, 34–35,

Lorenzetti, Ambrogio, 67–68, 112

Lorenzoni, Giovanni, 63,

Low Countries, 234

Macedonian Kingdom, 3

Macedonia (region of Greece), 71

Mahmood II (Ottoman Sultan), 34

Magnitogorsk, 17, 119, 242

Maliq (gorge), 6, 24, 33, 36, 56, 128,

Maliq (factory), 68, 93, 98, 139, 162, 199, 203–204, 206, 215

Maliq (plain), 1, 2, 6, 7, 16–17, 23, 39–40, 47, 49, 56–57, 63, 65, 68, 70, 74, 77–81, 83–86, 88–90, 93–94, 97–99, 102, 106, 108–112, 125–126, 129, 130–131, 136–137, 140, 146, 147, 149, 174–175, 178–179, 182–183, 201–202, 208, 218–219, 220, 222, 226–227, 245

Maliq (landscape), 67–68, 85, 103, 106, 107, 109

Maliq (project), 6, 10, 16, 20, 42, 82, 98, 102, 104, 109, 114–115, 119, 156, 158, 209, 240–241,

Maliq (refinery), 19, 86, 94, 114, 119, 127, 161, 195–197, 211, 219–221, 232

Maliq (scheme), 16, 20–22, 35, 57, 60, 62, 86, 114, 216, 220, 240, 244,

Maliqi (state farm), 117, 130, 167,

Maliq (sugar combine), 114, 129, 149, 173–176, 178, 184, 187, 200, 216, 221, 225

Maliq (swamp), 2, 6, 16, 21–22, 27–28, 30, 37–38, 45–48, 59, 65, 68, 70–71, 73–79, 82, 95, 117, 121, 224, 227

Maliq (town), 1, 3, 4–6, 8–9, 10, 21–22, 40–41, 69–70, 73–74, 76, 85–86, 92, 96, 99, 106, 116–117, 119, 122–123, 126–127, 138–142, 149, 151–158, 162–168, 171, 180–181, 185, 191, 193, 195–196, 206, 211, 215, 219–225, 227–231, 233, 236, 239–240, 243–246

Maliq (village), 2, 6, 7, 8, 9, 15–17, 19–20, 21, 24, 46, 48, 53–54, 65, 78–79, 85, 89, 99, 132, 136, 138, 148, 150, 161, 167–168

Maliqi Company, 38–39, 42, 48–58, 62, 64, 241

Martinez, Adolfo, 237

Marx, Karl, 98, 189–190, 209

Masllavica, 17

Massey, Doreen, 9

Mazower, Mark, 13

Mediterranean, 2, 25, 28, 78, 153

Melvin, Neil, 129

Memaliaj, 196

Mesolithic, 3

Mëhilli, Elidor, 14

Middle Ages, 109, 111

Middle East, 154–155,

Midwest (American), 68

Mihali, Ana, 237

Index

Milot, 196,
Mohammed, 228
Mokra (highland), 4
Molotov, Vyacheslav, 161
Monastir (vilayet of), 25–26, 31
Montenegro, 31–33,
Moore Jr., Barrington, 73
Morava (mountain), 2, 23
Moscow, 16, 18, 21, 153–154, 156, 161, 163–164, 167–169, 209, 224
Moscow Canal, 72, 109
Moss, Ron, 237
Mouzelis, Nicos, 13
Mozambique, 72
MTV (Music Television), 244
Musaraj, Smoki, 231
Muslim, 7, 24–26, 126, 154
Mussolini, Benito (see also, Il Duce), 46, 57–62, 70–71, 159
Myftiu, Manush, 114, 149

Naçi, Aneta, 237
Nasser, Gamal Abdel, 155
NATO (North Atlantic Treaty Organization), 170, 175
Nehru, Jawaharlal, 155
neolithic, 3
Netherlands/Dutch, 68, 104–105, 153, 169
Neuburger, Mary, 15
Nistri, Pierfrancesco, 63
Nkrumah, Kwame, 155
Norilsk, 196
North Americ,a 12, 197, 228
North Korea/North Korean, 153
North Macedonia (Republic of), 1, 25–26
North Sea, 211
Novoselë, 90
Nowa Huta, 72, 73, 119, 16
Nurekh (dam), 16

Ohio, 197
Ohrid (lake), 1–2, 164
Omodeo, Angelo, 56–57, 73, 78, 80
Opar (highland of), 2, 147

Orientalism/Orientalist, 11, 13, 34, 113, 170–171, 221
Orman Pojan, 132
Orthodox Christianity/Christians, 7, 23–26, 126, 228, 237
Ostrava-Poruba, 72
Otranto (strait of), 31
Ottoman Empire (see also, Sublime Porte), 25, 30, 35, 42, 48, 155
Ozersk, 73, 116

Panama, 211
Panama Canal, 109
Paris, 34–35, 47
Patos, 196
Peluso, Nancy, 87
Pennacchi, Antonio, 119
Pennsylvania, 230
Pernik, 196
Peshkëp,i 23
Pet Shop Boys, 244
Péteri, György, 172, 190
Petrilia, 196
Pindus Mountains, 1
Pirg, 54, 140
Pittsburgh, 230
Plasa, 108,
Plasa, Llazar, 176, 207
Pliocene, 1
Pojan, 108, 132
Pojani, Emin, 52
Poland/Polish, 16, 72–73, 85–86, 108, 153, 173, 168, 174–175, 184, 212, 234
Poliçan, 196
Pontine Marshes, 57–59, 70
Portugal, 159, 212, 234
Prague, 72
Preobrazhensky, Yevgeny, 118
Prespa (basin of), 2
Prespa Minor (lake), 83
Prifti, Ilia, 124, 126, 167
Prifti, Stavri, 219–220, 233
Pula, Besnik, 215
Pyongyang, 153

Index

Pyramiden, 196

Qarr (hills of), 2
Quran/Quranic, 24, 228
Qyteza, Sadik, 52

Rëmbec, 55, 90, 93, 132
Riesman, David, 238
Roman Empire, 3,
Romania/Romanian, 100, 153, 161, 174, 196
Rome, 32, 57, 63
Rozafa (fishing company), 22, 230
Rrëshen, 196
Rudder, Cynthia, 109
Russia, 12, 31–32, 72, 73, 162, 164, 179–180, 196, 217, 224, 227, 232–233
Rust Belt, 198, 209, 233

Samara, Thoma, 166
SASA (The Albanian Joint–Stock Sugar Company), 62–65
Schumpeter, Joseph, 189
Scott, James, 102–103, 108, 240–241
Secret Treaty of London, 32
Selenicë, 196
Selim III (Ottoman Sultan), 24
Serbia, 31–33
Shambli, Peti, 89, 91
Shehu, Mehmet, 99, 145
Sheqeras, 125
Shkumbini (river), 1
Siena, 67
Simmel, Georg, 197
Slavic, 25, 31, 61
Slovakia, 212, 217, 234
Slovenia, 234
Smith, Neil, 115
Soviet Union (see also, USSR), 6, 11–12, 17, 65, 69, 73, 79, 119, 127, 129, 143, 152–154, 161, 163–168, 172, 179, 209, 238, 242
Sovietization, 16, 18
Sovjan (lake), 23–24

Sovjan (village), 54, 90
Soya, Edward, 115
Sowerwine, Jennifer, 95
Spain, 58, 71, 104, 159, 212
Springsteen, Bruce, 228, 233
Stalin, 11, 17, 134, 242
Stalinism, 17, 20, 21, 67, 69, 70, 76, 99, 109, 115, 154, 156, 160–161, 165, 182, 232, 242
Stewart-Steinberg, Suzanne, 85
Sudetenland, 60
Sugarland, 17, 19, 21, 94, 206, 245
Sukarno, Koesno Sosrodihardjo, 155
Switzerland, 68
Swyngedow, Erik, 58
Syria, 154, 155
Szelényi, Iván, 129
Sztálinváros, 72, 116, 119
Škoda, 65, 83

Thana (pass of), 1
Thessaloniki/Salonika, 25, 31, 33–34, 36
Third World, 154
Thum, Gregor, 15, 85
Thumanë, 203
Tilly, Charles, 10
Tirana, 1, 15–16, 34, 45, 48, 51, 56, 62, 70–71, 79, 84, 86, 89, 92, 97–100, 110, 126, 132–135, 143, 145, 153, 160–161, 164–165, 167–169, 170, 172–173, 181–182, 185–186, 189–190, 192, 195–196, 203, 206, 214, 216, 221–222, 236, 240
Tito, Josip Broz, 155, 160
Tocqueville, Alexis de, 72
Todorova, Maria, 14
Torviscosa, 68
Turkey/Turkish, 176, 181
Turks, 50, 176

Ugolny Ruchei, 196
Ukraine, 126
United Kingdom, 32
United States/American, 4, 25, 46, 48, 179, 209, 213
Ural Mountains, 233

Index

Vahksh (river), 16
Vandergeest, Peter, 87
Venizelos, Eleftherios 33
Versailles (Conference of), 35, 47, 60
Vidin, 196
Vietnam, 29
Vila, Adem, 52
Vilm, 111
Vlachs, 25
Vlamos, Konstantinos, 49, 51, 54, 56
Vorkuta, 196
Voskopoja (highland of), 2
Vreshtaz, 125

Wallerstein, Immanuel, 115
Warsaw, 16, 72, 169
Weiner, Amir, 58
Western Europe, 12, 14, 21, 29–30, 47, 59, 169–172, 176–178, 181–182, 189, 197, 199, 209, 215, 226, 228, 232, 234, 238–239
West Germany/West German/FGR, 68, 153, 169–170, 173–176, 181–182, 184

White Sea–Baltic Canal, 71
Wilhelm von Wied, 32
Wilson, Woodrow, 35
Wittfogel, Karl, 238
World Bank, 222
World War I, 32, 34–35, 38, 45, 47, 210
World War II, 2, 5, 16, 26, 37, 48, 57, 61, 65, 70–71, 74, 85, 104–105, 118, 126–129, 131, 152, 155, 159, 183–184, 203, 211–212, 227, 234, 238, 241

Young, Craig, 214
Youngstown, 197
Yugoslavia/Yugoslav, 13, 35, 108, 153, 155, 160–161, 170, 174–175, 184, 215

Zedong, Mao, 171
Zhukov, G. A., 79–80, 83
Zog, Ahmet/King Zog, 51, 53–54, 56–57, 60–61
Zvirinë, 54
Zuiderzee, 68, 71